SHORTAGE AND FAMINE IN THE LATE MEDIEVAL CROWN OF ARAGON

IEE

IBERIAN ENCOUNTER
AND EXCHANGE
475–1755 | Vol. 6

The Iberian Peninsula has historically been an area of the world that fostered encounters and exchanges among peoples from different societies. For centuries, Iberia acted as a nexus for the circulation of ideas, people, objects, and technology around the pre-modern western Mediterranean, Atlantic, and eventually the Pacific. Iberian Encounter and Exchange, 475–1755 combines a broad thematic scope with the territorial limits of the Iberian Peninsula and its global contacts. In doing so, works in this series will juxtapose previously disparate areas of study and challenge scholars to rethink the role of encounter and exchange in the formation of the modern world.

SHORTAGE AND FAMINE IN THE LATE MEDIEVAL CROWN OF ARAGON

ADAM FRANKLIN-LYONS

THE PENNSYLVANIA STATE UNIVERSITY PRESS
UNIVERSITY PARK, PENNSYLVANIA

Library of Congress Cataloging-in-Publication Data

Names: Franklin-Lyons, Adam, 1978– author.
Title: Shortage and famine in the late medieval Crown of Aragon / Adam Franklin-Lyons.
Other titles: Iberian encounter and exchange, 475-1755 series ; vol. 6.
Description: University Park, Pennsylvania : The Pennsylvania State University Press, [2022] |
    Series: Iberian encounter and exchange, 475-1755 ; vol. 6 | Includes bibliographical
    references and index.
Summary: "Recontextualizes late medieval famines using contemporary concepts of complex
    human disasters, vulnerability, and resilience"—Provided by publisher.
Identifiers: LCCN 2021054030 | ISBN 9780271091747 (hardback)
Subjects: LCSH: Famines—Spain—Aragon—History—To 1500. | Food supply—Spain—
    Aragon—History—To 1500.
Classification: LCC HC387.A68 F74 2022
LC record available at https://lccn.loc.gov/2021054030

The Pennsylvania State University Press is a member of the Association of University Presses.

It is the policy of The Pennsylvania State University Press to use acid-free paper. Publications
on uncoated stock satisfy the minimum requirements of American National Standard for
Information Sciences—Permanence of Paper for Printed Library Material, ANSI Z39.48–1992.

Contents

Illustrations

Figures

Maps

Table

Acknowledgments

When I first started my work as a medievalist, I was primarily interested in the cultural expressions of food and the dietary choices of wealthy consumers. This interest brought me to study with my long-time mentor, Paul Freedman, whose work on spices and the medieval imagination bolstered my early interest in the more glamorous expressions of medieval recipes and diets. I first became interested in the subject of famine in an agrarian history course that Freedman co-taught with the famous political theorist James Scott. Through Freedman's work on peasants and Scott's writings on the moral economy and innovative views on how state policies do and do not filter down to individuals trying to survive, I became more and more interested in questions of food distribution, access based on social standing, and, ultimately, food shortages and crises. In the decade that I have been working on this project, Paul Freedman has been an invaluable mentor, putting me in contact with numerous people, suggesting publication venues, and always believing in the project.

With the help of a Fulbright fellowship and a grant from the Program for Cultural Cooperation Between Spain's Ministry of Culture and United States Universities, I spent more than a year working in several archives in and around Barcelona, laying the major groundwork for this project. While there, I received help from many people on everything from navigating the libraries to reading documents. Josep Baucells i Reig and Josep Maria Masnou were both generous with their time, helping me find documents and sort through the collections of the Barcelona and Manresa cathedrals, respectively. Carme Muntaner and David Montavi deserve special thanks for making my time in Barcelona both more productive and more enjoyable. Most important for this volume, I also met and began working with Pere Benito i Monclús. Pere, perhaps more than anyone else, has directly influenced every facet of my work. He has helped me in numerous ways, supporting my work at conferences, inviting me to be part of several research groups focused on medieval food production and famines, and even helping me read difficult manuscripts. Pere constantly pushes me to be more thorough, more rigorous, and more precise. I have benefited from his friendship as much as from his expertise and his own scholarship, which appears liberally throughout this book.

Over the years, I have received significant help and support from numerous people. Early on, I met Philip Slavin and Tim Newfield, who were both working on food shortages, but from different points of view and using very different documents. We three have talked, argued, and presented together at numerous conferences, and I enjoy working with them as much as I do sharing a beer together. I met many others through research meetings convened by Pere, often in Spain. Several people have provided valuable feedback and advice as I developed my ideas, among them Phillipp Schofield, Antoni Riera, Antoni Furió, and students doing similar work, including Pol Serrahima i Balius and Joan Montoro i Maltas. While working in Valencia, I met Abigail Agresta, who was using many of the same archival sources for her work on water and the built environment. I have learned a great deal from our conversations about Valencian history, and I greatly appreciate Abigail's willingness to exchange references and alert me to relevant documents in the municipal archive.

Many other scholars have encouraged my work, read chapter drafts, commented on data, and provided inspiring conversations. Jenny Adams, George Dameron, and Felicity Ratte have all been generous in reading drafts and providing feedback. Matt Ollis helped me make my graphs, maps, and statistical data as clear as possible. Though we are not often together in person, Marie Kelleher provided frequent and invaluable support. Ever since I started reading her blog, she has been something of a role model and has offered consistently sound judgment and advice. She read portions of my work and advised me on my proposal material; we have also worked as collaborators. She first suggested that I look into the Iberian Encounter and Exchange series at Penn State as a possible venue for publication. Working with the editors at the Press has been smooth and easy. As anyone who knows him can attest, working with Mike Ryan is always a joy. Ellie Goodman's forthrightness and clarity are exactly what I needed in an editor. Suzanne Wolk provided many improvements and meticulously edited the text, saving me from my own numerous small errors. Laura Reed-Morrisson and her team provided help in laying out the maps and graphics and excellent logistical support overall. I appreciate the time and effort they have put in and their overall faith in me and my work. The assistance of so many people has made me a better scholar and a better writer. Any faults that remain are my own doing.

Finally, this project would not have been possible without financial support from several sources. In addition to my year in Barcelona, I have received support from Marlboro College faculty development awards and Aron Grant funds and from the American Historical Association's Bernadotte E. Schmitt Grant, all of which have made my archival work possible. I also received a Heckman Stipend to spend a few weeks at the Hill Museum and Manuscript Library working with documents from the monastery of Sant Pere de les Puel·les—the staff were very helpful and the people at the Studium scholars' residence run by Saint Benedict's were most hospitable.

The world experienced a significant food crisis in 2007 and 2008, near the beginning of this project, which made the work feel even more timely. As this project neared completion, the world had spent more than a year confronting a new and more severe crisis in the 2019–21 coronavirus pandemic. The question of how institutional structures and social cohesion influence our responses to crises is as urgent today as it was more than a decade ago, let alone during the late Middle Ages. It is heartening to see the ways in which society has learned to respond better to disasters, but demoralizing to acknowledge how persistent inequality and social marginalization still shift the burden onto the most vulnerable. It is my hope that new research into the social dimension of disastrous events, to which this book is a small contribution, can help to change this grim reality for future generations.

Adam Franklin-Lyons
Somerville, MA

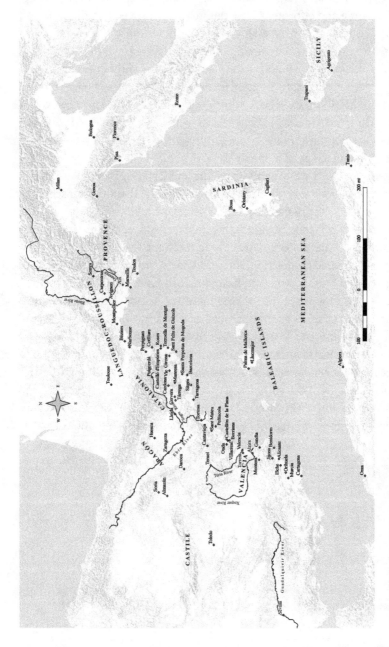

MAP 1. RELEVANT TOWNS AND REGIONS. The map was made using QGIS 3.14 "Pi" in the Europe Albers equal area projection with the Esri "World Terrain Basemap," with data from Esri, the U.S. Geological Survey, and the National Oceanic and Atmospheric Administration. https://www.arcgis.com/home/item.html?id=c61ad8ab017d49e1a82f580ee129893 1.

INTRODUCTION

In the twenty-first century, it is easy to identify the many ways in which human society can prepare for, mitigate, and quickly rebuild after significant natural shocks. Natural events may create particular hazards for humans, but in many cases we have developed methods to respond, including better building codes for earthquakes, river management systems of dams and levees to control flooding, and better weather forecasts that allow more lead time for major hurricanes. The more resilience we build into our societies, the more resistant we are to such disasters. Despite the systems at our disposal, we are not fully resistant to natural shocks. Japan has one of the best earthquake preparedness systems in the world but still was unable to prevent the disaster at Fukushima; clear playbooks and epidemiological warnings about how global pandemics spread have not prevented the widespread chaos, serious economic consequences, and high mortality of COVID-19. But beyond overwhelming our defenses, crises like these strike different individuals within society in very different ways. Most of the disasters of the past few decades have fallen unequally hard on the most vulnerable within societies. Hurricane Katrina swamped the poorest neighborhoods of New Orleans, and preexisting poverty left the marginalized portions of the city's population least able to respond or rebuild. Even in the global coronavirus pandemic, where people often repeat some version of how we are all in this together, the response has varied widely by country, and deaths and suffering virtually always hit disadvantaged communities most severely. Disasters occur when a natural shock exploits a vulnerability in human society and exposes preexisting weaknesses or divisions. Multicausal disasters—natural shocks that interact with structural weaknesses and social hierarchies—are often described as "complex human disasters." Of the many natural disasters, famine is one of the best examples of a complex human disaster. Our ability to produce and store food creates an array of different possible responses; natural shocks that influence the food supply run the gamut from floods to droughts, pathogens to wars. No famine has a single cause, and the resulting starvation and loss of life often mirror social hierarchies very closely.

The global food shortages of 2007 demonstrated many of the attendant complexities common to famine events. As the price of food rose steadily in the fall, commentators and politicians blamed a variety of factors, including low global food reserves, manipulative stock purchases by investment banks, growing demand for meat in Asia, drought in parts of the Ukraine, West Africa, Australia, and the United States, and a growing European and American subsidized demand for biofuels that took acreage away from global food staples.[1] News reports described bickering between countries attempting to lay blame for the situation.[2] While wealthier countries experienced rising food prices, poorer ones experienced real shortages. Food riots broke out in Egypt, Yemen, the Ivory Coast, Haiti, Bangladesh, and Cambodia. Local governments, fearing civil unrest, resorted to predictable measures to combat the food supply crisis: export bans, statutes against speculation and hoarding, and even price-fixing. These very measures exacerbated the problems in global exchange, causing markets to stagnate and inciting panic. Focus on the food crisis, particularly in developed countries, ended with the global banking meltdown in September 2008, which replaced the unresolved food issues with new, more dire economic concerns.[3] The events of 2007 included natural shocks, human economic and social decisions, market panic, and the filtering of suffering through global wealth inequality.

Medieval famines were similarly complex events, involving the same disparate array of environmental triggers, agriculture driven as much by societal choices as by survival tactics, and market failures. Patterns of suffering and starvation, then as now, ultimately followed the lines of social and economic inequality, striking vulnerable individuals considerably harder than elites. The central events of the major famine of 1374–75, which I describe in detail in chapter 5, resemble components of the 2007 crisis. Although the affected area was regional rather than global, 1374 witnessed diverse weather patterns across a wide area; frost, storms, drought, and hail ranging from Valencia around the Mediterranean rim to southern Italy created shortages in multiple regions. The western Mediterranean functioned as a major trade network for foodstuffs, moving fruit, nuts, and grain between multiple areas. As soon as large importers like Barcelona and Florence began buying up supplies and restricting exports, many smaller locations followed suit, shutting down the market and freezing supplies in place, regardless of need. Panic spread like a contagion through the market and prices spiked. Within individual towns and cities, the wealthy complained about not being able to buy bread and having to make do with less desirable foods like chickpeas, while the poor actually starved. Further, restrictions on the socially marginalized increased as cities forcibly removed foreigners and beggars in an attempt to reduce the number of mouths to feed. As they do today, famines in the fourteenth century contained a mix of natural shocks, human responses, political maneuvering, and the structural inequalities of power and poverty.

Understanding Medieval Food Crises

Research into premodern famines is often conducted in the shadow of Ernest Labrousse's distinction between modern and premodern crises. Labrousse described modern events as largely economic in cause and consequence. He contrasted them with subsistence or "old type" crises, where natural forces caused harvest shortages that translated directly into food crises in a simpler economic system.[4] Conceiving of premodern famines as largely subsistence crises reduces humans to passive agents in a narrative of larger forces. This view precipitated a long debate about causation, which was further wrapped up in various debates about the "crisis of the fourteenth century" and the perceived touchstones of a shift toward modernity, however conceived. Scholars described famines as manifestations of various structural causes, including overpopulation, the economic struggles of late feudalism, and, more recently, global climatic shifts.[5] One of the more famous early theoretical discussions of medieval famines, known as the Brenner debate, exemplified this focus on deep structural forces.[6] The debate pitted neo-Malthusian ideas about overpopulation and its accompanying economic stagnation against Marxist interpretations of inflexible modes of production and feudal lack of interest in land improvements as competing explanations of what caused the fourteenth-century crisis. Both sides saw the crisis as upending the previous socioeconomic order (through the population loss caused by the Black Death and the social mobility it ushered in) and setting the stage for new modes of production in the fifteenth century that made modern capital development possible.[7] The understanding of famines was secondary to the larger narrative, and the existence of significant disasters after the Black Death was largely ignored.

More recent debates, fitting our own contemporary concerns, have centered on the environmental backdrop to food supply. Again, the crisis of the fourteenth century fits neatly into a longer-term narrative in which the Medieval Warm Period slowly gave way to the Little Ice Age. The warm period provided optimal conditions for significant crop production and allowed for population expansion. The reversal of the climatic regime, which Bruce Campbell dubbed the "great transition," brought new restrictions and, ultimately, greater crop failures and crises.[8] In this model, the Black Death played a lesser role, but the decline in population still delivered some reprieve by blunting the impact of inevitable harvest shortfalls. In strong contrast to this model, Peregrine Horden and Nicholas Purcell adopted Amartya Sen's ideas about entitlement, which fit well into their own conception of diverse Mediterranean microclimates. In the 1980s, Sen had introduced the idea of famine "entitlements" as an analytical tool to describe how individuals fail or succeed at commanding access to food resources, particularly in times of scarcity. Horden and Purcell claimed that owing to high crop diversification and the pervasive connectivity of the sea, starvation was rare and resulted only from human failures.[9] It is certainly true that trade and exchange played a major role in medieval crises, as many of the examples in this book demonstrate. But Horden and Purcell described a climate with little long-term variation—its only persistent feature was its short-term variability. While Mediterranean models do not match northern Europe, significant climatic change in the fourteenth century did in fact influence the choices made by both individual and institutional crop producers.

The Great Famine of 1315–1317, one of the greatest food crises in European history, stands at a convenient junction in the early fourteenth century, a time when the multiple factors of climate, population, economic development, and feudal relations were all in flux.[10] Such a significant event makes a tempting foil in any number of historical arguments, but it can distract from the complexities of famine itself. While famines might be superficially connected to any one of those factors, as individual events they invariably weave together multiple causes and outcomes. Additionally, because of the narrative strength of the Great Famine and the crisis of the fourteenth century, research has mostly focused on crises prior to the Black Death. In the western Mediterranean, several famine events have competed to fill a historiographic niche similar to the one occupied by the Great Famine: 1328 and 1346 in Italy and 1325 in southern France.[11] For the Crown of Aragon, 1333, referred to as the "first bad year," has most often occupied that position.[12]

Recently, scholars have reconsidered many assumptions about the early fourteenth century. Collaborative projects such as the articles collected in *Dynamiques du monde rural dans la conjoncture de 1300* have described greater dynamism in peasant economies, including economic specialization, access to credit, and rural market integration.[13] Recent research has shown that small towns boosted systems of exchange and economic opportunity, counter to the prevailing narrative of stagnation. *Les disettes dans la conjoncture de 1300*, the companion volume to *Dynamiques du monde rural*, demonstrated the importance of exchange networks, political tensions, and war in exacerbating food shortages.[14] Several recent conferences, spearheaded by Pere Benito i Monclús, have investigated specific characteristics of famine, such as the links between famine and war and political responses to food shortages.[15] Daniel Curtis has applied the concepts of vulnerability and resilience to questions of economic development, especially in Italy, while very recent work by Philip Slavin has reconsidered even the Great Famine in complex terms, taking more seriously the role of social factors like poverty and war.[16] New works on the premodern climate have also complicated the connections between famines as individual events and the influence of the natural world; one recent work memorably described shortages as "socionatural entanglements."[17] These works all treat famine as a significant event in itself, albeit one that changes character and severity depending on its interaction with numerous other factors, including climate, politics, war, and social attitudes.

Despite these more nuanced discussions of the causes of famine, scholars still generally assume that the significant population drop brought on by the Black Death reduced both the frequency and severity of famines.[18] However, the Crown of Aragon and much of the western Mediterranean continued to experience food shortages after the Plague. For much of the region, the worst famine of the century hit during the mid-1370s, a time when none of the Mediterranean populations had significantly recovered. Treating famines as complex and unique allows us to better understand the conditions that underlie a society's food supply and also the character and distribution of suffering during a crisis, regardless of the underlying climatic or population regimes. As I show in part 1 of this book, the study of food supply provides a window into methods of environmental adaptation, cultural influences on agricultural production, the strengths and weaknesses of markets and economic institutions, and the moral restrictions behind food entitlements. Part 2 brings these observations to bear in understanding three famines of varying severity. For each event, considering the famine on its own terms involves multiple angles and cannot be easily subsumed into singular grand narratives.

While the fourteenth century saw a different constellation of overlapping causes than we see today in modern events, famines still involved a diverse set of factors, covering a wide geographic area. Long-term structural changes played a role, but no one factor proved decisive. Understanding medieval famines as complex disasters involves dissecting underlying vulnerability and resilience, but also considering the proximate set of causes that touched off individual events. The first part of this book dedicates a chapter to each of three fundamental aspects of society that helped shape how famines occurred and spread: agricultural production; trade and the economy; and systems of poverty and food access. In the fourteenth century, each of these areas had its own developments and shifts that changed the character of famines, determining who had better access to food, influencing the resilience of urban and rural people, and creating social filters that helped determine who, in the end, might actually starve.

Over the course of the fourteenth century, agricultural output fluctuated constantly in response to the weather. Scholars have debated crop yields and maximum caloric outputs for decades. However, other complexities of agricultural production influenced the outcome of shortages. Access to markets could encourage specialization at the local level, such as the increasing production of saffron in the counties northwest of Barcelona, or investment in vineyards, especially on land near large export markets. Responding to increasing demand and access to local markets, agricultural decision making was not primarily concerned with preventing famine at all costs. Producers balanced hedging against risk with strong cultural and market concerns. Even the heavy reliance on wheat responded as much to cultural tastes as to the goal of maximizing calories. In the Mediterranean, barley could provide more reliable yields and better resistance to drought than wheat. But the cultural supremacy of white bread meant that barley was planted only as a backup crop, consumed by the poor or even by domestic animals. In bad years, barley stored for animal consumption could be eaten by people in order to ward off starvation. Chroniclers regularly used the consumption of debased food—bread made of lentils, acorns, or even dirt or tree bark—as a measurement of suffering, because even in desperate times cultural food hierarchies remained in place. Agricultural output thus aimed to perpetuate cultural norms, not merely to maximize calories; preventing starvation was part of the goal, but not the entire goal.

6

If agricultural practices did not always seek to prevent famine, systems of economic exchange and trade could both reduce and exacerbate shortages. Contemporary scholarship has increasingly described the late medieval economy in dynamic and complex terms.[19] Over the course of the fourteenth century, western Mediterranean cities increased their direct legal and economic control over their grain supplies. Barcelona and Valencia, like major Italian cities, experimented with legal and economic measures, including monopolies, tax breaks, import subsidies, and direct purchases. These new initiatives often relied on support from the royal authorities, especially when granting trade licenses or acquiring new privileges was involved. This suite of options resulted in inconsistent outcomes. Some tactics, such as licenses and waiving fees, worked well in addressing local shortages but proved less effective in systemic crises. Violent coercion and export bans tended to shut down trade networks and channel grain away from areas with less clout toward politically powerful centers. Over the course of the century, urban governments, especially, learned which methods proved more effective and which only exacerbated the problem, and they leaned on methods with a better track record, although every response had its drawbacks.[20]

An important consequence of increasing market integration and control was a change in the geography of famines. As the western Mediterranean market became more efficient, local shortages became easier to cope with. But market breakdowns caused by shortages in multiple locations could heighten market panics throughout the region, increasing the severity of the crisis. Part of the complexity of famines during the second half of the fourteenth century arose from the occurrence of food shortages in multiple connected regions. If one region lost a harvest because of drought, while a second region experienced war or siege, it was the combination of these events that precipitated a famine. Hence the geographic breadth of the event contributed directly to its severity, an effect seen clearly in all of the shortages detailed in part 2 of this book.

Finally, individual access to food resources is not equally distributed throughout society. Amartya Sen, with his concept of "entitlements," codified the argument that inequality was more important than levels of production. Subsequent scholars have often distinguished between famines caused by bad entitlements (often caused by market failure or poverty) and those caused by an overall decline in food availability.[21] However, most modern famine scholars do not see these as mutually exclusive factors.[22] Crop failures caused by weather could reduce overall food availability, but not every individual starved. Measuring the entitlements of different groups during a famine helps identify those who are most likely to starve along with those who might even have profited from the shortage.[23] The particular character of suffering in a famine still depended on individual food access, rather than on a facile comparison between the amount of food produced and the number of mouths to feed. In the fourteenth century, the general treatment of the poor shifted in response to coalescing theological categories of poverty. Wealthy urban patrons donated increasing amounts of money to hospitals and other institutions that gave aid to the poor.[24] But most such donations were predicated on the spiritual rewards gained by the donor as much as on concern for the physical well-being of the needy. In order to ensure the salvific character of those who gave alms, churches, hospitals, and governments increasingly used theological categories of deserving and undeserving poor to criminalize economic marginality. Those criminalized often included the local poor, along with migrants or temporary residents.[25] During periods of food shortage, these laws took increasingly harsh effect, systematically denying food entitlements to large categories of people in an effort to preserve supplies for those deemed worthy. At worst, foreigners and the poor were both scapegoated, when in fact market forces were responsible for exacerbating an initial shortfall of food supplies.

Thus famine was not only a question of agricultural or market failures but always involved at least a partial breakdown in the general social order. In the most serious events, riots and unrest manifested the general feeling that the social contract had been violated (an idea discussed in scholarship on the "moral economy").[26] Even during minor shortages, though, suffering was filtered through individual vulnerability. When individuals in power aided the needy, they did so on their own terms and often for their own benefit. One of the better markers of famine severity is thus the level of social disjunction. Shortages encouraged governments and individuals alike to find methods of diverting suffering away from those who might cause direct unrest to those with less social standing. The cruel mechanisms of society determined who could suffer or die with the fewest overall social consequences.

While these patterns appear in other famine crises across Europe, the Crown of Aragon provides a particularly useful combination of factors for understanding medieval food shortages. The Crown combined several powerful trading cities—Barcelona, Valencia, and Palma de Mallorca, most notably—with a complex agricultural system. Inland areas of Aragon, along with large portions of Catalonia, like the Urgell, produced grain both for urban centers and for export into the wider Mediterranean market. Valencian irrigation systems shifted production toward crop intensification and required significant governmental oversight to function well. Records from the Crown of Aragon illustrate complex systems of production and the diversity of agricultural methods available in the fourteenth century. The urban centers participated in long-distance and local trade, providing evidence of the influence of market integration on the changing character of shortages. Additionally, the Crown of Aragon had an extensive system of hospitals with large record collections, enabling a close look at the treatment of the poor and the social structures produced by a changing theological view of poverty. The Crown of Aragon combines a rich documentary tradition with a diversity of institutions and practices that constitute an excellent laboratory for understanding the complexity of late medieval famines.

As noted above, medieval famines share many features with modern events. In 2007, the relative wealth and power of individual actors and political power centers determined the most likely destination for available grain. Such a global crisis necessarily involved a combination of long-term and short-term causes. Political leaders responded to fears of civil unrest with an array of increasingly desperate responses (hoarding, export bans, criminalization of individuals at the social periphery). In the end, the economic elites did not seriously expect to starve either in 1374 or in 2007. Both poor relief and international aid favored specific groups of people and excluded others, leaving the excluded even more vulnerable than they had been before the crisis. Modern and medieval shortages have these features in common, making the underlying structures of many famines ultimately legible and comparable.[27]

Sources

Famines are difficult to study because the shortage of food influences so many facets of social life. Documents that refer to the famine and provide insight into the responses of fourteenth-century society appear in royal, urban, baronial, and religious administrative collections. I have tried to be omnivorous in the inclusion of diverse types of sources from as many regions as possible, but the realities of archival work inevitably make certain collections more fruitful for research—notably, in this case, the urban administrative records of Barcelona and Valencia and the administrative documents from the poorhouse of the Barcelona Cathedral, the Pia Almoina.

The municipal archives in Barcelona and Valencia are well known and widely used. Both contain council deliberations, exchequer records, and letter collections (among other documents) starting in the early fourteenth century. Earlier research on urban food supply has often made use of these archival sources.[28] The financial records from Valencia in particular made possible a detailed study of import subsidies and the financial ramifications of urban interventions in the grain market. Such analyses form the basis of the first case study in chapter 4 and a significant portion of the argument in chapter 2. Similar documentation exists in other urban centers, and I have used additional resources from Manresa, Villarreal, and Tarragona, and have supplemented this information with published studies that draw on similar data from Cervera, Tortosa, Tarragona, and other locations.[29]

I have also relied heavily on poorhouse records for their extensive administrative documents, which often illuminate agricultural practices and the conditions of the grain market in addition to practical decisions on the treatment of the poor. For this study, the most important hospital records include the archive of Pere Desvilar in Barcelona, other hospitals of the Barcelona Cathedral (especially the hospital "d'en Colom" and the hospital "dels malalts" [of the sick]), the Hospital of en Clapers in Valencia, and the episcopal poorhouse in Vic.[30] Not only did poorhouses record the levels of aid available to the poor, but their donation documents often illustrate the restrictions placed on the poor when they received aid, the types of people singled out for assistance, and those denied public help. The poorhouse in Vic and the cathedral's hospital records also include food prices and land-use records that provide points of comparison for the study of agricultural production in chapter 1.

The most notable source for this work is the impressive collection of documents at the Pia Almoina, the almshouse of the Barcelona Cathedral. As a poorhouse, the Almoina served an increasing urban population and received large bequests and donations from wealthy Barcelonans. The managers of the house parlayed these donations into an extensive urban and rural patrimony that in turn produced copious managerial documentation. The details in the archive allow us to reconstruct every facet of the food supply system, from agricultural practice in demesne lands, to involvement in the powerful international grain market in Barcelona, to fourteenth-century conceptions of poverty and poor relief. Because of this variety, the records of the Almoina are cited regularly throughout this book.

Until very recently, the records of the Pia Almoina were poorly cataloged and relatively difficult to access. The Almoina's archivist, Josep Baucells i Reig, made a heroic effort to better systematize and describe the archive's rich resources, and oversaw the publication of several important catalogs of the institution's parchment charters and documents.[31] Apart from the studies written by Baucells i Reig himself, the only works to make extensive use of the Pia Almoina documents are those of Tomás López Pizcueta, particularly his book-length study of the Almoina's patrimonial holdings in the thirteenth and early fourteenth centuries.[32] Under the direction of Pere Benito i Monclús, new scholars have also begun to mine the resources of the Pia Almoina for studies on agricultural practice, poor relief, food supply, and famine.[33]

The Pia Almoina was overseen by a general manager, the *majordom*, who was supervised by a pair of canons from the cathedral. The *majordoms* kept a compilation of all financial transactions of the institution, now housed in the archive as the Majordomia and the first series of the "general administration." The first of these books has been edited and published by María Echániz i Sans.[34] The Pia Almoina doubled in size between the mid-thirteenth century and the beginning of the fourteenth, increasing the number and size of the registers. In the middle of the century, the *majordoms* consolidated diverse records into a single, large-format volume that contained a summary of all major income and expenses over a two-year period.[35] Each volume contains a section recording the income and expenses for each of two years. The payment sections provide perhaps the greatest new source of information: food costs. The books record all food purchased and served to the poor by the institution, including their bread, meat, wine, and accompaniments. Previous writers on the Catalan economy have either guessed at prices or provided only partial price series.[36] The Almoina frequently purchased its grain through privileged channels; thus the prices are probably slightly lower than those paid by an average consumer. However, the general fluctuations and the notes about the origins of the grain available in the Barcelona market provide a more complete picture of the city's economic tides than previously available.

Along with these centralized account books, several other series hold valuable information for the history of the Catalan food supply. The two main examples of agricultural land practices used in the first chapter, Sitges and Mogoda, both maintained local records that were compiled and summarized in the Majordomia. While many of the Mogoda books are now lost, Sitges retains several dozen that run from 1354, when the cathedral purchased the rights to the castle, to 1410. These volumes contain rents and expenditures, including extensive food and labor costs. Most important for this study, the records describe the work done on the demesne land of the castle, called the *llauró*, which allows for the calculation of crop yields and the description of labor practices. Apart from the wealth of English manorial accounts, European crop yield data are relatively rare until the fifteenth or even sixteenth century. Pere Benito i Monclús and I have each written an article investigating yields and harvest practices in Sitges based on these records.[37] Beyond these studies, there are no other comparable crop yield data known from anywhere in Catalonia or Valencia during the fourteenth century, so the importance of these books is hard to overstate.

In addition to using the Majordomia, I have added food prices from the financial records of the abbess of the monastery of Sant Pere de les Puel·les. Starting in the mid-fourteenth century, the abbess kept annual accounts of income and expenses similar in structure to the Almoina records (and possibly compiled under the supervision of members of the Barcelona Cathedral administration). The series is not as complete as the Almoina, but it provides additional evidence for labor practices and food prices. Sant Pere had different relationships to regional markets and to Barcelona itself, making it an excellent comparison to the data from the Almoina. Records of city administrations, including Perpignan, Manresa, Tarragona, Tortosa, and others, supplement the main observations from the archives in Barcelona and Valencia. Taken together, these sources cover a wide geographic area and take into consideration several different types of evidence. However, they are still only a fraction of the overall primary source base for a major famine event that left its mark in documents from Valencia north to Toulouse, and across many of the cities of the Italian Peninsula.

A Note on Weights, Measures, and Prices

One of the challenges of studying medieval economic history is the constantly shifting standards for both the weights of goods and the underlying values of coinage.[38] In Catalonia, even the most official weights and measures changed periodically. In 1381, King Pere the Ceremonious (r. 1336–87) adjusted one of the standard measures of wheat (the quarter, or *quartera*) in an attempt to normalize the measure for northern Catalonia so that it would match the same unit for barley. Prior to the adjustment, a quarter of barley held 20 percent more grain; this meant that the subdivision of twelve *quartans* to the *quartera* could be calculated as ten *quartans* of barley to twelve (or one *quartera*) of wheat. The adjustment brought the two *quarteras* into alignment, increasing the *quartera* of wheat by 20 percent. For several years afterward, numerous documents listed purchases in both the new and the old *quartera*. Because most of the events described in this work occurred under the old *quartera* system, I have converted all references to the Barcelona *quartera* to this older measure (just shy of seventy liters, as noted in the table below).

Beyond changes over time, measurements, especially for foodstuffs, sometimes varied from town to town. Thus, while Barcelona, Lleida, and Palma de

	Barcelona "old" quartera	Tarragona quartera	Tortosa quartera	Lleida quartera	Palma quartera	Girona quartera	Alicante cafís	Zaragoza cafís	Valencia cafís
Liters	69.5	70.8	70.3	73.4	70.3	72.3	249.3	179.4	201
Barcelona "old" quartera	1	0.98	0.99	0.94	0.99	0.96	0.28	0.39	0.35
Tarragona quartera	1.02	1	0.99	0.96	0.99	0.98	0.28	0.39	0.35
Tortosa quartera	1.01	1.01	1	0.96	1	0.97	0.28	0.39	0.35
Lleida quartera	1.05	1.04	1.04	1	1.04	1.02	0.29	0.41	0.37
Palma quartera	1.01	1.01	1	0.96	1	0.97	0.28	0.39	0.35
Girona quartera	1.04	1.02	1.03	0.98	1.03	1	0.29	0.4	0.36
Alicante cafís	3.58	3.52	3.55	3.4	3.55	3.45	1	1.39	1.24
Zaragoza cafís	2.58	2.53	2.55	2.44	2.55	2.48	0.72	1	0.89
Valencia cafís	2.89	2.84	2.86	2.74	2.86	2.78	0.81	1.12	1

TABLE 1. WEIGHTS AND MEASURES. These numbers follow Llensa i de Gelcen 1951 and Alsina i Català, Feliu i Montfort, and Marquet i Ferigle 1990; see also Gual Camarena and Druguer 1981.

Mallorca all used similar *quarteras*, each city's measure held a slightly different amount of grain (see table 1).[39] In this case, the differences are relatively small, fluctuating by less than 10 percent. In Valencia and parts of Aragon, a *cafís* was nearly three times the size of a *quartera*, but the variations could be larger. Valencia's *cafís* equated to around 201 liters of wheat, while Zaragoza's measured only about 180, with Alicante's measure yielding almost 250 liters, a difference of more than 20 percent. Moreover, Zaragoza broke its *cafís* into eight *fanegas*, while Valencia subdivided it into six, meaning that the size of the smaller unit diverged even further (22 liters versus 33).[40] This does not include the staggering variety opened up when we look at the whole of the western Mediterranean with multiple Italian measures, frequent use of the Sicilian *salma* for imports, and other, less common measures. When comparing grain measures and prices across markets, I have tried to include a conversion to a baseline of either Barcelona *quarteras* or liters, especially when estimating caloric yields and the overall grain needs of a population.

Fortunately, the monetary system was, relatively speaking, more stable. While the weight and value of coins varied, the general system remained consistent over the entire time period. Overall, as with much medieval coinage, the system mirrored the Roman monetary system. The basic silver coin was the solidus or *sou* (in Latin and Catalan, respectively). In earlier documents, this unit is sometimes called a *croat*, but the term is rare in late fourteenth-century records. Each solidus was worth 12 denarii or *diners* (the copper penny, again in Latin and Catalan), and the gold florin was generally worth 11 solidi. However, multiple mints in the western Mediterranean struck their own gold florin (most obviously its namesake, Florence), and the weights of those competing florins could sometimes be worth differing amounts of silver. The pound, or *lliure* in Catalan, worth 20 solidi, was not actually a coin and only appears in account books as a unit of measure for especially large payments or costs. In this book, I have tended to convert all costs to solidi whenever possible, as the solidus was the most commonly used currency for the purchase of grain.

I

LIMITS

I

THE MEASURE OF PRODUCTION

Agriculture formed the basis of both risk and resilience in the medieval food supply. Weaknesses in production and distribution usually correlate directly with both the causes of famine and how people experienced it. The desire to resist the inevitable shortage was not the only driver of agricultural choice. Farmers balanced that need with a set of decisions based on the natural conditions of their land, cultural dietary preferences, and marketability. Social norms alone could weaken resistance to shortage, especially when calculated in terms of pure calories. Symbolic, religious, and cultural factors helped guide food choice as much as risk mitigation did. Today, meat production is an inefficient use of land, but it is not healthy to eat almost exclusively yucca, corn, or potatoes either; spinach and tomatoes, let alone wine and whiskey, are terrible in terms of caloric yield but remain important parts of our diet. Medieval agriculture was no different in striving for some semblance of balance. Despite complicating factors, both individuals and institutions invested directly in efforts to insure their basic food supply. At the institutional level, large civic irrigation projects, and smaller projects by individual large landholders, protected crops against the most common cause of Mediterranean shortage: drought. But storage, especially of grain, provided the most direct resistance to shortage. Storage offered direct resistance in the form of reserves, but it also allowed large producers to play the market, selling some of their stock when prices rose. Food storage also allowed a balance between market integration and subsistence concerns.

Commercialization generated a strong influence on agricultural production. Growing crops for a market could increase a producer's resilience but could also be a gamble. Growers had an array of options given the varieties of produce available at regional markets. If those markets could in turn draw food toward them for further exchange, this increased local resilience and aided general famine resistance, especially with smaller-scale shortages. Crop reserves that could be sold and financial savings provided a direct buffer in the case of local difficulties like an enemy raid, illness, or destruction of crops by animals. Market crops frequently offered opportunities for enrichment that, if they paid off, granted longer-term resistance to shortage, even when such choices came with greater short-term risk. The appearance and disappearance of markets for certain crops could have a direct influence on the choices made in agricultural land use and thus on local resilience. Perhaps the clearest example is the growing of grapes for wine, which requires several years before the land begins to produce a profit. A strong demand for wine can make a parcel of land far more valuable than it would be if devoted to cereal rotation. The specific interactions of particular crops with the triggers of famine—bad weather, war, political breakdown—shaped a farmer's individual experience during a crisis.

After describing these influences, I turn to a unique case study: the castle of Sitges on the Catalan coast just south of Barcelona. The castle's administrative records demonstrate how efficient and productive fourteenth-century agriculture could be. Despite much archival digging, no other manor in the Crown of Aragon has come to light that can provide such a detailed view of how an important landholder balanced competing questions of farming practices, crop preferences, storage, and marketability.

Throughout this discussion, grain predominates over other foodstuffs. This is not to deny the importance of other foods in the fourteenth-century diet. Cities increased their consumption of meat as well as of wheat bread, and the thriving trade in wine helped shape both urban landowning practices and rural systems of land tenure.[1] There is an increasing number of good works on the cultural shape of the medieval diet, its social hierarchies, the demand for luxury products, and the influence of dietary choices on both agriculture and trade.[2] But the study of famines justifies a heavier focus on grain because it formed the core of most people's diets. Not only was grain the most common source of calories, but wheat and barley were the only crops that could single-handedly set off a food crisis when they failed. Shortages of wine, no matter how extreme, did not cause the same mass panic.

Natural Restrictions on Agricultural Production

Farmers did not ask whether they would have a bad year, but when. The fourteenth century brought with it changes in the overall climate that only increased the probability. As Bruce Campbell has demonstrated, the climate shifted away from the warmer, calmer weather of previous centuries and brought wetter, colder, and more volatile weather to much of northwestern Europe. The Mediterranean also experienced this shift in climate, though less abruptly and uniformly than in northern Europe. Campbell describes increased flooding and more frequent harvest failures in early fourteenth-century Italy as markers of the new extreme swings in rainfall.[3] As Richard Hoffmann notes, however, the Mediterranean did not experience the "steady cold and damp" that dominated northern weather patterns. Mediterranean variability mitigated the worst effects of new weather patterns on society because Mediterranean cultivators had already built agricultural systems that assumed a wider range of "normal" swings in yearly weather.[4] Over the second half of the fourteenth century, the weather became more prone to storms, but specific agricultural restrictions and crop destruction still tended to come from local weather conditions.

Given the constant shifts in weather and climate, producers worked under a "triple imperative: diversify; store; redistribute."[5] Crop variety shaped the core of agricultural resilience, not just in the rotations between grains, legumes, and fallow but also in cultivating multiple crops, including wine grapes in vineyards, tree crops such as olives and oranges, and commercial crops like saffron and carob. By the fourteenth century, most regions produced a mix of staples and exportable cash crops. Wheat, the grain in highest demand, could function as both. Part of Mediterranean diversification came directly from the terrain; wet river valleys produced grain or orchards of nuts, olives, or fruit. Better-drained hillsides were well suited to growing grapes, whether for wine or for the intensive production of raisins.[6] The high mountains of the Pyrenees and large parts of the Cordillera Ibérica in Aragon provided excellent terrain for raising large flocks of sheep for both wool and meat.[7]

In the heartland of the Crown of Aragon, coastal lands and broad inland valleys, especially the rich Ebro River Valley, produced high percentages of grain. The Vallès to the west of Barcelona and the Camp de Tarragona provided grain for those cities.[8] As the redistribution of grain became more routine, the plains of the Urgell between Lleida and the foothills of the Pyrenees and the river valleys of the Ebro and its tributaries in Aragon furnished the granaries for major cities from Zaragoza and Lleida to the coastal centers of Tortosa, Tarragona, Valencia, and Barcelona.[9] The Segre River in western Catalonia provided irrigation and rich soil for the grain growers of Lleida, but when it flooded, the results could be disastrous. Mountain runoff caused a large flood in 1379 that ruined homes and damaged irrigation systems, though it did not result in a major grain shortage.[10] The heavily irrigated plains of coastal Valencia, both around the capital itself and in the region south of Jijona comprising the cities of Alicante, Elche, and Orihuela, allowed the intensive grain production that made Valencia a grain exporter for much of the late Middle Ages.[11]

Hillier, drier lands along the Catalan coast and the inland regions of Valencia favored both vineyard and orchard crops such as olives and almonds. Regions of southern Valencia specialized in growing tree crops like carob beans and figs.[12] The extensive irrigation of lands in Valencia restricted wine production somewhat, since rice and wheat could absorb quantities of water that would drown grapevines. Meat supplies for much of Valencia came from the highlands around the city of Teruel and along the border with Castile. Large flocks of sheep traveling through the hillier lands could damage vineyards and led to routine disputes between Valencia and Teruel over animal pasturing and land-use rights.[13] Barcelona's demand for meat precipitated similar conflicts; many flocks came from the Pyrenees or the Catalan interior, often congregating in distant markets like Puigcerdà before beginning their journey south to Barcelona.[14]

Even Mallorca followed this pattern. Farmers along the coastline raised the most grain, while grapes and olives predominated in hillier regions. Population increases at the end of the thirteenth century pressed wheat fields higher into the terraced hills at the beginning of the fourteenth century.[15] The new grain fields displaced some olives, orchards, and vineyards, but coastal populations also began to draw more heavily on Mediterranean trade. Mallorca used its position as a waypoint between the mainland and the other productive islands—Sardinia and Sicily above all—to siphon off the necessary grains for urban populations.[16] Throughout the period, the craggy spine of mountains along the northwest coast of the island accommodated the animals sold in the markets of Palma.[17] In general, animals were more difficult to ship than their caloric equivalent in grain, which encouraged local production.

The landscape determined general patterns, but cultivators responded to natural pressures by both redistributing and diversifying. Inventories from small towns near the Pyrenees frequently recorded multiple lesser grains, including spelt, oats, rye, and even millet. Each grain came with its own resistance: rye to cold, oats to excessive rain, barley to drought. While farmers cultivated rice in the irrigated lands of Valencia, northern inventories could also contain rice or locust bean (another crop common in southern Valencia), showing that most grains were available throughout the region.[18] The practice of diversification blended all of these elements regardless of a farmer's particular microclimate. Farmers in the high terrain in northern Aragon produced wheat like everyone else, but rye's resistance to cold made it a preferred grain for bread. The region produced multiple cereals alongside legumes, almonds, and fruits such as apples.[19] Variety dominated, but the specific character of agriculture in a given location depended on the social, market, and legal forces and constraints in that region.

Finally, within this diversity of cultivars, practices, and land types, a handful of general practices are worth mentioning. First, most grain came from winter cropping. The Franciscan friar Francesc Eiximenis (ca. 1330–1409) offered hyperbolic praise of Valencia's *huerta* (literally, vegetable garden, in the case of Valencia the irrigated territory spreading out several kilometers from the city), claiming that it could sometimes produce three crop cycles per year, but normal grain crops came largely from one winter planting or a mix of winter and summer harvests.[20] Second, thinner Mediterranean soils, even on irrigated lands in Valencia, tended to encourage use of the scratch plow rather than the heavy moldboard plow favored in parts of northern Europe. The lighter plow reduced the need for heavy traction—most Catalan plows were usually pulled by pairs of oxen or mules rather than by horses or large teams of oxen—but also increased the need for frequent plowings and human labor.[21] Finally, cash crops varied throughout the kingdom, but the predominant crop was grapes for wine. Even small communities produced wine for local consumption as well as for export and often attempted to protect their local vineyards for economic reasons, as we will see in chapter 2.

Catalan agriculture occupied a diverse mixture of ecological settings that helped to produce an abundant assortment of crops. The handful of regional similarities are important, but they are hardly predictive of agricultural success. As Grove and Rackham note, "Harvests often failed. [But] in Mediterranean countries it is not easy to starve. The various crops made it less likely that all would fail at once."[22] These environmental restraints left extensive room for human choices and responses, choices that balanced competing needs for survival, cultural ideas about food, and economic incentives.

Social Influences on Agricultural Production:
Dietary Preference, Land Tenure, and Cash Crops

Resisting the environmental pull toward diversification was a deep reliance on culturally preferred crops. The foundation of virtually all late medieval diets was grain, but people consumed different grains depending on location and wealth. Cultural preference centered on wheat, a preference inherited from both biblical rhetoric and ancient Roman ideals of civilization. Pliny described barley as outdated and unappetizing: "Barley bread, which was extensively used by the ancients, has now fallen into universal disrepute, and is mostly used as a food for cattle only."[23] Barley hovered on the line between human food and animal food. In Catalonia during the high Middle Ages, most people's diet centered around the *olla*, or pot, in which people boiled a mixture of vegetables, meats, or fish that was thickened into a substantial stew with the addition of barley.[24] During the twelfth century, economic prosperity allowed more and more people to switch from the inexpensive barley stew to wheat baked into bread. At the same time, barley more frequently found its way into the feed of horses and mules. By the fourteenth century, mules, the main source of transportation and agricultural traction, consumed a diet of nearly half barley supplemented with other grains. The mixtures appear in the Catalan documentation as a general animal feed called *civada*. The *olla* still bubbled away, but Catalans ate their stew accompanied by bread and wine. Even if wheat could not be had, bread made of barley, rye, spelt, or other grains ruled the table.

The ratio of wheat to other grains in bread became a marker of class.[25] Catalan moralists Francesc Eiximenis and Saint Vincent Ferrer (1350–1419) both recommended the sober consumption of barley bread as a remedy for gluttony. "First, do not eat desirous bread," Ferrer preached, "nor beautiful wheat bread—better barley bread—nor meat nor wine nor other delicate thing."[26] Despite the sermons, people continued their turn toward "beautiful wheat bread." In cities, wheat bread or bread mixed with a minimum of barley accounted for nearly half of all calories consumed.[27] The association of barley with austerity or poverty drove the relative price of the two grains in city markets. Throughout the second half of the fourteenth century, barley prices in the major markets of Barcelona and Florence remained consistently around two-thirds the price of good wheat.[28] Other grains that could be used in bread, like rye, tended to hover around half that of wheat.[29] Consumers could thus save money without reducing their total caloric intake by purchasing mixtures, although this clearly represented a choice of hardship.

As long as wheat was in good supply and the price stayed low, all other grains remained secondary. Only when the wheat supply failed did the prices of the other grains diverge on the basis of their desirability: the price of barley rose fastest, followed by that of rye and spelt and finally oats.[30]

Despite the popularity of wheat, barley remained important.[31] Barley's resistance to salinity made it a resilient choice for farmers on the Mediterranean coast (what Emmanuel Le Roy Ladurie called "the Mediterranean of barley eaters"), and agricultural land often produced more barley than other crops.[32] Barley also provided higher yields and greater drought resistance than wheat.[33] In rural areas, wealthier peasants could afford to consume wheat, but poorer peasants ate mixed bread or even bread made without wheat. In the mountainous regions of the Pyrenees and the Alps, wheat was often mixed with rye (which has greater cold resistance), millet, or spelt. Beyond the steep hills of the Collserola to the northwest of Barcelona, records for the rents and lands of Santa Perpètua de Mogoda show that the house manager planted and collected wheat, barley, spelt, oats, and millet almost every year in the second half of the fourteenth century.

Even in cities, it was only in the wealthier and better-connected centers that many people could afford wheat as the primary grain of their daily diet. In Barcelona and Valencia, the wealthiest and most powerful of the Catalan cities, even the bread at some of the poorhouses was made almost exclusively of wheat.[34] A few other wealthy almshouses, such as the Almoina in Lleida, the Hospital of Santa Catarina in Mallorca, and the hospital at Coll de Balaguer, which sits halfway between Tarragona and Tortosa, also served mostly wheat.[35] Other regional centers, such as Girona, served a mix of wheat and barley bread depending on the harvest quality, a diet not unlike that of many peasants.[36] The poorer relief houses of smaller cities like Vic, where even the rents paid to the bishop were mostly barley and spelt, served bread largely made from barley.[37] Laws restricting how mixtures could be sold indicate that even in Barcelona and Valencia, people consumed a variety of grains on a regular basis.[38]

In good years, when humans consumed wheat and some barley, animals received the other grains. While animals ate grasses and roughage, work animals received much of their food directly from their owners. Mules, like their peasant counterparts, received payment in food whenever they worked. The standard diet consisted of a blend of lesser grains. In 1382, a fairly good year, almost all of the secondary grains harvested in the town of Santa Perpètua de Mogoda—spelt, millet, and some of the barley—were thrown in with the animal feed.[39] In 1352, in Mollet, just to the east, the procurator sold all the barley collected in rents, but he fed the spelt directly to the mules.[40]

Animal consumption also allowed people to plant nitrogen-fixing crops that might otherwise be inedible. Vetch, a hard seed consumed only in times of famine, was grown intentionally as a cover crop and fixed nitrogen as fava beans did. It also provided a high-protein addition to animal feed. The few years for which we have known prices for vetch, it cost the same as oats, despite being inferior even to the lesser grains. Hence the demand of animal consumption generated its own secondary market.[41]

Despite the omnipresence of other grains, the demand for wheat affected every level of society. During the rich harvest of 1373, the hired hands at the manor house of Mogoda, usually fed a barley and wheat mixture, received pure wheat bread as a reward for their labor.[42] In 1377, another good harvest year, the workers demanded bread made from wheat and barley instead of pure barley. Rations for the laborers had been cut back to barley and oats during the famine from 1374 to 1376, but with the crisis receding, the workers grew bold enough to demand the fruits of the improved harvests they had eaten prior to the shortage. The manager of the property mentions milling *mestall*, or "mixture," with the laconic comment that he "milled the wheaten mixture because they did not want to eat barley."[43] Barley was a better choice from his point of view, as it was cheaper but left the stomach just as full. The manager used the last of the previous year's stored wheat mixed with millet for the workers' bread rather than the fresh barley and wheat the workers themselves were helping to collect.[44] The manager himself would not suffer to eat such a diet; in the same year, he ate bread of pure wheat only.[45] The choice of cultivated grains reflected a balance between cultural preferences, environmental demands, and the desire for security in the face of perennial shortfalls, vectors that often pulled in opposite directions.

Dietary aspirations encouraged particular choices, even when they did not result in greater resilience. Land tenure, a widely studied subject, similarly constrained agricultural choice but generally lowered the resilience of marginalized producers. Extensive studies of northern Italy have investigated the relationship between urban land ownership and different forms of rents and dues.[46] The sale and purchase of land itself created a bewildering array of contracts, from straight cash rent to payments in kind, along with various forms of fees for alienation, subleasing, and other contractual forms. Tenure practices have been extensively researched elsewhere; what primarily concerns us here are the aspects of land tenure that directly influenced agricultural vulnerability and resilience.

The most salient feature of Catalan land tenure was the general division between the flexible tenure systems around Barcelona and south of the

Llobregat River (often referred to as "New Catalonia") and the increasingly onerous systems in the northern counties of "Old Catalonia," centered around Girona and the Urgell.[47] Even with the population slump after the Black Death, northern lords continued to try to increase the level of servitude, in large part to prevent peasants from fleeing to urban centers or new settlements to the south.[48] At the end of the fourteenth century, serfdom persisted under large landholders in northern Catalonia.[49] By contrast, both New Catalonia and large urban areas relied heavily on a resuscitated form of Roman land contract called an "emphyteusis."[50] These highly flexible contracts allowed peasants to alienate the land without explicit permission and often simply by paying a fee to the lord. Emphyteusis contracts allowed both flexibility for peasants and landholders' ability to raise quick sums of money without extensive oversight, creating more commercial agriculture and freer land use even around cities like Girona.[51] Around 90 percent of the land in the town of Sant Boi de Llobregat, just south of Barcelona, came under an emphyteusis contract by the middle of the fourteenth century.[52]

The kings of the Crown of Aragon had conquered this territory more than a century earlier. Much of the land was initially granted to nobles and members of knightly orders who had assisted in the conquest, who used flexible contracts to attract new settlers.[53] The appeal of the new territory initially increased some peasant obligations in the north, as lords attempted to keep them from leaving. By the beginning of the fourteenth century, much of the land of New Catalonia no longer offered incentives for colonization and the frontier had moved significantly further south, into more recently conquered areas of southern Valencia and parts of Mallorca. The lands around Orihuela and Elche continued to be partitioned until the 1330s.[54] The Ebro and Segre river valleys still fell largely under noble seigniorial control, while the southernmost region, around Alicante, Elche, and Orihuela, saw more commercial and urban land investments. However, both regions exported significant quantities of grain along with other products such as wine and olive oil.[55] Emphyteusis rents, particularly, provided long-term stability for both lord and tenant, often encouraging infrastructure work such as the expansion of irrigation.[56] Consistent surpluses and increased agricultural output in turn increased the production of cash crops. The specifics of cash cropping depended on location as well on the specific desires of landlords and cultivators. Several regions developed their own specialties, including dried figs and raisins around Gandía and Benidorm, chestnuts from the hillier territories of northern Catalonia, and saffron in the central Catalan plains.[57]

Wine and saffron in particular benefited from flexible land tenure, but in different ways. Landowners, especially urban elites investing in the hinterland, drove the intensification of wine production. As Stephen Bensch has shown, investment in vineyards provided some of the early wealth for Barcelona itself.[58] By the beginning of the fourteenth century, the division of wine into types and qualities encouraged not just routine consumption but also the growth of a luxury market.[59] Wines came not just in red and white but in particular types, such as the sweet white wine popular among the wealthy called *vi grec*, or "Greek wine."[60] Records from the monastery of Sant Pere de les Puel·les, just outside Barcelona, always distinguished between red and white wine and occasionally mentioned rarer distinctions such as *moscat*.[61] Large landholders drove vineyard expansion, largely because vineyards required intensive labor, which tended to exclude independent peasant producers.[62]

Saffron production in central Catalonia, by contrast, grew mainly out of individual peasant interest in market participation.[63] Merchants in Manresa and Cervera encouraged planting by providing a ready market, purchasing large quantities of the exotic spice for export.[64] Saffron did not involve the same capital requirements that encouraged institutional investment. Saffron was highly labor-intensive; each flower had to be picked individually and processed by hand into the slender threads of the spice. However, individual cultivators could plant small plots of saffron crocus that they could process entirely on their own, selling even relatively small amounts of the spice for their own benefit. The labor of saffron production intersected well with cereal production: saffron required very little water and grew well in dry summers. Because the plant flowered in August or September, the labor used to harvest, process, and dry the spice fell conveniently between early summer grain harvests and later fall wine making.

Participation in distant markets expanded food access by providing outlets for agricultural production that in turn improved purchasing power. However, such investment could be a double-edged sword. Lords rarely expected to starve, so a disastrous grape harvest usually resulted in reduced income or debt. Saffron production in central Catalonia proved more fickle. During the famine of 1374–75, peasants in the region around Manresa could not compete with the economic and political power of Barcelona and Lleida, and the crisis did nothing to make saffron more valuable. A letter from the chapter house of the cathedral in Manresa to the prince of Girona described the degradation of some of the surrounding lands owned by the church: many of the peasants in those areas fled toward Barcelona. The impoverishment of both the city and the collegiate chapter persisted for years after harvests had returned to normal.[65] The choice to grow grapes or saffron might expand economic possibilities in a good year, but the economics of shortage meant that a bad year could be devastating.

Extending the Harvest: Manure, Irrigation, and Storage

Once a given producer decided what to plant on his land, how much would a given area produce? This question lies at the heart of the debate about over-population in northern Europe in this period. The "population and resource model" of early fourteenth-century agriculture describes peasant holdings as increasingly divided between more and more children, relying heavily on marginal lands like marshes, and without new technological abilities to in-crease crop production.[66] The early proponent of this model, Jan Titow, also added soil exhaustion to the list of problems based on low animal stockage rates and decreasing fallow or cover crop use.[67] Bruce Campbell's broad re-consideration of the fourteenth century, which included climate as a central factor, still assumes that low yield and lack of surplus ensured that serious harvest failures dragged peasants further into poverty.[68] In this model, the demographic slump of the Black Death freed up large areas of land, reduced reliance on marginal soils, and increased peasant holdings.[69]

The population and resource model assumes that persistently low crop yields were compounded by persistent difficulties caused by soil exhaustion and cultivators' basic inability to solve this problem. Scholars throughout Europe have estimated standard yield ratios as low as 4:1 (four quarters har-vested, before tithes or taxes, for each quarter of grain sown); despite the oc-casional report of higher yields, as Georges Duby put it grimly, "They could hardly hope for more."[70] English husbandry manuals pegged yields at 8:1 for barley, 7:1 for rye, 5:1 for wheat, and 4:1 for oats; German evidence from the rich Rhineland suggests an average of 5:1 and a high of 8:1.[71] Duby de-scribes these estimates as "very optimistic."[72] The scant previous yield data available for the Crown of Aragon comes almost entirely from the fifteenth and sixteenth centuries and offers a divergent set of numbers. The average is roughly 5:1, but the rates range from a grim 2:1 up to a notably positive 12:1.[73] Historians often describe these yields as remaining at these dismally low rates for centuries, only finally rising during the Industrial Revolution.[74]

But producers did have the capacity to change their agricultural results. In the Crown of Aragon, with its often thin and sandy soil and the constant threat of drought, the two most common agricultural inputs were manure and water. Soil health and access to manure are key components of the debates on agricultural yields in the fourteenth century. Jan Titow's initial claim of late thirteenth-century soil exhaustion sent many scholars looking for relationships between animal stock and crop yields.[75] The combination of harvest failures and major epizootic diseases during the Great Famine reduced the number of stock animals, and thus of manure, just as harvests plummeted, making agrarian recovery that much more difficult.[76] English manorial agriculture relied more directly than other European countries on local animal stock for the manure used as fertilizer. However, Catalan regional markets developed an exchange in manure itself, alleviating some of the need for private animal stock on agricultural land.

Evidence of the manure trade remains relatively scarce, appearing in manorial records of small purchases but not rising to the larger level of contracts or credit that appear more frequently in notarial archives. As in northern Europe, plenty of manure still came from draft and production animals housed on agricultural land.[77] However, multiple managerial accounts from around Barcelona describe the purchase of extra manure from a regional market when necessary. The monastery of Sant Pere regularly paid workers to spread manure but also recorded its purchase. The records do not note any particular in-house shortages, only that manure was purchased.[78] In 1393, the manager at the Hospital Desvilar described purchasing forty-two *somades* of manure (roughly 5,250 kilograms) from a man who seems to have been visiting the hospital and offered the manure for sale.[79] Purchases often spiked after bad years, with several hospitals recording extra manure use in the late 1370s after the famine of 1374–75. In 1375, the Hospital d'en Colom purchased manure directly from the royal palace for its fields at the low price of 8 denarii per *somada*.[80] By the end of the season, the hospital had purchased more than two hundred *somades*, or several tons.

The benefits of manure were doubtless well understood.[81] Early Catalan agricultural manuals from the fifteenth century often describe the proper use of manure, which animals produced the best manure, and what crops needed it most.[82] The presence of the market implies that a large city like Barcelona might have had an active trade in reselling the manure produced by the myriad animals in the city. Horses, mules, and other transport animals coming and going, horses in the royal stables, and the many sheep, goats, and other types of animals brought to market for slaughter would all have produced significant quantities of manure that cities regulated.[83] The city of Valencia was already offering licenses to manure haulers in 1327; in the 1390s, the city trade was large enough that Valencia restricted storage of the manure within the city walls and also forbade the haulers from working at night or on Sunday.[84] Given the casual mention of manure purchases in the poorhouse records, it is somewhat surprising that urban and royal records do not offer *more* evidence of its regulation and sale.

While manure clearly had the potential to improve general soil fertility, it is difficult to know exactly how effective such additions were. Eric Schneider, using recent statistical analyses of numerous studies of English manors, argues that manure use did not correlate closely with agricultural yields. Perhaps unsurprisingly, weather played the most direct role, and the influence of animal manure was notably smaller. Schneider notes, however, that this could be the result of changing demand for oats on farms with large numbers of animals to feed. The balance of crops would have shifted away from wheat and barley, which might have received greater attention and subsequently greater yields.[85] In Catalonia, the manure market seems to have spread out, so to speak, the available fertilizer to more agricultural producers, perhaps resulting in more efficient use.

Lying at the crossroads of Roman and Islamic influences along the dry Mediterranean coast, the Crown of Aragon also made intensive use of its water resources. Irrigation practices, especially in Valencia, have garnered significant scholarly interest. Since the publication of Thomas Glick's landmark study demonstrating the Arabic influence on Valencia's irrigation systems, scholars have debated the origins of numerous irrigation practices in both Roman and Arabic science.[86] For the purposes of understanding famine and shortage, irrigation shares important features with the land tenure and wine production described above: while smaller projects were possible, irrigation generally required large inputs of capital, in contrast to the use of manure. By the end of the fourteenth century, the vision and desire for grand water-diversion projects could outstrip the available finances of even wealthy cities. Like emphyteusis rents, irrigation projects frequently derived from urban economic desires, but they ultimately benefited both cultivators in the hinterland and citizens.

Multiple large-scale irrigation projects left their mark on the agricultural system in the Crown of Aragon. One of the largest water-diversion projects proposed in the fourteenth century illustrates key aspects of late medieval irrigation systems, especially the vast amounts of capital involved and the direct relationship between crop failure and the need to manage scarce water resources. Valencia's famous irrigation system began a dozen kilometers upriver on the Guadalaviar (today the Turia), where four large canals branched off the river. Valencia suffered a particularly intense drought in

1372, a slightly better year in 1373, and then a second serious drought in 1374. In 1372, the council of Valencia petitioned King Enrique of Castile for permission to divert part of the Cabriel, a tributary of the Júcar that ran within twenty kilometers of the Guadalaviar.[87] By the winter of 1374, the Guadalaviar could no longer adequately supply the system, and the city redoubled efforts to build a canal from the Cabriel and expanded the plan to include the Júcar itself.[88] When the counselors of the city first proposed the idea in October, they explicitly cited the drought. They ordered architects and irrigation experts to draw up plans for a canal large enough to hold half the water of the Júcar River and bring it nearly forty kilometers from the south to join the Guadalaviar. When the experts finally submitted their report in the spring of 1376, they estimated that such a project would cost as much as 40,000 pounds.[89] The city balked at the cost and never started the project, but it is important to note the city's responsiveness to the extreme drought conditions.[90] This does not necessarily mean that fourteenth-century urban planners knew that their climate was changing or that extreme weather had become more frequent. But they did understand that drought was a persistent problem that was likely to continue, and they were willing to consider massive public works projects to mitigate future threats.

While the Valencian *huerta* boasted the most famous system of irrigation in the Crown of Aragon, it was far from the only large-scale irrigation project. The city of Manresa had recently undertaken its own project.[91] Manresa's irrigation canal, called the *sèquia*, took decades to complete. As in Valencia, the city began planning during a major Catalan drought, this time in 1333, but the work was not fully completed until nearly 1400, delayed in part over land disputes with the local bishops.[92] Other irrigated lands throughout Aragon used water for various purposes. Castellón de la Plana sought to extend its irrigation capacity in 1387, just two years after a significant shortage. The Ebro River and its tributaries, among them the Cinca and the Segre, all had significant irrigation systems that made the region around Lleida and Zaragoza an exporter of grain in all but the most extreme drought years.[93] In northern Catalonia—the lands around Girona, Cervera, and Castelló d'Empúries— noble landowners used small irrigation projects that often served the double purpose of supplying the lord's mills and irrigating nearby land.[94] The Segura River in southern Alicante flowed through both Murcia and Orihuela, feeding a rich band of agricultural land. The region was so well known for its grain supply that a poem bragging of its agrarian prowess appeared in the city register near the end of the fourteenth century: "ploga o no ploga blat ha en Oriola" (rain or no rain, Orihuela has the grain).[95] While grain surpluses enriched the merchants of Orihuela, they also meant that many of the peasants had significantly improved resilience. When a normal year meant surplus, a bad year might still mean survival.

Because of irrigation's capital needs, it often responded to changes in population in the opposite way that land did. Population decline could hurt irrigation systems because not enough people remained to keep the channels clean and maintain the walls and structures of the canals that flowed through their land.[96] The monastery of Sant Pere near Barcelona paid as many as a dozen workers nearly every year to clear and repair the channel that supplied its mills and irrigated some of its fields. In one notable instance, workers hired to clean the millrace tossed too much mud into the channel; the following day, the overseer had to hire an expert to supervise the workers and make sure the task was done right.[97] Without constant infusions of labor and capital, an irrigation system could become unusable, and its agricultural advantages would literally dry up.

Finally, storing food provided the most direct hedge against shortage. Storage protected against future losses resulting from bad weather, military depredations, or disease. Food storage took multiple forms in the late medieval world, depending on its goals and the resources at hand. Grain storage fell into three categories: above-ground storage houses, subterranean storage pits, and private cellars, jugs, sacks, and earthenware vessels. Private storage could not adequately keep grain for long periods but was an accessible form of storage generally used for commerce or to get from harvest to harvest. In the fourteenth century, most rural people used some form of small personal storage in their homes or cellars. A study by Joan Montoro i Maltas of the inventories reflected in multiple notarial archives shows that the amounts rarely exceeded twenty Barcelona "quarters"—roughly enough for a family of four or five to live on for one year. These personal stores were usually mixed grains, although wheat figured prominently, especially in the houses of the well-to-do.[98]

Both above-ground grain houses and underground pits provided longer-term storage and more robust resistance against shortages. Both forms of storage had advantages and disadvantages, but legal restrictions on grain sales tended to discourage systemic long-term storage. Agricultural treatises written by Muslims living in the Taifa kingdoms described almost unbelievably effective storage methods, improving on the Roman techniques they referenced. The twelfth-century Andalusian agronomist Ibn al-ʿAwāmm chronicled the use of large above-ground granaries with ventilation sufficient to keep the wheat dry, a method he claimed could store wheat for many decades.[99] These granaries, called *al-hurī* (a word probably taken from the Latin word *horreum*, or barn), were commonly large communal structures placed atop hills or embankments.[100] Ibn al-'Awāmm also described underground methods, all of which involved mixing some substance—oak ash, dry pomegranate or cypress leaves, even gypsum—in with the grain to prevent the growth of bacteria and mold.[101] All of these underground storage methods involved cylindrical pits dug directly into the ground, or jars that were filled with grain, sealed, and buried. Many of these pits have been unearthed in archeological excavations throughout the Iberian Peninsula.[102]

With new Christian systems of land ownership and market practices, the use of large storage buildings fell out of favor. Fourteenth-century Spanish translators of Islamic agricultural writers like Ibn al-'Awāmm and Ibn al-Wāfid used *hondo* or *silo* for storage pits, both earlier native Spanish words similar to their Latin roots in the manuals of Columella and Varro.[103] Lacking firsthand experience of such granaries, however, the translators had to borrow the Arabic term for the large, above-ground constructions: *Al-hurī* became *alhori* or, more commonly, *alfolies*.[104] Urban centers had abandoned the practice of centralized, state-controlled grain storage, preferring to regulate the private market of imports and sales. Even the early use of public granaries in Játiva and Valencia, called *almodí*, appeared to allow for better market regulation rather than storage.[105]

The underground storage pits did continue in constant use throughout the medieval period.[106] However, the chemical techniques described in the Arabic agricultural manuals disappeared in response to new legal requirements in the grain market. Market regulations set various grades of wheat and determined their relative sale prices and tax levels.[107] The quality of grain mixed with additions could no longer be determined accurately, which often decreased its value. In 1343, the majordomo of Barcelona's Pia Almoina had been promised a grain shipment from Urgell of the highest quality, but he declined to buy the wheat after he learned that it had been mixed with lime and could not be assured that the grain was of the stated quality.[108] In a remarkable document from 1383 in the city of Manresa, Pere Nadal, a citizen of Manresa acting as royal bailiff, interviewed a number of wealthy grain merchants about their practices.[109] Nadal asked the merchants whether they were aware of the many ways grain in storage could spoil. His prodding included references to both storage pits (*cigis* or *sitges*) and *orri*, basements or cellars with a constructed floor and walls for medium-term storage similar to the stores studied by Montoro i Maltas.[110] One of the merchants, Bernat Amargós, described the effects of overly humid storage: "He said that it depends on the house it is in;

that is, that if it is a humid house, then the grain should increase, but if it is a house made of rock or of stone slab, or if it is clean, then no."[111] "Increase" seems to have meant a larger volume with no actual increase in the caloric yield of the grain, and also a greater chance of spoilage based on the damp conditions. The merchant Bernat de Garmeçans confirmed that he himself had seen grain stored underground increase when the storage container was opened. "He testified that there was sold . . . a silo where there was a good 270 quarters of wheat or more, and according to the number that was put in and the number pulled out, . . . that there was more taken out than put in by a good six quarters or more."[112] As with the grain mixed with lime, the simple act of storage could change the value of the grain in possibly imperceptible ways. Especially with wheat, whatever grade went in could not necessarily be verified as the same grade coming out. If any additive recommended by the agronomists made the grain harder or even impossible to sell, merchants would be loath to adopt such practices. Regulation also made it illegal to sell any grain stored in an underground silo as seed grain, a restriction that doubtless lowered its desirability, no matter how long the stay underground.[113]

These restrictions encouraged heavier reliance on barley for storage.[114] In the Sa Fortesa property of the Pia Almoina, the house manager stored only a single quarter of wheat in 1353 but more than a dozen quarters of barley. Larger houses like Mogoda and Sitges had multiple pits that held one hundred quarters of grain each, all filled with barley or barley-oat mixtures.[115] Records from around Manresa mention even larger pits, holding hundreds of quarters.[116] Barley performed best in balancing the concerns of human consumption with the various uses for which grain was destined. During a moderate harvest, barley could be stored while wheat was either consumed or sold on the market at higher prices. If the wheat proved to be sufficient for the year, the stored barley could be replaced by the new harvest and the year-old barley fed to the animals or sold at a reduced price. Even when stored for long periods of time, barley would not go to waste, since it could both protect against human hunger and also keep livestock well fed long after the grain became unpalatable to humans.[117] The legal and mercantile advantages of storing barley, combined with a seigniorial preference for underground silos, probably also explain the high percentage of barley paid in rent over wheat in most Catalan surveys of land ownership and rents.[118]

In the face of volatility, risk-averse actors will usually take the safer position. For farmers, this often meant saving grain, but regulations tended to discourage storage. Laws placed more emphasis on short-term functionality than on long-term incentives for storage or famine resistance. At the beginning of the fifteenth century, Perpignan's leaders observed that people kept their grain in storage for up to eighteen years, until even animals would no longer eat it. In response, they restricted the storage of grain in silos to a maximum of four years.[119] Concerns about grade and quality broadly reduced the interest in long-term, systematic storage of grain. While this may have helped secure a smoothly running market, it created vulnerability to short-term shortages. While manure markets and irrigation could assist large groups in society, market restrictions often assisted certain groups at the expense of others.

Crop Yields and Agricultural Management in the County of Barcelona: A Case Study

Catalan archives do not often contain detailed land administration records like the English manorial accounts. However, the records of the cathedral poorhouse of Barcelona contain several detailed management records kept by overseers in the field, the procurators, concerning agricultural practices on the Pia Almoina's properties. The most remarkable series comes from the castle of Sitges, located about forty kilometers south of Barcelona on the Mediterranean coast. The agricultural practices at Sitges represent some of the more advanced agricultural capacities in the region, combining integrated irrigation practices, routine purchases of manure, and extensive use of wage labor to avoid bottlenecks. Additionally, because of the castle's connection to the cathedral poorhouse, the overseers had access to deep pockets for land improvements and the ability to ship grain to Barcelona to convert their production into cash when it proved beneficial.

In 1354, the poorhouse completed its purchase of the full rights to the castle. Beginning that year and continuing until 1411, the procurator began keeping a series of documents containing extensive information about seigniorial and agricultural practices: the rent he collected, how much laborers were paid, and, most important, the yearly rhythms of planting and harvesting on the demesne land.[120] The local record books from Sitges are divided into three sections. The first summarizes all of the castle's income, including rents, payments in kind, labor, and other tax revenues. The second, arranged chronologically over the fiscal year from May through the following April, lists all payments made by the house and their dates, including both paid labor and the seigniorial obligations that provided the agricultural work in the fields and vineyards. The final section usually records "extraordinary" payments such as building repairs, the sale or purchase of property, and the cost of trips to neighboring towns or to Barcelona. Occasionally, missing information such as sale price data can be filled in with the general management records of the Majordomia, recorded at the Barcelona Cathedral.

Both the format of the records and the agricultural practices were widely used, at least within the county of Barcelona. Other large properties under the Pia Almoina's ownership left similar books, though almost none have survived—fewer than a dozen such books remain from properties in Mogoda, Vilafranca del Penedès, and the Torre Baldovina. Similarly, hospitals run by the church, like the Hospital d'en Colom and the Hospital dels Malalts, kept records describing their own practices that offer a handful of good comparisons. Finally, the abbess of the nearby monastery of Sant Pere de les Puel·les kept general records of the monastery's income and expenses, starting in 1356, that often describe labor costs and agricultural practices, though they do not provide the kinds of details on agricultural practice and yields that we have for the castle of Sitges.[121]

The most remarkable finding from the Sitges data is the divergence in crop yields in the second half of the fourteenth century. The procurators at times reported yields in excess of 20:1 for both wheat and barley. Over the course of fifty years, barley yields averaged more than 12:1 and wheat averaged just below 10:1, both significantly higher than the averages given for other parts of Europe. The yields for fava beans are more modest but probably reflect their use as a cover crop rather than as a staple (see fig. 1).[122] Barley rarely produced less than a tenfold yield; in virtually all of the years that it did, the Barcelona city records mention problems in the grain supply, indicating relatively widespread shortages.[123] The lowest recorded yield of any harvest—a mere 5:1 in 1376—corresponds to the final year of the worst famine of the century in the Mediterranean. When the harvest was below average, procurators noted that it was lower in quality as well as quantity. In 1397, barley yielded only an 8:1 ratio, and the record describes the grain as "weedy."[124] The records of the Hospital dels Malalts, though sparse, reveal a few additional data points. In 1380, a year that marks the beginning of several rainy seasons, increased prices, and new imports to Barcelona from Sicily, the hospital yielded a barley ratio of just 7:1 in its own fields.[125] The following year, as rains continued, the hospital harvested a record low 1.8:1, a number commensurate with the "dismal" harvests frequently discussed in northern Europe. After 1381, records containing specific numbers end, as most of the grain was eaten in-house rather than sold. What little grain did grow was of poor quality.[126] Despite these few bad years, the general trend is quite good,

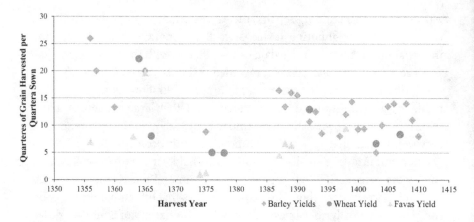

FIG. 1. CROP YIELDS AT SITGES CASTLE (SEED RATIOS), 1350–1415. The yields are recorded as quarters harvested per quarter sown. The lack of information on field size makes yield per acre impossible to calculate. While the numbers show a large spread, they average just over 12:1 for barley and 8:1 for wheat.

matching the famously productive lands of Sicily.[127] By any measure, average yields throughout the second half of the century were extremely high.[128]

There is no reason to think that the land in Sitges was more fertile than other areas. The castle sits against a steep backdrop of hills covered with thin, lightly watered soil, a terrain prevalent along the Catalan coastline. The overseer of the castle, and presumably many of the laborers, understood a great deal about the health of the soil, the productive potential of different grains, and how to maximize their output. Such practices gained priority under the direction of a class of economically savvy clerics motivated to increase profits.[129] Record keepers, always interested in cost and production (but never in explanatory prose), rarely spelled out the reasoning behind their agricultural choices. However, some of these reasons can be inferred from known weather patterns and harvest trends.

The records demonstrate that cultivators employed multiple methods for increasing their yields, relying on both capital and labor. The documents also reveal the decision-making processes of the property managers, especially their responses to the famines of 1374–75 and 1383. Supporting the conclusions of David Stone's work on the manor of Wisbech in England, the procurators responded to the best available market and weather information, using extra labor and varying crop rotations to maximize output and hedge against risk.[130] While some methods might not have been available to all farmers, poorhouse managers, seeking financial gain, adopted a number of methods that proved beneficial for organizations that could afford them. Because of the close proximity of the Barcelona market and managers' ability to ship or store grain—whichever method yielded the best price—their decisions reflect a mercantile attitude toward farming.

Sitges followed the general patterns of Catalan agriculture: frequent use of the scratch plow pulled by mules, a strong preference for winter cereal production, and a reliance on manure and irrigation to maintain fertility.[131] Of the available agricultural techniques, systematic and efficient use of labor was the single most important. Work on several farms, both at Sitges and on other agricultural land around Barcelona, involved a combination of paid day laborers, full-time retainers or servants (referred to as *macips* and *servents*), and labor obligations of both human labor (*tragins*) and animal labor (*joves*) performed as part of peasant rents. Individuals often worked for a single day's pay, which hovered between 1.5 and 2.5 solidi per day; women and youths received less, sometimes as little as one solidus per day.[132] In addition to pay, laborers received their food for the day, which usually meant only the main meal of the day and included bread and meat (or fish on fast days) and some form of *companatge*—that is, vegetables, cheese, eggs, figs, or other foodstuffs. Workers who performed particularly heavy work, such as plowing and harvesting, also received breakfast. The monastery of Sant Pere de les Puel·les employed a similar combination of paid labor, food, and obligatory labor. The payment books often recorded specifics about the workers' diet, such as when they were fed perch, and the periodic addition of higher-quality foods for the slaves, such as *botifarra* sausages on Christmas.[133] The abbess of the monastery also recorded amounts of money spent on both wages and food for women, whose rations could cost as little as half as much as those of male workers.[134]

Strategic use of market labor at the properties of the monastery and the Pia Almoina decreased the occurrence of bottlenecks in production. The labor-intensive periods of the year, particularly planting and harvesting, involved as many as ten men and multiple draft animals.[135] At the castle of Mogoda, a larger property of the Pia Almoina, overseers hired more than thirty people at a time.[136] In the vineyards of Sant Pere, dozens of men and women tended the vines, weeded, plowed between rows, and harvested the grapes.[137] The laborers could harvest larger-than-usual yields in good years, weed around the plants in wet years, and carry water to the fields in dry years. They frequently spread and plowed in manure, performing extra plowings when necessary. This doubtless allowed the managers of the land to keep soil fertility high and respond to the vicissitudes of weather in a way that individual farmers were less able to do.

The labor records also provide clues about specific planting and harvesting practices. All grains mentioned at the different properties were winter crops, usually sown in November. Prior to planting, the fields were cleared of weeds and plowed (often more than once), the remaining clods broken up with mallets or spades. Finally, the seeds were sown and then covered with a new layer of manure-enriched soil.[138] While they probably still used a broadcast method, it does appear that the planters paid close attention to how the seeds came to rest for germination. Leveling the soil or covering the seeds, and even watering if the ground was not sufficiently wet, could have greatly improved germination rates, thereby considerably improving the final yield.

Throughout the winter, overseers kept close track of plant growth. Hired hands watered the fields from the wells around the castle or pulled weeds that threatened to choke the young grain.[139] In the dry Mediterranean, the fields required frequent watering, but weeds threatened during rainy winters. In 1362 at Sitges, in addition to a man with two mules hired to sow fava beans, laborers included a second man and two women "who planted the favas and pulled weeds because there were so many."[140] Normally, only one man with a mule team working as a labor obligation sowed favas. In 1400, however, three teams of mules came to plow and had to do so twice because, "on account of the rain, it was all weeds."[141] Similarly, at the Hospital dels Malalts in Barcelona, during the shortages of 1381–84, extra laborers worked the fields in November to completely replant and refertilize the field because of heavy rains.[142] During the winter and spring, laborers routinely hoed the fields to help keep weeds down. This sort of careful tending doubtless also improved yields.

The economic resources of the Pia Almoina allowed the farm to invest heavily in materials. Immediately after the purchase of the land and rights in 1354, the Pia Almoina managers set about improving the fields. Hired laborers removed large stones from the land. In one note from 1356, the overseer hired men to come and repair what appears to have been a noria waterwheel, called a *cenia* or *sènia* in the sources. The device had collapsed and the drive wheel needed to be reset or replaced.[143] As noted above, capital-intensive irrigation technology often required institutional backing.

Another important aspect of the agriculture at Sitges was the use of crop rotation.[144] Echoing some of the patterns noted by David Stone in Ely, England, managers responded frequently to changes in economy and climate by rotating crops.[145] After the disastrous year of 1374, workers at Sitges planted an indiscriminate mix of barley and wheat, something not done previously. Presumably, they were attempting to harvest whatever they could

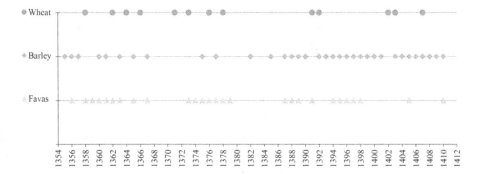

FIG. 2. CROPS PLANTED AT SITGES CASTLE BY YEAR, 1355–1410. In a given year, if the particular crop (wheat, barley, favas) is marked, the house chose to plant some quantity of that crop, although the quantities are not known. If no crop is indicated, the records are missing.

after the miserable harvest of 1374. In 1376, they returned to planting wheat but again reaped a poor harvest. After attempting barley and favas in 1377, they sowed wheat again in 1378, but with similarly disappointing results. These two years would have put Sitges at a strong disadvantage relative to other markets, since prices in Barcelona had already begun to fall in 1375, as wheat arrived from Sicily and Flanders. After 1378, the overall planting of wheat dropped considerably. In the twenty years before the famine of 1374–75, barley was planted ten times and wheat six, with a couple years of only favas and a handful of unknowns. After the failed attempts with wheat in 1376 and 1378, that grain appears only in two record years through the end of the century, whereas barley was planted fourteen times (see fig. 2). Dismal wheat harvests pressured procurators to rely on safer, though less lucrative, barley well after the difficulties in growing wheat had ended. During poor harvest years in the 1380s, the managers at the Hospital dels Malalts also responded quickly. After the dreadful harvest of 1381 (1.8:1, the lowest seed ratio recorded for barley in any source), only favas were planted in 1382, presumably with the goal of returning some fertility to the soil. In 1383, the hospital bought 1.5 quarters of high-quality wheat for planting, relying on the new grain to produce a superior harvest. Again, the rains thwarted this effort and the "poor" wheat harvested was all served in the hospital.[146] In 1384, the hospital managers returned to a crop of all favas with heavy manuring.[147] While the severity of those years overwhelmed the usual defenses, the general response of hospitals to climatic difficulties demonstrates a clear pattern: retreat from production for a year and maintain good fertility with cover crops or manure for when better weather returns.

All of these features—from high labor inputs to the use of irrigation and the resources of a manure market—demonstrate an integrated and resourceful agricultural system. It is unlikely that any one of these elements made the difference between the high yields recorded at Sitges and the relatively low averages found in other areas. However, the combination of elements allowed for greater responsiveness to the vicissitudes of weather and disease and resulted in increased yields in both good years and bad. Agriculture in the fourteenth century was an incremental science, and any small gain reduced risk. The managers of these properties certainly assumed that their efforts were both effective and worth the cost.

Agricultural Advancement in the Crown of Aragon

In the absence of widespread comparative data, it is difficult to know whether these practices were unique in the region around Barcelona. The general quality and output of agriculture in the Crown of Aragon are of paramount importance in determining the population's fundamental resilience or vulnerability to harvest shortfalls. The highly productive land around Sitges demonstrates that the use of irrigation, manuring, and storage described above helped to produce and regulate a healthy surplus in normal years. Consistent surplus across a wide area would translate to generally strong access to food and resistance to famine. Such surplus was also necessary to keep the more highly urbanized Mediterranean coast supplied with food. But we do not know how thoroughly these practices penetrated the extensive farmland throughout the Crown.

Studies from around the kingdom demonstrate the general presence of storage and the frequent use of irrigation, but documents describing specific agricultural results are relatively rare. Furthermore, even rich church records from around Barcelona have limitations. Without an indication of the area of land involved, yield per acre is impossible to calculate. It is thus also impossible to know just how much land made the difference between a comfortable peasant family and a family constantly on the edge of starvation. Studies of agriculture in England have found that yields were sometimes lowest in areas with the largest amount of available land.[148] The castle of Sitges could have increased its yield on a relatively small plot with extensive labor and nitrogen inputs, but this does not necessarily mean that these were widely desirable practices. Finally, because all of our data come from after the Black

Death, the numbers cannot speak to possible agricultural changes due to demographic decline. Agricultural managers did maintain a marked preference for high labor inputs even in a time of declining labor availability.[149]

What we can analyze with confidence are the influences of economic incentives and managerial practices encouraged by the presence of a large nearby food market. Both Barcelona hospitals and the monastery of Sant Pere relied heavily on their connections to the market. Sant Pere could decide to consume its own produce, sell it locally, or ship it to the city, depending on production in a particular year. Particularly with wine, the monastery produced significantly more than it routinely consumed.[150] As noted above, the use of grapes as a commercial crop appears regularly in other documents. At Sitges itself, the workers each year loaded a ship with all of the produce harvested at Sitges and surrounding towns like Vilafranca del Penedès. The grapes, grain, and other goods were taken directly to Barcelona, either to feed the inhabitants of the poorhouse or, more often, for direct sale in the markets of the large trading city. Pere Benito i Monclús has demonstrated that the procurators at Sitges were knowledgeable enough to decide whether it was more profitable to send grain to market, consume it in-house, or store it in large underground granaries. Using their storage capacity, the Sitges managers routinely maximized their profit by speculating on grain prices in Barcelona.[151] Evidence of large-scale storage on other properties, such as Mogoda, provides a tantalizing hint that this practice might have been common throughout the Pia Almoina holdings.[152] English agricultural management also "responded to economic conditions when deploying labor inputs, such as weeding, manuring, harvesting, and gleaning, on their manors as Stone has suggested."[153] Such incentives and the resulting practices are also consistent with Bruce Campbell's observation that strong nearby markets tend to correlate with agricultural intensification and increased yields.[154]

Valencia, Zaragoza, Barcelona, Perpignan, and even smaller cities like Lleida and Alicante extended significant influence over their surrounding agricultural land. However, the mere existence of such advantages does not mean that everyone had access to large markets. As Campbell has shown, the areas in England that adopted the most progressive methods "were those with natural environmental advantages, good market access, and few institutional constraints in the form of servile tenures and communal property rights."[155] The coexistence of customary and economic or contractual arrangements over land blunted the economic incentive by disguising the true cost of rent. False costs made it appear more profitable for both peasant and lord to employ methods designed for short-term gain in a land-rich world. The inability to participate fully in the grain and labor markets further diminished the incentives necessary to increase harvests consistently. The Catalan evidence for the intensive use of manure and labor shows the possibility of planning for harvests over a longer term. Reliable transportation to the Barcelona market and integrated management by the Pia Almoina itself ensured that Almoina land managers responded wisely to the institutional, natural, and economic factors that guided their agricultural decisions.

The data raise another question, however: just how aware and deliberate were the overseers and laborers in their choices? It is probably impossible to know whether certain cultivators were aware of available techniques but did not adopt them for whatever reason.[156] While the lands examined in this study constitute a minority of the county of Barcelona, it seems likely that many of their tenants would have been aware of the possibilities detailed in the Sitges records. Additionally, many of the techniques discussed above were not radical technological changes—using manure as fertilizer, pulling weeds, and watering and irrigation are all frequently documented routine techniques. As with crop rotation, what is notable is less the information at their disposal and more how procurators chose to act on it.

The skilled management of church lands around Barcelona created a model for the best agricultural practices of the late fourteenth century. But even if day laborers and small cultivators had access to information that could improve their yields, their ability to make use of it would have varied. Many techniques depended on available capital and a flexible labor market. The Pia Almoina, an institution that hired hundreds of workers throughout its patrimonial holdings, could afford the occasional spike in labor costs, particularly if it meant a larger harvest. Individual holders, lacking that freedom, were subject to stricter restraints. One of the tenets of the population and resource model stipulates that agricultural labor also suffered from diminishing returns.[157] Two people might double output, whereas five people might only triple it. One of the major explanations for this feature of medieval agriculture has to do with labor bottlenecks—the necessity of intensive labor inputs for only certain seasonal tasks, with low labor requirements in other months. Plowing might require a dozen men and several animals, but this could be the only time in the agricultural year when so much labor was needed. Excessive rain could ruin a crop absent an immediate and intensive intervention of labor (e.g., weeding), while other labor might be performed by only two or three workers. Given this aspect of labor-intensive agriculture, only the frequent use of wage labor would allow a cultivator to escape both the law of diminishing returns and the normal bottlenecks of the agricultural year. Individual peasants with sufficient wealth might be able to hire enough people to perform the work required, but, in general, institutions were better able than individual cultivators to generate consistently higher cereal yields.

Conclusions

Cultivators in medieval Aragon, like farmers everywhere, made their agricultural choices within a set of constraints, some of which increased their resilience in the face of shortages and some of which did not. Climate created the broad background requirements within which everyone lived, but cultural desires added social, legal, and economic constraints. The persistent desire for wheat tended to discourage, though not erase, the most effective use of crop diversity in the protean Mediterranean climate. Even the grading system of wheat deterred its effective storage. The storage of food persisted, but large-scale and longer-term grain storage favored barley, which provided both human and animal sustenance. Other influences proved effective at reducing the impact of the inevitable bad harvests. The intensification of agriculture brought on by high levels of urbanization reached a sufficiently commercial level that a market for manure created new avenues to renewing soil fertility. Increased use of emphyteusis contracts allowed urban landowners to collect stable rents in cash and enabled peasants to respond to market demands and improve their land. Multiple cities and nobles throughout the Crown of Aragon invested heavily in irrigation projects that bolstered the value of land and directly assisted in peasant survival when drought threatened crops. Although a project like the proposed Júcar-Turia canal proved too politically challenging and expensive to build, that plan demonstrates the scale at which late medieval actors could envision adapting their world to make agriculture more profitable and shortages less threatening.

In the end, the combination of cash crops, favorable land tenure, and capital investment created a robust agriculture system. Significant territory from Aragon to the Urgell to southern Valencia produced routine and effective surpluses. Surpluses appeared first in regional markets, where traders moved food for export from towns like Sant Feliu de Guixols and Castelló d'Empúries or down the Segre and Ebro Rivers through Lleida and Tortosa to the sea.[158] Some of the surplus came from the extractive tenures that made serfs more likely to starve. But the quantities of grain that flowed out the mouth of the Ebro River on ships indicate that many cultivators must have been able to produce more than enough to meet their own needs. In the south of Valencia, the lands between Alicante and Orihuela produced a surplus so routinely that droughts tended to cause political wrangling over exports rather than a sudden need for new imports. It is to this broader system of exchange that we now turn.

2

THE POWER OF DISTRIBUTION

Within the impressive bibliography on the economy and trade in the late medieval Crown of Aragon, two underappreciated features link trade and famine. First, over the course of the fourteenth century, urban councils and jurors in the coastal cities consciously experimented with available measures for controlling their grain markets (jurors, literally *jurats* in Catalan, were the executive members of the city government). Urban leaders understood the complex nature of famine, which could have many causes.[1] As the jurors of Valencia declared to Johan I of Prades (1335–1414), the seneschal of Catalonia, in 1374, "This shortage has come to us not just from the lack of grains this year . . . but even more from the large quantities of wheat that we secured in Sicily that have been seized and carried off in Sardinia for their own supply."[2] Because of the various causes of any given famine, cities experimented with their economic responses and found that some functioned better than others.

The second feature linking trade and famine was that as a consequence of increasing market integration, geography took on a new role in causing shortages and famines. Changes in the grain supply—increasing control over nearby markets, experimentation with incentives, connections to more distant markets, and general integration of markets—reduced the direct influence of local harvest failures. The expanded reach of markets meant that well-connected cities might not suffer greatly during minor shortages. Even smaller towns, when necessary, could access the grain supplied by large markets. Despite tightening legal controls, larger cities did allow such access when smaller towns were under duress from local harvest failures. Even with their consolidated control of nearby areas, city importers looked beyond their normal grain supply regions in times of shortage to a secondary set of distant production areas to cover nearby shortages. This created a double supply horizon, with significant overlap in the secondary supply regions of multiple cities around the Mediterranean rim. When multiple locations experienced shortage, however, too many secondary supply areas came into competition, exacerbating the crisis by spreading panic throughout the market.

Experimentation and integration frequently relied on economic and political dominance over nearby sources of food. Over the course of the fourteenth century, Catalan markets in general moved from being relatively open and largely privately controlled to being increasingly under the thumb of city governments and more tightly constrained.[3] As Stephan R. Epstein has shown, contrary to free-market expectations, increasing institutional control of markets in Italy contributed to their integration.[4] Institutional control went hand in hand with the self-interest of several elite groups. Royal and noble landowners used permissions and trade rights to generate revenue; and urban councils, often dominated by powerful merchants, used legal restrictions to promote their own trade. Contrary to modern ideas about corruption, new ideologies of the public good promoted the concept that the best way to rule was to align the economic interests of the rulers with the economic stability and success of the cities they oversaw.[5]

Over the course of the century, smaller and smaller towns gained market privileges and created new economic connections with their neighbors. The Black Death may have reversed population growth, but it did not significantly reverse the number of market privileges blanketing the landscape or the market integration of the Mediterranean region.[6] By the 1370s, most markets could weather even significant regional shortages. The locusts of 1358 devastated crops (and caused highly localized hardships), but increasing market integration meant that even rural areas were unlikely to simply run out of food in a bad year.[7] The flip side of the coin, of course, was that when multiple factors created shortages in overlapping supply regions, the entire system could collapse, causing widespread panic and serious famine across a wide geographic range.

Increased market integration, in short, created a situation whereby minor shortages became less frequent and more survivable but interdependence and panic spawned sharp price spikes during serious crises. Locally raised crops still provided the core of market resources, but imported grain from each city's secondary markets became increasingly important. By the end of the century, these imports came not just from the Mediterranean but from northern Europe as well, a market initially opened up by the dictates of food shortages themselves. Grain imports came to play such a large role in Barcelona that they could even change the normal seasonal variation of prices. Trade turned famines into vastly more complex events than they had been before. Local bad weather was insufficient to cause a famine on its own; only some combination of war, multiple bad weather events, and market panic was enough to bring down the regional supply systems and create a true crisis. To make matters worse, constrictive or counterproductive measures imposed during shortages fragmented the market at exactly the moment that greater integration might have helped.

Demography, Migration, and Market Expansion

Before turning to the distribution of grain, let us consider the distribution of people and markets. There are numerous demographic studies of the many regions in the Crown of Aragon, but they are all based on sources with significant shortcomings. Much demographic research begins with tax documents, whether the hearth tax in Catalonia (called a *fogatge*) or the monetary or head tax used in the rest of the kingdom (named after the types of coins collected—*morabatín*, *maravedi*, or sometimes *monedatge*).[8] Hearth taxes counted only households, requiring some estimation of normal household size. Monetary taxation relied on individual payments but left out anyone not required to pay (children, but also the poor). Both kinds of documents provide only snapshots of given moments in time, with very few sources before the Black Death, making trends difficult to discern.[9]

Broadly speaking, the Crown of Aragon comprised three different regional demographic regimes in the late fourteenth century.[10] First, a dense population of small landholders, often laboring under relatively onerous land contracts, covered the northern third of the territory, running from the various counties in the Pyrenees into the highlands of Aragon north of Huesca and the valleys in the older counties of Catalonia, such as Urgell and Girona. In the mountains themselves, population density was sparser and more land was given over to transhumance, the seasonal movement of livestock like sheep between mountains and lowland pastures.[11] Second, there was a wide area of both Catalonia and Aragon that had been conquered from Muslim Taifa princes or from the Almoravids in the late eleventh and early twelfth centuries. This zone included all of the agricultural land around the city of Zaragoza, much of the southern interior of Catalonia, and the important river valleys of the Ebro, the Llobregat, and the lower Segre, much of it highly productive and characterized by a mix of tenures, though frequently held by powerful independent lords.[12] After the unsettled period of conquest in earlier centuries, this territory had become densely settled by around 1300. Third, in much of the region south of the Ebro River, along with the Balearic Islands, the Christian conquests happened late enough that the king was still distributing territory as rewards almost until the eve of the Black Death. The southernmost areas of Valencia, including the towns of Orihuela and Elche, were not absorbed entirely into the Crown of Aragon until the early fourteenth century. Nobles often traded control of the land along the Ebro for new land in the Balearics or Valencia, areas that often contained subject Muslim peasantry but that lords could more easily control and begin settling with new Christians.[13] Because of the continued interest in new Christian settlement, this third band of territory served as an immigrant destination throughout this period.

Overlaid on top of these three demographic areas was an increasingly connected urban network that constantly drew in rural population. Each portion of the kingdom—Aragon, Catalonia, Valencia, the Balearic Islands, and territories in Roussillon—had a large capital city and several other cities of varying importance. Scholars have tried to define the boundaries between urban and rural areas and have subdivided cities into categories based on population size, government structure, privileges, economic connections, and other factors.[14] When it comes to understanding grain supply, economic and political clout tends to matter more than absolute population size or the explicit development of urban institutions. While these things are clearly important, economic muscle is more pertinent in explaining the importance of smaller cities like Palma or Tortosa, which vied with the most populous locations for supplies.

In 1348, the arrival of the Black Death erased any possible population pressures on available land across most of Europe. The Plague killed between 25 and 35 percent of the population within a few years, and repeated outbreaks produced a general downward pressure on population that persisted for decades.[15] Valencia probably recovered more quickly than the other regions because of strong immigration, but nowhere did the population reach previous levels until the fifteenth century.[16] The Black Death not only reduced the overall population but accelerated urbanization. Before the Plague, descriptions of overpopulation in the north often refer to lands in the immediate vicinity of towns like Girona, Huesca, and especially Zaragoza.[17] The epidemic broke some of the bonds that kept individuals in small towns, encouraging survivors to move to larger cities. All of the capital cities increased their relative percentage of the population throughout the period, although Palma de Mallorca began the fourteenth century with a larger share of its regional population than the other cities.[18] The densest agricultural population persisted in the irrigated *huerta* around Valencia, the plains around Zaragoza, and the wine-producing interior of Mallorca. Ultimately, population size was a poor predictor of famine in the Crown of Aragon. Any pressure that may have existed, particularly in the northern regions, was increasingly mitigated by expanding access to land provided by southward migration. Population pressure was usually local, compounded by socially restrictive arrangements that forced families to inherit divided plots and allowed relatively few outlets for economic expansion.

In contrast to population, rising access to markets and regional integration provided increasing resilience through exchange during the fourteenth century. Beginning in the late thirteenth century, the number of chartered weekly markets exploded. Throughout the fourteenth century, more new markets came into existence than in either the thirteenth or the fifteenth. Catalonia added forty-four new markets, Aragon nearly fifty, and Valencia almost forty.[19] With this growth in the number of markets came an increase in written contracts and new availability of money and credit. These social technologies developed, largely uninhibited by changing demographics. Access to midsized population centers with official fairs and markets drove significant changes in the overall economy.[20] Mark Bailey has noted that increased economic integration actually reduced the problem of marginal land by allowing poor agricultural land to produce market products such as stone, wood, metal, and wool for a higher price, relying on exchange for basic foodstuffs.[21] Throughout the Crown of Aragon, the areas between medium-sized cities like Vic, Manresa, and Tortosa in the north, Huesca, Teruel, and Lleida to the west, and Castellón, Alicante, and Orihuela in Valencia were interspersed with numerous smaller towns, both along major roads and down the coastline, that bound together agricultural producers, urban capitals, and commercial demand. Market access drove increased demand for agricultural land around cities like Zaragoza, Valencia, Barcelona, and Palma de Mallorca.[22] The growing importance of these towns created a dense new web of food access based on exchange and increased the ability to respond to local shortages by purchasing grain from regional sources.

The density of markets set the stage for competition for control of agricultural and trade zones. Such competition created conflicts between multiple towns, which pressured the king to act as mediator—with mixed success. For example, the town of Banyoles, controlled by the monastery of the same name, fought for greater and greater protections of its market, eventually gaining a privilege from Alfons IV (r. 1327–36) in 1334 to a monopoly on the goods coming to market from within a league (roughly a five-kilometer radius). That distance placed Banyoles in direct competition with nearby towns like Besalú.[23] Similarly, Alfons revoked the market privileges of Vilagrassa in April 1329 because of direct competition with Tàrrega, only three kilometers away. Tàrrega had a close association with the queen, which helped its case against the smaller market.[24] Eventually, in 1342, Pere the Ceremonious (r. 1336–87) reinstated Vilagrassa's market privileges because of its high tax base. Such demands often revolved around profit but had consequences for the ability of small towns to control the flow of agricultural goods during times of shortage.

Market integration, then, provided both resilience and risk. The combination of easily available contracts, broad monetization, access to credit, and the possibility of imported food allowed subsistence farmers to put off a minor crisis: food and seed could be purchased, even at a high price, with a promise of repayment based on future good years.[25] Of course, such purchases also involved the possibility of heavy debt and potential long-term impoverishment. Market access also increasingly allowed politically powerful cities to squeeze surplus out of rural areas in times of shortage. In general, increasing market penetration did not eliminate subsistence agriculture, but it did tilt the balance toward an exchange economy more than ever before.[26]

Importers, Exporters, and Waypoints

Critically, these interlocking trade systems included large amounts of bulk trade in grain. Because of growing levels of exchange, rural communities increasingly felt the impact of economic strife or food shortages in neighboring regions. Economic well-being, and by extension the ability to draw food toward local markets, was connected to faraway towns and cities with little concern for the stability of the producing region. Food shortages in Valencia had consequences for southern France and even Florence, while Barcelona's economic privileges could harm producers far inland in Aragon. This feature of trade created new competition and encouraged political actors throughout the network to experiment with multiple legal and economic means of controlling the grain supply. Depending on political power, local agricultural conditions, and geography, different strategies for control developed.

Generally, each political entity preferred to liberalize trade within its sphere of influence while exercising strict controls on trade at its borders. Nobles wanted easy movement to markets within their lands but the ability to control exports and charge money for licenses. Cities could force individuals to declare and sell their available grain, but they fought for the power to ban exports and regulate internal markets. The kings of Aragon passed legislation that sometimes ran counter to local measures enacted by both lords and cities, occasionally implementing remarkably bold legislation designed to change the entire regional market. Indeed, royal attempts to liberalize internal markets while restricting and licensing exports began early in the thirteenth century, well before similar urban efforts.[27] Most often, the kings acted as mediators in disputes between local powers. Even then, however, royal authorities frequently gave preferential treatment to powerful urban governments or to trade that benefited the royal treasury.[28]

In the fourteenth century, the most common regulatory experimentation came from urban governments. Cities in the Crown of Aragon had more uniform systems of government than Italian cities, where many complex dynamics were at play. Virtually all cities maintained their rights based on privileges granted by the king. As noted above, city governments included a small group of men, usually called *jurats* (literally "jurors"), who oversaw the running of government and received direction and consultation from a larger council. The councils worked together with royal representatives, notably the *veguer*, a legal official who helped enforce the king's laws, the *batle*, or bailiff, and, most important for the food supply, the *mostassaf*, who oversaw market regulations. The size of these groups varied, but generally the jurors numbered a dozen or fewer (six in Valencia, eight in Barcelona), while the councils could be quite large (eighty in Girona and a hundred in Barcelona, where the council was usually referred to as the Consell de Cent, or Council of One Hundred). Urban government structure was relatively uniform across cities because most privileges were modeled after a few original legal charters, like the customs of Lleida or the legal rights of Zaragoza and Barcelona. With the expansion of the Crown into Mallorca and Valencia, kings issued new urban privileges modeled after these originals.

Francesc Eiximenis famously described the three "hands" that combined to form these urban governments, including an upper (*major*), middle (*mitjana*), and lower (*menor*) status group.[29] The upper level included only the most influential patrician families in the city, a category defined more by social status and custom than by economic clout. The middle included wealthy traders, cloth merchants, and other economically influential families. The bottom tier generally included artisans and other laborers, but how many other workers were included depended on the city. In most cities, the upper two hands dominated the council, but not always. At one extreme, Barcelona's council came almost entirely from an overlapping group of patricians and wealthy mercantile elites, while, at the other, artisans had significant representation in Girona.[30] Even the highest-status category systematically excluded both ecclesiastics and the nobility.[31] Barcelona's council fought constantly for control of regional trade with cities like Tarragona and Tortosa, but it also frequently clashed with nobles and their export privileges. The notable exception was Valencia, where even in the earliest charters minor nobles appeared as part of the *mà major*, or upper hand. During the late fourteenth century, Valencia's jurors included four members of wealthy families (often merchants) and two nobles.[32] That Valencian jurors combined urban mercantile goals with the interests of landowning nobles contributed to the city's powerful control of the surrounding regions.

The relationship between hinterland production and demand and commercial access also directly influenced grain supply policy. Towns either had sufficient regional production to act as exporters, or they attempted to control trade, either through strategic locations and bottlenecks or through political dominance and privilege. Barcelona and Valencia, especially, exercised tight political control over nearby sources of routine necessities. Multiple regions acted as grain exporters throughout the century. Much of Sicily exported wheat from the ports of its largest cities that helped supply the entire western Mediterranean basin. King Pere often relied on Sicilian imports to keep his army in Sardinia fed; Catalonia's importers—Barcelona, Valencia, Palma—routinely received Sicilian grain. Some parts of southern France— Montpellier, Narbonne, Agde, Cotlliure—could export excess wheat during good years, although shortages reversed the flow, making the towns importers.[33] Within the Crown of Aragon, Zaragoza was the most notable urban exporter. Because of the densely populated productive land around the city, Zaragoza became a major market, drawing grain from around Aragon and exporting the surplus down the Ebro River to connect with the wider Mediterranean supply.[34] Zaragozan wheat exports paid for massive quantities of imported dried hake, herring, and sardines for fast days.[35] Located just upriver from the junction between the Segre and the Ebro, Lleida also brought grain exports from the Urgell through its market and into the Ebro system.

Some exporting regions specialized in crops of varying dietary value. Animals from the Pyrenees and from the Maestrazgo, on the border of Aragon and Valencia, supplied both wool and meat.[36] Manresa, as noted in the previous chapter, developed an export market by moving large amounts of saffron, often over great distances. The land just south of Valencia produced a number of tree crops, including apricots, dates, and almonds.[37] Further south, the land around Orihuela, Elche, and Alicante tended to produce barley for local consumption and turn over as much land as possible (including irrigated land) for grapes and wheat for export.

Several market centers relied on trade connections, combined with strategic geographic location, for their economic strength. In the Crown of Aragon, the two most notable examples were Tortosa and Palma de Mallorca. In contrast to exporting cities, the supply strategy of these waypoints was to encourage more trade than was necessary for local supply. In good years, these cities sold some foodstuffs on the local market while collecting fees and taxes on goods continuing to other locations. Palma used low anchorage fees to encourage high levels of ship traffic.[38] Cagliari, especially after the Catalan invasion, also functioned as a transit point between Sicily and the Crown of Aragon.[39] Tortosa controlled most of the river traffic leaving the Ebro, including huge quantities of grain exported from Aragon.[40] For these waypoints, bad years generally meant restricting the outflow of their already expanded resources, rather than attempting to create new market connections. Moderate shortages did not cause needless panic, for the quantities arriving still met the needs of the local market. The main risks during a famine came when exporting regions stopped their outward flow of grain, or major importers intensified their political pressure. For both Tortosa and Palma, the goal during a major crisis was to restrict exports enough to keep their own markets supplied without angering the major importers unduly.

The largest cities managed a multilevel system of local supply, regional imports, and a wide but loose network connecting them with distant exporters in times of crisis.[41] In the Crown of Aragon, Barcelona and Valencia fought with exporters large and small for control over the grain trade, and both cities exercised political power as their preferred means of maintaining their supply. Barcelona remained the largest and most politically powerful importer of grain until the late fourteenth century, when it was slowly overtaken by Valencia, and significant scholarly work has detailed its development.[42] During the fourteenth century, Barcelona's primary grain supply came from regions in Catalonia itself, especially the city's own hinterland around the Llobregat River and the agricultural land just inland in the Vallès.[43] Barcelona also routinely imported grain overland from the Urgell and Segarra regions, and sometimes from some of the smaller coastal ports, such as Torroella de Montgrí, Sant Feliu de Guixols, and Castelló d'Empúries.[44] The city's rulers constantly attempted to control the substantial flow of Aragonese grain

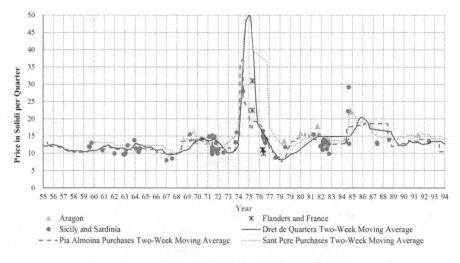

FIG. 3. MOVING AVERAGE OF BARCELONA PRICES WITH KNOWN IMPORTS, 1355–1394. The trend lines show the moving averages from the Llibres d'abadesses from Sant Pere de les Puel·les, the market purchases from the Pia Almoina, and the *dret de quartera* from the Pia Almoina. Sales of grain from Sicily and Sardinia are clustered around years with elevated grain prices. Grain from Flanders and northern France appears almost exclusively during significant price spikes, such as those in 1374 and 1384 (and also in 1401, not included here).

through the port of Tortosa at the mouth of the Ebro River. The Ebro was navigable as far inland as Zaragoza and could carry grain from the highlands of Aragon and from parts of the Urgell down the Segre River to Lleida, where it joined with the Ebro.[45] Internationally, Barcelona also routinely imported grain from Sicily and parts of southern France. However, grain imports from Sicily and Roussillon remained consistently more expensive than grain from closer sources and thus tended to increase only during shortages. Records from Sant Pere de les Puel·les and the Pia Almoina often indicate when market purchases came from farther afield and map closely onto years with price increases (see fig. 3). While Barcelona maintained the constant possibility of more distant imports, consumers preferred cheaper grain from local sources when available.

Valencia has also received its share of research on grain supply, particularly its irrigated hinterland and its relationship with the surrounding kingdom.[46] Because of the inclusion of nobles in city government, which helped Valencia consolidate political control, the city focused more heavily than Barcelona on local resources. Valencia's market encouraged regional production of both rice and wheat, usually at the expense of "lesser" grains like barley and oats.[47] This allowed a higher percentage of its calories to come from production within the kingdom, only extending outward during particularly intense shortages. Years with particularly bad harvests prompted Valencia to import from Sicily, southern France, North Africa, Aragon via the Ebro River or overland, and even from Seville in Castile.[48] Valencia's relatively abundant urban letter collections are full of communications with officials in Palma de Mallorca arguing over the ability of ships carrying Sicilian or North African grain to pass unimpeded on their way to Valencia.[49]

These differing economic relationships with grain supply were common throughout the western Mediterranean.[50] The historian of Italian grain supply Giuliano Pinto has categorized many of the Italian city-states in similar terms, although his criteria are less about individual supply than about the role of the commune in the overall grain trade.[51] He posits four urban forms: the first two, exporters and importers, are similar to those described above (exporters included Sicily, Sardinia, and parts of Naples; importers were large cities like Florence, Pisa, Bologna, and Milan). Pinto's third category includes cities on the verge of outgrowing their hinterland and becoming major importers—incipient importers, as it were. The final category involves cities whose merchants controlled large portions of the trade itself, primarily Genoa and Venice. These actors could influence the market in much the same way that Palma and Tortosa could, but they relied more on political power than geography to do so. These categories help highlight the diversity of political choices available and clarify how urban areas responded to shortages and crises.

Legal and Political Control

The basic suite of options used to influence the grain markets is both well known and, in many cases, still used today. Some market control methods could effectively combat temporary shortages: market inspections and inventories, import subsidies, or direct purchasing combined with an official urban market.[52] However, some strategies, notably the export ban, tended to ignite panic and restrict the ability to ameliorate shortage through trade. With the expansion of urban legal controls, markets in the Crown of Aragon shifted from loosely regulated and privately controlled, often by local nobility, in 1300 to generally dominated by urban political power later in the century.[53] Notably, political and economic responses demonstrate how many actors treated famine as a complex event requiring multiple actions. The strength of merchants in governing councils in cities like Barcelona and Valencia meant that response to famine included a healthy dose of self-interest. In many cases, merchant members of these councils participated in the grain trade they regulated. Wealthy urban families sometimes lent money to the city government to subsidize grain imports controlled by other members of the council. Beyond helping to keep imports running smoothly, these close political connections meant that the various incentives enriched the very members of the councils who made economic decisions, creating what Amrita Rangasami calls famine's "winners" and "losers."[54] Luciano Palermo has described similar outcomes of shortages in Italy.[55] The same measures that might counter the worst effects of a food shortage also lined the pockets of the wealthy.

Previous studies of the politics of urban grain supply have focused on two parallel goals: keeping the market well stocked and ensuring that it was free of deceit.[56] In normal years, the smooth and fair running of city markets was essential to civic life. By the fourteenth century, many cities had a permanent official, called a *mostassaf*, with responsibilities to both the city and the king, in that some market regulations covered the kingdom (some weights and measures and restrictions on quality), while others (sanitation, taxation, licenses) varied from market to market.[57] These officials monitored all of these regulations but worked closely with urban magistrates, who had the most direct urban control.[58] For grain markets, regulations governed the taxes on milling and baking, the weight of prebaked loaves, the quality of the grain, and prices. These market regulations were more stable and less experimental than the methods employed by cities during crises, although infractions and market crime frequently spiked along with the price of food.[59] The most notable changes in general market regulation came from attempts to prevent price swings caused by panic by fixing daily prices. In 1374, the *mostassaf* of Barcelona mandated that the price of wheat could not change by more than 2 denarii per day.[60] Similarly, one modern method of preventing prices from spiraling out of control, particularly in the stock market, is simply to close the market, thus allowing panicked sellers to calm down.

Other response tactics involved both blunt instruments and more nuanced strategies. In the latter category, cities lowered or temporarily suspended both harbor fees and market taxes. Towns frequently paid import subsidies to merchants, guaranteeing a certain profit on grain sold (usually called an *ajuda* or *aventatge*).[61] The subsidies took the form of a reward payment to the importer on top of the market price of grain, or, less frequently, a guaranteed minimum price. Such practices became more routine over the course of the fourteenth century. Towns raised and lowered subsidy rates gradually in response to their perceptions of the market, reaching their highest points during the worst crises. However, subsidies increased the danger of trade wars. When multiple towns employed subsidies at the same time, it reduced their effectiveness in attracting grain. Tarragona enacted a subsidy at the outset of the 1374 crisis, but the regulation stated explicitly that other cities had already passed similar laws.[62] Subsidies and changes in taxation tended to work best for local or regional shortages; intense competition during a major shortage blunted their effectiveness.

The most extreme direct market intervention involved large-scale purchases of grain to be sold at fixed prices. Direct purchases worked hand in hand with official markets. These markets functioned alongside regular markets for grain but functioned as a price regulator, selling less in good years and more in bad, even if it meant a financial loss for the city.[63] Initially, official markets sprang up sporadically to respond to crises, but eventually they became permanent. Valencian cities adopted the practice earliest; the *almodí* of Valencia appeared around 1300, followed by other towns, including Castellón de la Plana, Alzira, and Játiva, in the first half of the century. In Barcelona, the city-run market started late and was first instituted only during famines. However, it became so effective at regulating prices that the city governors made the institution permanent and expanded the structures that housed the grain in 1357.[64] During famine conditions from the summer of 1374 to the summer of 1375, the official Barcelona market sold enough grain to account for a quarter of the entire market, more than enough to influence overall prices.[65] Other cities used markets only temporarily; Tarragona formed its market in the midst of the 1374 crisis.[66]

To better regulate the city-run markets, councils demanded clear information about supplies. Jurors often began by ordering full surveys of all the grain available so as to determine the overall level of need. Tarragona's jurors commissioned a survey on July 28, 1374, and found that enough grain remained for only a couple of normal days.[67] Tortosa's inventories routinely included the surrounding townships in order to get a more global sense of market availability.[68] The surveys were sometimes accompanied by a demand that all available grain be brought to market, an attempt to prevent hoarding. Once the councils had a sense of local availability versus need, they sent out representatives either to purchase grain directly or to coerce other markets into selling their stores. All of the importing cities sent representatives to their neighbors: Barcelona to Girona and the Urgell, Tarragona to the towns around Valls and Reus. Tortosa routinely communicated with Lleida and Zaragoza, while Valencia was in touch with towns from Castellón to Alzira and Gandía. The distances representatives traveled expanded quickly even under only moderate strain. Valencia sent people deputized to purchase grain to North Africa, Sicily, Montpellier, and Castile, all during years of moderate shortage.[69] Tarragona sent representatives to Tortosa, Barcelona, and Lleida to defend its grain supply during crises.[70] The movement of these representatives followed the normal channels of grain supply, but in reverse. As nearby grain resources contracted, communications needed to reach the broader networks of trade to keep the markets stocked.

Under extreme conditions, large importers leaned heavily on their expanded trade networks, while smaller cities searched for ways to trade with people beyond their normal supply horizons. Early in 1374, Valencia sent representatives to both Tortosa and Girona in search of grain. When the king forced Tortosa to send grain to Valencia, the Valencian representative, Bernat Sicard, was already in the city, waiting for just such an order.[71] On November 18, 1374, the exchequer of Tarragona paid Francesc Castlar 300 pounds to find and purchase grain for the city, enough money to buy hundreds of quarters in a normal year.[72] Barcelona maintained two hired men in the province of Urgell from the summer of 1374 through the summer of 1375. Over several months, the pair spent 150,000 Barcelona solidi on grain to be sent directly to the city-run market.[73] Whole castles could be bought and sold for less. Such actions were extremely expensive, but at least they proved effective. The direct purchase of grain worked particularly well for coastal cities that could send ships long distances. Barcelona paid handsomely for the grain that merchants brought back from Flanders in April 1375: 45 solidi for the wheat and 35 for the rye, a price several times above normal. But the injection of so much grain into the city market had an immediate effect. As we can see from figure 4, the imports dropped prices back to only slightly elevated levels by May, in contrast to the soaring heights of December and January.

While the use of subsidies and direct purchases could be scaled up or down depending on the level of crisis, other methods were more blunt, particularly price-fixing, export bans, and the use of outright force. Early in the century, Barcelona received a royal right called *vi vel gratia*, which amounted to legalized piracy. By the middle of the fourteenth century, Palma de Mallorca, Valencia, Tarragona, and even Cagliari had received similar though more restrained rights, and they routinely used armed ships to force grain merchants to dock at their ports. As Marie Kelleher has shown, Barcelona made liberal use of its privilege, intercepting even ships with grain destined for neighbors like Girona and Tarragona.[74] Like the escalation of subsidies,

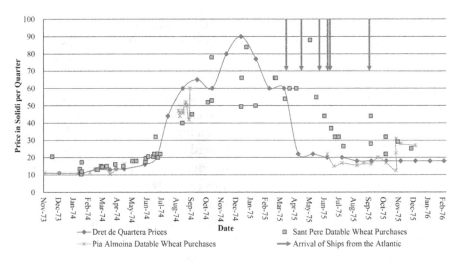

FIG. 4. WHEAT PRICES IN BARCELONA WITH SHIPMENTS FROM THE ATLANTIC. This figure shows all the available wheat prices from the monastery of Sant Pere and the Pia Almoina in Barcelona. The arrows show the arrival of grain ships from the Atlantic coast. The data on grain ships from the Atlantic come from Tutusaus i Canals 1986, 102–4.

the use of force by cities like Barcelona encouraged other towns to arm ships as "escorts" for grain shipments they purchased from more distant locales.

Relying on force could temporarily increase supplies at the expense of competitors, but further regulations attempting to fix prices generally failed. Price-fixing encouraged black markets and speculation. Because local price-fixing invited nearby black markets, major attempts to regulate prices generally came from the king rather than from individual city governments. In 1375, both King Pere the Ceremonious and the duke of Anjou attempted to fix prices in all the cities under their control. The duke fixed prices in Toulouse, which had just banned all exports. Possibly aware that price-fixing encouraged the worst temptations during food shortage, such as black market sales, he also toured the city to monitor measurements and make sure that sales occurred only in designated markets.[75] Pere the Ceremonious attempted to fix prices across all of Catalonia, a bold attempt at broad market regulation. On September 27, 1374, he mandated a slow drop in grain prices starting on October 1, with wheat at 45 solidi per quarter and barley at 35. Each month thereafter, the price would drop by 5 solidi until it reached 30 solidi for wheat in January.[76] The markets completely ignored these demands—prices stayed high throughout the early spring. In the end, price-fixing was probably more ignored than destructive.

In contrast, export bans proved destructive while encouraging further use of force on the part of city authorities. The earliest export bans came from the Crown, not to prevent shortage but to establish a monopoly on export licenses (which involved fees paid to the royal treasury). These licenses and restrictions had become routine by the middle of the thirteenth century.[77] City governments only slowly accumulated the privileges necessary to exercise violent control over the grain market in subsequent decades. Enforcing these bans and privileges required extensive policing and use of force. Armed ships that set to sea to force merchants to port also monitored the coast for unauthorized exports. Guards routinely patrolled late medieval cities, but during times of shortage their work focused on the grain supply. Barcelona hired guards to monitor the roads in the surrounding territory to prevent merchants from removing grain supplies.[78] Valencia employed not only armed guards but secret enforcers whom they called "spies," men who both monitored the surrounding territory and could also entrap merchants by tempting them with illegal export deals.[79] Smaller cities, including Villarreal and Tarragona, also record payments to guards hired to prevent similar exports during shortages.[80]

All the resources put into enforcement do not seem to have clearly increased the grain supply in any market. Not only did the export bans usually fail to improve the situation but they frequently made matters worse by inciting panic and shutting down the movement of grain supplies to those who needed them. In a particularly bold move during the 1374 famine, King Pere attacked such trade restrictions, even though his own royal privileges often made export bans possible. In October, along with the price mandates described above, Pere criticized both urban governments and nobles for shutting down trade, arguing that harvests had been plentiful in previous years and that they were still plentiful in the mountains in 1374. He claimed that famine did not arise from shortage but was "the fault of the depravity of evil men."[81] The edict admonished market overseers to purchase only as much grain as the town needed, and reprimanded nobles who collected high rents yet refused to move their surpluses onto the open market. While Pere's claims of sufficient harvest may be overstated, the king clearly believed that shutting down the regional market unnecessarily restricted access to grain, making the situation worse than it had to be.

Subsidies, purchases, export bans, and force all tended to be short-term responses to price fluctuations. Fears about market volatility also inspired longer-term legal changes to the rules governing the grain trade. Permanently expanding trade access buttressed cities' defenses against future strain. Cities like Tortosa and Palma de Mallorca held distinct geographic advantages that other cities attempted to supersede through legal means. Over the course of the century, Barcelona and Valencia both expanded their legal control of an increasingly large territory. Valencia consolidated a tighter grip on the surrounding kingdom. Often responding to shortages, the city petitioned for and accumulated privileges similar to Barcelona's, including the right to patrol the coast with armed ships to prevent grain from leaving any harbor without permission. Armed ships "escorted" grain merchants from ports stretching from Alicante to Castellón de la Plana, forcing them to sell their grain in the city of Valencia. Agustín Rubio Vela describes how the grain trade throughout the kingdom went from being relatively permissive and unrestricted in the late thirteenth century to being dominated almost completely by the capital city a century later. As noted above, the participation of nobles in city government meant that the goals of the council aligned with those of large landlords instead of competing over noble exportation rights. Rubio Vela highlights a conflict between Alzira and Valencia in 1380 (a year with normal grain supply), when first Alzira and then Játiva passed export restrictions.[82] Valencia responded immediately, stating that the restrictions came "not from necessity, but more from mischief and in injury of the city [Valencia]."[83] By the end of the century, it had become standard practice to defend fiercely all possible legal challenges to this hegemony.

Barcelona never managed to dominate the Catalan grain supply as thoroughly as Valencia did. In large part this was due to older, better-established competitors. Barcelona had to contend with powerful bishoprics and local nobles in Girona, Vic, and Urgell, and with the archbishop in Tarragona, in addition to the political strength of cities like Lleida and Tortosa. While Barcelona started down the road of legal domination with privileges similar to Valencia's, it eventually moved to control some of its grain supply directly rather than through abstract legal rights. In the later fourteenth century, Barcelona felt increasingly constrained by having to deal with Tortosa for grain from Zaragoza and Aragon. During successive shortages in 1360, 1374, and 1384, Barcelona had to persuade Tortosa to continue exporting while competing with merchants from Tarragona and Valencia for the Aragonese supply. In 1398, Barcelona purchased two strategic castles upriver from Tortosa—Flix and La Palma—for 15,000 pounds (300,000 solidi), that they might "be the key and principal granary of all the grains that proceed from the Ebro."[84] Barcelona also bought the towns of Banyoles and Miramar (currently Guardamar in Mont-Roig del Camp) so as to secure points along the road to the coast and a reliable Mediterranean port.[85] Because the route was more expensive and handled less grain than shipments through Tortosa, the castles acted more as a pressure point in negotiations than as a direct threat to Tortosa's control. Such competition continued throughout the fifteenth century, when, during the Catalan Civil War, Flix was burned by the archbishop of Zaragoza as an indirect attack on Barcelona.[86]

Thus, at the beginning of the fourteenth century, cities throughout the Crown of Aragon employed a variety of measures to ensure smooth imports and prevent exports. Deployment of these strategies became more targeted and finely tuned over the course of the century, as urban leaders weighed their costs and consequences. During the minor food shortage of 1310–11, Barcelona's Consell de Cent passed a number of laws in bulk and then repealed them as soon as the shortage was over.[87] During the larger crisis of 1333, multiple cities in the Crown of Aragon, among them Valencia, Barcelona, Mallorca, and Tortosa, acted similarly, using subsidies, armed ships, and export restrictions and then dropping these measures after the crisis had passed.[88] By midcentury, city councils had figured out that some of these provisions were more effective than others. Valencia, especially, used more graded import subsidies to keep its market supplied and relied more heavily on direct purchasing only in serious crises. Tight control of shipping routes and market regulations became more standard, or even permanent, while cities resorted to more draconian measures less often.

Effectiveness, Motivation, and Choice

Urban councils consciously experimented with changes in market regulation over the course of the fourteenth century. Although regulation was always experimental to some degree, mercantile leaders came to understand the fundamental economic forces that determined grain prices. Stark contrasts between grain regulation and laws regulating meat, wine, and other products demonstrate both the centrality of grain and the conscious application of economic controls. Even as market regulations lessened some of the volatility of earlier decades, city councils usually enacted restrictions that bolstered their own personal positions. Smoother market functioning provided both political legitimacy and financial gain for those who enforced the law.

Before looking at the economics of these regulations, it is worth quantifying the effectiveness of urban market controls. Larger ships and expanded trade connections enabled importers to purchase an increasing percentage of their annual grain supply over time. Even a few well-supplied ships could have a drastic and immediate influence on grain prices. In order to calculate the market impact of a given ship full of grain arriving in port, one must be able to make an educated guess about global demand. As noted in chapter 1, diet varied according to class, geography, preference, and other factors. There is no universal number for annual grain consumption, but several local studies, often based on poorhouse records similar to those of Barcelona's Pia Almoina, provide a useful ballpark figure for how much grain cities might have needed. Estimates vary from around 250 grams of bread per day in Girona to 715 grams in Lleida; Valencia ordained that prisoners receive 680 grams. At around 775 grams per liter of wheat, this would translate to between 120 and 340 liters of wheat (from two to just under five Barcelona quarters) per person per year.[89] But these are austere diets, in contrast to what laborers would have required. Girona in particular was known to serve poorer rations than other cities and usually served high quantities of barley.[90] Estimates of total grain consumption and recipients at Barcelona's Pia Almoina by María Echániz i Sans, in conjunction with fourteenth-century purchase totals, show that the institution usually purchased between four and four and a half quarters of grain per person per year.[91] Because the Pia Almoina catered to students and the relatives and widows of wealthy individuals, the more generous diet compared to institutions in Girona is unsurprising.

Other studies have focused on rural workers. Louis Stouff used land-management records in Aix and Arles in southern France to estimate that in 1338 most workers consumed between 400 and 600 liters of grain annually (45 percent of their overall diet and between six and nine Barcelona quarters).[92] Sitges castle records corroborate Stouff's work. At the end of each year, the castle's overseer noted how many quarters of wheat had been served and to how many people. The managers of the house usually milled and cooked between 420 and 490 liters (six or seven quarters) per person per year.[93] During the food shortage of 1361–62, which was worse in Sitges than in Barcelona, annual consumption was reduced to just over five quarters of wheat per person.[94] While this figure is an average that included laborers, slaves, the overseers, and even visiting dignitaries, it provides us with some idea of how much grain was needed to feed a rural labor force an adequate daily diet. Other small references corroborate these numbers. An apprentice tailor in Sant Feliu de Guixols received nine *mitgeres* of wheat (around 340 liters, or just shy of five quarters) along with a ration of wine, bacon, and oil for his wages in 1316.[95] Thus six or seven quarters per year represents a reasonable average consumption of grain, falling to five or even four quarters per person during years of shortage.

Given these numbers, how many people could a ship of grain feed? While ships routinely carried multiple products as cargo, even partial ship-loads could be substantial. During the fourteenth century, Italian and Catalan traders started using square-rigged cogs that required less wood for the same hold space, allowing increasingly larger shipments of foodstuffs. A fully loaded cog from Sicily could carry several thousand quarters of wheat.[96] Ships arriving in Valencia often carried smaller quantities but sometimes brought as much as 500 *cafiços* (nearly 1,500 Barcelona quarters; see table 1 in the introduction).[97] Relatively small ships routinely appeared in Valencia from southern France with 100 to 200 *cafiços* (280 to 500-plus Barcelona quarters).[98] These smaller shipments could have significant market impact. In 1355, Valencia had around 25,000 residents, rising to nearly 40,000 by the end of the century.[99] Barcelona followed a reverse trajectory, beginning with 40,000 before the Black Death and steadily declining to closer to 25,000 by 1400, meaning that these cities needed between 400 and 600 quarters per day.[100] Thus the grain from one well-stocked ship (1,500 quarters) could supply the needs of these larger markets for several days. For smaller cities, a group of ships could supply enough grain for a few weeks or months. Hence even news of ship arrivals could influence urban prices. The purchase of multiple shiploads of grain could set market prices for an entire season. In 1401, Barcelona purchased nearly 40,000 quarters of grain from southern France—between a quarter and a third of the entire market supply for the year.[101] Even the power of subsidies could be significant. In 1360 and 1361 (years of minor shortage), Barcelona paid subsidies for 36,000 and nearly 60,000 quarters of wheat, respectively. This means that import subsidies influenced the retail price of half the market in 1361.[102] While most of the imported grain might still arrive on private ships, the legal and economic influence of subsidies and direct purchase could be considerable.

Contemporary writers understood these economic forces. In 1383, Francesc Eiximenis wrote a treatise dedicated to the merchant class of Valencia called *Regiment de la cosa pública* (Government of the republic), in which he described how grain markets functioned. Eiximenis understood the importance of keeping grain prices stable and providing financial incentives when necessary. Citing "wise men," he wrote:

> If, the grain having a convenient price, a ship loaded with grain arrives and unloads, the [price of] grain will fall so much that the merchants will lose much on the grain that arrives at an acceptable price. As such, these thinkers state that the community, with good

conscience, can allow the merchants to buy the said cargo and to store the grain, because it is more useful to the republic that the grain might cost a little more and that those who transport it will make their cost and will be helped. Because if not, even if it is for a short time, when the market has excess product, the merchants will be discouraged.[103]

Eiximenis understood that oversupply could be as risky as undersupply. New grain arrivals immediately caused prices to fall, sometimes to the detriment of the merchants themselves, who therefore had to be considered. This provided direct reinforcement for policies like the import subsidy, a payment that reduced the risk of oversupply for the merchant while still encouraging price reduction through new imports.

Eiximenis's writings probably confirmed what Valencians already knew. Political responses to famine combined concern for a stable market with the self-interested desire for profit. The Valencian council that commissioned Eiximenis's work understood the basic economics of supply and demand and saw market regulations as the solution, not the problem. In this regard, the different regulatory regimes for meat and wine are instructive. For meat, urban councils in the coastal cities dictated market price but understood that shortages required some increase in cost to keep the market supplied. For wine, a product with strong connections to urban land investment, regulators enacted protectionist measures, safeguarding the economic interests of urban landlords. In contrast, grain regulations balanced all of these concerns with the moral obligation to keep people fed.

During the winter of 1371–72, the council of Valencia responded to a temporary shortage of meat with regulations that confirm the understanding of these market forces. At the council meeting on January 7, the leaders acknowledged a "great shortage of meats as much of lamb and goat as of salted pork." The council added 1 denarius per pound to the price of all meat "in order to have a greater abundance."[104] When the shortage continued, it injected more cash into the system by distributing a certain amount of money to some of the city's leading butchers so that they could purchase extra supplies.[105] The councilors understood that simply injecting money into the market could increase animal stocks. The politics of the meat market tended to balance urban consumers' desire for cheap meat with the demands of herders and butchers for reasonable profits.[106] Meat shortages neither caused panic nor created particularly large profits, so small injections of new cash tended to be sufficient. Butchers also had limited influence on the council, so while the infusion of cash kept them employed, it did not particularly enrich them.

Wine functioned in nearly the opposite way. While wine was widely consumed, shortages did not threaten anyone's health or survival. Urban patrician families and wealthy merchants, however, both of them well represented on urban councils, often made a great deal of money from their ownership of vineyards. Urban hinterlands routinely encouraged wine production as a more economically profitable use of land than grain production, a practice that underpinned Barcelona's early prosperity.[107] Some of the regions around Girona created economic wealth by producing wine destined for export through the Mediterranean Sea. Girona's patrician Bell-Lloc family, like Barcelona's Grony family, made its fortune in the thirteenth century by switching from grain to large-scale wine production.[108] Already in the thirteenth century, Marseille relied on Sicilian grain for the express purpose of encouraging local wine exports.[109] Describing shortages in particular, Luciano Palermo has noted that this form of hinterland development often aimed at creating economic advantage rather than the consistent supply of the market per se.[110]

Because wine production was geared toward economic profit and shortages did not create panic, virtually all markets in the Mediterranean implemented protectionist measures, exactly the opposite of the pattern that prevailed in grain markets. Towns of all sizes in the Crown of Aragon—Huesca, Cervera, Alicante, Tarragona, Balaguer, and others—enacted laws preventing excessive imports.[111] When shortage threatened, the normal practice was to lift the protectionist measures for a short period. In 1372, a drought reduced both the grain and the wine supply in Valencia. While the city council spent thousands on direct grain purchases and subsidies, the wine shortage resulted in only a temporary lifting of the import ban. For the three months of summer, the council allowed in foreign wine, but with a maximum of five hundred barrels per shipment, and only with a license issued by the city.[112] Such local flexibility provided sufficient relief, in stark contrast to the expansive measures needed to ensure the grain supply. In times of severe shortage, when the urban population began to complain, leaders temporarily loosened restrictions, but snapped them back into place as soon as supplies improved.

As with wine and meat, self-interest also influenced grain market legislation. Through subsidies or guaranteed prices, merchants who brought grain into a city during a shortage could expect to be paid handsomely. Merchants could even earn money running official markets themselves. When Tarragona switched from offering subsidies to setting up its own official city market in order to regulate prices in August 1374, the city sent representatives out to purchase supplies. By spring of the following year, two merchants, Johanet Salmonia and Nicholau Pallerès, offered to pay the city council for the privilege of running grain sales for several months; Pallerès offered 100 florins (1,100 solidi), enough money to buy a house. He claimed that the work would be purely altruistic, but with the money collected from the city for every quarter sold, coupled with consistently high prices, it is hard to see how he would not have turned a handsome profit. On March 22, 1375, when the city announced the importation of a shipment of grain, Pallerès persuaded the city to protect his sales and profits against both robbers and the fickleness of consumers. The council not only agreed to post guards but went so far as to pay damages for lost grain even in the case of rats or other vermin![113] The subsidies even directly benefited merchant members of the very council that approved the payments. During the crisis of 1384, Johan Laver, a well-connected member of Tarragona's merchant elite, personally collected more than 350 solidi in subsidies for wheat he imported. Furthermore, he first lent the city 7,000 solidi specifically for subsidizing the grain. Johan thus lent the city money at interest and then collected payment *from the same loan* for his work as a merchant. In the icing on the cake, the city even paid for the transaction costs and expenses involved in preparing the documents for both the loan and the subsidy payments![114]

Such practices did not constitute graft but rather conformed to normal market expectations. The money that merchants earned from such practices was considered fair recompense for a smoothly functioning market that benefited the population.[115] By the beginning of the fifteenth century, when municipal control had become normal even in good years, cities often continued to import more grain than they actually needed. While this could be read as a general concern with maintaining constant supplies, it is equally likely that the political economy of the city encouraged such spending.[116] Multiple merchants elected to the city council of Valencia received lucrative contracts for large grain imports. In 1418, just a couple of years after being elected councilor from one of Valencia's parishes, Jofré de Meya signed a contract with the city government to import more than 1,500 *cafiços* of wheat from Sicily and Sardinia. In this context, export bans during shortages appear similar to protectionist practices for wine. The restriction and licensing of all grain sales directly benefited those involved in improving the urban supply. The coupling of city power with merchant desires, sometimes in the body of the same person, helped ensure good business for the merchants while, it was hoped, improving the grain supply for the general population.

Import subsidies and direct purchasing could rapidly change the market price of grain. Export bans and protectionism often had the opposite effect, keeping prices relatively high. However, the legal regimes created in the fourteenth century make better sense when seen not as a persistent buttress against famine but rather as a set of restrictions originating in the complex motivations of conflicting governing bodies, including nobles, urban councils, and even the king. Most ruling elites understood the basic functioning of market demand and prices and tailored their laws with an eye to balancing dietary demands, moral responsibility to residents, and their own financial interests.

Competition and Famine Regions

Increasing market controls ultimately changed how famines spread. The relatively unregulated market tended to transfer small fluctuations in harvests and prices directly into nearby markets. As Stephan R. Epstein has argued, markets in the fourteenth century tended to suffer from a lack of integration, and much of the time greater urban control served to regularize transactions and ease rather than impede this integration.[117] By late in the century, the heavy regulation of commodities had integrated much of the western Mediterranean by creating more predictable arenas for merchant action. While the legal environment gave large cities greater control over their nearby grain-supplying regions, these cities simultaneously expanded the use of the more distant secondary markets. Access to information and clearer understanding of regulatory impact on the market gave cities like Valencia and Barcelona more flexibility, which could mean the difference between panic and mere high prices. By the end of the century, these expanded market connections tamped down smaller crises but expanded competition during genuinely large-scale events. More complex import networks created the possibility of new and more explosive region-wide crises, while simultaneously ameliorating local shortages and sometimes alleviating seasonal price variations in urban markets.

In the late medieval period, harvest rhythms created natural price seasonality for many commodities.[118] Scholars looking at market prices have postulated two types of years: those in which prices followed the harvest (prices rise through April or May and then drop back again with the new harvest), and those in which prices followed their normal course before the harvest but then continued to rise in a bad year, creating crisis situations.[119]

However, long-distance imports could interrupt the normal course of prices during mediocre and crisis years. While the influence of these imports might have been minimal in earlier centuries or in smaller inland towns, by late in the century, Mediterranean trade networks had created a new price regime in the major cities, independent of local agricultural production. Because a group of ships could provide such significant market shares, price volatility depended as much on the arrival of cargo as on the agricultural cycle.

Unfortunately, we lack sufficiently robust price data for such analyses in multiple towns in the Crown of Aragon. Several years' worth of price data in Barcelona, however, demonstrate the decisive importance of imports. During the famine of 1374–75, the highest price spike in Barcelona began dropping almost immediately upon the arrival, on April 6, 1375, of 15,000 quarters of wheat from Flanders, Normandy, Harfleur, and Sluis on the northern Atlantic (see fig. 4 above).[120] Over the course of the next few months, more than 30,000 quarters of grain came in from the Atlantic, and a further 20,000 arrived from Sicily over the late summer and fall of 1375.[121] This meant that Barcelona received adequate supplies for most of the summer months only from long-distance imports, without any recourse to the new harvest. Grain from Flanders also ended a smaller price spike in 1385 in Valencia. The city received more than 2,000 *cafiços* (almost 6,000 Barcelona quarters) in mid-May, much as Barcelona had a decade earlier.[122] In both instances, prices dropped significantly prior to the new local harvest.

Beyond such dramatic events, large enough shipments arrived in multiple years to move the needle on grain prices. In 1361, the price began to rise in the fall after a mediocre harvest, but with the arrival of ships from Sicily in December, the price dropped back for several months. With a second mediocre harvest in 1362, the price jumped to 15 solidi per quarter in May, but, again, ships from Sicily supplied Barcelona in July and August, bringing the price back down to only 9 solidi per quarter by October. In contrast, in the coastal town of Sitges—also a trading town, but without the reach of Barcelona—the price of wheat kept rising through both years, reaching 18.5 solidi per quarter by the spring of 1363. In the seasonal year starting in 1403, both imports and seasonality played a role. Initially, grain prices rose after a moderate harvest, but the arrival of ships in November brought prices back down to their original level. Prices stayed low through January, but then, the ships having sold off all their supplies, rose again until the following year's harvest (see fig. 5).

Separating the Barcelona price data into years without subsidies or major foreign imports and years with significant shipping demonstrates this point clearly. In years with few imports, we see the expected seasonal variation:

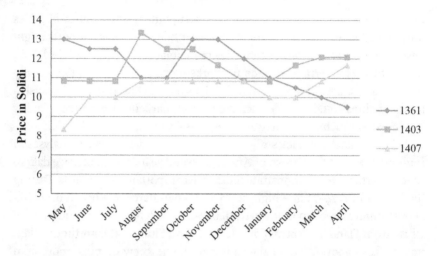

FIG. 5. MONTHLY PRICE FLUCTUATIONS IN YEARS WITH LARGE GRAIN IMPORTS, 1361, 1403, 1407.
Each of these three years demonstrates a different response to local harvests and the arrival of
imports. The diversity of possible outcomes is more important than the particular curve of any one
year. While seasonality played a role in the Barcelona market, the vicissitudes of shipping had an
equally strong impact that often overrode seasonal prices.

prices rise slowly, from a low in June, just after the harvest, through a high
the following April. In years with large imports, we see a double price fluctuation: prices tend to reach a peak in November or December and then fall
back, depending on the arrival of ships. There is sometimes a secondary rise
around May, as in 1403, but this secondary increase is often weaker. The
extensive connections of Barcelona allowed it to weather the smaller ups
and downs of the grain harvest, despite the city's continuing dependence
on regional production. Lacking equivalent fine-grained price data for other
cities within the Crown, we can only guess that price patterns were similar.
As already demonstrated, multiple cities responded to shortages in similar
ways, suggesting related market dynamics.

The dense trade networks throughout the western Mediterranean also
created integrated famine regions by tying together the supply regions of
major importers of grain. These famine regions could mitigate more local
instances of shortage. Massive imports allowed urban centers to recover
from potentially catastrophic, if localized, harvest failures. Even a significant fall in regional production could be made up entirely by imports from
farther afield. But famine regions created overlapping trade demands that
could exacerbate famines when shortages threatened large areas simultaneously. As shortages or supply problems threatened entire trade networks, the

legal control each city exercised ran into the efforts of its competitors, creating panic and increasing restrictions and violence. This dynamic meant that geographic breadth contributed directly to the severity of the crisis.

Local shortages precipitated a search for nearby producing zones that had generated enough surplus to allow exports. The winter of 1372–73 saw bad harvests in the hinterland of Valencia but did not cause significantly broader disruption. In August 1371, early in the crisis, Valencia sent a member of the city government, Johan Renouart, to act as its representative in Montpellier. Renouart had full power to negotiate the direct purchase of grain and to promise import subsidies to any merchant willing to sign a contract.[123] Part of Renouart's work included negotiating contracts with two merchants from Montpellier and a subcontractor from Mallorca who sent grain to Valencia on four different ships captained by both Catalans and people from Montpellier. Such contracts proved very successful. By the following July, the city had already imported so much grain that it revoked some of the promises of high subsidies in Montpellier and sent a runner to find Renouart, who had left for Avignon.[124] Renouart's efforts continued to move grain through the system toward Valencia. In December, two more merchants from Montpellier, G. de Tornafort and P. de Vernujols, arrived with a load of grain and a promissory note from Renouart for 5,641 solidi, a huge sum of money. Despite its improved supply, the city unloaded the grain for sale in the *almodí*, specifically to avoid possible future shortage.[125] Furthermore, the city eventually paid several of the fees and other costs accumulated by the ships under Tornafort's command. The three ship captains, Huc Ramon, en Valenti, and en Golart, submitted their anchorage fees from Tortosa and Peñíscola and their official market taxes for reimbursement, as described in the original contract.[126] Valencia paid a similar set of fees for the shippers of Vernujols's grain, including some to the same captain, Huc Ramon.[127]

These few shipments alone represent a complex set of actors with multiple allegiances. Most shipments came with similar complexities: Barcelona merchants sent Sicilian grain on Genoese ships; Valencian merchants brought Sicilian grain on Castilian ships; Tortosan merchants supplied grain from Zaragoza on Mallorcan ships. Barcelona sometimes restricted the access of foreign traders, giving preference to its own merchants and ships. There is plenty of notarial evidence, however, especially during times of shortage, for foreign traders. Tortosa and Palma, because of their geography, described above, often encouraged merchants from other locations.[128] During two shortages, in 1327 and 1333, Montpellier imported large amounts of grain from the Black Sea, often on Genoese ships.[129] While numerous subsidies still ended up in local hands, subcontracting, multiple ship contracts, and reliance on intermediary ports created a complex web of actors. If at any point any of these actors or their governments decided that their interests were threatened, the network would begin to unravel and create the panic that led to systemic breakdown and famine. Montpellier could decide to ban exports if it felt that its own supply was threatened. Captains and merchants alike might decide that dealing with Barcelona or Palma was more lucrative than honoring its contractual agreements with Montpellier or other towns. In the case described above, Tortosa and Peñíscola could have chosen to impound the ships or force the sale of their cargo, though in doing so they would certainly have risked Valencia's anger and possible retribution. Indeed, earlier impediments in the supply from Sicily and restrictions on cargo passing through Cagliari had necessitated dealing with Montpellier in the first place.

Interlocking supply networks meant that fighting shortage required imports from regions that came into conflict during larger events. During a crisis, most large cities in the western Mediterranean could import grain from North Africa, Sicily, Sardinia, Apulia, Montpellier, Cotlliure, Ebro River towns, and even the Atlantic coasts. A few had their own distant sources, such as Genoa's reliance on parts of the Black Sea, which supplied grain that Genoa sometimes turned into lucrative exports of its own when the price was right from buyers like Montpellier and Valencia. When shortage threatened more than one area, whether the cause was agricultural, military, or political, the ensuing competition spread restrictions that threatened the supply of other locations. Even a rumor could spread fear through the system and lead to market shutdowns.

Hoarding, Private and Public

In contrast to the market competition described above, both medieval writers and modern scholars have often blamed hoarders for market crises.[130] By withholding supplies and waiting for prices to rise in order to turn a larger profit, merchants might increase the suffering of a population. The moralist Eiximenis captures succinctly the medieval attitude: "Because the hoarder always desires bad weather and shortage, and buys large quantities in hopes of raising prices, he is absolutely contrary to the good merchant."[131] Morality tales described saints who gave away their own grain only to find that they miraculously had more than before, and sinners who hoarded grain only to see it rot.[132] In response to private hoarding, authorities conducted house-to-house inventories of grain, attempting to root out reserves and force them into the market.[133] In more and more towns controlled by noble lords and independent town councils, royal privileges granted the right to ban or restrict excessive storage. One of the first major statements of such privileges appeared during the 1333–34 famine.[134] In 1385, Valencia attempted to force merchants to sell their grain at one fixed price for the duration of a market day, allowing day-to-day changes of only 2 denarii per *fanega* in order to prevent price spikes. With this regulation, the council implicitly restricted regrating (buying low and withholding the grain to sell high) by forcing all merchants to sell all the grain they brought to market on a given day. Any grain they attempted to withhold from the market could be confiscated and sold at the fixed price by the official market regulator.[135]

These legal restrictions on hoarding were implemented during shortages infrequently, however. By the late fourteenth century, financial market incentives generally outweighed efforts to control individual actors. In 1371, as prices began to rise in Valencia, the council acknowledged that while it would continue to restrict hoarding, it was unlikely to be a real problem:

> First, it was proposed and considered that in such a manner the republic suffers great harm on account of the regraters who purchase and monopolize foodstuffs and other things necessary for human life using advanced purchases and other methods, such that great and inexcusable shortages follow. And, although on account of the regraters, the council has and will have mandated certain provisions and ordinances, however, the said council doubts that, perchance, there might be very many of them, especially when considering those who are not from the region of the city.[136]

Doubting the severity of the problem, in other words, the council declined to enact new regulations and instead mandated that the market officials simply be vigilant and strictly enforce existing rules. Despite its strong initial rhetoric against regraters, the council singled out foreign merchants as *less* likely than locals to be regraters, which makes sense. Anyone who received news of high prices in Valencia, or even a subsidy contract from a representative in a distant city, arrived already chasing high prices. Arriving with grain that they hoped to sell at a profit is exactly what the council wanted merchants to do. Those with a subsidy contract had to sell in the public market or they would be unable to receive their extra payment. These merchants were much more likely to sell their goods and then leave on new business than to intentionally wait for prices to rise still higher. Merely seeking to sell at a profit did not in itself constitute hoarding.

Some of the archival examples of hoarding amount to merchants' looking for the best price, which probably reduced shortages rather than exacerbated them. In February 1376, a Barcelona merchant named Raimon Pellicer deputized a Tarragona merchant, Berenguer Martí, to sell his stock of wheat and other grains at the best price he could find, "either in Tarragona or in other towns or places in Catalonia."[137] Against the backdrop of the famine in 1374 and 1375, reducing Barcelona's grain supply in search of profit might seem self-serving and morally suspect. But by late 1375, regional competition was driving Barcelona to resort to distant import markets in Seville and Portugal and on the Atlantic coast.[138] These imports lowered the market price by more than half. Imports, especially from Sicily, continued to arrive well into 1377, and by then the market was so saturated that the price dropped to its lowest level in decades. It is likely that by 1376, nearby cities such as Tarragona really were in greater need of grain than Barcelona was. The very actions of merchants who imported grain had reduced the price enough that new arrivals to the market were driven to seek other markets, with higher prices, inverting the trajectory that had first spread the crisis. Thus Barcelona's panic spread fear and shortage into new markets, but Barcelona's massive response eventually spread some of the newly imported grain to other towns in the region, relieving their burden as well. Despite medieval rhetoric and distrust of merchants who sought high prices for their grain, such practices usually reduced prices fairly equitably at the regional level.

In the end, concrete evidence of hoarding is often quite minimal. Kevin Mummey has described several notarial contracts prepared for Berengar de Roig, his wife, Margarita, and a second woman named Blancha de Pertagatio in Mallorca.[139] In January 1374, before markets had shut down and prices had spiked, Berengar and his wife purchased forty-nine quarters of wheat, enough for a household of ten for an entire year. Over the spring, they purchased another twenty quarters. They also purchased bonds and property at the same time, giving the impression that the grain represented a sort of investment rather than a routine food purchase. The quantities were certainly high enough to raise a red flag for urban councils with their grain surveys. In November, however, at the height of the famine, Margarita transferred fourteen of the quarters to her brother, perhaps using her outsized resources to assist potentially starving family members. Even assuming that these grain purchases were meant to be withheld for sale at the highest price, the presence of dozens or even hundreds of hoarded quarters would have paled in comparison to the thousands that could arrive by ship at the nearby port of Palma. The direct evidence we have of hoarding, then, tends to be much less impressive than the rhetoric leveled against the practice.

This rhetoric contrasts notably with the frequent use of export bans that acted as a de facto hoarding practice. If restrictions on hoarding were more moralizing than practical, export bans often conspired to feed panic and exacerbate crises, even spreading the problem to areas not affected by harvest failures. As Adam Smith first noted, laws against regrating and forestalling probably encouraged the very panic and overbuying that they were meant to prevent.[140] As urban leaders railed against the hoarding of grain, they simultaneously launched ships and militias to force other territories to surrender their supplies; urban mercantile elites who often controlled city councils told people not to panic or hoard food while using their political power to hoard their own supplies. Almost immediately after Valencia armed and outfitted a galley to patrol its waters in 1374, it sent the ship to Castellón de la Plana, where two ships purportedly bound for Valencia had been impounded by Castellón's council. In a letter dated May 24, Valencian authorities made veiled threats about what the galley would do if Castellón did not release the two grain ships, urging the town to "consider the circumstances in which you have placed yourself."[141] Religious and noble landlords could enact similar legislation over territories under their control. In Rome, edicts issued during the same crisis explicitly condemned local hoarding but enacted region-wide restrictions in the same breath. On July 24, 1374, the pope in Avignon ordered his vicars in Italy to prevent grain from leaving the Papal States. Individuals could purchase only as much grain as their families would use in a year. The edict sanctimoniously called grain hoarders "murderers of the poor." But Avignon also restricted exports to Florence, with which it was intermittently at war, proving that the church was not above using the poor as pawns in its own power struggles.[142]

Just as cities worried that hoarding by individuals would drive up grain prices, so hoarding and frenzied purchasing by cities had the same effect on the regional market. In this scenario of systemic competition and panic, the capacity of cities and towns to keep their markets running smoothly mirrored their general political fortunes. For cities with little influence, the fight for grain could be disastrous. During the 1374 crisis, Tarragona, desperately watching the little grain remaining in its market flow to larger centers, attempted to ban exports (just as nearby cities had already done). The law was passed in the winter of 1375, late in the crisis, after the city had already dispatched representatives to purchase grain. When a shipment actually arrived from Cambrils, Tarragona prevented it from continuing north to Barcelona. Barcelona reacted violently. On March 6, the city sent a militia to lay siege to Tarragona and force the town to give up its supplies.[143] Tarragona attempted without success to negotiate, at the same time preparing the city's defenses. In the end, the council of Tarragona had to send a representative, supported by the archbishop, to the king's court to request mediation. Under pressure from the king, the siege was lifted a short while later, narrowly averting disaster for Tarragona.

The panicked collapse of the grain market can be seen most clearly in the timing of export bans. Political fighting between larger cities forced smaller city councils and noble-controlled towns to respond with their own export bans to prevent grain from being forced toward the larger markets. In 1374, because of previous years of shortage, Valencia responded early, attempting to lure as much grain as possible away from cities like Girona and Tortosa. At the same time, the Valencia council passed the first of many export bans. Barcelona, always nervous about its own large supply, similarly applied political pressure to keep grain flowing into its port.[144] As the northern towns grew anxious about their own supplies, they in turn attempted to restrict exports.[145] Once all the cities in a given region had passed export bans and other protectionist measures, grain distribution followed the lines of political power and economic might rather than need. For a time, Girona continued exporting grain to both Barcelona and Valencia; more than two thousand quarters of wheat and barley left the city between April 17 and May 17, 1374. But these large and rapid exports dragged Girona more quickly into crisis, and the town council complained to the Crown in an attempt to stop the outflow of grain.[146] Tortosa found itself in the same position. Valencia requested wheat supplies, which Tortosa refused, citing its royal privileges. Valencia appealed to King Pere the Ceremonious, who, citing Valencia's stronger privileges, ordered Tortosa officials to release their grain to Valencia.[147] Comparison of the export ban time line with Barcelona prices illuminates clearly the effect such laws could have on a shortage (see fig. 6). Prices in Barcelona had barely risen in April 1374 when the various city governments began their conflicts. By the time the prices really began to shoot upward in July, much of the political infighting had already concluded and the export bans established. Instead of securing grain, the intense new protectionism only exacerbated the coming crisis.

As many of the previous examples demonstrate, royal intervention was routinely necessary to prevent the worst excesses of interurban violence. Although King Pere had granted multiple cities the right to legal piracy through

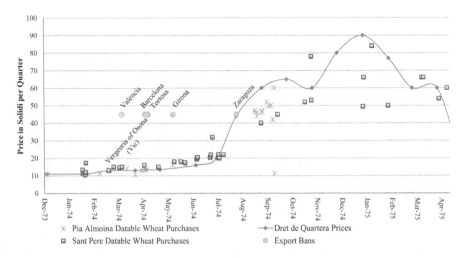

FIG. 6. EXPORT BANS AND GRAIN PRICES. The passing of export bans in 1374 preempted rather than responded to the price spike. Urban councils understood that a bad harvest was coming and sought to exercise more direct control over the grain market. As larger cities passed export bans, their nearby neighbors followed suit regardless of the price of grain in their markets. The time line follows the supply of grain in reverse, up the chain from the importing coastal cities inland, to the waypoint of Tortosa, to Vic and Girona, and upriver to Zaragoza.

the use of their galleys, he explicitly exhorted Valencia not to attack ships sailing between Blanes and Sitges, creating a buffer between the otherwise legal violence of Valencia and Barcelona.[148] But royal preferences markedly favored the most politically influential locations, as Tortosa discovered when it tried to prevent exports to Valencia. In his role as mediator, King Pere himself demonstrated an understanding of the dangers of excessive protectionism. In August 1374, he issued an order that all royal officials, bailiffs, and town councilors should refrain from restricting the market in grain because of great need throughout the kingdom.[149] He urged them not to enact restrictions that would prove damaging to their neighbors and other parts of the kingdom, claiming that there was sufficient grain if only it was distributed fairly, and observing that market restrictions themselves had caused the panic. In the price-fixing legislation he enacted in September, he repeated this claim, using the explicit language of hoarding: "whenever there are poor harvests and shortage of food in the world, they are by the will of God . . . yet because many distrust the goodness of providence, when they feel any shortage of grain, they buy up one, two, or three years' worth, even as everyone else is ruined by famine."[150] Rather than target individuals, however, the king singled out cities and towns that purchased more grain than their local markets could use, along with nobles who collected rents in grain and refused to put those surpluses up for sale.[151] This accords well with reports of some of the more egregious hoarding in England during the Great Famine. Using detailed manorial accounts, Philip Slavin has demonstrated that lords with-held large grain stores during the Great Famine, both to buttress their own supplies and to seek higher prices.[152] Similarly, as described in chapter 1, the castle overseers at Sitges did actively seek higher prices by using their storage capacity, though almost exclusively with barley. It is remarkable to see the royal authorities level the same criticism at towns and cities that urban coun-cils in turn directed at hoarders and regraters. The king attempted to respond with the same measures, too: surveys of available supplies, official markets, and threats of confiscation or fines for illicit grain reserves.

At each level of government—towns, cities, nobles, and even the king—leaders wanted to enforce liberal market operations within the limits of their control while exercising strict limits at the border. Despite the boldness of his effort, King Pere lacked the power to inventory and regulate all grain sales within the Crown of Aragon. Nobles and cities, by contrast, did have the local resources and coercive force at their disposal to enforce such regula-tions, especially when their efforts were thwarted by the legislation and re-strictions of their neighbors. In the end, royal authority generally fell back on mediation in such conflicts. Thus corporate groups, like town governments with sufficient political power, could act to their own political and economic advantage, not just surviving famines but using them as an opportunity to profit. Hypocritical concerns about hoarding did not prevent the law from privileging some actors over others.

Conclusions

Better communication and access to increasingly distant exporters helped integrate fourteenth-century grain markets. As Stefano Magni has noted for Italian city-states, the procurement of grain by urban institutions made pos-sible the transfer of information and knowledge that allowed for widespread trade in staple grains.[153] Such integration allowed cities to respond to, and even escape, local shortages, but it also set the stage for massive regional shortages. As Stephan R. Epstein puts it, food crises tended to turn urban governments into "decentralized monopolists" willing to break rules for their own advantage, while simultaneously snapping back into place many of the barriers that increased transaction costs. Export bans were "coordination failures (institutional arrangements which persist despite being collectively damaging because no individual actor wishes to change them and no actor wishes other actors to change them either)."[154] Food shortages created a prisoner's dilemma for any trading city, giving it a strong incentive to deviate from the normal practices of trade, which often led to temporary but damaging disruptions to normal market practice.

Despite the king's efforts, shutdowns of regional markets caused by panic could restrict the access of even the largest importers. In 1374, the implementation of export bans in the Crown of Aragon spread to parts of southern France and many Italian city-states. The bans appealed to a simple logic of grain supply: increase imports and reduce exports. But export bans appeared prior to actual price spikes, ultimately shutting down markets and expanding the use of violence. While banning exports, city councils also searched individuals' houses, forcing those with stocks of grain to sell them on the city market. On July 28, 1374, the councilors of Tarragona, accompanied by a group of armed citizens, went door to door through the city, searching for all grain supplies. The councilors decided how much each family needed, and all grain in excess of that amount was confiscated for immediate sale.[155] Tarragona complained bitterly when Barcelona in effect showed up at the door with a large group of armed men, but when dealing with citizens under its control, the town did the same thing. Such systemic breakdown ultimately forced cities to search far beyond their normal horizons: Barcelona sent ships as far as Flanders and the French Atlantic coast; Valencia attempted to work with its enemies in Seville but also received ships from Bilbao in the Basque Country and Pontevedra in Galicia.[156] Marseille looked for supplies from northern France overland and from the Black Sea. Valencia sometimes encouraged ships from Sicily to steer a direct course and stay well away from intermediary ports like Cagliari and Palma.[157]

Famines and shortages themselves created a feedback loop, encouraging greater legal controls. In turn, increased market control reshaped the causes of grain crises. Increasing political competition created a new type of crisis in which importers scrambled for access to border regions where exports were still available. Control of information, shipping lanes, and long-distance imports became critical to surviving a crisis. In Italy, the cities that emerged victorious in their efforts to capture and control the grain market often achieved dominance in the fifteenth century.[158] In the Crown of Aragon, Valencia in particular developed more nuanced control of its grain market and improved the city's access to good information when attempting to respond to shortages. By the end of the century, Valencia had increased its control of both its grain supply and its coastline. Safeguarding its grain supply system in this way may have contributed directly to Valencia's economic success and dominance early in the fifteenth century.

Once the panic of a famine takes hold, reversing it is extremely difficult. Just as the human body cannot recover from starvation simply by resuming a normal diet but needs a much larger and richer diet than normal in order to regain strength, a society needs a greater influx of supplies than would be required in a normal year in order to quell fears and change perceptions.[159] Even a small drop in the food supply can cause panic and famine in a population, necessitating a large influx of food to counter the shortage. This helps to explain why prices in Barcelona spiked at the beginning of a famine but then often bottomed out afterward, as the market became saturated in an attempt to overrestore normal food supply. After Barcelona's initial spike ended in May 1375, excess grain continued to flow in from Sicily and elsewhere in the Mediterranean. By the time the harvest of 1376 arrived—by many accounts a normal harvest—food prices in the city had dropped to the lowest level in almost thirty years.

Despite mixed responses to shortage and famine, the largest and wealthiest urban centers tended to weather the crises of the second half of the fourteenth century. The main lingering problem stemmed from the significant amount of debt that cities accrued in financing their subsidies, purchases, and arming of ships. Many scholarly works describe the increasing debt load of Catalan cities over the course of the fourteenth century.[160] Scholars have identified systemic population changes, taxation difficulties, and the intense economic demands of war as the main drivers of debt. Towns from Palma de Mallorca, to Tarragona, to smaller towns like Villarreal struggled with long-term debt that was exacerbated by the crisis of 1374.[161] But the debt tended to come from the financing of the patrician members of urban councils themselves. Valencia routinely took on regular loans from the Jewish residents of the city, but authorities also used short-term loans to raise money directly from local elites that the city coffers would then repay.[162] Thus merchant councilors often voted to take out loans from themselves to pay themselves subsidies to bring in grain to sell at a profit, and then pay themselves back with money raised by the city.

These long-term shifts in the methods of urban grain supply started before the Black Death and continued moving in the same direction afterward. As a structural element of famine, market integration and market control increased over the century regardless of population levels.[163] The increasing role of the market created a devil's bargain in which urban markets gained the upper hand over smaller or local shortages while simultaneously laying the groundwork for large major famines that occurred when the entire system collapsed. The wider the geographic scope of harvest failures, the more pronounced the famines became, though these dynamics were not absent from earlier shortages. In 1276, the Crown of Aragon, Genoa, and parts of Tuscany and Lombardy all experienced harvest failures and looked to southern Italy for exports. The demand for grain created political tension with Genoa and internal strife between Zaragoza and Valencia. Possibly because of the royal preference shown for Valencia, prices in the Aragonese town of Daroca rose to almost triple the price recorded in the coastal town of Cullera.[164] Pere Benito i Monclús has demonstrated how shortages and restrictions in one region could create fears in neighboring regions during even earlier centuries.[165] The same characteristics of a famine region sometimes existed in earlier times, allowing crises to spread like a contagion because of fear, panic, and overheated competition, rather than simply because of bad weather.

3

THE LIMITS OF INDIVIDUAL ACCESS

Despite the expanding access of wealthy cities, individual access to markets remained deeply unequal. The individual ability to buy food, especially among the poor, related to one's occupation, family ties, and social networks. In this chapter, I look at the layers of food access available to the poor, both the working poor and those deemed "deserving" of aid who survived on the pious distribution of alms. Between these two poles were a range of people who scraped by thanks to the support of family and friends, and others who fell through the support network to become "vagabonds" and undesirables. Outside direct agricultural production, wages provided substantial food access. Many people earned money through physical labor, although their tasks and income differed. Even day laborers could earn decent wages, but their food access depended on the terms of their employment. Within the paternalistic system of late medieval employment, many laborers were paid in part with food. Those without direct access to land and with only meager income or unreliable employment often fell into extreme poverty. Individuals often turned to the social connections of families, employers, confraternities, or guilds for safety nets. In the fourteenth century, the increasing number of hospitals also ensured a minimal diet for a growing number of people.

When actual shortages struck, both informal social support networks and institutions relied on conventional wisdom and shared beliefs to determine how to address the emergency of elevated need. Many employers and hospitals increased their handouts to the deserving, but their largesse was paired with corresponding downward pressure on, and even the criminalization of, those considered undeserving. The distinctions between the deserving and undeserving poor helped determine who received aid and who did not. Starvation most frequently afflicted low-level laborers who could neither rely on the generosity of their employers nor gain access to free assistance. Those with no other option might resort to begging or crime. The largest safety networks were located in cities, which helped attract the destitute and vagrants from the surrounding countryside who hoped to find work or charity. This migration, more than the controlled poverty of those who relied on hospitals for sustenance, caused further dislocations, loosing people from their bonds to the direct entitlements of land or work and laying the groundwork for future crises.

Labor and Wages

A large proportion of medieval people earned at least some income from wage labor. Peasants without sufficient land supplemented their livelihood by working for nobles or wealthier peasants who owned or controlled land. Rural youths could be apprenticed to families to learn agricultural skills or could work as domestic servants called *mossos*.[1] The labor of townsfolk ranged from artisanal crafts, to semiskilled work like construction, stonecutting, or woodwork, to basic manual labor like providing transport. Different forms of employment offered varying degrees of resistance to shortages based on the balance between wages, reliability of work, and other benefits.

It is important to establish a baseline of economic need in order to understand how economic resources translated into access to food, especially all-important grain. Assuming 1,500 calories' worth of grain per person per day (roughly half the calories burned by a physical laborer), most individuals needed around 70 solidi of grain per year. This accords with the calculations of around seven quarters per person described for urban imports in the previous chapter. Obviously, this is a highly variable number, and relative poverty/wealth would probably have significantly influenced the quantity and quality of food available to different individuals. At the level of mere survival, however, 70 solidi of grain, another 50 solidi each for meat and wine, and a further 25 solidi spent on other foods (fish, cheese, favas, garbanzos, vegetables, salt, etc.) would provide a diet moderately better than the one available in the Barcelona hospitals. Thus 175 solidi was sufficient to cover individual basic needs for a year. Teresa Vinyoles i Vidal estimates that food, clothing, and heat would have cost roughly 200 solidi per person per year near the end of the century.[2] From 1350 to 1400, prices rose between 30 and 50 percent—a substantial increase but a relatively low level of inflation over fifty years. Notably, neither Vinyoles's calculation nor mine includes the cost of housing, taxes, or other expenses. It is also difficult to estimate the specific increase in cost from an individual to a family, but 200 solidi per year is a good place to start.

Salaried positions generally paid workers monthly or biannually, especially for tasks that required inexact amounts of time. Many privileged jobs paid annual stipends that all but ensured a stable and comfortable livelihood. The Pia Almoina of Barcelona, the Cathedral of Lleida, and other large institutions maintained lawyers, agricultural overseers, financial managers, and procurators with annual salaries. The lawyers and procurators earned between 100 and 120 solidi per year and the financial overseers between 200 and 300 solidi per year, usually in two or three fixed payments.[3] Government officials in smaller towns made similar amounts: Villarreal paid lawyers between 160 and 200 solidi per year, depending on how many cases they worked.[4] Overall, these salaries are not high. A lawyer for the Almoina might earn only 100 solidi, around half the cost of a reasonable diet. But lawyers routinely held more than one such post; their work for the town was not full-time. Urban and institutional documents also reveal that large court cases often involved additional payments for the preparation of specific documents.

Salaried positions were not always privileged. Urban guards earned significantly less than councilors did. Barcelona's city guards received the largest salaries, of around 480 solidi per year; in Valencia, the men who patrolled the surrounding *huerta* were paid around 350; guards of the port received only 200, perhaps because this was not a year-round position. Guards of the land surrounding Villarreal earned only 75 to 100 solidi per year, but they could supplement this income with a portion of the fines levied on anyone they caught breaking the law. It was common in many jobs, such as that of market regulator, to receive as much as a third of the fines collected.[5] City street cleaners, public entertainers, and the town crier earned between 200 and 300 solidi, a wage that would barely cover an individual's expenses.[6] If these men had families, it is likely that more than one adult, and even older children, also worked to earn income and keep the family solvent. At times, salaried workers complained of poverty in petitions to their employers. The monitor of weights and measures for the city of Barcelona petitioned the council to help pay for a dowry. He claimed that he lacked sufficient resources for the extra expense because of "the costs that he ordinarily has to meet to sustain his life and the lives of his wife and children."[7] Even an urban inspector with stable employment might be unable to make ends meet in the event of a crisis, or even the more predictable extra expense of marriage.

Servants routinely received long-term contracts, getting paid for several months rather than by the day. Many institutions hired employees to carry messages, transport goods, and do other menial tasks. Citation officers, called *saigs*, in Villarreal earned a meager 30 to 60 solidi per year, although their income was frequently supplemented with payments of food. Other tasks performed by the poor, especially wet nursing (a long-term job with inexact hours if ever there was one), also received a more predictable, fixed salary, based more on working conditions than its prestige.[8] The Hospital of en Clapers in Valencia paid its wet nurses only around 17 solidi per month; Barcelona wet nurses earned 20.[9] Distinct from even the city guards, wet nurses came from both the urban and rural poor. The death of mothers from illness or childbirth resulted in the movement of children between nurses and often cut contracts short. Despite the salaried nature of these positions, stability did not necessarily protect people from destitution.

Payment for wage labor similarly varied, depending on the work. Some jobs paid per task: porters were often paid according to the weight of the materials they moved. A quarter of grain might cost 1 or 2 denarii to move across Barcelona, while a pile of firewood could cost three or four. Many jobs paid by the day, although workers might get a contract that promised a month or more of ongoing work. Agricultural work paid roughly 2 solidi per day; skilled workers such as stonemasons or master carpenters received more. Women's manual labor—which ranged from sweeping out threshing rooms, to cleaning wine fermenters, to planting, harvesting, and other field work—routinely paid less.[10] Women agricultural workers earned between 1 and 1.5 solidi per day, increasing to between roughly 20 denarii (1.6 solidi) and 2 solidi by 1400. Skill and experience influenced how much one earned doing many jobs, such as cloth production or metalworking. Wages in Marseille could often vary as much within a profession as between professions; some cloth makers made more than twice as much as workers doing similar tasks.[11] As with salaried positions, wages for these jobs increased moderately but slowly over the course of the second half of the fourteenth century.

The Black Death forced the one notable exception to the slow rise in wages. The sudden drop in the labor force at midcentury upset the balance between workers and available labor.[12] In October 1349 in Valencia (only months after the first wave of the Plague), the city council voted to increase the salary of the notarial office from 1,200 to 1,500 solidi because Pere

Rovira, the head notary, complained that he was unable to find workers at the normal rate. In November, the king mandated a wage freeze across the entire Crown of Aragon in a futile attempt to fight the sudden drop in labor supply. Valencia posted twelve men throughout the city to ensure that the rule was followed and threatened anyone who tried to overcharge with a public whipping.[13] Barcelona passed some of the more draconian laws, mandating a maximum wage of 2 solidi per day for farm work and 2.5 for planting garden crops. The penalty for breaking the regulation was the cutting off of the perpetrator's hand![14] Despite complaints, most of the kingdom saw wages level off within a few years.[15] Reports from other Mediterranean locations, such as the areas around Florence, Marseille, and other parts of southern France, also showed wages first spiking but then leveling off.[16]

Fundamentally, wage labor was highly unreliable. Planting and harvesting, balanced between different crops, needed to be done most of the year, but the number of workers hired varied wildly from day to day. The monastery of Sant Pere de les Puel·les and the properties of Barcelona's Pia Almoina routinely went weeks without hiring anyone, but during planting, harvest, and wine making, they could hire forty or fifty people per day.[17] Short-term interruptions such as excessive rain could send workers home early without pay. Presumably, it was rare that a manual laborer could find steady work year-round. Estimates based on institutional labor costs peg wages in Valencia at around 12 pounds (240 solidi) per year at the beginning of the fifteenth century, suggesting roughly 120 working days.[18] At times of special need, individuals might fill their empty days with transporting materials and other poorly paid kinds of work.

Within the paternalistic structure of late medieval social relationships, day laborers and servants also received meals and sometimes other essentials, such as clothing, from their employers. Broadly speaking, the lower the cash wages for a given job, the more likely it was to include these other types of compensation. At the more paternalistic end of the spectrum, Valencia's Pia Almoina paid a wet nurse's rent, in part for her labor and in part as alms because of her poverty.[19] For common manual labor, the heavier the work, the more food people received. Within the Crown of Aragon, laborers generally received the main meal of the day, early in the afternoon. On meat days, they were fed lamb, pork, or other meat cooked into a stew with vegetables or garbanzo beans, a diet similar to what was served at hospitals. Fish days could include fresh or salted fish, depending on the location and time of year. Even mules, whether part of patrimonial labor obligations or wage labor, received cheap grain mixtures of oats, barley, and perhaps vetch when they plowed.[20]

Recompense for heavy labor such as pruning vineyards or harvesting crops could include quite a rich diet while the work lasted. At the castle of Sitges, hard work meant liver for breakfast, a pound of pork or salted fish for an afternoon snack (called *barena*), and a small amount of lamb mixed into a stew for dinner.[21] In one memorable instance, workers who came to uproot a dead olive tree (a backbreaking process involving animal traction and lots of digging) were served this repast. Among these workers were a pair of Genoese prisoners who, despite receiving no wages, did partake of all the meals.[22] Similarly, when the Barcelona Cathedral sent a team of workers early one morning to fetch a tree trunk for repairs, its overseer gave them bread, wine, and nuts before they set out.[23] Some laborers, like the baker at the monastery of Sant Pere, received supplements based on their type of work. To make up for his low salary of 1 solidus per day, the baker was allowed to take home almost two pounds of bread each evening. As with wages, because women were barred from harder physical labor, they were also deprived of the richest diet. Women who spent long days washing out wine fermenters were given some fruit for breakfast, meat or fish for the main meal, and possibly dried fish for *barena*, though rarely all of these meals.[24] The cost of these meals could total as much as 15 percent of men's daily wages but was closer to 10 percent for women.

The practice of paying in part with food was not necessarily universal. Monique Bourin's study of economic development in towns near Narbonne and Beziers indicates that employers preferred to pay entirely in silver rather than feed their day laborers. Bourin sees this as a reflection of the highly monetized economy in the area.[25] Francine Michaud's study of labor contracts in Marseille, by contrast, suggests that food payments for servants, slaves, and agricultural laborers were common. Some notarial contracts, in fact, include specifics only about the food, clothing, and shelter workers would receive, and say nothing at all about monetary payments.[26] Both Marseille and Barcelona were also highly monetized economies, so even in major commercial centers, the paternalistic practices of payment in kind persisted alongside cash wages. Agricultural employers might have preferred this type of payment in kind because it typically came from their own harvest.

Reliable access to food, however meager the portions, helped balance out low cash wages. Servants and some slaves lived at one end of a balance between stability and opportunity. While these individuals lacked freedoms, many of their caloric needs were met by their masters during shortages. Their legal and financial access to food was fixed, but usually dependable. In one contract from 1399, an elderly woman agreed to free her slave as long as the slave continued working for her; the contract also states explicitly that the slave, now servant, would receive all her food and clothing as well.[27] Her legal status had changed, but her food entitlements remained fixed and formally recognized. The Barcelona Pia Almoina and Sant Pere de les Puel·les both owned slaves who performed multiple duties, including cleaning buildings and moving supplies. Payment records confirm the extent to which the houses furnished basic necessities for the slaves; they were provided with shoes, shirts, bedding, and basic medical care when necessary.[28] The slaves at Sant Pere received new shoes as often as the sisters at the monastery did (roughly every couple of years), though of notably lower cost.[29] Similarly, the slaves received all their meals at the house where they lived, though, as with their shoes, they received only inexpensive foodstuffs. While their diet contained no perks such as liver, they could count on a base number of calories from stew and bread every day, a diet that continued largely uninterrupted even during shortages.

The diet of slaves was similar to that of mules in that the food was sufficient if not good. Also like mules, when shortages were extreme enough, slaves became expendable. Poorer individuals like mariners and craftsmen might own slaves, and when the master went hungry, so did the slave.[30] When slave numbers rose, masters could and did release them rather than feed them. The influx of Sardinian slaves in Mallorca during the Catalan invasion in the 1350s created large manors with dozens of slaves. During the famine of 1374, owners let go of some of these slaves so as to maintain the rest, creating a clear group of impoverished and marginal people at immediate risk of starvation.[31] Many of these released slaves wandered around looking for food, first by seeking work and eventually by theft, inviting punishment and crackdowns on their freedom.[32]

The Character of Charity

In normal years, agricultural and other forms of manual labor supplied most people with their daily needs. Amartya Sen's set of food entitlements included the power and control of one's own labor as one of the last resources of the poor. But charity routinely provided food and resources to those who maintained no stable entitlements of their own. Even in good years, the overall distribution of wealth in medieval society remained highly unequal, enough so that the poorest people routinely lacked sufficient access to daily necessities.[33] Urban centers contained significant numbers of public beggars who often congregated around shrines, churches, and other central places. Even in relatively well off families, some members could find themselves destitute from causes that persist to the present day: incapacitating injury, serious illness, or merely old age—a hazard we all must face eventually. Some were forced to rely on institutional charity, whether prevented by age or infirmity from working to meet their needs or condemned to the margins of society for some other reason.[34]

Throughout the twelfth and thirteenth centuries, new poorhouses, both religious and secular, sprang up around Catalonia and throughout Europe. By the fourteenth century, these institutions fed and housed an increasingly large segment of the population. Corporate generosity began to supplant private charity. Even when families or social groups wished to continue to give alms, they often donated their assistance to an institution that could better manage the resources while explicitly protecting people from their own extended family. Many large institutions began as part of the work of cathedral canons attached to larger dioceses. Barcelona, the Seu of Urgell, and Vic are the oldest.[35] By the late fourteenth century, the landscape of Catalonia included dozens of charitable institutions—even a small city might contain three or four—under a wide variety of administrative frameworks.

Wills often designated money for hospitals, along with money for masses to be said in the donor's honor. Sufficiently large bequests of landed property endowed hospitals with the resources to serve multiple poor people in perpetuity.[36] Pere Desvilar and Joan Colom in Barcelona, Bernat des Clapers in Valencia, and Ramon de Terrades in Vic all started private hospitals, initially under the control of the executors of their wills.[37] Both famine and plague precipitated a spike in the number of wills produced, as the threat of death inspired even those less likely to die to contemplate their spiritual duties. In one will, written during the famine of 1375, the widow of Guillem Salamó, named Margarida, explicitly finalized her will "on account of the famine and deadly pestilence which by the divine authority rages and strengthens daily in the realm of Catalonia and in all the world."[38] Previous scholarship has used these spikes in the number of wills as a proxy for the severity of both famine and plague.[39]

Medieval charity, like modern practices of social support, was refracted through the lens of economic and theological attitudes about individual moral worth. By the fourteenth century, Christian theology's traditional opposition to the accumulation of wealth had given way to a grudging acceptance of its existence in Christian society. Francesc Eiximenis's treatise on government lionized the value of merchants to society but also emphasized their obligation to those less well off. Citing an apocryphal reference to Philologus of Sinope, Eiximenis wrote, "merchants must be favored above all secular people in the world, because they are the life of the earth where they are found, . . . the sustenance of the poor, the branch of all good business." Eiximenis clarified the obligation of this new merchant class to the poor, noting that God himself "has placed [the poor] in every community so that the rich and others who have the obligation shall have the opportunity to give alms and redeem their sins." He tied the virtue of wealth to the importance of alms, citing a passage from Proverbs 13:8: "riches have been given to man specifically to redeem himself."[40] Churches reinforced this moral teaching by appealing directly to the piety of their donors. In 1398, the church in Daroca offered 140 days of indulgence to anyone who gave money to the hospital, which was in dire need of funds at the time.[41]

Eiximenis and other writers saw poor relief as one of the best ways to balance concerns over wealth. Donations were inextricably linked to the character of the donor, spiritualizing and ritualizing the care offered to the poor during the late Middle Ages.[42] This ritualized character of charity directly encouraged limits on who might receive aid. Before seeking hospital assistance, individuals sought support from their employers, from their status as citizens or their membership in guilds or confraternities, and often from their own families. After these resources failed, individuals had to fit into the proper theological categories to receive charitable donations. While these categories had precedent in Byzantine and monastic practices, Scholastic writings helped solidify a set of distinctions that underpinned medieval poor relief and set the stage for a modern understanding of poverty. The variety of legal and social restrictions surrounding the poor—such as bans on begging and the expulsion of immigrants—helped regulate the entitlements of the lower classes. Just as cities magnified their economic controls, they increasingly controlled people in a similar fashion, using preexisting ideas of how to classify, help, or remove the poor. Those with the weakest claims to entitlements were held in the lowest esteem by society and were the first to go hungry—it was socially acceptable to let them starve.

The most important late medieval distinctions revolved around the voluntary and involuntary poor, the latter being further divided into the deserving and undeserving poor. These distinctions originated in commentaries on canon law in the late twelfth century and had gained widespread use in legal codes by the fourteenth.[43] The voluntary poor included various monastic professions, including the newer friars and other minor orders. The involuntary poor included all who found themselves significantly below their station in life. In Catalan (with similar phrases in both Spanish and French), medieval writers described the deserving poor as *els pobres vergonyats* (the shamefaced poor).[44] Such language enshrined an attitude that the recipients of aid should feel remorseful about their station; their shame should help excuse their potential laziness. The undeserving poor included a diverse group of people, most often men, who were able-bodied but destitute. Often, these poor held jobs but persistently found themselves lacking the minimum resources necessary for survival. Both theology and legislation focused charity on the "deserving" and placed increasing restrictions on the "undeserving." Access to charitable aid followed an individual's social connections but provided extra protections to those who came to their poverty in theologically faultless ways.

Because charity was so closely tied to the salvation of the donor, medieval charitable institutions often put as much effort into restricting people's access to food as they did into securing resources for charity. Concern for the donor's soul generated the need to distinguish the true poor from the false. Legislation bears out this overriding concern for the donor over any real need of the recipient. In 1321, King Jaume II (r. 1291–1327) granted a privilege to all cities in the Crown of Aragon, allowing them to create restrictions and punishments: "Whenever any unfair person, under false pretext of poverty or necessity, goes through the city and locations of our realm begging for or unhesitatingly receiving false alms, through which they have unjustly carried off those alms given to them by faithful Christians, ignorant of their condition; consequently, that person has defrauded the poor of Christ of their alms and offended the divine majesty."[45] The two primary reasons for punishing false begging were that the beggar had taken alms from the deserving poor, and that he or she had deceived the donor and offended God. To be sure of absolving their sins, donors needed to know whether the beggar was a true "poor of Christ." If the alms went to a false beggar, not only had a true poor person been denied help, but the gift became spiritually ineffective for the donor.

As the distinction between the "shamefaced" poor and the poor who lacked moral standing (vagabonds, cheaters, evildoers, and ne'er-do-wells) strengthened in the thirteenth century, legal codes attempted to codify the differences in increasingly harsh ways.[46] In 1365, Barcelona issued restrictions on donating alms to children, hucksters, wet nurses, jugglers, and servants. The law explicitly exempted people if they gave "for the love of god, to a religious person or a miserable person."[47] In 1387, the city required that people wear visual identifications of who was a genuine *vergonyat* to prevent fraudulent alms; Valencia had already created a system of licenses in 1350 to restrict begging.[48] By the end of the century, Barcelona had published a list of "pimps, gamblers, and vagabonds" who had been obligated to leave the city; if the prohibition against donations to undesirable individuals failed, the next step was to remove the temptation.[49]

The mere act of begging became tantamount to a desire to avoid work. Eiximenis placed a high bar on even the disabled, arguing that the blind could ring bells or run the bellows of a blacksmith, and that those missing hands or arms could carry mail or other material on their backs.[50] The city of Valencia frequently used the same language that Eiximenis did, condemning "laziness" (ociositat) in its statutes against begging. The council was determined "to avoid the laziness of the vagabonds" and the "wickedness or dishonor or disgrace" brought on the city by actions seen as offensive to God.[51] Teresa Vinyoles i Vidal has noted that these same concerns about laziness and public nuisance drove an increasing intolerance of the disabled more broadly.[52]

Because charity was a form of atonement for sin, the setting and quality of its distribution reinforced the trappings of holiness. During the 1374–75 famine, King Pere the Ceremonious donated money for the foundation of a hospital explicitly focused on the healing of souls.[53] Some of the cathedral poorhouses required entrants to donate their remaining property before receiving their daily rations.[54] The donation of property reflected a monastic ideal of exchanging one's claim on the volatile entitlements of the outside world for a theologically narrow but more reliable (divinely provided) set of resources. The austere rations, the presence of priests, and the constant saying of masses for the anniversaries of the many donors enhanced the monastic feel of the late medieval hospital. The nobleman Pedro Fernández de Híjar (1245–1299) wanted all of the poor in his hospital to be constantly reminded through liturgical commemorations of his and his descendants' souls as they received their generosity.[55] Such donations created what Raúl Villagrasa Elías has called "an entire system of propaganda for [the donor's] posthumous glory."[56] The Hospital Desvilar in Barcelona included instructions for prayers and liturgies to benefit the souls of the patients but also to advertise the spiritual merit of the donors.[57] For students who expected to return to work after a fixed time relying on charity, their time at the hospital perhaps provided a reminder of the prayerful attitude attached to the act of learning itself. For wealthier individuals who retired to a hospital in old age, the act might have been tantamount to taking a monastic vow—a choice to ensure not just their daily bread but also their salvation. The sacralization of charity and poverty reached its apex in the late medieval hospital, with people from varying class backgrounds all reduced to a theologically uniform group of "shamefaced" poor whose prayers provided salvation for themselves and their benefactors.

Restrictions on those who received formal charity perpetuated their lives as agents of the salvation of donors. Jenny Edkins describes a similar demand on famine victims in the twentieth century. Depoliticized famines, viewed as natural rather than complex disasters, become unrelated to political and social destruction. Famine aid (often large quantities of grain) only sustains "bare life," without restoring agency to the victims. Aid agencies often demand that victims of famine receive their food in work camps or adopt the agricultural norms of the donors. The victims do not get a say in how to reconstruct their own broken society.[58] If famine's chief destruction comes from social breakdown, then the sustenance of bare life does not repair the disaster. Such aid preserves the life of idealized victims rather than assisting fully human people. Medieval charity, similarly, preserved the life of those willing to conform to the correct ideals of poverty, molding the poor to shape the needs of the better off.

Poverty and Survival

The theological categories of "deserving" and "undeserving" poor tell us who late medieval society marked out for acceptable starvation, but the distinction does not necessarily tell us who did and did not starve. Not all of those whom we would consider marginal were necessarily poor or particularly vulnerable. Marginality included the economically disadvantaged—beggars, itinerants, the working poor—but also those disadvantaged by other factors, such as religious minorities, people with diseases like leprosy, the physically and mentally disabled, and women.[59] Complicating all of these categories of privilege is the fact that "wealthy" and "poor" were relative terms. Modern understandings of poverty, and particularly of food insecurity, are generally expressed in absolute terms: what are the minimum nutritional requirements to feed an individual? What is a minimum income that can sustain these requirements and supply basic clothing and housing?[60] Medieval writers were concerned as much with the qualities of poverty. "Poverty was never seen purely in economic terms," James Brodman explains, "but rather viewed as a form of degradation that rendered the individual vulnerable or dependent."[61] As such, the medieval "poor" were those whose entitlements either no longer matched their social standing or came entirely from a source outside their control.[62]

Certain forms of marginality carried greater risks than others. There is no good evidence that Jews or Muslims starved in significantly larger numbers than Christians during a crisis, although their marginality did produce other problems. In Valencia, rural Muslim populations suffered greater levels of poverty than their Christian peasant counterparts owing to their increased servile status after conquest. Famines are generally not associated with increases in anti-Jewish acts that came with the Plague. Early in the famine of 1374, the city council of Tarragona lumped its Jewish inhabitants together with foreigners and ordered all those who could not find provisions for themselves to leave or else lend the city the money to purchase provisions for them.[63] While restrictions on foreigners and beggars were common, including the Jews in such restrictions was quite rare. The wave of anti-Jewish violence that broke across Spain in 1391, hitting Valencia especially hard, also did not derive from rhetoric about food supply or shortages. Instead, grain riots often targeted urban elites for failing to uphold their social contract. Gender and disability, by contrast, did map closely onto poverty. Research on and evidence of women's labor has increased steadily over the past few decades.[64] However, women were routinely paid less for their work, while their perceived position of inferiority also encouraged certain forms of aid. Recent scholars have also found that disability was a chief cause of loss of income. Without any form of insurance, a severe injury that impeded the manual work of a laborer could suddenly and permanently dry up his livelihood.

Before seeking charity, many people—whether injured, landless, or destitute—found refuge in family structures. Aging parents stayed with their children, and the injured stayed with extended family. The norms of familial obligation also gained new and more concrete structure in the legal thinking of the thirteenth century. Gratian's *Decretum* suggested that children who failed to support their parents in old age could be stripped of their inheritance. With this legal backing, many town statutes systematized these obligations. Town charters throughout the Crown of Aragon adopted language requiring that children feed and clothe their parents when they became too old or infirm to work.[65] David Herlihy has noted that thirteenth-century preachers in northern Italy began to discuss in more detail the obligations of children and grandchildren toward their elders. He speculates that urban norms had broken down the more systemic familial obligations of earlier decades.[66] María Luz Rodrigo Estevan and María José Sánchez Usón have studied wills from the period that required children to provide for their parents' upkeep. In one example from Barbastro, a town northwest of Lleida, Pascual Garaza and his wife received from his widowed mother, Leanor, several houses and properties that he was to manage. He was to use the income to provide for Leanor's upkeep in her illness. The contract stipulates that he could not sell any property until after Leanor's death.[67] It is possible that legal restrictions attempting to force this sort of family care helped fuel large donations to hospitals, with stipulations that these institutions care for family members.

In the founding documents of the largest nonecclesiastical hospital in Barcelona, Pere Desvilar laid out a primer on the social hierarchy of destitution, stating in the charter that his donations were to assist "all the poor of Christ who are citizens or residents of Barcelona." Others might be admitted, but the people of Barcelona came first. Three years later, in 1311, Desvilar's will provided more specific instructions: the resources for donations were to be divided in thirds, the first two-thirds to go in equal parts to two of the standard recipients of late medieval charity, widows and captives, with preference for captives who were citizens of Barcelona or at least Catalans. The final third was to be distributed among the "deserving poor." Desvilar further specified that they should be "first and foremost of my lineage and after that other poor of the city of Barcelona and no others." Later donors, including Pere's brother Jaume and the wealthy merchant Arnau Ballester, continued the precedent, reserving as many as half the beds they endowed for members of their own families and the remaining beds for citizens of Barcelona first.[68]

Most hospitals in the Crown of Aragon demonstrate preferential patterns similar to those of Desvilar. At the Hospital of en Clapers in Valencia, almost all the people listed in a document from 1374 came from the Christian population of the city itself.[69] Jaume II had an agreement with the Pia Almoina of Barcelona where three people specifically chosen by the king could receive their rations from the institution. Some of the first royal choices were Bartomeu Carbonell, a student and the cousin of the king's chaplain, and Agnès, the widow of Pere Burgès, a poor citizen of Barcelona.[70] Wills designating funds for Barcelona's Almoina routinely noted a preference for the education of family members.[71] This form of support was meant to be temporary (often specified as between three and eight years) as the family members learned a trade to support themselves. Ripoll de Cortades in 1302 required that his money go to a scholar of his family, but if no scholar could be found, the money could be used for other poor members of his family, especially if they came to Barcelona to learn a trade. In 1365, Simó Rovira split his inheritance between the Pia Almoina and the Hospital Desvilar, each receiving the same instruction to provide first for a member of Rovira's family seeking to become a cleric, or, failing that, for other poor members of his family.[72]

Some hospitals focused on providing aid to specific populations. Confraternities and guilds both endowed beds specifically for their members.[73] Two specific examples appeared in Valencia: the confraternity of Sant Jaume in the city founded a hospital specifically for Castilian refugees from the famine that raged there in 1377, and Pere Bou, a merchant, founded a shelter for fishermen who were too old to work.[74] In Mallorca, Moisés Cabrit founded a small establishment specifically for poor Jews.[75] One confraternity of freed black slaves kept a pool of money available for assistance so that their orphans and needy could stay within their group rather than be forced to rely on the charity of the broader community.[76] Some of these institutions, such as the shelter founded by Pere Bou, acted as a social security system or retirement plan as much as they did as a house for the poor. This meant that even when poor people fell into the category of "deserving," their entry into a hospital or poorhouse hinged as much on their social connections, or even their occupation, as it did on actually being poor.

Donations demonstrate the intentions of the donors, but records of admissions to hospitals are extremely scarce. A small handful of examples provide a useful balance to the information above. Pere Desvilar's will delegated the responsibility of choosing new administrators to the main council of Barcelona.[77] Starting with the election of Pere de Vilafranca and Ferrer de Moià in 1325, the councilors annually elected new administrators throughout the century.[78] On rare occasions, these councilors entered the comments of petitioners who sought aid. These brief entries provide an important glimpse of some of the people who described themselves as poor and the arguments they made to gain access to the assistance provided by the urban hospital. In the first case, a woman named Alitsen, wife of the farm worker Salvador Gila, applied to the administrators Bonanat de Valls and Ferrer Alot for admission on February 7, 1357. The councilors noted that she had "demonstrated to us at length that she is poor and of the lineage of Jaume Desvilar, deceased."[79] The document provides no specific proof of her poverty beyond her word. But equal in importance is the evidence of her lineage. Whatever the particular circumstances of her poverty, she received aid on the basis of her relation to Desvilar himself. It is possible that her gender also contributed to her claim that she could not support herself. Two other claims demonstrate the kind of evidence that those without specific lineages needed in order to receive aid. On March 8 of the same year, the administrators granted a daily ration to Pere Johan, a mariner. While of no particular lineage, Johan did pass the citizenship requirement. The petition goes into greater detail about Johan's poverty, noting that he was "old, poor, and in pain, on account of which he cannot work and requires a portion or ration from the hospital for the sustaining of his life."[80] In a similar case in 1407, two men previously employed as city guards received what was essentially their pension. The two had been relieved of their duty because they were "old, with failing vision," but received their assistance "because they had served well and were poor."[81] For the mariner and the city guards, the hospital functioned essentially as a retirement home. Both jobs paid well enough to sustain day-to-day life, but not necessarily enough to save for the day when these individuals could no longer work. Charity gave preference to retirement for those who had worked hard during their lives, proving that they were not lazy. Those with family connections often did not need to provide the same rationale in order to receive similar assistance.

Although the city of Valencia does not have similar cases for entry into hospitals, the city council did pay pensions that note similar conditions. In 1381, Agnes Ferrandez, a well-connected noblewoman from Castile, arrived in Valencia seeking what amounted to asylum. Her husband, the Castilian nobleman Garcia Ferrandez de Villodres, had died and been stripped of his land and patrimony. In response, Agnes "had arrived fleeing to this city where she is and lives in great poverty and misery."[82] The city's councilors were moved by pity to provide her with an astonishing 500 solidi per year. This was more than many poorer families lived on but represents the level that the councilors perceived as necessary for a noblewoman with good connections.[83] The city also periodically extended small amounts of charity to those in more dire straits. In July 1367, the Valencian exchequer paid a mere 20 solidi to one Maria, who was "poor and old and powerless who came crying."[84] Donations to other poor people routinely note their "powerlessness" as a qualification for membership among the deserving poor. Finally, rather than place its long-serving retirees in local hospitals, the city sometimes simply granted them a stipend. This was the case with Johan de Sessa, a city bailiff who, like the Barcelona guards, had served long and faithfully but was now "tro vellea" (too old) to support himself.[85] He received more than Maria but less than Agnes— a guaranteed 360 solidi for his upkeep even after he stopped working.[86] Valencia's systems of poor relief appear less formal and institutionalized than Barcelona's use of the Hospital Desvilar, but the same connections, history of service, age requirement, and general loss of previous position applied.

A few programs specifically targeted youths. Such efforts often arose from the general fear that theologically protected orphans could grow up to become unwanted vagabonds if not properly guided. In March 1338, the Valencian council, working with the king's blessing, created a system that placed orphans and those "afflicted with poverty" directly under the control of an official tutor, "so that [they] might not refuse appropriate labor and fall back on begging, miserably consumed with infamy and wastefulness."[87] Under threat of whipping, children could be coerced into working with their tutor. Parental fears drove some poor people to place their own children under the tutelage of others. At midcentury, two widows living near Marseille placed their children with a master, the first with a mendicant monk who would teach the boy to read and write, the second with a maker of bags and sacks. In both cases, the goal was to prevent the youths from outgrowing the public assistance that was easier to acquire for children and widows and becoming able-bodied adult beggars.[88]

While I have focused on forms of assistance in the Crown of Aragon, the same theological distinctions governed the treatment of the poor in other regions. Italian cities, driven by the same urban wealth enjoyed by Valencia and Barcelona, also expanded their charitable institutions in the early fourteenth century. Hospitals appeared in most Italian communes, similarly founded by wealthy individuals, confraternities, or other groups.[89] These institutions restricted entry using the same theological methods. Leaders in Bologna worried about the bad influence on its populace of those who begged under false pretenses, accusing beggars of being foreigners and con artists.[90] Such accusations persisted throughout late medieval and early modern European history and indeed to the present day. Sixteenth-century writers described masters in the "art of begging" as faking all manner of wounds, handicaps, and disabilities. Bologna eventually took monasticism to a new level, passing laws to forcibly enclose the poor in 1563. Poor people were paraded to the archbishop's palace and then taken to a deserted monastery beyond the city walls where they could be both fed and monitored. Despite the show, some late medieval institutions did cater directly to other poor. The Congregazione dei Buonomini di San Martino in Florence routinely used its funds to help the working poor and even artisans with debt or financial struggles, and also supplied aid to widows and pregnant women.[91] Aid did sometimes reach the needy, but it virtually always came inflected through a system that marked off certain types of individuals as meritorious and others as suspicious.

Resources in Times of Famine

Systems of redistribution and protection never came close to meeting the collective needs of all medieval people. During times of crisis, individuals leaned harder on available aid. While there is no clear definition that distinguishes famine from shortage or dearth (for further discussion of this point, see chapter 4), the modern understanding of famine as a complex disaster reminds us that social breakdown and loss of community are key markers of the boundary between events that people can weather and those they cannot.[92] "Famine, as a humanitarian disaster, uncovers the underlying contradictions in the constructed social order and in the codified system of relationships."[93] As Pere Benito i Monclús has shown, in chronicle accounts from the eleventh and twelfth centuries, the breakup of families was the most severe consequence of famine. Thus the continued functioning of social support systems represented a robust response to crisis and a sign of society's resilience.

No single shortage event produced enough of a shock to cause the systemic breakdown of all social institutions, but the number of structural problems can indicate the level of an event's severity. Elites most often feared the specific social rupture of riots. Despite the descriptions of chroniclers who emphasized their unruly nature, these riots followed an internal logic that often targeted precisely the social structures that rioters felt were responsible for failing to uphold their side of the paternalistic social bargain.[94] Fourteenth-century grain riots were fundamentally similar to anarchist rioters who threw bricks through bank windows: violent, yes, but targeted rather than simply desperate or random. When bread riots broke out in 2008 in Senegal, Egypt, and Bangladesh, rioters often paraded effigies through the streets and torched government-sponsored bread handouts, demonstrating their specific ire with the inadequate government response.[95] Violent responses to economic inequality are neither "modern" nor born of mere desperation.

In much the same way that work restrictions or bureaucratic prerequisites can be used to strip needy individuals of government assistance, medieval towns and governments doubled down on requirements to restrict access to certain paupers. Needy individuals who did not meet the proper criteria were criminalized. Perhaps the most violent public response to famine was the restriction placed on migration; those who fled their previous lives seeking food were frequently branded "undeserving." The import networks cities offered were more malleable than rural production. Particularly as famines dragged on into a second or third season, urban trade resources guarded or restored food supplies through political pressure and economic incentives, even as rural resources dwindled. These efforts tended to lower prices in large markets before rural agriculture in the hinterland had fully recovered, creating economic and survival pressures on rural inhabitants to migrate to the cities. Manual labor in a city, such as being a porter or servant, offered narrow economic entitlements but could be easy to come by and provided quicker resources than waiting for a new harvest. Urban areas varied in their responses to the influx of poor people, but legal restrictions could be extremely severe in times of shortage.

Documents that describe crisis migration often came from those who complained that peasants or workers had left the countryside. Both famines and plagues produced *masos ronecs*, or deserted farmhouses. It is impossible to know whether the original owners of these lands had died of hunger or disease or simply left.[96] Occasionally, documents tell clearer tales, even indicating where people might have gone. After the famine of 1374–75, the cathedrals of both Mallorca and Manresa complained about the sudden evaporation of their workforce. Francisco de Campo, a citizen of Manresa, wrote to the prince of Girona, Joan I (eventually king of Aragon from 1387 to 1396), seeking restitution for the sale of land in the Vallhonesta because the land had ceased to be profitable. The "sterile time" had left the land unusable, and the peasants who were originally tied to it, now "oppressed by hunger and poverty," had fled.[97] In Mallorca, a miller named Pere Bisanya apologized to the abbot of the monastery of Santa Maria de la Real for not paying the census tax because everyone in the region had fled to Valencia and Catalonia and he had no work.[98] We cannot know whether his claim that everyone had fled was true, but both documents reflect a common belief that in times of food shortage in the countryside, people would find better options for work and sustenance in the city.

Many people who fled to cities saw their relocation as a temporary response to crisis. Changes in available work and food resources created an ebb and flow during shortages. Francisco de Campo wrote his letter from Manresa in 1376, months after food prices in Barcelona had already fallen back to levels only slightly above normal but toward the end of a second consecutive year of rural scarcity. The city of Valencia experienced both an outflow of people at the beginning of the famine and rural depopulation and urban influx at the end. On June 10, 1374, in the early days of the crisis, the Valencian council wrote a desperate letter to King Pere asking him to divert any available grain ships to the city; otherwise, the council feared, Valencia would be depopulated.[99] In the winter of 1375, after the initial crisis, the city had begun to secure its grain imports. In June, the councilors of Valencia wrote to the leaders of Gandía, a rural coastal town just south of the city, complaining of a growing shortage of workers in the kingdom. Valencian leaders worried that Gandía must ensure sufficient grain for itself to prevent its population from becoming migrants as well.[100]

Scholars continue to debate, even at the level of terminology, how best to understand migration that occurs in response to crisis. Today, the United Nations and other organizations debate the use of such terms as "environmental migrant" and "climate refugee."[101] Climate change may be a slow-moving hazard that promises to uproot millions, but most individual migrants still move in response to shorter-term events. During late medieval food crises, people responded to sudden environmental change by seeking a new environment, in both economic and natural terms. Unable to wait months for the next harvest (which might also fail), laborers went searching for quick work (always more plentiful in cities) and the cheaper grain that was imported long distances and subsidized by powerful urban councils.

Excepting laborers who might be paid, at least partially, with meals, urban centers were reluctant to share food with migrants. As we have seen, urban charity tended to go to citizens first; access was limited when it came to regional refugees and more distant foreign migrants (represented by the hazy categories of "vagabonds" and "foreigners"). Beginning in the early fourteenth century, Castilian, French, and Italian cities all enacted laws restricting vagrants and begging. In 1308, Fernando IV of Castile (r. 1295–1312) required all able-bodied beggars to leave Burgos, the old Castilian capital. The pronouncement targeted those perceived to be able but unwilling to work, thus shutting them out of the category of the "deserving" poor.[102]

Within the Crown of Aragon, Barcelona restricted entry most severely. The Barcelona council notably switched from grants of citizenship in the early fourteenth century to increasing preference for more restrictive grants of residency in the decades after the Black Death, strengthening its control over even legal immigration.[103] New laws also further restricted new migrants. The repeated passage of these laws and increasing punishments suggest that people continued to flow into the city. The timing of laws often corresponded to food shortages or military strife; such laws clearly were efforts to respond to social dislocations caused by these events. The first evidence of such action comes in 1322 with a restriction on the entry of beggars and the removal of some members of the lower classes from the city.[104] Restrictions grew more sweeping and severe after the Black Death. In March 1361, following a minor food shortage in 1360, Barcelona's Consell de Cent upped the ante by allowing any citizen to carry a sword in public, "on account of all the scandal occurring and so that nothing bad would come to pass in the city of Barcelona from the passage [through the city] of foreigners, who are many."[105] In October of the same year, Barcelona gave visitors three days to find work, at the end of which they were whipped publicly and then expelled.[106] During the more severe famine of 1374–75, punishment increased. Anyone caught in the city after eight days without finding work would be flogged, but if they were caught in a second offense, they would be "hanged by the neck without mercy."[107] "Foreigners" included not only people from other kingdoms but also migrants fleeing other parts of Catalonia itself, including peasants fleeing a military invasion in the fall of 1374 and winter of 1375. Almost a year after the invasion, the council clarified the restrictions on entering the city to beg, singling out poor people fleeing from the Urgell and other northern counties in Catalonia, in addition to foreigners.[108] The same promulgation expelled all beggars, prostitutes, and "gamers" from Barcelona under threat of the same punishment. However, the law also stated that "neither mendicants nor the useless who are naturals of the city are to be included in the present ordinations."[109] In order to protect the entitlements of the city and its residents in times of desperation, Barcelona resorted to the only sure means of ending someone's need for food: execution. Such extreme punishment was imposed only rarely. One of the few examples of capital punishment is suggestive. The city leveled the threat of hanging at those who helped Genoese prisoners after the war with Genoa in 1355, suggesting that assisting the foreign poor during a time of famine was tantamount to treason.[110] Given that Barcelona was willing to send militias against even its Catalan neighbors to ensure an adequate food supply, it is not surprising that city authorities would have taken this additional step as well.

Social unrest could prime an area for further difficulties. While social bonds remained weak in the wake of crises, smaller harvest troubles, which might have required only some belt tightening after a series of good years, could escalate. Unlike the Black Death, which struck all levels of society, famine tended to disrupt poorer and rural people—those most in need of stable food production. In this light, some famines appear not as crisis events in their own right but as famine "aftershocks." The Great Famine in northern Europe initially lasted from 1315 to 1317, but William Chester Jordan points out that "conditions so often degenerated over large regions from 1319 to 1322 that it is no exaggeration to link these years with the earlier years of the catastrophe."[111] In other words, although the Great Famine can be seen as a single event in 1315–17, it was followed by a series of aftershocks visited on a society that lacked draft animals, manure, and even the human labor necessary to recover.[112] The structural breakdown caused by major famines created a more susceptible society, which helps explain Amrita Rangasami's observation that famines are rarely single events, but are often a "recurring condition" that strikes a society in which large portions of the people are already at the margins of access. Starvation was only the last in a long string of events that degraded people's resilience, social ties, and ability to maintain robust access to food.[113]

The interaction between civil unrest, violent social responses to natural forces, and the changing legal climate for the poor provides an excellent example of what Dominik Collet and Maximilian Schuh call "socionatural entanglements."[114] Natural and social events interact and influence each other, but not always with linear causes and effects. The restrictions of the poor responded both to plague and to food shortage. Migration into large cities increased after the Black Death, but restrictions on the poor began increasing years before the Plague struck. Disasters tended to increase restrictions and punishments, and once the crisis had passed, things did not always revert to their previous state. Like political control of the grain supply, changes in treatment of the poor demonstrate the ways in which natural shocks can impel long-term social change. The increasing theological precision surrounding the *vergonyats* was a social precursor. Weather-induced food shortages and disease outbreaks pressured government elites to act, and the confluence of factors created an increasingly hostile environment for the destitute.

Despite these conditions, some measures helped to ensure social stability and mitigate negative outcomes. Urban responses were not always as draconian as Barcelona's violent crackdown. Employers offered temporary wage increases, informal loans, and even what amounted to insurance arrangements that assisted individuals in the case of death or injury. Particularly for short-term price spikes, such measures surely allowed better survival and greater social cohesion for those who received these extra entitlements.

Valencia in particular approached its perceived duty to the poor with more nuance and at times greater leniency than Barcelona did. Like its northern neighbor, Valencia's government passed laws removing those who preferred begging to "honest work" in 1338.[115] After the Black Death, the city created a system of licensing for "deserving" poor. It also required the able-bodied poor to be supervised by tutors and accept the work chosen for them. Such forced labor is its own sort of violence (and it was backed by the threat that anyone who refused would be whipped and exiled). However, the city responded more pragmatically to labor shortages after the Plague. In 1353, the city council protected migrants in order to reduce wages, threatening to punish local laborers who committed violence against newly arrived people looking for work. The law accused local workers of wanting to maintain artificially high labor prices by keeping others from entering the market.[116] Those who received the city's protection were people who wanted to work and had not resorted to "undeserving" begging, but they were still noncitizens. This law was passed around the same time that Barcelona increased penalties for all people entering the city, whether they arrived to work or to beg.

During the worst of the famine in 1374, Valencia did expel from the city those who could not feed themselves. In November, however, officials noted that the usual alms available from begging no longer sufficed. In response, the council exhorted each parish in the city to centralize and encourage greater almsgiving (though only for *vergonyats*, who presumably were licensed) that could be distributed from the parish churches. Alms were again increased in 1376 and 1377. Starting in August 1376, Valencian authorities noted an increase of foreign beggars, including an increase in nobles and knights begging in their streets, confirming the pattern described above in which faster urban recovery drew in rural individuals still suffering from poor harvests. The city initially fined those begging illegally and threatened repeat offenders with banishment.[117] By 1377, however, the council of Valencia was describing these new foreigners as refugees from a serious famine in the neighboring territory of Castile. Perhaps inspired by Valencia's recent experience with food crisis, the council made new arrangements. The individuals from Castile (fleeing the very sorts of laws Valencia had recently enacted) built tents and lean-tos on the grounds of the Franciscan monastery within the city. Rather than evict or regulate these refugees, the city voted, "with reverence to God and compassion for the many poor come from Castile," to distribute alms, and a couple of months later bread as well, from the public funds to help them survive.[118] Eventually, the city constructed an entirely new poorhouse near one of the city gates to house the influx.[119] Between actual increases in spending on poor relief and the welcoming of refugees from a nearby food crisis, Valencia improved at least some entitlements for its poor, even as it restricted those seen as lazy or indigent.

Some Italian evidence also reflects a more lenient urban response to poverty and migration. A chronicle from Siena lauds the large hospital of Santa Maria della Scala for offering bread three times a week throughout a famine to whoever arrived, "and there arrived so many people."[120] During a food shortage in 1329, the chronicler Giovanni Villani commended the city of Florence for its merciful treatment of the hungry. Even as Lucca, Pistoia, and other communes expelled beggars and vagabonds in order to conserve their food supplies, the city of Florence expended huge sums of money sending ships to Sicily to ensure its own imports and feed its population. Villani explicitly rejected the violent treatment of the poor, "regarding the piety of God, which would not endure it."[121] These Italian chronicles represent a counternarrative to the more common effort to restrict access to urban wealth and charity.

Other institutions, and even individuals, extended smaller but still effective forms of assistance. In response to the food shortage of 1374–76, Pere the Ceremonious ordered his royal shipyards to increase their pay for eight months.[122] The order appeared in January 1376, late in the crisis, the king noting that while the worst of the crisis was over, prices were still high and workers were having trouble sustaining themselves. Predictably, the highest-paid jobs got the largest raises, with youths receiving both less pay and a smaller raise. Still, this move by a large employer probably put upward pressure on wages more broadly, at least in the short term. Bad agricultural conditions themselves increased the amount of work available because they increased demand. Labor requirements at large manors like Sitges and Mogoda, owned by the Pia Almoina, and lands owned by the monastery of Sant Pere increased during shortage years. As described in the introduction, records at several hospital properties outside Barcelona reflect an increase in the number of workers needed for hoeing and tending grain fields, especially when rain threatened crops. While these were not wage increases like those at the royal shipyards, these manors created more jobs that paid at least partly in food, even if the bread included a great deal more barley than in good years.

Paternalistic employment provided limited protection during a crisis. In 1374, Sereneta, the wife of Ramón de Tous, the head steward for Queen Maria de Luna, sent several letters to her husband detailing her experience of the famine and plague. Through October and November, she begged her husband to use his connections to send wheat or barley to her in Barcelona because their entire household was running short. Finally, at the end of November, Ramón sent a bit of grain, but not enough for long. By December, Sereneta was rationing grain for everyone in her household to only fourteen ounces per day (four ounces less than the Hospital Desvilar ration mentioned above). Throughout the fall, the servants in her house continued to have a reliable food supply, despite their reduced rations. On January 2, however, Sereneta again wrote to her husband to say that they could no longer afford to feed the servants. She recommended that he release a slave named Joana and her illegitimate son (called simply "the bastard"), but asked him to make the decision. She noted that "there are very good houses who have had two and three [servants] who now have only one."[123] The letter seems to imply that she sent the pair to her husband, but there is no further mention of Joana or her son. While this sort of employment provided strong support for a servant's food access, reducing the size of the household labor force was a common solution for the wealthy who could not afford sufficient grain. Loyal service came with some benefits and access to the entitlements of the wealthy, but there were no guarantees.

Institutions also extended protection to some of their employees. The Pia Almoina of Barcelona gave an extra food allowance to its own servant during the same famine; the document explicitly cites his poverty as the reason for the additional assistance.[124] Because the servant received barley, it is easy to see this particular handout as an explicit buffer against starvation rather than any great reward for employment. The Almoina also stepped in after one of its residents in Sitges, Pere Sales, was killed defending the castle from a Genoese assault in 1358. The manager of the property provided Pere's widow with enough grain to feed two or three people for an entire year and a stipend of cash for the "love of God" and because "she was left with many children."[125] This was not a response to famine, but it shows an employer responding to poverty driven by sudden crisis. Like the servant's ration, the widow received barley, including some barley that had been in storage. Love of God helped keep people alive but did not bring luxury.

The final form of moderately effective crisis assistance was the extension of credit. Peasant credit markets were quite well developed by the late fourteenth century. Scholars have shown how credit could drive an individual into permanent debt and ruin, but also how peasants could use short-term debts to improve their circumstances.[126] Loans taken in desperation, what José Ruiz Doménec calls "hunger loans," drove their recipients further into poverty and proved difficult to recover from.[127] The historian Maurice Aymard captures the double-edged nature of the sword when he asks whether peasants were "constrained more by selling to pay than by being able to buy."[128] Whether the debt helped or hindered, by the fourteenth century every echelon of society routinely took on debt, especially to weather hard times.[129] Large landholders extended both formal and informal credit to their peasants to help them endure shortages. In his study of Santa Coloma de Queralt, Gregory Milton found many debt contracts that explicitly use future harvests as promised payment.[130] Accepting cash for the purchase of food in the short term for a fixed percentage of a (hopefully) improved harvest was a reasonable bet for a peasant trying to scrape by. Many peasants received other informal deals from their landlords that amounted to the same temporal displacement. Several times during short years, the monastery of Sant Pere de les Puel·les put off its collection of customary dues, sometimes for months or even years. During the 1374 famine, the monastery permitted Berenguer Asona from Montmeló and Ferrer Sala from Sant Andreu to pay their rent in grain based on the prices in a normal year rather than at the elevated shortage prices. Sala paid his grain rent at a rate of 12 solidi per quarter in mid-1375, when prices in many places were double that figure. In both cases, the monastery cited the peasants' poverty as the primary reason for leniency.[131] Similarly, the monastery allowed Berenguer Folguer from Granollers and Ameler from Palaudàries to postpone payment and use the cash equivalent for their rent during the crisis year (both paid in 1376 for rent due in 1374 and 1375, respectively). In this instance, the monastery also permitted the peasants to pay based on the price in the subsequent, more abundant year, rather than the high prices that prevailed during the harvest failure.[132] These acts amounted to credit for the peasant. With no interest and sometimes paid at a lower rate, this extension of credit also represented a genuine drop in income for the monastery. Like the royal decision to increase wages in the short term as an antipoverty measure, such restructuring of rent payments provided real relief to individuals suffering during a crisis. Impoverishment has always been a mark of vulnerability, before any form of economic or climatic shock that might occur. Relying on the charity of others, accepting the informal reprieves of a landlord, and assuming debt were all risky means of propping up shrinking food resources. But as a temporary fix available to individuals with even moderate resources, these measures could significantly improve resilience at the moment of need.

Conclusions

The ability to survive a famine depended on preexisting social structures. Each individual maintained his or her own food access through the availability of land, paid work, or participation in different social groups. People's access to food did not necessarily have to do with their absolute level of poverty; those with political or family connections could count on better aid than those without. In times of crisis, access to formal institutions or informal assistance highlighted the social connections of the starving to the structures of power that defined and constrained their available resources. As Amartya Sen famously wrote, "The law stands between food availability and food entitlement. Starvation deaths can reflect legality with a vengeance."[133] The structures of poverty and assistance in late medieval Europe followed increasingly rigid paths that favored the "deserving" poor. The categories applied to the poor ultimately derived from the religious needs of the donors rather than the circumstances of the poor. For those perceived as able to work, the act of begging became tantamount to laziness. Alms given to grifters, wanderers, freeloaders, and prostitutes did not count in the economy of salvation. Royal privileges and early restrictions on the poor first appeared in the cities of the Crown of Aragon in the decades leading up to the Black Death, but the attitude behind these actions would have a long life. Multiple studies of later centuries echo the same concerns; as Cissie Fairchilds put it bluntly, charity "was a way for a rich man to buy salvation."[134]

The sacralized character of charitable donations created establishments that cared as much for the souls of their charges as for their physical survival. Lineage and citizenship generally trumped actual need. Barcelona could hang "undeserving" beggars who entered from outside the city walls but allow natural residents to remain and beg as they might. Beyond family support and hospital relief, many individuals remained desperately poor. For the destitute, a wide variety of ad hoc measures taken by urban governments, religious institutions, and large landowners could make a difference during times of crisis, but even these resources favored those with social connections. Landowners in Catalonia extended credit to their tenants, allowing them to pay rent late and at a reduced level. While such small forms of support surely helped, they were not enough to provide a systematic buttress against the threat of starvation. In the face of widespread collapse of food access, the first response of families, institutions, and governments was to protect their own, even when this meant violently rejecting those who lacked the right social connections.

It is clear that charity, combined with economic measures by urban governments, provided better food supplies even for the lower classes. When food shortages occurred in consecutive years, the greater charity and privilege available within city walls drew people toward them from the countryside, where prices remained high. This encouraged cities like Barcelona and Valencia to pass various protective measures that favored their own citizens over those from their hinterlands. Combined with the rapid depletion of urban markets at the beginning of a food crisis, this created a flow of people moving out of cities early in a crisis but flowing back in as urban markets restocked and rural storage ran out. The pull toward urban areas could help keep the countryside in chaos long after a food shortage had ended, proving detrimental to rural production but also to city imports, potentially making future crises more likely.[135] The interacting forces of agriculture, trade, and poverty offer the clearest example of how real declines in food production could act as a trigger. But the shape of the crisis then followed legal and social lines, which produced a disaster in which individual food entitlements were determined by poverty, resilience, and the unequal distribution of power.

II

DISRUPTIONS

4

TWO SHORTAGES OF LESSER MAGNITUDE

The system of food production and distribution in the Crown of Aragon could function surprisingly well, keeping people supplied with basic necessities. Effective agricultural management, economic knowledge, and integrated trade made it possible to surmount small shortages. Even so, the strict hierarchical society of late medieval Europe routinely denied resources to the needy. Almost no one thought of universal resilience as a priority, or even as a good.[1] Fluctuating agricultural, economic, and social factors created the dynamics of famine resilience and vulnerability.[2] The complex interaction between these forces explains why the experience of the Crown of Aragon, and to a great extent of the entire western Mediterranean basin, does not match northern Europe's famine time line.[3] Regional market integration after the Black Death made famine less likely than before—multiple overlapping areas of hardship were necessary for famines to occur—but growing climatic variability meant that broad geographic shocks increased.

Establishing a secure chronology is difficult, not least because scholars routinely disagree on the definition of famine itself.[4] One problem is determining whether a given year or event meets the threshold of a famine and how many lesser events ("dearth," "shortage," "subsistence crisis") are included. In general, scholarly attention has focused on a narrow set of clear starvation events. Cormac Ó Gráda relies on a classic and fairly straightforward definition of famine: "famine refers to a shortage of food or purchasing power that leads directly to excess mortality from starvation or hunger-induced diseases."[5] The definition allows for economic as well as natural causes, but it bases the measurement of famine on mortality. For the Crown of Aragon, Albert Curto i Homedes and Antoni Furió have contrasted good years with two types of shortage: those that occur in mediocre years and those that occur in bad years.[6] Classifying shortages by whether they have agricultural or market origins, Antoni Riera Melis delineates two lesser categories: *carestía*, meaning shortage caused by high prices, and *penuria*, or shortage caused by a lack of supply. For major famines, Riera Melis relies on the physical definition of nutritional deficiencies that lead to illness or death.[7] Pere Benito i Monclús has suggested that medieval writers and chroniclers understood these distinctions and used their terms more carefully than we tend to assume.[8] By the standards of all of these scholars, truly bad years are rare: Furió notes only four in the space of almost two centuries. Mediocre years, however, came as often as once a decade.

Modern writers have also made several attempts to categorize famines according to their severity, a project related to attempts to create a fundamental definition of poverty.[9] Such attempts imply the need for action: if the United Nations accepts a clear definition of severity, the categories imply levels at which international intervention should occur. Yet modern famines still go hand in hand with other serious social, economic, political, and climatic conditions; the Saudi-backed war in Yemen has disrupted food supplies and created a massive rise in malnutrition and mortality, but death attributable to starvation occurs against the backdrop of a massive increase in violent death from the war itself.[10] Even with clear definitions, aid often does not target underlying political and social problems. Jenny Edkins, using the concept of "bare life," criticizes definitions that focus only on restoring base caloric needs rather than restoring people to socially and economically rich lives.[11] Ó Gráda's definition relies heavily on the criterion of "bare life" rather than on social disjunction. Because underlying conditions can involve a wide range of conditions of poverty and food insecurity, a key difficulty in defining famine comes from the huge variation in what is considered the "normal" functioning of society.

When it comes to the fourteenth century, it is important to acknowledge these complexities and to understand that shortages occur on a continuum between "normal" life and catastrophe. Famines are the sum of multiple elements, no one of which alone is sufficient. Famine can involve harvest failure across multiple geographic areas, but also the depletion of earlier food stores, hunger-driven migration, the use of wheat substitutes, market controls enacted by cities, legal restrictions on the poor, increases in personal and public debt, war, elevated rates of disease, and the breakdown of public order. Several of these elements—particularly war and disease—could, on their own, constitute a crisis and cause elevated mortality, while others, as we have seen, were regular features of late medieval life. Famines, then, are the late stage of a number of interlocking crises, the enumeration of which must serve as a proxy for severity.

Finally, focusing on the points of overlap between multiple causal factors encourages temporal specificity. Many authors discuss broad periods of hardship rather than specify the years or even the months of a given crisis. The early years of the fourteenth century, the 1590s, and the early seventeenth century were all periods of hardship in Europe.[12] Scholars have made such designations about several periods in the Crown of Aragon, including 1310–14, 1320–25, the 1330s, the early 1340s, and the 1370s.[13] Within these years, most notably 1333–34 and 1374–75, are embedded real and extreme famine events. However, focus on the broader time period tends to give the impression that these are vast waves of difficulty that slowly engulf society and that nothing can be done about them. What these descriptions miss is how a series of minor crises do not necessarily add up to a major disaster; they also miss how quickly a major disaster can develop. When only one region suffered a harvest failure, social and economic measures could soften the effect of a poor year, or even several in a row. Only when harvest shortfalls occurred across a very large area, often in combination with multiple other systemic shocks, did suffering become acute.

Geographic scope, then, is often better correlated to the level of crisis than duration is. Historical works often include the geographical area that a famine covers, but without acknowledging its causal force.[14] In contrast, scholars routinely describe famines as increasing in severity over the course of two or three years.[15] Tim Newfield has noted, however, that famines are necessarily geographically widespread.[16] Because of the strength of trade networks, regions often exchanged increasing temporal severity for geographic severity. In a survey of the grain supply in Barcelona, Eva Serra i Puig identifies numerous difficult years: 1302, 1311, 1315, 1322, 1324, 1333–34, and 1374–75.[17] Agustín Rubio Vela prepared a similar study on Valencia, and the two series overlap at key points, notably 1324 and 1333.[18] These overlaps occur not necessarily because either place had a more intense harvest failure, but rather because both had harvest failures at once. Including studies on Castile and Italy, the years that stand out suddenly become those known to be the most severe famines of the century: 1333–34 and 1374–75 above all, but also 1324–25 and 1347.[19] Thus overlapping crises across a wide area contributed to the severity of a given event.

In this chapter and the following one, I present three case studies: a local shortage in Valencia in 1371–72, a regional crisis in 1384–85, and the major famine of 1374–75. I have focused my research on the years after the Black Death in part to balance the extensive research on the years before the Plague, but the basic understanding of famines as complex disasters applies equally well to events before the Black Death. The two events I examine in this chapter also expose the line between routine shortage and famine. As many scholars have noted, shortages were common, famines rare.[20]

The first event, a series of poor harvests in Valencia between 1370 and 1373, never developed into a famine, despite lasting for several years. Social mechanisms designed to find new supplies, especially in the city, functioned surprisingly well. There were no riots, no social breakdown, and no evidence of a major mortality crisis. The second event struck the coastal territories of the Crown of Aragon during the winter of 1384–85. Because of the fresh memory of the major famine of 1374–75, people in the affected area and their neighbors tended to overreact, fearing the worst. These reactions became the most notable feature of 1384–85. The sudden demand for supplies along the Catalan coast created a spike in demand for Sicilian grain. Fear-inspired export restrictions in Aragon and a military blockade by the city of Cagliari compounded the supply problems. The crisis ended quickly, however, when supply regions like Aragon realized that a major shortage was not developing and reopened their export markets. Neither of these two events exhibits the features of severe famine. However, because of their narrower scope, they provide excellent examples of different forms of cultural resiliency mitigating food supply shocks that could potentially lead to disaster.

Shortage in Valencia, 1371–72: A Local Crisis

Historians have generally acknowledged the occurrence of minor shortages, but they have less frequently described mediocre years in detail, preferring to write about the most intense disasters. In 1370, Valencia suffered a mediocre harvest, followed by two bad harvests in 1371 and 1372, with moderate improvement in 1373. In 1374, Valencia suffered a catastrophic harvest failure, but it was exacerbated by a huge array of other factors, including failures throughout much of the Mediterranean basin. While it is possible to view the entire period from 1371 to the end of 1376 as a single period of hardship (indeed, to the residents of Valencia it might have felt that way), I believe that the time line is best understood as two events. In 1371, the city of Valencia used its political and economic resources to respond successfully to a sequence of poor harvests, largely preventing a full-blown crisis. In 1374, by contrast, numerous factors conspired to overwhelm the defenses not just of Valencia but of cities and towns throughout the western Mediterranean.

While not a famine, the events of 1371–73 did cause a crisis. Valencian city government officials described the shortage using common words for difficulties with the grain supply: *carestía* and *fretura* (both meaning shortage or lack), eventually adding intensifying adjectives: *gran neccesitat, gran fretura*, or *molt gran carestía*.[21] They stopped short of using the explicit terms for famine that appeared in 1374. Even the urban leaders understood that this was something short of a famine: a dearth, or perhaps a "market break."[22] Over the course of 1371 and 1372, the city of Valencia successfully pulled out all the stops in an attempt to keep its market supplied. The government sent deputized representatives throughout the kingdom and beyond to make contracts with foreign merchants and exporters. Members of the city council petitioned the king and the city of Barcelona to temporarily ease certain shipping restrictions so as to aid Valencia. And, finally, the city poured significant amounts of cash into the grain market in the form of tax reductions, import subsidies, and direct purchases. It is clear from the council discussions that the leaders understood the pros and cons of many of their decisions. Because of the relatively slow buildup of the crisis, the shift from regional to international grain sources is particularly clear.

A Slow Start

The harvest in the Valencian hinterland during the summer of 1370 was below normal. The city of Valencia did not complain immediately, but there are small hints that the authorities were nervous. Late in September, the jurors sent a messenger to Denia, Gandía, and Benidorm to remind each of those towns of the restrictions on sending grain outside the kingdom without Valencia's permission. At the same time, the council arranged for a few advantageous contracts to ensure that the available surplus from the hinterland made it to the city. Only a day after the runner returned from Benidorm, the council contracted with Vicent Amoros for grain from the region around Sant Mateu and persuaded the commander of the military order of Montesa, Ambert de Thous, to export grain from its demesne.[23] The council still believed that sufficient grain could come from regional surplus as long as the city put its thumb on the political scales.

However, the Valencian council quickly moved to buttress the regional surplus with more distant supplies. A couple of weeks later, it sent a runner to Tortosa to determine the availability of grain there. The runner did not carry money for purchases; the council only wanted information. Early in November, it went a step further and sent a local merchant, Ramon de Palou, with 1,000 florins (11,000 solidi) to find and purchase extra supplies "in the parts of Aragon and of Catalonia, or wherever seems good to him."[24] The record does not say whether Ramon de Palou's mission came in response to information gathered in Tortosa, but news of a fluid market would surely have made it clear that grain surpluses existed around Aragon and Catalonia, making his mission likely to succeed. Aragon and Catalonia would also have been routine sources of grain during any minor shortfall, and the search for grain there does not, in and of itself, suggest a crisis. Only Barcelona's heavy-handed control kept Tortosa from being a routine source of grain for Valencia.

Valencia continued to tighten its control over the grain supplies of the kingdom. Any minor shortage could be an excuse to lobby for greater royal privileges. In mid-November, the city received royal permission to purchase five hundred *cafiços* of wheat from Orihuela, the southernmost grain exporter in the kingdom and a town that frequently butted heads with the capital over control of its own exports.[25] Valencia also successfully petitioned the king for a temporary right to restrict exports of rice. Instead of an outright ban, the city allowed rice exports in exchange for specific amounts of wheat: for each *carrega* of exported rice, the merchant had to import two *cafiços* of wheat, a roughly one-to-one exchange in volume.[26] This was initially meant to be a short-term privilege, but because of continued bad harvests, the king extended the right for several years. These maneuvers demonstrate how much shortage relates to perception and demand. Orihuela routinely exported barley and probably had grain to spare, but what Valencia wanted was wheat. The second privilege, especially, indicates at least a moderate surplus of rice in the capital itself, meaning that there was no serious shortage of calories, only a shortage of the culturally valuable wheat.

Both of these privileges eventually led to the threat of violence, as the granting of royal privileges often did. In order to ensure the exports from Orihuela, the Valencian jurors paid Pere Torrella, the official in charge of shipping and the port, to hire an armed ship to sail to Orihuela and the nearby port of Guardamar and escort "a small galley and other ships loaded with wheat" back to the capital.[27] Unlike in more serious shortages, the council did not pay the high cost necessary to have its own galley on permanent patrol. Instead, they hired a private gun, as it were, for the specific enforcement. In February 1371, in order to monitor rice exports, the jurors hired an extra guard, Andreu Paga, to inspect all ships entering and leaving the port of Valencia to make sure that the restrictions on rice exports were observed. Paga also reported to the council on the quantities of wheat in each ship that arrived, presumably to ensure that none of it disappeared into the black market.[28] Even minor shortages highlight how legal and economic privilege translated into better supply.

Over the course of the spring, a second poor harvest threatened. The city jurors enacted new import subsidies and price guarantees. At the beginning of February 1371, Ramon de Palou returned from his trip. The city paid for his expenses, including numerous runners to relay communications back to Valencia. The accounts do not record the quantities of grain purchased, but Ramon did succeed in spending most of the 1,000 florins on large grain purchases, mainly from Tortosa.[29] On April 16, the city of Valencia paid its first of many import subsidies to the merchant Berenguer de Roials, who imported 400 *cafiços* of wheat "from other parts outside the kingdom."[30] These subsidies continued through May and ramped up considerably over the following year.

Finally, Valencia experimented with a modified import subsidy in the form of a price guarantee. The city promised a lucrative grain contract to a merchant from Barcelona named Pere Fontelles. The agreement stipulated that Fontelles could sell up to 1,400 *cafiços* of wheat in Valencia for the guaranteed price of 46 solidi per *cafís*. Specific Valencian prices are relatively scarce in surviving records, but prices during the 1360s appear to have hovered in the thirties.[31] Through the spring of 1371, wheat sold in Barcelona for roughly the equivalent of 40 solidi per *cafís*. Although this was an elevated price for Barcelona, the increase of as much as 6 solidi per *cafís* represented an attractive offer. When Fontelles arrived in Valencia, however, the first 746 *cafiços* of his cargo sold at only 42 solidi each, forcing the city to make up the difference. The following day, possibly because of the influx of grain, the price dropped another solidus, forcing the city to pay 5 solidi apiece for the remaining 254 *cafiços*.[32] The final 400 also sold at 42. While this method allowed the urban government to gamble on the market, hoping that high prices would adequately compensate merchants and cost the city nothing, it did not work out that way. Valencia ended up paying its usual subsidy rate or more. Probably for this reason, the import subsidy dominated the city's subsequent economic responses and the experiment was not repeated.

Subsidies still cost money. In part because of the significant cost of repairing damage from the siege of Pedro the Cruel of Castile in 1365, Valencia took on a handful of loans in May 1371, at the end of the fiscal year. The financial officers understood that these economic measures were successful and stated their aims in the payment descriptions. Both when purchasing extra grain from Montesa and when paying Fontelles for his large imports, the records stated that the imports were intended "to avoid a shortage and rising grain prices."[33] They meant to avoid a crisis before it became critical, and they knew that these systems should work because they had used them before. During the grain shortage of 1347, the city of Valencia combined the same regional supplies, such as those from the order of Montesa, with privileges that allowed merchants to import grain from the Ebro River and Catalonia.[34]

A Broader Crisis

It gradually became clear that the initial measures were insufficient, as a second poor harvest unfolded in 1371, exacerbated by drought in the summer and fall of that year. Valencia sent runners throughout the kingdom to collect information about possible grain supplies. Once they understood the scope of the problem, Valencian officials ramped up the response, vastly expanding their import subsidies, extracting new privileges that allowed previously banned merchants to enter Valencia, and dispatching representatives to distant ports with advantageous promises to new merchants.

Supplies were already flowing in from the areas around Sant Mateu and Orihuela, albeit largely by force. At the end of April 1371, the Valencian council sent Paschual de Fonts south into the mountains inland from Denia and Benidorm.[35] While there is no indication that this mission succeeded, additional supplies arrived from northern Valencia, although under increasing threat of force. In October, the city contracted with Antoni Astruch to purchase 5,500 solidi worth of grain from around the northern town of Onda, just inland from Castellón de la Plana.[36] A runner also traveled to Burriana with a letter about "grain that we have purchased from the royal official [the batle]," although the quantity is not specified.[37] These few purchases supplemented probable imports that came from nobles looking to sell their produce at a profit, along with whatever grain came from private contracts.

As winter arrived, the entire kingdom began to run short. On December 10, three days before the feast day of Saint Lucia, the city council met and declared that it would use the feast to hold a procession praying for rain. "At present there are great adversities and drought which have been and are in the city and kingdom of Valencia. So much so that through all the past autumn and into the present winter it has not rained, for which reason a very great shortage of grain has entered in the land."[38] After two paltry harvests, the continuing drought threatened to extend the crisis for a third year. Clear proof of the drought's extent and impact on the anticipated 1372 harvest came a few weeks later, when two messengers returned to Valencia with bad news. Domingo Calbo spent a week traveling north to Villahermosa and other towns further inland from Onda and Burriana, where Valencia had previously purchased supplies; Antoni Jorba traveled for ten days further north to Cantavieja and other towns along the Aragonese-Valencian border.[39] Both men reported having purchased nothing and found only shortage and new export restrictions. With a third poor harvest looming, it was clear that no significant supplies would be forthcoming from Valencia's neighbors.

Because the shortage was slow to develop, however, Valencia had already started searching farther afield. The first grain from Barcelona had arrived early in 1371, prior to the second poor harvest. Exports from Tortosa began in 1370, around the time of Ramon de Palou's trip to Aragon and Catalonia. The insufficient new harvest, combined with bad news from around the kingdom, had prompted the immediate expansion of these efforts. On July 4, 1371, the council had already bolstered the subsidy program, offering assurances of good prices to anyone bringing in foreign grain.[40] The city placed oversight of the new efforts in the hands of the juror Pere dez Puiol, a man who would be called on to oversee grain imports again during the famine of 1374. The jurors sent Guillem Pujada and Bernat Sicard to negotiate new contracts in Tortosa, trying to secure more grain from the Ebro River supply.[41] Subsidy payments on grain from Tortosa were made throughout the rest of the year. By early May of 1372, Pere dez Puiol himself traveled to Tortosa with 1,000 florins for prepayment of contracts.[42] In late July of 1371, the Valencian city official Johan Renouart left for Narbonne and Bezier, deputized by the council to make contracts and promise subsidies on its behalf to merchants in southern France.[43] By April 1372, Renouart's work had yielded results, and grain merchants from Agde, Aigues-Mortes, and Montpellier began arriving in Valencia, carrying Renouart's contracts.[44] Around the same time, Valencia sent another merchant, Pere Ramon, on a longer trip through Tunisia and Sicily with similar powers; he did not return to Valencia until October, several months later.[45]

The jurors of Valencia made many specific moves to expand access to grain, especially to Italian supplies. Normally, because of competition in the wool market, royal decrees restricted or banned outright the participation of foreign merchants in direct dealings in Catalan and Valencian markets.[46] Restrictions often targeted the Genoese in particular because of periodic military tensions. Given the Genoese access to grain from the Black Sea, however, and the increasingly severe shortage at home, the jurors petitioned the king to relax restrictions on Genoese merchants. Genoese ships had already arrived in March, but legal threats remained in force.[47] Indeed, on April 13, 1372, the royal official in Valencia, Francesch Marrades, using his royal authority, moved to impound and confiscate the goods of all Genoese ships entering the port.[48] However, with word from the king, the city council presented Marrades with new privileges granting special protection to any merchant from Genoa who arrived with grain. Marrades relented.

The council worked tirelessly to uphold its privileges during the shortage. It even indicted its own king, noting that he had been seizing some of the cargo of ships passing near Cagliari. The Valencians thus found it safer to rely on shipments aboard Genoese ships that could pass Cagliari without the threat of royal confiscation. They protested that if word of this poor treatment of Genoese ships reached Sicily and other parts of the Mediterranean, ship captains would no longer attempt to deliver grain.[49] The council also reiterated its own promise to protect Genoese merchants bearing grain, and they dispatched messengers and payments to publicize this fact in Sicilian ports. They also sent representatives to the king to petition for updated privileges ensuring their demands for safe conduct, because of the "great shortage and scarcity of wheat and grains in the said city and in its kingdom."[50] Within a couple of weeks, the council decided to pay its guards to unload Genoese ships and deliver the grain to the city, so as to protect both the sailors and their cargo, rather than leave the ships floating in the port, their cargo vulnerable to confiscation.[51]

April and May 1372 became critical months in the crisis: if Valencia's efforts succeeded, they would significantly ameliorate the crisis, while failure could very well lead to increasing starvation. Securing Genoese assistance represented a significant opening of new grain supplies. In May, the council held a meeting and published a long explanation of the causes of the food shortage, as the authorities understood them, and another expansion of the city's efforts to combat it. The document notes the shortages brought on by continued drought and the "extreme deficits of the present months." The central point of debate was whether to extend the terms of the contracts of merchants bringing grain from Sicily. "Men of good faith" told the council that "much time had passed when many vessels in places in Sicily loaded with the grain of the said merchants left to come [to Valencia] and that because of contrary winds they were not able to unfurl their sails such that sometimes they were forced to return to the same ports from which they had departed." Given the political impediments in Cagliari and Valencia's new contracts with Genoese ships, the council strongly supported the jurors' requests to modify any and all contracts at almost any cost, as long as they kept grain imports coming. Jurors were given the ability "to sign with whatever merchant or private or foreign person any and all contract, agreement, understanding, terms, and assurances, and offer to them as to whatever other person, in particular or in general, they promise, insure, and pay, or are able to promise, to insure, and to pay all those subsidies, prices, and advantages, with any and all obligations or restrictions that to [the jurors], or a part of them, or even to one of them elected according to what is stated, will seem best to do."[52]

The rising panic turned out to be at least somewhat overblown. Within a week, multiple ships did arrive from Sicily carrying so much grain that the jurors returned to the council to debate whether they should store some of it so as to prevent too great a financial loss on the contracts. Notably, the council debated whether to act like the very regraters it so often decried for withholding grain, but, in this case, with the aim of avoiding a sudden price slump. This influx is visible in figure 7, which shows the quantity of subsidized grain in the market tripling suddenly in June 1372. Tellingly, the council recommended the distribution, at a good price, of as much grain as possible to the city's bakers.[53]

Finally, the city also made overtures to Barcelona in the hope of shoring up supplies from Tortosa. While Valencia purchased Aragonese grain from Tortosa early in 1371, Barcelona kept strict limits on the valuable supplies. At the end of August 1372, around the time Valencian imports hit their peak, the city council sent a runner specifically to enlist the aid of the queen in petitioning the city of Barcelona for a short-term revocation of its restrictions.[54] By September 7, the runner had returned with a sealed royal letter formally (if temporarily) revoking Barcelona's restrictions on exports from Tortosa to Valencia. The council immediately had copies of the letter read out in public markets in both Valencia and Tortosa, informing all merchants that commerce with Valencia was not against regulations and could be undertaken freely and without fear.[55] As in its dealings with the Genoese, Valencia understood the importance of accurate information in the smooth running of its market. Barcelona's acquiescence also illustrates how the flexibility of the larger supply system could bend toward areas of need, working effectively to reduce local shortages. If the markets in Barcelona had also been experiencing shortage, it is unlikely that that city would have released its control over Tortosa.

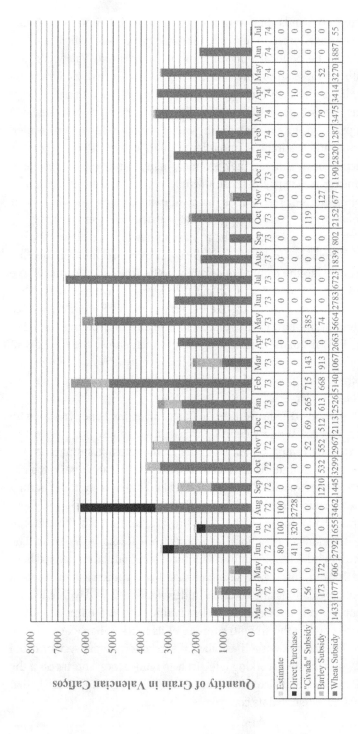

	Mar 72	Apr 72	May 72	Jun 72	Jul 72	Aug 72	Sep 72	Oct 72	Nov 72	Dec 72	Jan 73	Feb 73	Mar 73	Apr 73	May 73	Jun 73	Jul 73	Aug 73	Sep 73	Oct 73	Nov 73	Dec 73	Jan 74	Feb 74	Mar 74	Apr 74	May 74	Jun 74	Jul 74
Estimate	0	0	0	80	100	100	0	0	0	0	0	0	0	0	0	0	0	0	0	0	0	0	0	0	0	0	0	0	0
Direct Purchase	0	0	0	411	320	2728	0	0	0	0	0	0	0	0	0	0	0	0	0	0	0	0	0	0	0	0	0	0	0
"Civada" Subsidy	0	56	0	0	0	0	0	0	52	69	265	715	143	0	385	0	0	0	0	119	0	0	0	0	0	10	0	0	0
Barley Subsidy	0	173	172	0	0	0	1210	532	552	512	613	668	913	74	74	0	0	0	0	0	127	0	0	0	79	0	52	0	0
Wheat Subsidy	1433	1077	606	2792	1655	3462	1445	3299	2967	2113	2526	5140	1067	2663	5664	2783	6723	1839	802	2152	677	1190	2820	1287	3475	3414	3270	1887	55

FIG. 7. VALENCIAN IMPORT SUBSIDIES, 1372–1374. The "estimate" category represents money allocated or spent for which there is no quantity. I have used the prevailing price in purchases from the same time period to estimate the quantity imported. A few direct purchases contain insufficient data to support even an estimate.

The broader absence of shortage throughout the western Mediterranean made expanded access throughout 1372 possible. Valencia had to contend with threats from the military conflict in Sardinia,[56] but studies of Barcelona, Girona, and Tortosa found no supply problems.[57] Barcelona's Pia Almoina documents show that prices rose moderately, between 10 and 20 percent, in 1371 and 1372. The increase may have been an echo of Valencian problems' driving up prices throughout an integrated import market. That Valencia and Barcelona regularly quarreled over supplies from the Ebro River probably meant that Valencia's high import subsidies had a knock-on effect, driving prices slightly higher in Barcelona despite a normal harvest. The only notable exception occurred in Florence, where prices of multiple commodities, including wheat, oil, and wine, started rising in 1369, spiking in 1371 before falling again in 1372.[58] Siena's wool carders also rioted in the summer of 1371, protesting both low wages and rising grain prices caused by mercenary raids on the hinterland. The violence and fighting continued for weeks, adding chaos to Siena's strained market.[59] Had these problems in Italy persisted into 1372, they could have impeded Valencia's ability to import grain from both Sicily and parts of southern France. Thus Valencia's economic solutions benefited from geopolitical good luck as well as from adept financial management and effective communication.

An Effective Response

To avoid a crisis, the city of Valencia relied on an adaptive mix of direct purchases, price guarantees, and subsidies, while largely avoiding draconian legal measures that tended to shut down the market. Valencia had consolidated much of its control over exports from its own region and could transmit messages and news of economic need quickly to distant regions. The council spent vast sums of money, going into significant debt, but succeeded in encouraging merchants throughout the western Mediterranean to flood Valencia's market with foreign grain. By the end of the crisis, as much as 90 percent of all grain consumed in the city had been imported from outside the region under a subsidized contract or through direct purchase by the city council.

A global look at the numbers gives us a good view of the changing methods, the high point of the crisis, and the cost. First, the numbers clearly show that the crisis reached its peak early in 1372 and slowly abated through the middle of 1373 (see fig. 7). The city began a kingdom-wide search in earnest in January 1371, but it only began reaping significant rewards several months later. Many of the regional purchases in 1371 were still direct purchases made by the council's representatives. Despite the expansion of subsidy powers, Mediterranean imports did not really ramp up until June of the following year, shortly after the city failed to secure sufficient Sicilian grain. By August, only a couple of months later, that failure had turned around with the arrival of thousands of *cafiços* of grain under subsidy or direct purchase contracts. Despite the rapid communication, it took months for the subsidies to reach their full potential. In October 1372, as high-subsidy imports continued, the council lowered the import subsidy rate from 4 solidi per *cafís* to 2, reflecting recent successes.[60] In November, it rained so much that there were reports of damaged roofs; this surely dispelled continuing fear of drought.[61] By December the council had relaxed the regulations on grain resale, allowing middlemen to return to the market. Originally, it had banned all sellers working for a wage, forcing grain sellers to sell only their own grain. Forcing middlemen out of the market to keep prices down was consistent with the moral distrust of hoarding and regrating. But laborers who earned their living transporting and selling the grain of others complained to the city and the council relented.[62] Thereafter, few discussions of ongoing imports appear in the records. In April 1373, the council declared a more permanent end to the crisis when it offer a reward to G. de Barbera, a resident of Tortosa who routinely served as Valencia's representative, purchasing grain and disseminating information. For his completed work, the council presented de Barbera with a silver chalice and a jewel.[63] Despite these indications of the end of the crisis, subsidized imports continued, though in September they fell below 1,000 *cafiços* for the first time in sixteen months. Such measures probably helped allay continuing uneasiness by keeping the market well saturated until confidence had returned.

The time lag involved in many of these grain contracts also helps explain the evolving methods preferred by the city government. All of the direct purchases were front-loaded. Purchasing grain was the fastest and surest way to increase imports, but it carried greater financial risk and volatility than simply promising fixed subsidies. In July 1372, the jurors in Valencia sent a runner to find Johan Renouart in southern France and revoke the order for more direct purchases.[64] The continuing subsidy contracts would suffice. A year later, in July 1373, the city extended its two-solidi subsidy for several months despite a functioning market—but it explicitly limited the subsidy to 20,000 *cafiços* of grain, around half the quantity subsidized in the previous year.[65] At the same meeting, the council explicitly endorsed its preference for subsidies over direct purchases because of their greater flexibility and pre-dictability for both city and merchants. Despite several decades of evolving market controls, the council was still debating the various methods available to it. Indeed, after the council's experiences with these varying methods, it eventually settled on subsidies as the most effective. During another minor shortage in 1390, the council empowered the jurors to enact the usual grain control measures, but explicitly admonished them to offer subsidies as much as possible and "not purchases nor other contracts . . . as experience has frequently shown, purchases and other forms of sale are unprofitable for the city."[66] After years of experimentation, the council had settled on a pre-ferred method, but the continuing debate drives home the fact that medieval elites attempted to deal with food shortages by drawing on the most reliable information and using the best understanding and means at their disposal. While not every decision had the desired result, late medieval food shortages were hardly the result of a long string of failed responses to routine natural shocks inflicted on a hapless population.

Finally, the massive amount of money poured into the market highlights the degree of overlap between public and private grain supply efforts. From June 1372 to June 1373, between subsidies and direct purchases, Valencia influenced the delivery of more than 45,000 *cafiços* of grain. Assuming a (very) rough population of thirty thousand and a median consumption of two *cafiços* per year, the city required around 60,000 *cafiços* of grain per year. A second reference point is taken from a 1402 letter from the Valencian jurors noting that the city required roughly 40,000 *cafiços* of grain per year above and beyond the production of its hinterland.[67] Thus the estimate of 60,000 *cafiços* is probably not far off as a ballpark figure for 1372. We can conclude that the city's grain subsidies and purchases represented around three-fourths of the entire grain market, more than a normal year's imports. Crises presumably required greater imports, but this also shows just how much the market shifted in response to the council's policies. Through its representatives in Tortosa, France, and Sicily, the council's financial leverage influenced a majority of all "private" grain imports to Valencia (see map 2). Furthermore, significant imports came through Valencian merchants them-selves, often men connected to the council. To take only one example, almost 5,000 *cafiços* of the annual total came through a single merchant, Vicent Carbonell, the relative of a future city magistrate. The level of municipal ma-nipulation of the market and the close connections between "public" and "private" actors left little room for casual grain sales.

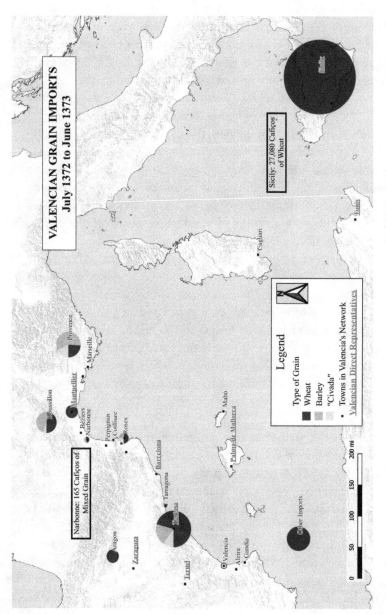

MAP 2. VALENCIAN GRAIN IMPORTS, JULY 1372 TO JUNE 1373. The payments marked "Other Imports" are quantities recorded as imports but without a specific origin. The quantity is fairly modest and presumably represents a blend of the other identified sources. The map was made using QGIS 3.14 "Pi" in the Europe Albers equal area projection with the Esri "World Terrain Basemap," with data from Esri, the U.S. Geological Survey, and the National Oceanic and Atmospheric Administration. https://www.arcgis.com/home/item.html?id=c61ad8ab017d49e1a82f58o0ee1298931.

The End of the Crisis

In the fall of 1373, Valencian import subsidies largely tailed off; for the six months from August 1373 to January 1374, the city paid for fewer than 10,000 *cafiços* of grain. Subsidies probably would have continued to fall had bad weather not returned in February. As noted above, the events of 1372 and 1374 are connected insofar as Valencia never completely left its crisis footing. Despite suspending its direct purchases and winding down its subsidies late in 1373, by March 1374 the city had once again increased both in response to the new and rapidly expanding crisis. Perhaps because of continued nervousness after the shortages of 1372, Valencia was the first city in the Crown of Aragon to pass an export ban in 1374, when it became clear that it would be in fierce competition with Barcelona, Tortosa, and Mallorca in a way that it had not been before (how and why this happened in 1374 is the subject of chapter 5).

This fine-grained account of a minor crisis reveals aspects of medieval food shortages that scholars have tended to overlook. Like many crises in the food supply, Valencia's shortage developed slowly over the course of several years. The long-term buildup helped to keep panic out of the markets and allowed people to respond and prepare. The messengers whom Valencia sent to France and Sicily took months to produce major returns, but once the system was in place, the quantities imported into Valencia made up for local shortfalls. The spread of accurate information about the state of the Valencian market encouraged distant merchants to adjust their strategies. Far from causing the crisis, merchants' search for the best price, encouraged by official subsidies, kept prices under control. It is hard to see how hoarders could have profited in this environment, when storing grain for the future would only allow more time for cheaper imports to arrive. Also, there is no evidence in the extant records of expanded bread handouts, and the only actual charity came during citywide processions—and was more about the performance of piety during religious events than it was about actual support for the needy. The political goal was economic stabilization rather than aid for individuals. If most of the money spent and financed by debt went into the pockets of merchants, including members of the council, rather than to feed the poor, this was considered theologically acceptable and financially sound.

Finally, Valencia's council understood its economic system well and disseminated information and money in targeted ways. It used its nominal competitors, the Genoese, when Valencian ships were impounded by the king. It understood that negative rumors could interrupt needed supplies, while positive news and publicizing government subsidies would grease the wheels of commerce. All of these actions cost money. The city had already refinanced a number of outstanding debts in 1371 in order to pay for new grain subsidies. The council gave the city's jurors full license to take on whatever debt was necessary to continue funding Valencia's grain supply. The council convened far more often to discuss its economic strategies than to organize prayers or alms. Indeed, council records show more organized prayers concerning the Plague in 1371 and 1372 than addressing the food shortage.[68] The many systems in place allowed Valencia to respond effectively and provide ample evidence of the evolving pragmatic character of the fourteenth-century response to food shortages. Three poor harvests in a row severely stressed the Valencian supply system, but ultimately it did not break down.

Panic on the Mediterranean Coast: 1384–85

In 1384, harvest troubles and food supply difficulties struck several areas around the western Mediterranean. While only the kingdom of Valencia suffered in 1372, the events of 1384–86 influenced large portions of the Crown of Aragon and beyond that shaped the contours of food imports. Effective political and economic responses to shortage had kept panic and price spikes at bay in 1372. By contrast, the shortages of 1384 developed into a hybrid crisis, neither a serious famine nor merely a series of market troubles. From late 1384 through the spring of 1385, prices spiked throughout the Crown of Aragon. Compounding the problem, residual difficulties with supply and continuing bad harvests kept prices volatile until 1387. As we will see, the spike was not as drastic as in the famine of 1374, but the initial panic, combined with persistent supply issues over subsequent years, suggests the profile of a famine rather than a local shortage.

The increase in complexity was critical to the increased severity of 1384. In 1372, a small region was affected and the shortage sprang from relatively simple causes: the central and northern areas of the kingdom of Valencia suffered two or three years of drought and harvest shortages. In 1384, both Catalonia and Valencia suffered harvest shortages. Political conflict and violence threatened both northern Catalonia and the region of southern France around Avignon and Marseille. While the conflict among the towns in Provence never threatened the Crown of Aragon, it increased competition for Sicilian grain by forcing several towns to look beyond Provence for supplies. Demand in Tortosa, Barcelona, Tarragona, and Valencia converged on the Ebro River and on Sicily. Fear of inadequate supplies eventually compelled both Zaragoza and Castile to restrict exports, diminishing regional commerce at a critical juncture. Multiple areas experienced concomitant disturbances, including wine and meat shortages in Valencia and milling strikes in Tarragona. The conjuncture of multiple restrictions in overlapping geographic areas created a more significant set of difficulties overall.

Additionally, fear of a major crisis hung over a populace whose memories of the famine of 1374–75 were still vivid. Panic and social breakdown play a role in most famines, but the visceral fears of 1374–75 drove multiple actors to take extreme measures in 1384. Import subsidies offered a fine-tuned response to food shortage, but once multiple actors offered to pay high subsidies, it became difficult for small towns to compete with wealthier cities. Valencia never ended its subsidy program after 1374, putting other cities at an immediate disadvantage even ten years later. In response, Tortosa elected to go straight for direct purchases. Tarragona sent overseers to inventory all the grain in the surrounding territory in order to assume as much direct control over the markets as possible. At the same time, Valencia took the extreme step of arming multiple warships, including a small flotilla specifically to guard the entrance to the Ebro River. The armed ships and the shutdown of the local export market exacerbated the general panic. Competition for Sicilian grain became intense, especially when Cagliari and Sardinia implemented a blockade on ships attempting to sail from Sicily to the Catalan coastline. Overlapping demands fueled by fear created a spike in the price of grain across the region that was probably higher than it needed to be, given the actual harvests.

The shortages ended relatively quickly. By June 1385, only six months after the peak of the crisis, conditions throughout the Crown improved dramatically. Better harvests in Valencia, a reversal of the Castilian export ban, the ending of armed conflict in the north, and the opening of new ports in Sardinia all added more grain to the system. Faced with the sudden increase in supply, importers found themselves incurring debt for stores of grain that in some instances they no longer needed. Tarragona attempted to sell off its grain as quickly as possible and ordered grain still in the port of its erstwhile competitor, Tortosa, to be sold in place rather than incur additional shipping costs. Such liquidations caused the price of grain to plummet, lessening competition for the Ebro River supply. The knock-on effect encouraged other areas to drop their most severe antishortage measures. Valencia brought its expensive warships back to port, Zaragoza ended its export ban, and Tortosa suspended direct purchases. Even with the panic and overreactions, many actors in the Crown remained attuned to the overall grain supply system and attempted to respond as much to positive changes as to negative fears.

A Regional Event

The famine of 1384–85 in some ways mirrors that of 1374–75 (see chapter 5). Valencia had suffered minor shortages in the years leading up to the actual crisis. In the winter of 1380–81, Valencia had already engaged in the same tactics it used in 1372. Its import subsidies increased and hit high levels in midwinter. In December, the city paid subsidies for 1,329 *cafiços* of grain, and in January it financed more than 2,500 more, including a large shipment from Cadiz in Castile. Although the quantities fluctuated in later months, high imports generally continued, with more than 4,000 *cafiços* recorded in April. The origins of the grain mirrored the previous crisis, with a few exceptions. In December, the city contracted with Genoese merchants to assist them in bringing grain from Sicily. G. de Barbera, the Tortosan merchant, still acted as a representative, drawing up subsidy contracts (just as in 1372, the city rewarded him with an expensive silver vessel at the end of the year).[69] This time, however, the city had no representative in southern France. Instead, a number of city merchants, notably many of them Jews and Muslims, succeeded in purchasing thousands of *cafiços* from Oran and other cities along the North African coast. The city also transported moderate amounts of grain by pack animal through the highlands around Teruel from Aragon, bypassing the need to deal with merchants in Tortosa or the capricious political demands of Barcelona.[70]

These conditions continued in 1382, with Valencia again importing and subsidizing significant portions of its yearly requirements for the market: more than 29,000 *cafiços*. In March 1383, the council of Valencia ordered a citywide procession to pray for the end of a "great drought which is and has been in the recent winter and current beginning of spring."[71] The procession reflected the city's ongoing anxiety about the situation. Shortly thereafter, the newly sworn-in council voted to continue all necessary subsidies for the foreseeable future. As in previous crises, the council gave jurors wide latitude to make payments "in whatever quantity of money . . . above the price which the sellers can acquire in the public market, and for all those quantities of grain that to [the jurors] seems good." However, the council notably restricted the actions of the jurors, allowing them to encourage imports "only by way of subsidies."[72] In part because of the actions of the previous year's council, many contracts had already been signed, and those shipments continued into the new year. In June alone, only weeks after the council reauthorized the payments, more than 4,000 subsidized *cafiços* arrived from Sicily and another 1,800 from Oran and North Africa.[73] With the addition of grain from Aragon, June was one of the highest import months recorded.

In light of the arrival of so much grain, the strong statement of the council might seem like an overreaction. But 1383 also heralded a handful of important developments that set the stage for full-blown panic in 1384. Unfortunately, the Barcelona council's records for these years are missing, but other documents indicate an unsettled supply chain. In an undated deliberation from 1383, the Barcelona council gave the city leaders permission to arm galleys if necessary, a clear sign that shortages were anticipated.[74] Esteve Gilabert Bruniquer, a later chronicler of the city, recorded a procession asking for rain in October 1383.[75] Like the procession in Valencia, this one also asked for deliverance from the Plague, which was making a new round through the western Mediterranean.[76] However, another document notes that such large grain shipments were arriving from Sicily that some could not be sold in the city market. The council allowed surrounding towns to purchase the excess grain, something it would never do when faced with imminent shortages.[77] It is likely that the subsidies, approved in response to the perceived threat of shortage, proved more effective than anticipated.

The crisis reached its peak in the winter of 1384. While the troubles of 1383 had increased competition between the perennial rivals Barcelona and Valencia, other actors, sufficient to trigger a regional famine, were not yet involved. By mid-1384, supply problems combined with both proximate and distant political conflicts to produce panic and price spikes throughout the coastal cities. In March 1384, Tortosa declared a drought and expressed its increasing fear of food shortage. The initial response of town leaders was to require greater local storage by all merchants, effectively limiting exports to those who could first provide sufficient grain for the Tortosan market.[78] By May, Tarragona had begun paying import subsidies, and by July it had restricted grain exports without a permit.[79] In August, Barcelona upped its subsidy level for imports from distant markets, especially Sicily.[80] In October, Tarragona followed suit.[81] The first critical moment came in November 1384 when Zaragoza banned further grain shipments down the Ebro River.

Until that point, both Tortosa and Barcelona had been relying heavily on Aragonese grain. The Valencia city council began paying increasingly large subsidies for grain carried overland from Aragon and shipments from Sicily and North Africa. Immediately after the Aragonese ban, Tortosa sent a delegation to Zaragoza, insisting on Tortosa's right to ship grain down the Ebro. The delegation argued that the river was a public waterway and therefore could not be blocked. While the argument was novel, it is unlikely that the leaders of Tortosa really believed it themselves: less than a month later, they passed their own prohibitions on grain exports from the mouth of the river.[82]

This pair of export bans from Zaragoza and then Tortosa forced Barcelona into direct competition with Valencia as it began looking for imports from the Mediterranean. Both Tarragona and Tortosa also attempted to import grain from the same sources. To make matters worse, Castile banned exports early in February 1385. The king of Castile broke off exports because of his war with Portugal and the internal demands of military supply, rather than owing to any particular harvest failure. The political nature of the ban is especially transparent given that exports were reinstated only a couple of months later and did not correspond with the harvest year.[83] Just as Tortosa had done with Zaragoza, Valencia sent a delegation to argue its case at the court of Castile. However, the travel and debate took time, and there are no records of subsidies for Castilian grain for several months (the Valencian council did hire smugglers to transport grain, but the quantity was limited).[84] The closure of the Ebro, Castile, and southern France through competition with Barcelona sent Valencian merchants scrambling. The city resolved many of its problems in the early 1370s with heavy imports from all three regions.

After the Castilian ban, Valencia repeatedly described its situation as one of "almost extreme necessity."[85] The city was forced to rely heavily on the more expensive overland transports from southern Aragon and on politically unstable imports from North Africa, especially the city of Oran. Late in the crisis, in May 1385, a handful of grain shipments also arrived in Valencia from Palatia, the medieval settlement on the island of Marmara near Constantinople (referred to in the documents as part of Torquia).[86] Barcelona's sparser records note shipments mostly from Sicily, with a few others from Seville, the island of Rhodes, and the coast of "Romanía."[87] Palatia and parts of the Balkans formed part of Genoa's complex grain supply network but represented a distant and more extreme search for Catalan cities.

Competition ultimately focused on Sicily. While Sicilian exports were strong, several factors conspired to make relief supplies more tenuous. First, owing to a series of disputes surrounding the succession of the queen of Naples, Joanna I, several Provençal towns banded together into the "Union of Aix" to back their preferred successor. Military actions between competing towns, including sieges of several ports, destroyed significant amounts of crops between the Rhone and the Durance Rivers. Cold weather in the winter of 1384 further reduced rural supplies, forcing cities like Toulon, Aix, and Marseille to turn to Sicily themselves. Interior towns like Carpentras, Serres, Auriol, and others reported famine conditions from the deadly combination of weather and war.[88] While the crisis in Provence was not related to the turbulence in the Crown of Aragon, the cold winter of 1384–85 drew the two crises together at a crucial moment in their competition over Sicilian exports.

Furthermore, royal military demands in Sardinia created a shipping bottleneck that the king exploited, to the consternation of the coastal cities. Sardinia had long been a conquest goal of the Catalan kings, and military action simmered on and off for decades. Cagliari, the Catalan stronghold on the island, exported grain in the 1360s, but renewed military conflict during the 1370s increased the demand for imports.[89] In response to an alliance between the Judges of Arborea (the leaders of Sardinian resistance against the Catalans) and Genoa, Cagliari armed a galley in 1383 to patrol against hostile ships. As more ships left Sicily with grain, the royal governor in Sardinia used the galley to force some of those ships into Cagliari's harbor to keep the city and the military supplied.[90] Barcelona, Tarragona, and Valencia all lost imports in 1384 as a result.[91] Valencia even sent secret messengers to attempt to create an alliance with its erstwhile competitors in Barcelona and Palma and to pressure the king to rein in the actions of his governor.[92] Barcelona and Valencia set aside their perennial rivalry in order to approach the king with a unified front.

Finally, several other localized problems increased the complexity, and therefore the severity, of the crisis. In northern Catalonia, rebellions exacerbated the shortage. The count of Empúries, Joan I, was involved in longstanding arguments with King Pere over land rights. In 1380, Joan entered open hostilities with Bernat Alemany, a knight associated with Pere's wife's household. Pere forced the two men to come to a truce, but it did not hold; hostilities resumed in 1383. In the winter of 1384, Joan I's wife, Joana, a daughter of King Pere himself, attempted to intervene on her husband's behalf. Pere apparently beat her for her perceived insubordination and she died shortly thereafter.[93] Pere then moved to invade Empúries and Joan I responded with open revolt, hiring groups of mercenaries from Armagnac to assist him. The mercenaries came from well-supplied counties. The nearby towns of Tou-louse and Albi both recorded good harvests throughout the early 1380s.[94] In contrast, Pere's army was in constant need of new supplies. More than once, Barcelona and the king fought over grain shipments destined for the king's men in Sant Feliu de Guixols, the safe port nearest the battle.[95] Although Pere drove Joan out of Empúries (he had fled to Avignon by the end of 1385), the depredations of mercenaries and the demands of military supply destroyed lands in the northern counties and disrupted shipping along the Catalan coast in a way that must have felt disturbingly similar to 1374, which also involved an invasion from the north.

In Valencia, the grain shortage was accompanied by a shortage of meat and wine. Some weather patterns (especially hard winter frosts) can reduce grain harvests and destroy vineyards, but this is not consistent. Hailstorms damaged vineyards throughout Valencia in the fall of 1383, hitting at a time when there was little grain in the fields.[96] Through the spring of 1384, much of the kingdom ran short on wine, importing small amounts from its usual trading partners. In April 1385, the vines in the irrigated area around the capital were described as "sterile and thin."[97] Because only Valencia suffered, imports were easy to come by. The normal exporting regions around Elche and Alicante stopped exporting, but even the city of Valencia kept the brakes on imports to prevent foreign wine from glutting the market.[98] The end of exports from Elche and Alicante did not threaten urban consumption, but it did reduce the income of peasants who grew grapes, requiring recourse to debt or rent deferments. Further north, Tarragona also ran short of wine in May 1384 but only moved to survey wine supplies in order to avoid "scandal"; eventually, in November, it relaxed import restrictions but made no further moves to control the wine market.[99] Despite the relative ease of importing wine, the shortage in Valencia compounded economic woes throughout the kingdom during the peak months of shortage.

Similarly, meat supplies ran short throughout 1384 and into 1385, prob-ably thanks to severe cold that killed livestock in the spring of 1384 around Teruel.[100] The first whisper of the shortage in Valencia came in October 1384, when the council sent a secret messenger to visit fairs and markets in Aragon and report on animal prices.[101] City officials wanted to know if merchants were telling the truth about the rising price of meat at its source. The council eventually decided that the butchers were lying and laid the blame for meat shortages at their feet. City documents accused the meat merchants of "col-lusion or bad intentions," claiming that they refused to slaughter enough animals for the demands of the market.[102] Butchers might provide an easy scapegoat, but the urban meat market of the fourteenth century was a complicated and often tenuous animal, as it were, as butchers were routinely caught between fluctuating prices for animals in the countryside and a strong and fairly constant demand for cheap meat in the cities.[103] Disputes over pasturage and the right of movement for flocks between Valencia and Teruel and other towns in the Maestrazgo created shifting political blockages in the meat supply, and butchers may well have had trouble acquiring meat at normal prices.

The meat shortage, predictably enough, caused significantly less panic and required less intervention than the grain shortage did. Because of the political regulations that helped drive prices, direct responses by the city government proved both effective and relatively easy to implement. The jurors of Valencia paid several men to rent and man some of the tables in the public market and made several large direct purchases of flocks of animals to be butchered and sold at those tables.[104] In late February and early March, the city sent a representative, along with a shepherd and his assistant, to the town of Pego in the south to take possession of several flocks from the mountainous area between Pego and Benidorm. The same messenger who traveled to Castile to protest the export ban on grain also requested the right to import meat animals from the Castilian borderlands.[105]

The combination of rebellion, trade embargoes, multiple regional shortages, and supply problems for other food staples created an intense but short-lived crisis. Known prices from the monastery of Sant Pere near Barcelona, the few prices from the Pia Almoina, and the direct purchases from Tortosa all show a focused price spike with a rapid increase and moderate decline during the early months of 1385. A handful of price points from Valencia corroborate these data (see fig. 8). The spike is quite synchronous, showing the integration of market prices in multiple locations. Even the knowledge that grain supplies ran short in surrounding markets drove the corresponding price rises. However, the close connections between the various markets also meant that as soon as tensions eased in one area, the crisis quickly abated elsewhere.

Panic in the Shadow of Disaster

The spike in prices resulted primarily from a series of overreactions. Several factors contributed to the overzealous response, but most obvious was that the entire region had only recently suffered a terrible famine. Areas from Navarre to the west, across all of Aragon, including the entire Valencian and

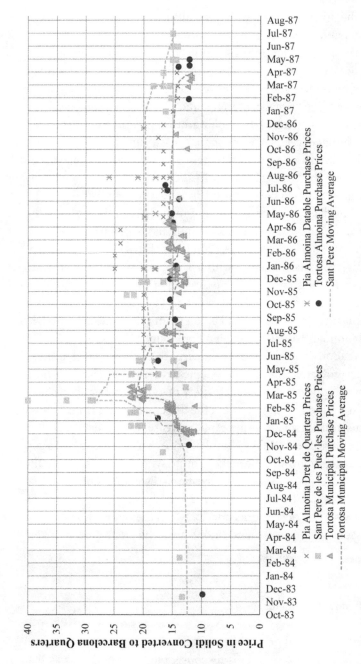

FIG. 8. PRICES IN TORTOSA AND BARCELONA, OCTOBER 1383–AUGUST 1387. The prices for 1384–85 do not have the same intense spike that occurred in 1374, but they do show a similar abrupt rise and more volatile fall. In this instance, the rise came in November. Valencia's extreme, even violent, pressure on Tortosa may have kept Tortosa's supplies more unstable, and for longer, than those of Valencia or Barcelona. We see a similar price dynamic in Castelló d'Empúries (see fig. 10). I have converted the prices from Tortosa, which are measured in *cafiços*, into Barcelona quarters for the sake of comparison. There is some debate about the correct conversion of a Tortosa *cafís*; I have used the rate suggested by Carrère 1967, 91. See also Curto i Homedes 1988, 37–38; Tortosa prices come from this work, 44–48, 106–15.

Catalan coasts, all had seen their highest prices in a century less than a decade before the events of 1384, so even rumors of shortage, and the attendant possibility of high prices, created very real, visceral fears. Additionally, the Papal Schism that began in 1378 realigned politics in the region, creating dangerous tensions and exacerbating religious fears. The schism appears in urban documents as one of the main sins that might have incurred God's wrath in the form of disease and shortage in the 1380s, a reference lacking in the earlier crises. Fear of another disaster pressured people into unnecessary and costly responses. The use of galleys and other armed ships proliferated, raising local debt and resulting in lawsuits and claims of damage after the crisis abated.

The long-term effects of the 1374 famine had not even been entirely resolved. As late as November 1383, Valencia had made final payments to a pair of merchants who brought grain from Flanders in 1375. The city had forced the merchants to sell the grain at a lower price than promised in the original contract. The merchants sued the city for restitution and payment of back subsidies, which the city finally paid almost ten years later.[106] Even as officials settled old contracts, the city of Valencia never entirely wound down its subsidy program; there are stretches of at most a couple of months between 1374 and 1384 without subsidized imports.[107] In Barcelona, it took several years of good harvests before the authorities began to relax the stringent laws against fraud and the new controls placed on grain sales. Even in the 1380s, laws covering both begging and the grain market remained in place, with severe punishments.[108] Because of these measures, cities had few new regulations and incentives to offer when a fresh crisis hit.

Finally, numerous regions suffered from the Plague in the years preceding the 1384 crisis. Several cities in Italy, including Lucca, Siena, Pisa, and Florence, all suffered from outbreaks of the disease in 1382 and 1383.[109] The Florentine chronicler Marchionne di Coppo Stefani described a general shortage during the 1384–85 winter and noted that excessive rain rotted some wheat supplies and that wet weather ruined the wine harvest, creating the worst wine shortage in a long time.[110] He also reported that meat was expensive but blamed this directly on the wars in Lombardy and Puglia. Wine shortages did not develop into general food panics. Rather, the return of the Plague tended to heighten general fears of disaster. Legal and religious responses proliferated early in part because of these fears. Castellón de la Plana enacted new regulations attempting to keep the fish market clean, while Valencia looked at new drainage systems for the marshes to the south so as to avoid disease-causing stench.[111] Just as drought drove irrigation projects, the Plague inspired new public health responses, some more successful than others.[112]

Early religious processions prioritized relief from disease; both Barcelona and Valencia held processions in 1383. Barcelona's records mentioned drought but prioritized Plague, while Valencia's did not mention food shortages at all (despite the fact that Valencia had held a public procession against drought in March 1382).[113] Even in 1384, Valencia distributed alms as a religious hedge against disease rather than to ensure the food supply.[114]

The general religious fears spread by the Great Schism of 1378 also prompted public processions. In part because of the technocratic responses available for food shortage, generally only the most serious droughts impelled the authorities to respond with official religious actions. Documents from March 1384 that detail the financing for a large public ritual in Valencia—months before the food crisis peaked—specifically cite the schism among their concerns. The city organized a series of pious works because they found "so many adversities today in the world . . . such as the schism of the holy Roman church, and the disagreements between the king and his officials and his clerics. . . . [There is] drought for lack of rain, so much so that the grains predominantly in dry land fields are in danger of being lost, and finally there are some signs and already some presence of a general mortality and other evils because of the sins of the people."[115] There was a clear threat to crops without irrigation, but serious shortage had not yet begun. The Great Schism also loomed large as one of the grave problems threatening the city, as real a peril as plague and famine.

The schism itself was partly the result of the famine of 1374. That year, papal authorities used grain exports as a lever against Tuscan towns and cities that resisted papal policies. Export bans from papal territory in central Italy enraged the cities, helping to convince them that the conflict was not the religious affair that Pope Gregory XI claimed, but rather a political battle with secular stakes. Gregory's successor, Urban VI, reacted violently to the continued unrest in central Italy, and his actions contributed to the eventual election of Clement VII, who resumed the papacy in Avignon, cementing the schism. In turn, when Queen Joanna I of Naples decided to back Clement over Urban, Urban declared her a heretic and gave his blessing to her niece's husband, Charles of Durazzo. This set the stage for Charles, backed by the pope in Avignon, to contest her inheritance, a move that eventually split Provence and began the conflict described above. The complexity of the disasters of 1374 and 1384 thus became cyclical. The conflicts over food in 1374 contributed to the political instability that fomented the Great Schism, which in turn fueled political instability that exacerbated the food supply problems during the famine of 1384.

Overkill

In this context, many of the decisions made in 1384 and 1385 were panicked overreactions. Unnecessary export bans, expensive measures like direct purchase, and the prolific use of galleys and armed merchant ships all proved excessive responses to what was ultimately a short-lived problem. In a handful of records, urban elites acknowledged that they had moved too quickly in spending huge sums, financed by debt, to keep markets supplied. This kind of overkill probably made the crisis worse than it needed to be. There is no other evidence of shortage in either Aragon or Castile beyond the decision to ban exports to the Mediterranean coast. While fear of shortage in new regions was clearly justifiable, these moves to prevent it exacerbated the intense competition for Sicilian grain, including the use of military force to control the narrowed shipping lanes. Even rumors of violence among the merchants could be enough to dampen trade. Italian merchants tempted by high prices to transport grain would think twice before delivering it to a city where they risked getting impounded or captured and forced to do business outside their control. Merchants who were still trying to recuperate lost goods and debts from 1374, nearly ten years earlier, provided a cautionary tale.

Direct purchases and the use of armed ships also proved extremely costly, far more so than import subsidies. Tortosa opted almost entirely for direct purchases during the 1384 crisis, paying only a pittance in import subsidies. During previous crises, the city had relied more heavily on subsidies, spending significantly less for the same amount of imported grain.[116] It is likely that after 1374 Tortosa's leaders understood the challenge of competing with Barcelona and Valencia. Given that Valencia never stopped offering subsidies, as Tortosa's leaders were surely aware, the decision to resort to direct purchasing appears less rash. Additionally, Tortosa lacked the legal right to use violence that Valencia and Barcelona relied on. Direct purchases meant a stronger claim on the grain than the mere promise of a subsidy. Despite these mitigating factors, Tortosa went into even greater debt than it had in 1374.[117]

Sending armed galleys to support military ventures cost the cities in the Crown of Aragon dearly. As late as the summer of 1384, Valencia still used a galley to patrol against pirates between the mainland and the island of Ibiza. Late in June, the city disarmed that ship and dragged it ashore in the Júcar River near Cullera; it was mothballed for several months to spare the city operating costs. In August, the Valencian authorities considered putting the ship to sea again, but the launch was delayed because the captain demanded three months of funding and the city only wanted to promise two.[118]

In January, the city authorized the use of galleys specifically to combat the grain shortage, and by the spring of 1385 Valencia had assigned additional soldiers to regular merchant ships. By May, Valencia had three ships, two galleys and a support ship, specifically to patrol the area around the mouth of the Ebro River. A third galley patrolled the Balearic Islands, and several smaller ships, including armed merchant ships, monitored the coastline to prevent exports from competitor towns like Denia, Alicante, and Orihuela.[119]

The coastal patrols prevented other towns in the kingdom from exporting food and forced passing ships into Valencia's port. Valencia even used a small *llaüt*, basically a large rowboat with armed men, to prevent a ship carrying carob nuts (a common export from the region and a useful secondary source of calories) from leaving the port of Denia.[120] The armada at the mouth of the Ebro had its own subexchequer who represented the city and could force ships to sign new contracts for their cargo on the spot. At least once, the armada assigned soldiers to a ship after the contract was signed, both to ensure delivery and to prevent interference from other armed boats.[121] These ships caused so many problems for the northern grain supply that Tarragona sent representatives to the port at Salou to signal the ships and try to pay them off directly; eventually, the king intervened and revoked part of Valencia's right to such violence for abusing its privileges.[122] However, other cities continued using the same tactics. Cagliari in Sardinia used its galley to patrol grain shipments out of Sicily. Barcelona, too, had galleys, although less documentation of their actions survives.[123]

Panic was so high that Valencia armed more ships in 1385 than it had in 1374–75, resulting in huge expenses. Direct purchases were costly, but the city could recover some of the money by reselling the grain. Galleys, by contrast, sucked up massive amounts of money for soldiers' pay, armaments, and supplies, but returned little more to the city than the promise of captured ships and their cargoes.[124] In four months between January and May of 1385, Valencia paid more than 120,000 solidi to arm its vessels. On the massive import subsidies of 1372–73, the city spent 150,000 solidi for the entire year.[125] Because merchants expected reasonable treatment, as evidenced by the long-lasting legal troubles from 1374, the city tended to pay the subsidy rate on the grain from captured ships anyway; in one case, a merchant explicitly agreed to renounce any further legal action against the city in exchange for a subsidy payment plus reimbursement of port fees.[126] Similarly, in at least a couple of instances, the subexchequer of the Ebro River armada promised merchant ships the going subsidy rate and reimbursements when the ships reached Valencia.[127]

Legal restrictions on the poor also sharpened in the wake of the 1374 crisis, exacerbating problems a decade later. Barcelona's laws against begging and its threats of forced removal remained in effect. In 1383, the Valencian council created a new position, hiring an official whose job was to oversee licenses for the "true poor," help the city identify "false beggars, vagabonds, or tricksters," and round up and imprison such people.[128] The council of Játiva passed laws only a few years after 1374 that forced all jobless individuals to find a master. The law implied that any able-bodied person without work was unemployed by choice, a situation that would "promote all manner of harm."[129] These restrictions were enacted in response to crisis but remained in force after the crisis had passed.

By May 1385, the entire coastline from Empúries to Alicante had geared up for a major famine. In this context of general panic, even the export bans in Zaragoza and Castile appear peremptory. Increasing demand on the Ebro market surely made the supply feel precarious, but it appears that Zaragoza could have maintained moderate exports with no ill effects. Thanks to the rapid disappearance of most of the exacerbating factors, however, and to a harvest that was better than expected, the crisis mentality dissipated quickly. The rapid resolution of the problem left many places with outstanding loans, contracts, and countermeasures that suddenly became unnecessary. In response, multiple administrations attempted to wind down their measures quickly and recover as much money as possible. High debt might be acceptable if it resulted in survival in the face of a major disaster, but adding extra grain to a saturated market was a problem.

Possibly because of the city's heavy debt, Tarragona's records describe in detail the attempts to wind down grain imports and recover costs. By May 1385, even before the new harvest, the councilors of Tarragona wavered on their commitments. On May 15, the two officials in charge of the city-run market reported that they had sold all their wheat and had funds left over. Normally, funds would continue to pay subsidies, but the merchants who had lent the city the money wanted it back because they did not believe it was needed. The city decided to liquidate its remaining stocks of barley and bread and distribute the money between the debtors as the exchequer saw fit. At the same meeting, however, the councilors agreed to honor a contract already made to pay an import subsidy to a merchant named Garcia del Son. As the city continued to honor such contracts, the official market absorbed new grain deliveries and the pressure from creditors mounted. At its June 15 meeting, the council decided to accept its losses and ordered all remaining supplies brought to the public market rather than the price-controlled city market. It provided an additional incentive by increasing the size of a fixed-price loaf of bread called a *doblera* by two ounces, amounting to an immediate price reduction—in effect, a fire sale.[130] By early summer, debt had become a more pressing issue than shortage.

The sudden saturation of one market reversed the panicked accumulation of grain and freed up supplies back through the system. After liquidating the grain stores in Tarragona, the council attempted to unwind other contracts as well. On July 11, it sent a messenger to Tortosa to request that all grain purchased by the city of Tarragona be sold in Tortosa itself.[131] The council hoped that prices would remain higher in Tortosa than in Tarragona, although it further requested that any unsold grain should be transported to Tarragona for sale there. Finally, the councilors demanded that any merchant in Tortosa who had money from the city to purchase grain should immediately return the funds. Tarragona's desire to sell its excess supplies added a sudden influx of grain to Tortosa's markets. With the export ban from Zaragoza lifted and Tarragona no longer buying, Tortosa had no need of ships from Sicily, avoiding conflict with Valencia's galley blockade. In the same week that Tarragona ordered its grain sold in Tortosa, Valencia sent a messenger to negotiate with Tortosa over the purchase of grain from its port. With the markets suddenly full, negotiation cost significantly less than committing legal piracy (although Valencia was also responding to pressure from the king to account for its actions!). By November, Valencia had ordered the galleys rowed back to the shipyards of Valencia, stripped of armaments, and unloaded.[132] Just as Tortosa had been one of the important focal points of the beginning of the crisis, the normalization of Tortosa's market quickly helped panic dissipate throughout the region.

Conclusions

The winter of 1384–85 represents a moderate or perhaps near famine, a severe crisis that fell short of the kind of terrible, memorable event inscribed in chronicles. As the councilors of Valencia stated several times, there was "a great and almost extreme necessity on account of the shortage of grain."[133] The following chapter describes the truly disastrous famine of 1374–75. The particulars of 1374 must have made the events of 1384 seem terrifyingly familiar: war in northern Catalonia, unreliable trading partners, sudden border closures, tension with Castile, and overlapping shortages of other goods. The similarities (right down to the use of French mercenaries to invade across the Pyrenees) played directly into the panic that contributed to price spikes in the first few months of 1385. In the end, the crisis was short. Prices spiked in December of 1384 but had dropped almost back to normal levels by late summer of 1385.

Just as multiple factors contributed to the onset, so too did several events combine to end the crisis more quickly than expected. Wine and meat supplies stabilized quickly in Valencia. The direct purchase of regional flocks brought down prices quickly after Easter, and by July Valencia had closed its official table in the meat market.[134] To ease fears about the grain shortage, the city reduced the meat tax by 1 denarius per pound.[135] Initially feared to be insufficient, the grape harvest in 1385 was larger than expected. Valencian officials initially paid vineyard guards half their salary, foreseeing minimal work, but they restored the full salary in the spring, noting that there was plenty of wine and thus the guards had to work "assiduously and continuously until the end of March."[136] Joan's invasion in the north was short-lived and only influenced the most northern counties. Early in May, the king resolved the tensions around Sardinia and allowed Valencia to begin exporting grain from Oristany and Bosa, ports to the north of Cagliari.[137] A month later, Barcelona and Valencia signed a set of agreements on grain importation to avoid further direct competition (and presumably conflict between their galleys).[138]

Several factors kept the crisis from becoming more serious. The productive regions around Toulouse and Albi continued exporting foodstuffs.[139] Despite fallout from the Papal Schism, problems in Tuscany did not overlap with problems in the Crown of Aragon. Florence experienced a shortage in 1384, but of wine, not grain—a more solvable problem. Most important, the inland regions of Aragon and Navarre and the neighboring provinces in Castile never actually ran short. The 1384–85 crisis had a greater geographic range than the Valencian shortages in 1371–73, but the limits still left some supply routes open. Panic drove people to take excessive steps: heavy direct purchases in Tortosa, export bans in nearby Castile and Aragon, and significant use of armed ships by Valencia and Barcelona, more ships even than in 1374. By the end of 1385, most of the coastal cities found themselves deeply in debt because of these excessive measures. Tarragona quickly reversed course, attempting to recover losses and dissolve recent contracts. Notably, the cost of warships dogged Valencia longer than the city's other expenses. In May 1386, more than a year later, the council was still debating how to finance Valencia's debt.[140]

Despite these costly mistakes, the frequent changes in policy and attempts to reverse course reflect the flexible, deliberate nature of late medieval responses to averting famine. In the midst of the crisis, on January 25, 1385, the council of Valencia put forth a clear directive. During a debate on renegotiating older loans so as to continue funding grain subsidies, the councilors noted that "it is not reprehensible, but rather expedient and wise to change the statutes according to the changing of the times."[141] As is clear even in modern disasters, sound methods of responding to crisis do not ensure that responses are always adequate. The backpedaling by government actors and the realization that shortages would end sooner than expected give a clear indication that late fourteenth-century officials understood both famine warning signs and indications that heralded the end of a shortage. As other scholars have pointed out, chroniclers are often prone to describing a disaster as the "worst in memory" or "most dire of their life."[142] Those who recorded the events of 1384–85 knew that the crisis was not in fact the worst in memory. It fell short of the severe famine of 1374–75, a widespread famine approaching in magnitude some of the most catastrophic crises of the Middle Ages, to which we now turn.

5

THE FAMINE OF 1374–75

On September 18, 1374, Berenguer Catala, the *majordom* of the Pia Almoina in Barcelona, canceled all bread handouts for the foreseeable future. Instead, the canons began handing out small cash sums—a mere 2 denarii per person—and allowing the people in their care to search for whatever bread might be found in Barcelona. Initially, as the price of grain skyrocketed, the hospital mangers attempted to supplement the usually all-wheat bread with barley and rye, but even those grains quickly became prohibitively expensive. The city also cut off the purchase rights held by the cathedral, known as the *dret de quartera*, in August of what Catala called "the current year of the great famine."[1] For six months, the Pia Almoina continued to distribute small sums of money rather than bread, but 2 denarii would not have sufficed for even four ounces of bread a day. What the people purchased to eat, we do not know. By the end of October, the canons decided that even the monetary donations were becoming too expensive and reduced the number of daily handouts by twenty people. How Berenguer Catala implemented these restrictions, and how he chose which people to cut, he did not write down.

Berenguer Catala's decisions were not rash; the Pia Almoina had known for months that the crisis was coming. Barcelona, Valencia, Mallorca, and Tortosa had been wrangling since March over legal and economic rights to the shrinking grain exports from Aragon. By May, Valencia, Barcelona, and Mallorca put armed galleys to sea. Mallorca began preventing any ship carrying grain from leaving the harbor, forcing the duke of Valencia to demand that ships from Sicily destined for Valencia be allowed to pass with full cargoes.[2] The king, Pere the Ceremonious, sent messengers and representatives of the city of Barcelona to smaller towns such as Cervera and Urgell in the grain-producing interior of Catalonia. There, they purchased or demanded grain exports to alleviate the crisis in the capital. Although the harvest was short, it had not been severe enough to plunge the entire western Mediterranean region into immediate crisis. Under political duress, some grain continued to move down the Ebro or from Sicily.

For Valencia, in particular, 1374 was one in a string of bad years, and city leaders had already implemented multiple response measures. The consumption centers of Murcia and Cartagena relied on imports from neighboring Andalusia, especially shipments from the port of Seville. Valencia might expect Barcelona to ease its political control during a good year by allowing Tortosa to export grain, as it had in 1368. Barcelona renewed its permission in 1372 and Valencia continued importing from Tortosa into 1374. At least a couple of agricultural reports from Catalonia in 1373 mention that harvests were acceptable, even plentiful; workers and servants on the agricultural lands in Santa Perpètua de Mogoda received all-wheat bread for their work rations rather than the usual combination of wheat and barley.[3] Even with the continuing supplies from Tortosa, the Valencian exchequer paid more than half of the city's imports subsidies for grain from Sicily. While Sicily did experience a harvest shortfall locally in 1374 and more generally in 1375, the island did not shut down its ports. Sicilian production was so reliable that only one shortfall during the entire century (in 1340) resulted in the widespread restriction of exports. As the largest exporter in the region, a decision in Sicily to stop exports could spread grain shortages faster than restrictions in any other major production center.[4]

By the summer of 1374, conditions had changed. The extent of harvest failures in 1374 ignited a firestorm of political and economic problems. Valencian officials declared a crisis on March 16, when they received news from Sardinia that two of their ships coming from Sicily had been forced to unload their supplies to provision the king of Aragon's military efforts on the island.[5] In Languedoc, excessive rains fell from Easter until Saint John's Day in late June, ruining harvests. Three towns north of the Pyrenees, Toulouse, Albi, and Castres, removed import taxes on grain and then moved to ban exports.[6] In Tuscany, late rains in November and December exacerbated shortages. Florence itself had just recovered from several years of high prices accompanied by civil unrest in 1368.[7] Similarly, both Siena and the Papal States in central Italy experienced a minor crisis in 1370, and the new famine in

1374 caused riots in Siena.[8] Despite some local control of markets, the papal power situated in Avignon held final authority over imports and exports from the church properties in central Italy around Orvieto and Spoleto. In June, Avignon banned all exports from its lands and directed the surplus to be brought to one of the pope's vicar-generals. The move incited social unrest and provoked the ire of cities like Florence and Bologna, which usually relied on supplies from the Holy See. Further ordinances continued through the summer, until in August the pope demanded the transport of all excess grain into the walled city of Perugia or another fortified location. In part, these moves were responses to the growing military tension between the papacy and Florence that would erupt in the War of the Eight Saints during the summer of 1375.[9] The cruel mercenary John Hawkwood, hired by Pope Gregory XI to harass Florence, used the shortages for pure political leverage.

In the Crown of Aragon, the son of the deposed king of Mallorca invaded Catalonia from the north, bringing war to the provinces around the Pyrenees. Like the pope, Pere the Ceremonious of Aragon demanded that food supplies be moved to fortified towns in response to the invasion.[10] Many of the upland regions around the headwaters of the Ebro River were experiencing shortages, and heavy snows hit the area around Teruel early in 1375. To the west, the kingdom of Castile held Valencia under constant threat of invasion until a lasting peace was signed in April 1375. However, at the edges of the crisis in the Iberian Peninsula, neither Granada, nor Andalusia in the south, nor the bulk of the kingdom of Castile felt any negative effects.[11] The famine also spared most of France north of the Mediterranean coast.

The events of 1374–75—caused by a variety of weather patterns, western Mediterranean in scope, lasting in many places for two years and occurring simultaneously with several small wars and military skirmishes and a bout of the Plague—display all of the important features of most late medieval food crises. The collapse of normal access to food began with multiple atmospheric problems, namely, drought, hail, and excessive precipitation. However short the actual harvest was in 1374, the geographic breadth of the problem prevented the habitual practice of shifting urban imports to new markets to cover periodic shortages. The overlapping crises in multiple production and consumption centers meant that small towns, usually able to draw extra resources to their local markets, found trade channels closed. The storage capacity of the countryside might have provided moderate relief, but the general panic kept these extra supplies locked up in rural areas and able to sustain only local consumers. The usually flexible distribution systems froze under economic, political, and even military pressure. Plague further dampened the willingness of merchants and ship captains to enter disease- and famine-stricken regions with supplies. Despite a second year of bad harvests, an end to several military conflicts, the return of productive harvests in key areas like Valencia, and the extreme measures of searching out distant markets like the Low Countries meant that by the fall of 1375, the general food crises of 1374 had subsided and most of the largest markets had returned to more normal functioning.

Foundations of the Crisis

Like all major famines, 1374 combined wide-ranging causes over a broad region. As with other fourteenth-century food shortages, these began with the weather. Despite the importance of underlying structural causes, every famine still had a trigger. Some of the confusion around modern famine response comes from the mismatch between responses to long-term problems and short-term triggers. According to the UN Food and Agriculture Organization, for example, long-term use of cheap US grain exports—an ideal solution to a short-term price spike—has lowered much of central Africa's own yearly grain production.[12]

Extreme weather precipitated most famines in Europe during the Middle Ages for the obvious reason that bad weather can reduce production across a vast landscape. In the shifting microclimates of the Mediterranean, adverse weather frequently hit relatively small areas without triggering region-wide shocks. But when periodic bad years stacked up geographically, chaos resulted. Valencia had short harvests from 1372 to 1374 and northern Catalonia and Languedoc in 1374 and '75, but the Papal States in Italy, the county of Spoleto, and Tuscany suffered only a single bad harvest in the fall of 1374. The geographic overlap of these poor harvests, clustered in the fall of 1374 and winter of 1375, provoked famine. Wars and sieges might also act as triggers, but only at the local level. Josephus's description of starvation during the siege of Jerusalem by the Romans is one of the most often referenced passages in medieval chronicles that describe extreme responses to hunger, like madness or cannibalism.[13] The Hundred Years' War (roughly 1337–1453) and periodic fighting between mercenary groups in northern Italy emptied out smaller villages and caused economic and social chaos akin to the effects of famine in their wake.[14] Whatever long-term causes might reinforce or worsen famine, most major food shortages in medieval Europe began with bad weather.

The connection between meteorological events and climatic shifts make weather both a trigger and a long-term cause. Today, many Mediterranean scholars see famines as multicausal events that involve both human and natural elements.[15] Many historians also attribute an important role to the Little Ice Age, a period of cold temperatures that began in the fourteenth century and reached its apex in the late sixteenth.[16] Tree rings, glacial cores, bog sediment, and other climatic proxies indicate a long period of warm weather, appropriately called the Medieval Warm Period, from the tenth to the thirteenth centuries, followed by an expansion of glaciers and colder, wetter weather in the following few centuries.[17] Two well-studied glaciers in the Alps, the Great Aletsch and the Gorner, both reached a three-hundred-year peak between 1360 and 1390, indicating significantly colder weather, at least in central Europe.[18] Such forces may have played a growing role in the famines of the fourteenth century, particularly as adverse weather probably increased after the Black Death.

Finally, the proliferation of different forms of bad weather often proved critical. Virtually the entire coastal strip from Valencia to southern Italy, along with Sicily and the other islands, is part of the broader Mediterranean climate, characterized by cool, wet, often stormy winters and dry, relatively hot summers. The drier climate often, but not always, meant that shortages were the result of drought. The Mediterranean world is well known for its pockets of unique weather from one region to another. Peregrine Horden and Nicholas Purcell write, "thanks to that climatic variability which cannot be overestimated as a factor in Mediterranean history, food crises have by all accounts been frequent in the Mediterranean. Therefore, we should not place too much trust in the concept of a normal year."[19] Corroborating this view, city records from Barcelona and Valencia show their councils discussing responses to some form of shortage at least once every ten years. However, it was rare that multiple places would all suffer bad harvests in the same year. The weather in 1374 depended on location: cold in Languedoc and some of the Aragonese highlands, storms in Provence, drought in Catalonia and Valencia, and excessive rain in Tuscany. In the Papal States of central Italy, a terrible drought persisted from Christmas to Easter, killing much of the new grain crops. This drought was followed by several months of soaking rains that ruined previous grain stores.[20] In 1374, the type of bad weather varied even over relatively short distances. But multiple forms of bad weather conspired to create shortages in virtually all the regions within the trading zone of the western Mediterranean. Unable to rely on Sicily or the other islands, cities had to turn to the Black Sea, Andalusia, or northern Europe. As noted in the previous chapter, this geographic breadth contributed directly to the famine's severity.

The typical short-term triggers in a given region depend on the structures of society through which the crisis is reflected. For the medieval Mediterranean, these triggers were almost always weather. This might seem self-evident, but it is not always the case, even in premodern society. Virtually all of the famines recorded during imperial Roman times occurred during war. The more extensive or protracted the war, the worse the famine.[21] Agricultural and economic systems interacted in such a way that climatic famines were rare, particularly in major cities, whereas military problems could adversely affect large regions of the Roman Empire. In medieval Europe, even with the extensive trade systems developed by the fourteenth century, the local character of legal control and administration created a situation in which famine triggers came generally from diverse weather patterns. Largely because of the geographical breadth of weather anomalies in 1374, many sources describe the famine as the worst in decades.

Famine's Trajectory

Despite the severity of the famine and the continuing bad weather in 1375, for many people the famine of 1374 was a single-year event. By April 1375, prices in the major cities of the Crown of Aragon had already begun to drop. Barcelona market prices fell in response to new imports from Flanders, while Valencia ensured a new supply of Andalusian grain from Seville. In May, the Pia Almoina returned to serving bread despite continuing price volatility. The record book of 1374, written by Berenguer Catala, is full of dire financial actions taken by the institution and expressions of Catala's shock at market conditions. The 1375 book, however, written by his successor, Pere Çaquinal, contains very little on the crisis. In Valencia, the Hospital of en Clapers continued serving bread throughout the year, although at much reduced levels. At the height of the crisis, it dropped back to around two-thirds of the normal ration and began mixing in inferior grains, first adding sorghum and eventually adding rye and rice flower for all but the sickest patients.[22] To restock its public market, Valencia secretly sent Bernat Periç to petition the king of Castile to allow grain exports from Seville in Andalusia in May 1374. The mission had to be done in secret because of the ongoing War of the Two Peters between the Crown of Aragon and Castile; neither side wanted to be seen aiding the enemy. Valencia received word from official messengers about the Peace of Almazán, ending the war on April 17, 1375, a mere five days after its signing. A few weeks later, Valencia sent out new ambassadors to renew officially (and openly) the city's export rights.[23]

Throughout the Crown of Aragon, areas with political power and connections saw their crisis end significantly sooner than those without. It is not clear how widely the grain coming into Barcelona from Flanders was available. The monastery of Sant Pere de les Puel·les continued to purchase wheat at the high price of more than 25 solidi per quarter even in December 1375. Barcelona's Pia Almoina was already working its political connections and paid less than 18. At the end of 1376 and again at the end of 1378, the Almoina paid a fairly handsome sum (22 and 44 solidi, respectively) to one en Leonich and thanked him for assistance in securing imports.[24] Because of its privileged buying power, the Almoina managed to pay only around 50 percent above the normal price rather than double that price as at Sant Pere. In addition, because much of the poorhouse's income came from rents, often paid in grain, the high prices made for profitable years. The Almoina essentially used its wealth and influence to turn rural suffering into urban charity, aimed most often at students and families of the well-off. Sant Pere still had access to the regular Barcelona markets, which lowered their prices, but not as far. Such forces made for different experiences of the famine between social groups as well as between urban and rural people.

In addition to the political connections leveraged by large institutions, wealthy individuals used their social networks to acquire supplies. The widow of Vice Admiral Guillem Morey in Barcelona wrote to a friend in Aragon asking for her personal grain supply, complaining, "I was not accustomed to eating bread made of chick peas and fava beans and now I have to eat them."[25] At the highest levels of society, famine caused logistical difficulties and dietary compromises rather than real pain. In October and November, the royal household continued its consumption of almonds, peaches, oranges, and other fruits. In part because the aristocratic diet was based more on meat and finer foods, the wealthy felt the shortage of grain less acutely. While most city inhabitants ate half their calories in bread, for aristocrats it could be as little as a quarter.[26] If bread became too expensive, royalty could consume more meat than usual (the fixed price of which appears not to have varied), cutting back on bread without sacrificing calories or health. Even for wealthy urban citizens, the shortage meant a little belt tightening and perhaps the consumption of some unsavory food at most.

Almost everyone else felt the threat of real starvation. In November 1374, the Valencia city council posted notices in all parish churches announcing that it would increase donations to the poor throughout the city. Many more people than usual had begun begging because of the high price of food, and "the alms that were ordinarily given to the poor in the parish churches did not suffice."[27] As described in chapter 3, however, the city also placed multiple restrictions on begging. Laborers who depended on the wealthy for work saw the support of their patrons shrink. Ramon de Tous's wife, Sereneta, reduced the rations of her servants to fourteen ounces of mixed barley and wheat bread per day, around half the normal amount.[28] To lose the security of payment in food just as prices rose must have left many of these servants and porters feeling quite desperate. In all but the wealthiest centers, the availability of secondary sources of food and charity generally waxed and waned in sync with the quality of harvests.

Nor could poor relief come close to reaching everyone who needed it during a famine. One great benefit of living in a city like Barcelona was not necessarily better access to food but the shorter duration of the shortage. Major difficulties lasted only a little more than a year. By June 1375, with grain arriving from Seville, Sicily, and Flanders, the official chronicle in Barcelona declared the famine over.[29] Prices remained elevated, but from June onward there was a consistent trend downward. Valencia picked up its imports from Seville after the end of the War of the Two Peters. Valencian vessels continued to patrol the main shipping line, often hiring armed guards for the merchant ships themselves. By May, after only a year of crisis, Valencia had hauled the two largest armed galleys into the Júcar River and left them unmanned.[30] Entries in the payment books began referring to the famine in the past tense in June, recalling "the great necessity and anguish that there was then because of a shortage of grain."[31] On May 11, 1375, the city leaders judged the new barley harvest of sufficient quantity and quality and considered lifting their export ban.[32] Despite the general relief, Valencia declined to lift the restrictions on rice purchases until January 18, 1376, and did not end the general export ban until May 1376, when they described the crisis as "largely alleviated."[33] Over the winter of 1375, the poor did begin to starve, and many doubtless suffered from malnutrition, but new imports rectified the situation in a matter of months.

Market dynamics meant that rural areas suffered less than cities and towns in the first year but as much or more in the second; urban areas suffered more acutely but could respond more quickly. Harvest shortages lasted between two and three years starting in 1374, depending on location. Unfortunately, harvest yield data from Sitges record only the harvest for fava beans in 1374: a miserable 1:1 ratio, leaving no extra produce for consumption. As discussed in chapter 1, fava returns were generally lower than those of grain because of their use as a cover crop. The Sitges harvest for 1375 includes barley, with a somewhat better ratio of almost 9:1 though still on the low end for that crop. For rural producers, poor cereal yields continued into 1376 and 1377, after most cities had moved past the crisis. Even in 1378, Sitges records a wheat harvest ratio of barely 5:1, one of the lowest on record. If this were a peasant property, what was left after deducting tithes and seed would scarcely support survival. Poor harvests exacerbated urban/rural wealth differences because the general price in urban markets had already dropped, depriving farmers of the higher sale prices that might have compensated for reduced harvests. Agricultural prices from properties in Barcelona indicate that 1375 fell just as short as 1374 and then improved moderately thereafter. Prices paid to convert the agricultural census in wheat and barley to cash from several Pia Almoina properties, including Sitges, show identical prices for both years. Only Gravalosa experienced a sharp price spike in 1374, although the documents provide no explanation. Harvest prices in 1376 improved somewhat but did not return to the mean (see figs. 9a and 9b). It is possible that the pull of Barcelona helped increase prices in the region; the relatively distant Sitges had the lowest sale price. However, it is equally likely that Sitges's coastal location and intensive storage practices helped reduce fears of shortage. All of the locations except Gravalosa record prices several times above normal but well below the peak of the spike in Barcelona. In 1375, the situation was reversed. The city of Barcelona's market prices fell below the harvest sale price in many towns. Similarly, income from the properties of Sant Pere shows some improvement in 1375, though the numbers are still double prefamine levels. Even the expensive imported grain from Flanders cost less than the newly harvested grain from Sitges, Santa Perpètua de Mogoda, and Sant Feliu de Llobregat. Just as the spike hit the urban center and radiated outward, prices dropped in response to new imports in the markets closest to Barcelona.

It is likely that the increased prices continuing into 1376 reflect ongoing concern about long-term supplies as much as they do fears of a third year of poor harvests. The attempts by city merchants to drain rural stock, especially to exhume any grain stored in underground pits, greatly reduced the resilience of rural producers. Small towns continued to export stored grain even as large cities entered full crisis. In early November 1374, the monastery of Sant Pere sent representatives to Castelló d'Empúries to secure grain purchases. The same month, the monastery recorded two purchases, one for grain from the Empordà (possibly the same grain the representative went to Empúries to

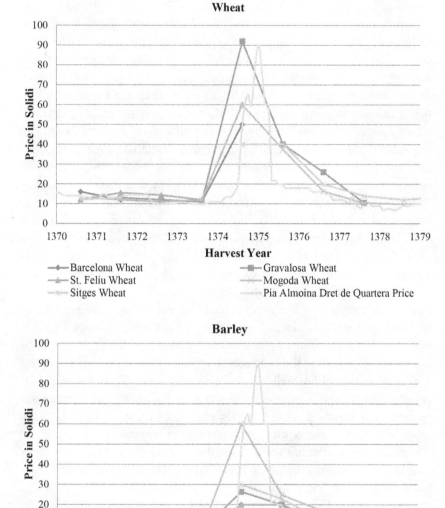

FIGS. 9A AND 9B. YEARLY GRAIN HARVEST SALE PRICES—WHEAT AND BARLEY. The prices for the harvested grain come from various properties of the Pia Almoina and are pegged to late August, as they were usually sold sometime between mid-August and mid-September. The barley prices are also compared to the moving price of wheat, as there are insufficient purchases and prices for barley to create an equivalent trend line.

purchase) and a second for grain from Urgell. The purchase from Urgell cost 78 solidi per quarter, a price comparable to the prices from the Pia Almoina. For the shipment from Empordà, the monastery paid only 52 solidi per quarter, close to the 58 recorded during the same month by the royal administrator of the mills in Empúries.[34] Prices in Castelló d'Empúries rose throughout 1374, though they always lagged a month or two behind Barcelona prices (see fig. 10). As in Barcelona, they reached ten times normal by the winter of 1375, but whereas Barcelona prices began to drop in March, Castelló's remained fully at crisis levels; prices there were still elevated in 1376, though no longer at the astronomical heights of the previous year.[35] The inland towns of Cervera and Tàrrega relied on silos of stored grain for both local supply and sale to larger towns like Manresa. In the south, Valencian towns like Elche and Orihuela still had stores available for export in 1375, although their marketability had been severely restricted by the military pressure of Valencian warships. Once these stores ran out—the outrageous prices paid in urban centers made the impulse to sell them all but irresistible—rural towns found themselves even more vulnerable to another poor harvest. High demand in wealthy urban centers actually helped set the stage for more severe shortages in the hinterlands in the second year of the famine. In some cases, barley prices did not see the recovery that wheat prices did, perhaps because of increased demand for the secondary grain in the face of a wheat shortage. With a second decent harvest in 1377, even rural prices returned to normal, although it seems doubtful that depleted grain stores would have been fully replaced.

Midsized towns like Vic and Manresa felt the worst effects in the intermediary period between the first urban price spikes and the lingering rural difficulties from a second bad harvest. The royal official (the *veguer*) of the region surrounding Osona issued an early export ban on April 15, 1374, with the support of Vic's council, just two days after the export ban in Barcelona.[36] The ban coincided with a demand from the king to move all grain to fortified areas in preparation for an invasion from the north. A few months later, on August 3, despite opposition from peasants, who knew that their situation would soon become worse, the king's councilor Ramon de Planella ordered Vic to export some of its grain to Barcelona for the city's provisioning in case of siege. By the end of August, Planella's representative Bernat de Bellveí had managed to extract and send to Barcelona 630 quarters of grain, including wheat, barley, and spelt, from Vic and its surrounding region. Vic lacked the political clout to prevent its grain stores from being drained by the most powerful player—the ever-rapacious Barcelona. For its part, in October, Vic sent Pere Feliu west to purchase wheat stores from Calaf in the Urgell, with

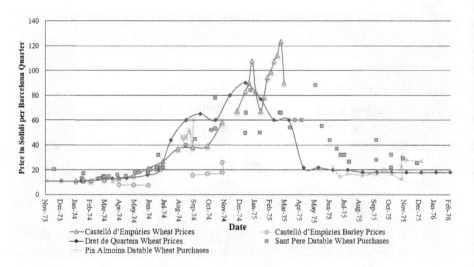

FIG. 10. GRAIN PRICES IN BARCELONA AND CASTELLÓ D'EMPÚRIES. The prices paid by both the Pia Almoina and the monastery of Sant Pere de les Puel·les in Barcelona began increasing around the same time as the prices in Castelló, but faster. The lower prices paid at Sant Pere, particularly in October, were actually for grain purchased from Castelló d'Empúries itself. The chaotic nature of the "Barcelona market" thus stems in part from the fact that prices include both Barcelona prices and regionally lower prices that institutions in Barcelona resorted to for grain purchases in times of crisis. The prices in Castelló were originally measured in solidi per *mitgera* (just over two quarters in size); for purposes of comparison, I have converted all measurements to Barcelona quarters. The Castelló prices are drawn from Gironella i Granés 2010, 320–22.

only partial success.[37] Despite the exports, some of Vic's grain supplies lasted longer than Barcelona's. On May 8, 1375, the Almoina of Vic declared that no more grain could be purchased and resorted to donating money to the poor, just as the Barcelona Pia Almoina had done months earlier.[38] Also in May, the same royal official of Osona banned sales of wheat still on the stalk, "with grass," presumably sold to hide the poor quality or quantity of the grain. In September, the official reissued the ban on exports without a specific license.[39] The export ban continued, with high fines for violations, until the fall of 1376. Despite a slightly better harvest in 1375, it took Vic longer than similar Catalan cities to return to a secure grain supply.

In Manresa, early export bans indicate that shortages developed quickly, fueled by the heavy demands of the city of Barcelona. As early as August 14, 1374, a secondary royal overseer (the *sots-veguer*) confiscated three quarters of flour from a porter who was trying to transport it to Barcelona in violation of the regional export ban. By March 1375, Manresa's government had taken on several large loans and attempted to send a representative to Barcelona to purchase grain, claiming that Manresa was suffering while Barcelona had grain to spare. While this claim was almost certainly rhetorical, the councilors of Manresa had no doubt that Barcelona enjoyed better access to grain than they did. On August 7, the city government announced that people could purchase Manresan wine for export only if they also supplied the city with wheat, mirroring a political move by Valencia a year earlier. The few prices we have from Manresa suggest that the grain shortage abated slightly in 1375 but then worsened in 1376. Prices rose more slowly than in Barcelona, reaching only 32 solidi per quarter by October 1374. In March 1376, the price was 29.5 solidi per quarter, but it had risen again, to 41, by April. On July 5, 1376, the councilors of Manresa even sent a delegation to the equally beleaguered Vic, petitioning Vic to circumvent its prohibition on exports.[40] These inland towns, lacking both ocean access for shipping and political clout, might have staved off the worst of the price spikes, but they continued to suffer from food shortages and financial troubles long after the large coastal markets had returned to normal.

At the tail end of the famine, resources from large markets did spill back out to more rural regions. In the midst of Manresa's continuing struggles throughout the spring of 1376, grain prices still hovered around three times higher than normal. The city council again sent a representative to the well-supplied Barcelona market with money to purchase one thousand quarters. Manresa could draw on the secondary effects of Barcelona's economic power despite having earlier prevented grain from heading in Barcelona's direction.[41] Several of the properties of Sant Pere near Barcelona saw reductions in prices in the fall of 1375. Sant Andreu, just outside the city walls, sold its grain harvest in 1375 at only 12 solidi per quarter, a return to the 1373 price. The flow of grain at the beginning of the famine went from smaller towns to large centers. By the second year of shortage, international supplies allowed this flow to be reversed. With a stronger barley harvest and secure imports from Seville, Valencia also began loosening its control of the market. By January 1376, its council allowed old grain to leave the city for Alzira, which was still suffering. The record documenting this decision comes across as condescending, explaining the export on the basis of the "special friendship" between the cities, even though only old millet and sorghum was shipped, while Valencian markets enjoyed new wheat imported from Seville.[42] The availability of grain might have mitigated the price, but large cities still guarded their access to good grain.

These price data allow a more nuanced understanding of the time line of famines in medieval Europe. The price of wheat in Barcelona shot up with the advent of widespread shortage. The actual wheat harvest began in June, and by July 28 the council of Tarragona was already holding a secret meeting to hear the councilor Francesch Foguet interrogate Berenguer Rodera about the state of the grain supply in the market. Rodera attested that there remained no grain at all in the market, but that bakers still had enough grain and flour to supply the town until the coming Sunday—three days.[43] The political fighting between trading cities helped fuel speculation about possible impending shortages. Catalonia had seen an excellent harvest in 1373, but the harvest had been marginal in Valencia. Despite having just recovered from a serious shortage in 1370, Florence saw prices that were also normal or below normal. It took only a single year of broad enough climatic shocks to cause famine, particularly in urban areas. This fact is echoed in descriptions of other famines as well; chronicles note the sudden onset of crisis with terms like *repente, statim,* and *subito.*[44] During the 1384–85 crisis described in chapter 4, prices in Tortosa spiked quickly, reaching their peak in April and May 1385 before dropping in the fall of 1385. Bad harvests in 1386 forced prices marginally upward, but not to the exaggerated levels of the initial panic.[45] For more rural areas and inland towns, additional years of shortage could potentially deepen the crisis, as they did in Manresa, Vic, and Alzira, but it is equally likely that the extra time gave certain areas time to respond.

Notices from other parts of the Mediterranean corroborate this narrative of urban panic and persistent rural struggles with supply. In rural parts of Languedoc, the bad harvests lasted for two years, returning to normal in 1376. The smaller towns of Tarascon and Draguignan further east in Provence suffered continuing shortages in 1375, though less severe than in the province of Languedoc.[46] Prices in the urban center of Toulouse reached their peak before the harvest of 1375 in April and May.[47] Florence saw prices rise dramatically starting in September 1374, partly in response to the depredations of mercenary companies. In the wider region of Tuscany, prices began rising in November or December, and did not reach a peak until May or June of the following year. The same preparations for war that reduced Vic's ability to govern its own famine response also hurt towns like Orvieto, Città di Castello, and Perugia, which had to respond to the demands for military preparation issued from far outside the region by the pope's vicar, the abbot of Marmoutier.[48] Despite two years of bad harvests, the trajectory of the shortage and the worst point of the crisis depended on location and political access to resources.

Rural capacity to store and provide grain throughout the year contrasted with city stocks, which ran out almost immediately, causing drastic price spikes. In rural areas and smaller towns like Vic, there might be sufficient stores to survive for almost a year. Prices still rose, but more gradually. Rural prices remained higher for longer, unassisted by long-distance imports. When Flanders grain entered the Barcelona market, prices dropped quickly below those in the hinterland. Prices remained high and volatile, reflecting the cost of such extensive shipping along with the anxiety over long-term supplies. However, such access gave the people of Barcelona a very different experience of the famine. Andalusian grain similarly relieved the city of Valencia sooner than it did the surrounding region. Early in the famine, Barcelona and Valencia, often with the king's help, managed to extract grain from those regions that had not yet reached crisis levels. However, by the end of the crisis, the capitals were so well supplied that regional towns sent representatives to their markets to bring back supplies for their own famine relief.

Religious Responses

Scholars today understand famine in deeply human terms, often using such language as "natural hazard," which only becomes a "disaster" when combined with human poverty or vulnerability. When these ideas came to prominence in the 1980s, the same writers tended to describe the technocratic ability to limit disaster as a modern achievement. Persistent ideas about the natural or divine origins of disasters were attributed to superstitious, underdeveloped societies, including the premodern Western past. Prayers for rain or respite from plague implied a desperation born of the inability to understand or respond to the magnitude of the disaster. Recent disaster-response ideas have brought back the importance of working within local religious frameworks, but the assumption is still that Western and other developed countries do not require this sort of religious deference.[49] The link between superstition and underdevelopment still colors our assumptions about late medieval Europe. Superstition is seen as a natural extension of premodern people's "impotence in the face of a real threat [that] made them turn to magical or religious solutions."[50] Even as the Catholic Church attempted to tamp down magical or "unorthodox means of weather control," religious ceremonies persisted into the sixteenth and seventeenth centuries regularly enough to allow us to use reports of processions as proxy data for weather and climate.[51]

More recent work takes seriously the medieval understanding of economic responses to shortage and famine.[52] Medieval actors had political, economic, and technological tools at their disposal to prepare for and respond to food crises, even if those technologies were less effective than modern ones. However, technocratic responses never removed the use of religious ceremonies and prayer from the toolbox of responses employed during famines. Instead, the core religious explanation for the origins of natural disasters blended seamlessly with technological responses. During the "first bad year," a famine that hit most of the Crown of Aragon from 1333 to 1336, the Barcelona Consell de Cent worried that crops were "in danger of being lost if God and good friends do not help quickly."[53] A letter from the city of Valencia, written during the famine of 1374 to Ramon Alemany de Cervelló, the royal governor of the kingdom, contains an explicit statement of the same sentiment. The letter petitioned the king and governor to allow grain ships through from Sicily because of the increasingly dire shortage. "The great necessity and anguish . . . have come from two things: the first by reason of drought and fog, the most that has ever been seen; and the second and more important is from the great quantity of grain we secured, which has been carried off and seized in Sardinia by those from Barcelona all this past year and still continuing until recently."[54] The letter is dated May 30, when drought threatened but before genuine famine arrived in the winter. While praying for rain, the city identified the principal cause of the shortage as the seizure of its ships in Sardinia. (Note, however, that the letter is written to someone with the power to solve the problem, so there is also an element of rhetorical flourish at work.)

Many places responded to the 1374 famine with religious supplications. The assumptions and desires behind religious processions are clear enough. If most medieval famines started because of drought, flood, excessive rain, or other meteorological phenomena, the root cause was assumed to be divine disfavor. But medieval disaster response never took a singularly religious form, in part because the medieval concept of disaster encompassed multiple forms of suffering. Many Latin sources use terms like *tribulatio* (tribulation); the Valencian council repeated the Catalan words *tribulacions* and also *adversitats* (adversities).[55] The religious imagery of the Four Horsemen of the Apocalypse includes the inexplicable and unstoppable (plague and death) along with the human (war). In fourteenth-century thought, famine fell clearly within these extremes, encompassing natural and human elements within its complex set of causes. Like the mix of religious and secular responses today, public religious responses often appeared when the magnitude of the disaster overwhelmed the usual secular coping mechanisms.

The time line of responses to the famine of 1374 illustrates the mixed use of religious and political responses in a late medieval disaster. Valencia and Barcelona both held large religious processions and public prayers for the mercy of God. Valencia, coming off previous years of drought, held a procession in February 1374 and again in October; the latter procession came a few weeks before Barcelona's first ceremonies. On Friday, October 27, the Valencian council paid for several days' worth of processions and prayers with religious and civic leaders. These began the following morning at the Cathedral of Santa Maria, processing down the street of Saint Nicholau toward the church of the same name. From there, the procession turned south along the street *de la bosseria*, passing through the central market and eventually arriving at the church at the Benedictine monastery of Sant Vicent, today the church of Cristo Rey. There, the clergy performed the divine office along with "solemn sermons." The following Monday morning, the churches handed out "general charity and alms as much to the mendicant poor in the diocese of the city as to the shame-faced poor and [also] to the religious to serve in reverence to our lord God and to soften his wrath."[56] Barcelona held its first large public procession on November 17, starting similarly at the cathedral and processing as far as the monastery of Valldonzella just to the southwest of the city walls. Priests and clerics from all the Barcelona churches and religious orders accompanied the procession, offering prayers and sermons, as in Valencia. Instead of a day of alms and offerings, Barcelona held a second procession the following day.[57] These processions took place late in 1374, well after the onset of the crisis and political responses. Valencian leaders described the crisis as a famine (*fam*, as opposed to the words for shortage—*fretura* or *carestía*) on July 18, 1374, and upped their import subsidies.[58] Both cities launched armed galleys to patrol their corner of the Mediterranean prior to the fall processions.[59]

The differences in the language describing the different processions are instructive. In Valencia's first announcement, on Tuesday, February 21, the council declared that a general procession should be held on the following Friday, the feast of Saint Matthias; this would be followed on Saturday by a day of almsgiving, "to encourage divine mercy . . . as it is of great necessity for the persons and for the harvests."[60] In their description, issued before the crisis had become widespread, the city's leaders asked only for "rain and health and good weather." War and plague were not yet major concerns. In its October discussion, the council included a list of religious and penitential acts to be performed "in search of divine mercy, through penitence, affliction, fasting, prayer, alms, and other good works." These events were to beg for God's "grace and blessing for health, abundance, rain, peace, and fair weather" in response to a laundry list of problems, among them "famine, drought, illness, death, war, and other adversities."[61] The list includes both "divine" acts (drought, illness, death) and tribulations of a more human sort (war and famine). Barcelona, which was not suffering from the Plague in 1374, did not include that problem in its litany of prayers, only "praying to God that he would send them ample foodstuffs and suitable rain."[62] In January 1375, at the height of the crisis in Barcelona, a woman wrote to her son in Aragon asking if he could send wheat. She mentioned both responses, saying that they only needed one to work. "If God does not help us with rain and the ships do not come loaded with grain . . . they will die of hunger, and I am one of them."[63] These overlapping responses show a clear awareness of the multiple causes involved in the crisis.

In Montpellier, the city chronicle, called *Le Petit Thalamus*, echoed these changing purposes for its own processions. On April 27, 1374, the city created a peculiar and very large wooden wheel and "had fabricated out of cotton and wax a cord [1,900 rods, or almost four kilometers!] long and of finger thickness." The wheel was placed on the altar of Saint Mary in the cathedral, where "it was lit to burn continuously on the altar in honor of God and the Madonna, Saint Mary, and to placate the ire of Our Lord, and to make cease the said plague." Then, on July 23, the city "thanked the Lord God who had removed the plague from us, and implored him that he give us health and peace and save the fruits of the earth."[64] These prayers continued but could focus on the most urgent problem of the day.

Other political debates firmly blamed human action rather than divine displeasure. At its meeting on March 16, the council of Valencia discussed a recent meeting of the courts with the duke and noted their "great differences" with the ecclesiastic and noble branches of the court. Councilors cited the pair of grain ships that had been confiscated by representatives of the king in Sardinia, sparking a more severe grain shortage. "There was disagreement over the compensation from the money of the stated offer . . . to those merchants of the said city [who were] damaged at the island of Sardinia." They do admit, even in their disagreement, that the grain unloaded by the officials of the king went toward the "provision and sustenance of [the island.]" The council appears to have distrusted the possibility of a forthcoming solution. In the next couple of paragraphs, it passed an export ban, citing growing fears and shortages in both Sardinia and Mallorca. It also enjoined the jurors to make "all those arrangements and provisions that should be necessary and that seem good to them,"[65] including sending messengers or ambassadors directly to the king and arming ships to patrol the waters and escort grain shipments. Long before the payments for the processions, the jurors of Valencia put these actions into motion. Barcelona's description of its export ban is more laconic, but the acts speak to the importance of shipping, alongside the weather and other divine acts, in maintaining the city's grain supply.

Finally, medieval responses to disaster could comfortably blend the mundane with the religious. Citing the use of Aristotelian "natural" explanations of earthquakes, Christopher Gerrard and David Petley argue that "a duality of views of a single event, involving both a natural and a supernatural explanation, was not uncommon." They place medieval responses within the major categories of disaster management today, including mitigation, protection, and adaptation. Medieval examples included tax relief and charity to mitigate economic losses, embankments and drainage ditches to protect against flooding, and updating building codes after a major fire to require more use of brick or stone.[66] Given the complexity of famines, late medieval society engaged in all three approaches. Producers and cities alike stored significant amounts of grain in preparation. They used charity and social organizations to redistribute resources, albeit unevenly. Subsidies and economic measures encouraged importation of distant grain supplies. None of these preparations prevented them from turning to prayer for extra assistance. The commonly invoked *pro pluvia* prayers could invoke God's help with good rains even as field owners cleaned and expanded their irrigation channels.

These dichotomies lived side by side in the minds of medieval people as comfortably as they can today when an American president prays for the victims of a flood or hurricane; prayers do not absolve one from organizing a robust relief program. Then and now, angry protests attest to the fact that suffering people require both prayers and secular aid. The two are so closely tied that it created no dissonance to pray for the fast arrival of supplies on ships sent by the same leaders, delivered by merchants paid well to accomplish the task. Instead of these sacred responses demonstrating the irrationality of the Middle Ages, such religious responses should make famine feel quite modern. It is clear that medieval people understood their religious supplications to be one of the many tools available for the alleviation of food crises. No historian would be surprised to find extensive prayers preceding a battle occurring side by side with repairs to castle walls, investment in weapons, and consideration of tactics; response to famine was no different. Economic competition required trade subsidies and reinforcement of privileges. Conflict with other towns and piracy required negotiation and armed escorts. Acts of God required prayer "to placate the ire of Our Lord."

The Edges of Famine

The famine of 1374 came about initially because of bad grain harvests. Prices for wheat, followed by barley and other grains, spiked far beyond normal levels, often remaining high for two or three years. The shortage of only a couple of fundamental staples—rice, wheat, potatoes—often provides the spark for a famine. Beyond this narrow causation, however, famines include a variety of other markers and events. Both historians and theologians frequently associate famine with war or plague. In spite of their frequent overlap, those three horsemen are not always causally connected.[67]

Unlike the crisis of 1384, the famine of 1374 involved only moderate price fluctuations in foodstuffs other than grain. The fluctuation in other commodities can relate to weather or external shocks, but price fluctuations in other goods, even staples like meat and wine, never caused famine. In Barcelona, prices of wine became more volatile than usual but experienced no spike (see fig. 11). The cost of wine was elevated because the same drought that killed the wheat reduced the grape harvest. Italian sources in Florence and Bologna complained of a shortage of bread and the high cost of wine.[68] But unlike the general panic produced by grain shortfalls, wine shortages moved cities like Perpignan or Valencia to modify existing import bans, protecting the interest in local wine production over a glut of inexpensive foreign products. In August 1374, the king granted Perpignan and the royal governor of the region the right to lift the ban temporarily without damaging their general privilege to restrict imports.[69] In Valencia, the city council discussed the shortage of wine in its ongoing deliberations about the drought, but only chose to lift the city's import ban for one year.[70] In 1377, hail damaged the grapevines and heavy rains ruined much of the grape harvest around Valencia, such that the council again allowed for a bending of the wine privileges. But the councilors made it clear that this move was only temporary, allowing imports only "from now to Saint Michaels" and ensuring that the imports were "without prejudicial repeal or revocation of the said privileges or prohibitive establishments [restricting imports] which remain in their force and efficacy."[71] Manresa, in addition to its wheat regulations, banned the export of wine unless the buyer had brought an unspecified amount of wheat into the city.

Other products had little impact on the overall famine. In 1374, the kingdom of Valencia also experienced an oil shortage, prompting an early export ban similar to that on wheat on June 23, 1374.[72] But the city provided no financial incentive for imports and oil was rarely mentioned in the deliberations

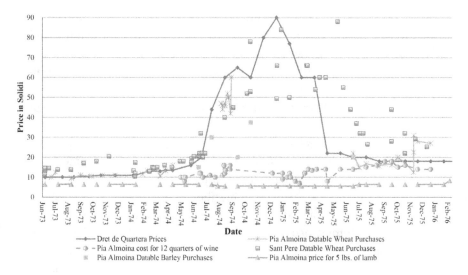

FIG. 11. FOOD PRICES IN BARCELONA DURING FAMINE. These prices include the same grain purchases from the Pia Almoina and the monastery of Sant Pere shown in fig. 10. The *dret de quartera*
shows a more predictable curve because the prices are only reported, not the actual prices paid
in the market. The wine prices shown here demonstrate some volatility but do not spike the way
wheat prices did. Lamb prices show virtually no change.

after the initial ban. On the Barcelona market, meat prices remained constant. Partly, this reflects the fact that animals have less inherent seasonality than crops. Additionally, as discussed in chapter 1, the lower volatility of
meat prices in general made them easier for towns to regulate or fix. An
overlapping epidemic disease in the animal population, such as the cattle
murrain in northern Europe at the tail end of the Great Famine, could have
deepened the crisis, bringing further loss of capital and reduced chances of
survival.[73] But the smooth operation of the meat market could not prevent
the extensive chaos and panic of 1374.

It is more remarkable that, far from spiking, prices of commodities such
as meat stayed constant. Often, in famines in the premodern West, prices
of other goods actually fell during severe grain shortages. Chronicles from
ancient Rome to the Great Famine note the poor selling off their cattle, wine,
furniture, and even houses if necessary in order to purchase bread.[74] In one
instance in Tarragona, on January 19, 1375, a woman named Catarina sold
the workshop that her husband, a weaver or cloth maker named Guillem
Vidal, had willed to the family just a few years earlier. She was the executor
of the children's property only until they came of age, so she had to justify
the sale, which she was not technically entitled to make. She proclaimed

specifically that the high price of grain had forced her to sell the property in order to feed herself and her children.[75] In Manresa, one man sold his land "because of the shortage of grain and the pestilence of famine . . . having been in poverty and in order to escape famine and on account of the imminent danger of death."[76] He claimed he had no further goods to sell. Beyond the sale of property, there are numerous reports of large debts.[77] As the man in Manresa noted, he was already in a state of poverty, possibly indebted and already below survival level before the famine hit. But the sale of property did not happen on a wide enough scale to affect the prices of other commodities.

If grain shortage alone could cause a famine, the prices of other commodities might spike without changing the price of grain. In 1373, Sitges suffered a bad grape harvest and the price of wine rose fairly steeply. The castle overseer complained about the high cost and difficulty of shipping wine, but no other ills seem to have arisen from the problem. In 1379, heavy rains damaged the cabbage and spinach around Barcelona, causing prices to spike during Lent.[78] Over the course of the fourteenth century, the most notable jump in meat prices occurred in the late 1350s. Sometimes this price increase is attributed to the demographics of the Black Death, as the labor shortage resulting from diminished rural populations forced an increase in the wages of shepherds and other meat-related workers. But prices did not rise evenly over the decades after the Black Death. The price of lamb in particular rose from 1356 to 1359 and again in 1366 and 1371 (see fig. 12).[79] It is possible that these spikes accompanied increased military demands rather than long-term availability. Whatever the explanation, these fluctuations do not correspond to grain shortages.[80]

Beyond the price of staples, famines are still invariably complex events. Similar climatic conditions could play out very differently depending on political and social situations and particularly on complicating factors like war or disease. Several of the regions that suffered from poor harvests in 1374 also saw military campaigns reduce general security. The city of Florence had to contend with the mercenaries of Pope Gregory XI. When John Hawkwood threatened the city in the spring of 1375, in the midst of the famine, city leaders found it prudent to pay him off in exchange for a promise that he would not attack for three months.[81] Towns in southern Valencia like Elche and Orihuela near the Murcian border spent much of 1374 and early 1375 fearing a renewed invasion from Castile, although an attack never materialized. A decade earlier, in 1365, Castile had laid siege to Valencia for a year, necessitating relief from Barcelonan ships. Just prior to the signing of the 1375 Peace of Almazán, numerous letters from the city of Valencia warned

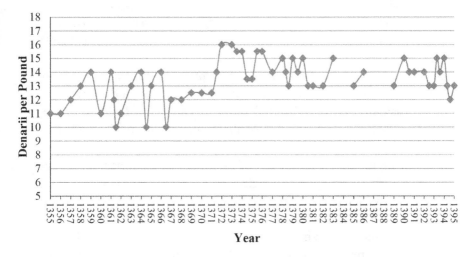

FIG. 12. LAMB PRICES IN BARCELONA, 1355–1395. Long-term lamb prices are taken from the purchases at the Pia Almoina of Barcelona. Purchases of meat were made daily throughout the year, with the exception of Lent. Prices rarely varied, largely because of the ability of the municipal authorities to set meat prices.

its ships and diplomats to tread very lightly when dealing with the Castilians and avoid setting off hostilities. If such an invasion had occurred during a famine year, the results could have been disastrous. Certainly, no relief ships from Barcelona would have been forthcoming.

In Catalonia itself, a claimant to the throne of Mallorca, Jaume IV (d. 1375), invaded from the north with a group of mercenaries. Jaume's father, Jaume III (r. 1315–49), was king of Mallorca but died at the battle of Llucmajor fighting the armies of Pere the Ceremonious (Jaume's cousin and brother-in-law). Pere had deposed Jaume III for failure to recognize his vassalage to Pere himself. Both Pere and Jaume III had legitimate claims through their shared ancestor, Jaume I "the Conqueror" (1208–1276). Jaume IV himself had been imprisoned by Pere in Barcelona. The invasion was an attempt to force Pere to return control of his kingdom. Assisted by the kingdom of Naples, Jaume gathered together an army of French and English mercenaries in the areas around Toulouse and Narbonne.[82] In August, circumventing the city of Perpignan, Jaume entered the province of Roussillon and crossed the Pyrenees. For several months the army moved southward, causing panic and confiscating supplies in undefended areas. Because of stiff resistance, Jaume moved west through the Conflent and split the army in two. One part continued west toward Cardona, taking the town of Els Prats de Rei near Cervera, where Pere the Ceremonious had begun massing his own troops. The larger portion crossed the valley of Osona near Vic and made it all the way to San Cugat del Vallès, virtually on Barcelona's doorstep.[83] Before the imposing walls of San Cugat and because of the imminent winter, Jaume returned up the Llobregat valley toward Urgell and the other half of his army. The invasion ended in failure and Jaume fled almost 400 kilometers west through the heart of Aragon. He eventually took refuge in the Castilian city of Soria before dying of illness in February 1375.[84]

During the short war, the city of Perpignan saw the most intense disruption of its food supply. Through February 1375, Pere the Ceremonious continued directing supply ships toward Perpignan because of the quantities of food stolen by Jaume's army. It is doubtful that Perpignan would have had sufficient food supplies even without the theft, but the war moved the city higher on the royal list of priorities, allowing it to compete with Barcelona and Valencia for supplies and privileges.[85] Pere commanded Catalan citizens in regions from Roussillon to Barcelona to move all available food supplies to fortified areas.[86] Vic's town council found itself stuck when Pere eventually demanded that it move all supplies elsewhere owing to the poor state of the walls around the town. Vic responded with frantic work on the walls and certified inspections. Those hit hardest were doubtless the smaller parishes outside the town walls in the Osona region, who saw their local barons use violence, authorized directly by a representative from the king, to force them to give up their grain for relocation; removal during famine was tantamount to theft, as it was unlikely that they would ever see any of that grain again.[87] Despite the suffering caused by the attack, the poor harvest, combined with the transport of staples to fortified areas, may very well have made matters more difficult for the invaders and might have contributed to the brief duration of the war. Over the summer in Roussillon, raiding kept mercenaries better supplied, but in December near Barcelona, the invasion force began to suffer shortages just like the surrounding population.

After the initial panic of facing an invasion, most lingering difficulties were fiscal. Pere the Ceremonious had experimented with several methods of financing the defense of the kingdom through various wars with Jaume III and Castile. The king often invoked a privilege, called *princeps namque*, in which he could demand a group of soldiers from the cities, towns, and castles of noble lands. After a series of obstacles to gathering such troops in 1368, the king looked for better ways to organize the finances without having to wait for soldiers to gather or for promised payments to materialize. In a meeting of the courts in 1372–73 in Barcelona, the branches agreed to create a fund of 130,000 pounds designated for the kingdom's defense.[88] Several towns and provinces had trouble meeting the new tax demand, however. The list of places that pled financial difficulty corresponds closely to areas with the most intense shortages and those hit hardest by the combined invasion and famine. Several towns in the Camp de Tarragon, including Reus, Valls, and Tarragona itself, sent messengers to the king requesting a reduction in their payments. Tarragona cited both the continuing famine and the military requirement of repairing their walls as causes for their financial difficulty.[89] In January, the king was still attempting to collect money from multiple provinces, including Tarragona, Cervera, Lleida, and others. To cover the costs of the invasion and for future defense, he asked the court for a forced short-term loan totaling 90,000 pounds. By May 1375, the king had still come up short enough on funds that he ordered the collectors from several provinces to be brought to account for the missing money. With the exception of Tortosa, the list of provinces matches almost perfectly those provinces hit hardest by the invasion: Roussillon, Cerdanya, Manresa, Vic, Girona, and Berga.[90] The war may not have brought on the shortage, but the extra costs of defense and the chaos of the invasion made recovery that much more difficult.

The war destroyed crops in Roussillon and forced the consolidation and export of precious grain. The added taxation impoverished the northern Catalan counties. Both results contributed to making the crisis a famine rather than a shortage. Crop failures began in Valencia in April, prior to any action on the part of Jaume IV. The few provinces affected by war were a minority of the number hurt by drought. Osona and Urgell were rich grain-producing regions, but so too were much of Aragon and the *huerta* of Valencia. While wars might complete the destruction of the harvest in some regions, it is just as often the case that famine interferes with the extensive preparations and supplies necessary for war. Until recently, war alone could not destroy as broad a swath of harvest lands as bad weather could.

Famine's connection with plague has deeper roots. Chronicles repeat the phrase "famine and plague" throughout the Middle Ages. King Pere the Ceremonious used this formula in his own chronicle: "in Our kingdoms there was plague and famine."[91] Pere was presumably referring to the return of bubonic plague to Valencia. However, writers referenced the pairing before the Black Death; they do not always mean what we refer to as *the* Plague, that is, the bubonic plague pandemic that ravaged the region starting in the 1340s and '50s. The link appears in descriptions of the Great Famine in northern Europe and in the *mal any primer* in Catalonia in 1333.[92] Often, plague in this sense probably refers to a host of common diseases that attack people's weakened bodies. Typhus fever, actually spread by the common louse, frequently becomes endemic in starving populations. Typhus causes high fever, delirium, possibly gangrene, and a darkening hue in the face for which the Irish called it the "Black Fever" during the potato famine of 1845–52.[93] Edema (fluid retention), also known as dropsy, from lack of protein can cause swollen limbs and eventual kidney failure.[94] While these ailments were probably present in medieval famines, the referent for each chronicle is difficult to know. Historical diagnosis of disease is notoriously unreliable.[95]

Additionally, attempts to connect famines specifically with the Black Death have not proved particularly effective.[96] Even when outbreaks of the Plague overlapped with famines (after the initial bout in 1348), the Black Death usually took its own course. In the Crown of Aragon, the first wave of the Plague did follow a shortage in 1346 and 1347. After the locust infestation of 1358 and the bad harvests of 1360, the next wave of disease struck, starting in the countryside and moving toward the cities. However, the third episode of famine and plague happened in reverse order. Late in 1371 and continuing through 1372, the Plague spread through Catalonia, killing mostly the young. In Tarragona, the archbishop canceled a planned council because of the outbreak of the disease in 1373.[97] For much of the Catalan coast, the Plague had ended prior to the onset of the 1374 famine. This bout of bubonic plague had also reached England by 1375, possibly even brought by ships seeking grain for Barcelona and Valencia. England and much of northern Europe experienced good years and excellent harvests in the 1370s. Although the people were well fed, this did not prevent the disease's return.

But plague and famine could still overlap, with deadly results. In Siena, the Plague appears to have arrived the same winter as the famine.[98] Valencia included the disease in its list of tribulations prompting public processions in October 1374. By early February 1375, the Plague had worsened enough that the city government petitioned for a general indulgence and forgiveness of sins for all citizens dying of disease. On May 11, 1375, at the same meeting where the council discussed the possibility of allowing some barley exports, it allocated 2,000 solidi to aid in burying Plague victims, the "many and diverse poor and miserable persons that have nothing with which they might make a shroud."[99] While the famine did not bring on the Plague, malnutrition and hunger would have increased its death toll.

As with the impact of war, part of the continuing difficulty of the Plague was financial. On December 22, 1374, the council of Valencia tasked Miguel Dapiera and Pere Marrades with assessing why the taxes and fees collected in the fall of 1374 had been so much lower than normal, specifically asking whether the harvest or the Plague was to blame. At their first report on January 15, Pere Marrades himself was ill, and the report was postponed until February. When the men did report, they blamed only deaths from disease for the reduced tax base.[100] Famine and war might not significantly reduce income, but they vastly increased expenses. Plague created fewer costs but reduced the administration's ability to raise funds. In addition to killing many city inhabitants, the Plague tamped down on trade, discouraging outsiders from entering the city and limiting the funds raised through tariffs and fees. Valencia lost income suddenly just a couple of months after expenses had spiked precipitously. In this context, it is unsurprising to see a constant stream of loans in the city's financial records stretching into 1376, long after the end of the crises.

When the book of Revelations describes the Four Horsemen of the Apocalypse, each is given dominion over a fourth of the world to go and destroy. Famine usually failed to reap its share, however, and disease picked up the slack.[101] One of the few actual records of mortality in Catalonia comes from the well-studied Arxiu de Capbreus in Vic.[102] Between 1374 and 1377, Vic recorded around 350 deaths above the normal death rate for the town. Other years of bubonic plague in the same records indicate around a hundred deaths or more per year from the disease alone, meaning that most of the 350 over the three-year period can be accounted as victims of the Plague. The monthly deaths show the clear seasonal pattern found in bubonic plague mortality. The spike in deaths started in September, before the city had run out of grain. By January and February, the worst of the Plague was over and the death rate fell. Again, in September of 1375, the disease returned and deaths rose, falling again by December. The monthly average was generally three or four deaths.[103] Months in 1375 with elevated death rates, particularly March, April, and May, with nine, eight, and eleven, respectively, probably represent a rise in mortality based on hunger. These deaths are around double the normal amount but still pale before Plague deaths. Famine victims in Vic probably numbered almost one hundred for the entire period; disease killed almost as many before the city had even run short of grain. Valencia does not have comparable records, but the dire descriptions of the ravages of the Plague indicate that the situation was undoubtedly similar. Descriptions of mass death appeared and disappeared with the Plague—not the case with famine.

In 1374, famine struck some areas free of war and disease, such as the interior areas of Aragon and the French Pyrenees. The Papal States in central Italy also suffered no military conflict, although the threat of war with

Florence influenced their grain policy. As mentioned above, medieval writers used a variety of words in addition to the term for famine (*fames*): *carestía, fretura*, and *penuria*, all meaning "shortage" or "dearth," and even *inopia annonae* (scarcity of grain).[104] The notary records from Manresa's cathedral repeatedly use the phrase *sterilitas temporis* (sterility of the time) and the pair *fames et paupertas* (hunger and poverty) to describe the harvest failures and their subsequent economic woes as rents plummeted.[105] The overlapping crises of 1374 show how widespread famines develop and how levels of complexity relate directly to levels of suffering.

However, none of the complexities, like geographic breadth, disease, or war, are especially compelling indicators of actual human suffering. Some aspects of the famine even imply that it might not have been so terrifying. Manresan authorities complained that "at present in the said city of Manresa there is a scarcity or lack of grain and in Barcelona it is sufficiently fertile."[106] This statement was made by the councilors of Manresa to a man they sent to Barcelona to purchase wheat; the phrase appears verbatim in two different documents. They surely overstated the case in the hope of garnering extra supplies. But still meat and wine prices in Barcelona stayed relatively stable. In King Pere the Ceremonious's own chronicle, the famine is depicted as little more than a nuisance that forces him to back down from certain political goals. "And We had to accede to the requests the said king [Enrique] of Castile made to Us referring to the marriage of Our daughter," writes Pere. "Although it displeased Us greatly, because this was a time when foreign companies were ready to attack Us from the kingdom of France. Besides, in Our kingdoms there was plague and famine, so We had to accede to the will of the said king."[107] Pere felt forced to accept a disadvantageous treaty because of the mounting costs of the invasion, disease, and famine, but he hardly mentions the crisis beyond this complaint.

Three other narrative descriptions support the connection between complexity and severity. One comes from perhaps the hardest hit area in the Crown of Aragon: Vic. The other two come from locations increasingly at the periphery of the disaster: Teruel, further to the west, and Montpellier, at the northern edge of the crisis. In each case, the overlapping of secondary events shaped the intensity of the famine. In Vic, a townsman named Johan Toralles wrote in his private recollections of the city that in 1374 "in Catalonia there was a great shortage [*gran carestía*] and in Valencia even more." After briefly listing the high prices, he describes how "in many places [people] ate no more than pine nuts, chestnuts, and acorns, and the people went crying through the cities and towns at night: Hunger! And one could have a beautiful woman for a piece of bread. Many people died of hunger and no field or garden remained to harvest nor mill from which to steal . . . and this last continued almost three years."[108] Although he makes no mention of the common trope of cannibalism used in some chronicles, the recourse to consuming undesirable foods is a hallmark of famine conditions. The displaced and the poor felt the worst effects, despite the fact that they were more likely to die from disease than from actual starvation.

The *Crónicas de los Jueces de Teruel* similarly delineates several of the classic markers of shortage: "In this year [1375], in the month of January, it was necessary to write . . . of the cruelty of the strong winter, such that men and livestock, young and old, were lost"; "in this year [it was] so difficult, so dry, so expensive, so bellicose, and ended so badly that many things must be written." The chronicler focuses most intently on the invasion by Jaume and his French mercenaries. He mentions several towns near Teruel ravaged by war—Torriente and Bronchales in particular—stressing the immediate impact of invasion over the longer-term travails of food shortage. Like the narrator from Vic, the Teruel chronicles also compare the situation in that town to that of Valencia: "So terrible was the shortage that bread in all the land cost twelve solidi per *fanega*, and in Valencia twenty-five solidi per *fanega*, and as many as five thousand people were in extreme necessity; and as they went from here to there, the people died in the streets and along the roads."[109] But still this writer ranks Teruel's problems as less severe than those of Valencia, where grain prices are more than twice as high.

Unlike Vic and Teruel, Montpellier escaped the worst of the famine. The city first experienced the Plague that was sweeping the Mediterranean for two straight years. The *Petit Thalamus*, reflecting the official view of the crisis, stated that the Plague arrived during Lent of 1374 but had run its course by Saint John's Day (June 21) of the same year. It returned the following year, killing "many notable and well-known men, both clerics and lay alike." During the spring of 1374, the text describes bad weather that caused harvest failures, overlapping with the arrival of the Plague. "All that year, from Lent to Saint John, there lasted fog and corrupt air; and thus the grain and the vines in the vineyard and the fruit was ruined and much of the wine in the cellars went bitter." Along with the bad weather, Montpellier also suffered from "many armed men who were all around this country in the month of June and ravaged a large portion of the said grains and wines and fruit." Despite the combined hardships of military and natural destruction visited on the harvest, the chronicler makes an unusual distinction between the various terms available to describe famine, writing, "All this year there was a pestilence of mortality and of shortage and *almost* a famine" (emphasis added).[110] Distinctions like this may have become more common in the fourteenth century. In 1347, a Florentine chronicle made a similar distinction: "Not only a shortage, but famine arose in the city [*non solum carestia sed fames insurget in civitate*]."[111] The shortage forced "the town [Montpellier] itself and the surrounding countryside to be reprovisioned from Bourgogne, from Champagne, and from France, where there was a great abundance of grain."[112] Cereals from well-supplied regions to the north kept food prices down and prevented an actual famine. The *Thalamus* notes that this was more effective in the city than in the surrounding countryside, an unsurprising fact given the course of famines in large cities and their surrounding hinterlands.

Famines have their epicenters and their edges. However we look at it, the events of 1374–76 were extensive and harsh. The proliferation of epicenters had a direct negative influence on the depth of the crisis; commercial capacity, especially in well-connected regions like the western Mediterranean, could generally prevent extensive suffering in a smaller number of epicenters. But the mortality and suffering of any famine cannot be easily disentangled from other events of the time. Famine's edges run close alongside those of its fellow disasters, war and disease: the greater the overlap, the greater the suffering. Montpellier stood on both the geographic and the definitional edge of the famine. Shortages, military destruction, and the Plague struck the city, but it escaped largely unscathed from panic and extensive suffering. Teruel suffered famine and death but acknowledged even in its own records that other areas were worse off. Both grain shortage and war influenced food availability in Teruel, but it experienced the Plague earlier in 1373. Similarly, the invasion of Jaume of Mallorca narrowly missed the walls of Teruel itself. Unfortunate Vic, by contrast, felt the brunt of multiple disasters all at once. Ultimately, which segments of the population were hit harder by starvation and which were more devastated by war depended on their station. Some city governments concerned themselves more immediately with protection from the depredations of war than from the ravages of hunger, which afflicted those at the top of society much less than those at the bottom. The king was preoccupied with the threat to his rule and considered the famine a mere annoyance inhibiting his political goals. City officials worked constantly to improve their grain supplies, but as privileged individuals they probably feared the threat of disease more than that of outright starvation. Survival depended as always on individual resources and political associations.

Return to Normal

Drought caused bad harvests in most of Catalonia and Valencia in 1374. The Catalan drought, combined with storms and cold in the mountains of Aragon and parts of southern France, destroyed crops from the Midi to Languedoc. Drought reduced yields in central Italy as well, and too much spring rain ruined both grain and hay harvests. Dry conditions on the islands of Sardinia and Sicily spawned a famine that stretched across most of the northwestern Mediterranean region. European climatic shifts might have made famine more likely, but a single year of geographically extensive bad weather was enough to touch off the crisis. Some inland agricultural areas, buffered by their grain stores, only began suffering in 1375, while large coastal cities began to panic almost immediately. Cities at the edge of the region, especially those with political affiliations beyond the afflicted area, like Montpellier and Murcia, made up their shortfalls relatively easily with imports (in this case, from northern France and Castile, respectively). Making matters worse for several locales, bubonic plague had arrived in Catalonia the year before. In 1374, the disease reached several areas in tandem with the grain crisis. War added to the chaos in the Pyrenees, and Tuscany suffered from pillaging by bands of mercenaries. These complicating factors were not always decisive. Valencia, in the end untouched by battle, experienced a more severe food shortage than some of these northern regions, combined with a serious outbreak of the Plague. Generally, the farther one traveled from the Mediterranean coast, the more the famine dissipated—but this was not true of the Plague. The unlucky city of Vic managed to sit right at the crossroads: the Plague arrived in September 1374 and war in October and November, with food shortage beginning slowly in the fall and peaking the following year.

In the fall of 1375, the barley harvest in Valencia recovered, and a promising harvest in central Italy began easing concerns across the region. By 1376, the extreme weather had ended in most areas. Despite continuing mediocre harvest numbers in Sitges, the overall sale price of wheat dropped across the Crown of Aragon, and very few places still reported shortages or maintained protectionist market measures. The largest cities with extensive import abilities had already begun allowing grain exports by the fall of 1375. By 1377, prices in some major cities had dropped below even their prefamine levels. Economic difficulties and debt persisted throughout the region for years after the crisis, but cries of panic in the records disappeared much faster. In Barcelona, Tarragona, and Valencia, the massive mobilization of resources to feed the people had disappeared from the records by late 1375.

The two hundred poor people still housed in Barcelona's Pia Almoina resumed receiving their normal bread ration. If anything, the continuing high prices regionally boosted the income of the Almoina, feeding the urban poor at the expense of their rural tenants. The economic inequalities that famine brings into stark relief existed before and persisted after the crisis. How many people died from starvation in 1374–76 is difficult to estimate. Records from Vic offer the vague suggestion that around 2 percent of that town's population may have died—largely the poor and the displaced. But many more undoubtedly died of the Plague; measuring the exact overlap of the two causes is almost impossible. The persistent threat of such crises could and did inform future plans, including large irrigation projects, new trade networks, and crop rotations. But the persistent economic inequality of late medieval society gave famine its particular shape and remained unchanged long after the recovery of sufficient grain supplies.

CONCLUSION

The frequency and severity of late medieval famines were influenced by many factors. As complex disasters, famines balanced human resilience and vulnerabilities, successful and unsuccessful responses, and internal and external shocks. The three "limits" surveyed here—agricultural production, market distribution, and social access—gave famines their shape. Increasing agricultural resilience, overlapping networks of trade, and social stratification and rarefaction of charity determined what food got produced, where it traveled, who had the ability to influence its destination, and which individuals could access it. Crop choice, storage capacity, and infrastructure influenced the resilience of producers. Crop systems structured around exports, including wine, could provide greater wealth to landowners and sometimes to individual producers, but they could also erode the buffers against shortages provided by the robust storage of staple grains. Regional and long-distance systems of trade enabled city managers and merchants to respond to and even solve local crises, but at the expense of a greater risk of systemic failure in the case of widespread shortages. Heavy reliance on trade created competition and bottlenecks for needed supplies, often resulting in conflict and violence. Finally, people in the fourteenth century paid significant attention to economic needs at the individual level. The adjustment of wages or increased payments in food provided some protection for workers. Systems of informal debt allowed peasants to pay their rent sometimes years late if a bad harvest made routine collections impossible. However, new scrutiny of the nature of charity and poverty also progressively restricted access to public assistance, as definitions of the deserving and undeserving poor became stricter. As cities gained economic power and the ability to command greater imports, they systematically denied grain access to undesirable outsiders and even some city residents.

Because of the fundamental resilience of agriculture and trade, moderate shortages became less likely to turn into famine over the course of the century. As Antoni Furió has noted, severe famines were rare. Furió observes that chroniclers described only four actual famines in Valencia over two centuries: 1347, 1374, 1435, and 1475.[1] Catalan chroniclers added 1333 to the list.[2] Fourteenth-century famines had to be increasingly complex events in order to genuinely break down society's preparations and responses. While late medieval famines usually involved some form of crop failure, multiple social and natural factors shaped their outcome. Thus food shortages became more serious famines not because of the uniform depth of harvest failures but rather owing to how many concomitant crises overlapped in time and space. The complexity of a famine was a strong proxy for its severity. Regions at the intersection of multiple difficulties—political unrest, military action, poverty and economic inequality, bad weather—suffered the most, as described by chronicles in Teruel and Vic. Conversely, regions at the geographic edges that lacked complicating factors—like Montpellier in 1374—often suffered only mildly. The chronicle of Montpellier described 1374–75 as "almost a famine," a phrase echoed in Valencia in 1384, when the city records speak of "almost extreme necessity." These events fell short of severe starvation.[3] Measured responses to local shortages, including reliance on stored grain, the use of import subsidies, and increased grain handouts, could keep even fairly severe local crop failures in check, as in Valencia in 1371–73. In 1384–85, panic, driven by the memory of the 1374 famine, led to excessive attempts at control and significant overspending. Panic tended to inspire overkill, such as armed patrols and export bans that both worsened problems in the short term and made the distribution of grain supplies even more lopsided, with plentiful supplies for the privileged and insufficient amounts for those who needed it most.

Despite increasingly adept responses to shortage, multiple causes still combined to create major deadly events. The famine of 1374–75 struck a huge geographic area stretching from Valencia to the French Pyrenees and all the way around the western Mediterranean basin to Sicily. Almost every region experienced both destructive weather patterns and complicating factors such as political strife, war, disease, and social breakdown. Indeed, the presence of violence during major shortages is so prevalent in the events surveyed here that it is hard to imagine a severe crisis without the complicating factor of war, just as we see in the twentieth and twenty-first centuries.[4] The regions that experienced the worst of the disaster did not suffer the worst weather but rather the largest number of overlapping causes, often combined with less political clout, making the usual resilience and preparations unequal to the task of responding to the crisis. The consequences of 1374–75 were also determined by personal access. The wealthy could move to new regions with better supplies, sometimes taking their slaves and servants with them. Wealthy employers increased wages for workers, such as the laborers at the king's shipyards, or gave informal credit to peasants, as on the monastery lands of Sant Pere. Those without land or connections found themselves shut out even from begging as cities policed shrinking public and private handouts.

As Dominik Collet and Maximilian Schuh put it, complex disasters are in many ways "a rediscovery of earlier pluralities. Premodern societies understood famines to be caused by a combination of extreme natural events, human neglect, and divine intervention."[5] In their prayers for divine aid, urban councils distinguished between "drought" and "famine" as distinct problems. Even as they worried about bad weather, they also complained constantly about economic access to distant grain markets. Letters from the council of Valencia reflect the clear understanding that bad weather caused shortage, but also the awareness that starvation would follow if Sicilian grain shipments could not pass the ports of Cagliari and Palma de Mallorca. Even the king grudgingly forged a lasting peace to end the War of the Two Peters in 1375 in order to reduce the overlapping crises and make responding to the famine easier. Valencia had already been in covert contact with the king of Castile for supplies, but the official end of the war allowed open exports to flow from Seville, an outcome that everyone involved anticipated. Similarly, informal charity and expanded food handouts tacitly acknowledged that poverty has as important an impact on starvation as a bad harvest does.

Understanding fourteenth-century famines as complex disasters reduces the separation between contemporary and historical events. Most human societies are characterized by complex interactions between agricultural production, trade, labor, poverty, power, and food access, regardless of where the boundary between subsistence production and market consumption may fall. Students of food shortages often debate the relative merits of various economic and social responses. Given the persistence of poverty as a key factor in starvation, even famines that occurred centuries ago highlight how structures of aid can support or undermine local resilience. Malthusian models, by contrast, tend to discourage the provision of aid, on the grounds that if we feed everyone this year, overpopulation will only become worse in the future. Price controls tend to arise when there are strong suspicions of mercantile malfeasance in the service of greed. Modern food aid highlights our continuing reliance on moral assumptions about the personal value of the recipient. Assumptions about laziness often translate into requirements of labor in order to receive certain forms of relief.[6] Aid programs that provide direct resources, including cash, have the potential to create resilience just as effectively as more tightly restricted handouts do.[7] A more complex understanding of famine can help create a more responsive system of aid that can create future resilience rather than perpetuate economic inequality and vulnerability.

In the end, it is worth remembering that while food supply disasters can last for months or years, individual lives are measured in days and weeks. While death may become more likely, and disease more widespread, as food shortages drag on, there are usually signs that normal expectations and obligations persist. I will end with an odd story from February 1375, at the height of the famine. Early in the month, the city of Valencia levied a fine against a Frenchman named Enrich Juboner for serving forbidden food, specifically goat, at his wedding. On February 6, the city revoked the fine, citing Juboner's poverty but also noting that because he was a recent immigrant and did not speak the language, he was ignorant of the law. At the same meeting, the council described the extent of the famine and discussed how shortages in Valencia's usual import territories continued to stymie efforts to lower prices. Because of this problem, they granted the usual blank check to the city jurors, allowing them to sell land, take on loans, and finance imports in any way possible.[8] Among the broad trends of urban market supply, access to rural production, economic disparities, restrictions on the poor, and other, more panicked actions, this story turns on their head many of the patterns we usually see in response to shortage and famine. A poor man was accused of purchasing the wrong kind of food, but for a wedding celebration (an act of particular confidence and faith in the midst of shortage!). He was pardoned because he was both poor and foreign, a very different experience from that of many poor foreigners desperately seeking food at the time.

The council gave no special reason for showing mercy to Juboner, but perhaps the city leaders were feeling lenient that day. In the same record, they declared that the food crisis did "not fall within the power of any individual, but rather of the whole."[9] City residents, especially those "of low condition," lacked the power to secure their grain from distant lands, so the job fell to the city collectively, and especially to members of the council and their representatives. Despite the crisis, the councilors acknowledged their obligation to the whole city, proving that social bonds could hold even in a time of widespread panic. In the midst of economic and social breakdown, individuals still made everyday decisions to get married, have children, throw parties, and uphold their sense of a normal society. Cultural norms excluded many people, but social obligations endured, demonstrating a core resiliency when fending off disaster at both the individual and the larger social level. Even a complex view of famine may resort to simplifications that fail to capture the many small choices individuals make that allow them to survive.

Notes

Introduction

1. Piesse and Thirtle 2009; Kaufman 2011; UN Dept. of Economic and Social Affairs 2011, 61–74.
2. *New York Times* 2008; Sullivan 2008; Jiao 2008; Lakshmi 2008.
3. UN Dept. of Economic and Social Affairs 2011, 61.
4. Labrousse 1944. More recently, Cormac Ó Gráda and Jean-Michel Chevet (2002, 2004) have used this system to argue for a "transitional"-style crisis in the eighteenth and nineteenth centuries that contained elements of premodern and modern crises. See also Benito i Monclús 2013b, 17–20; Dameron 2017, 977–81; Devereux 2007, 3–11.
5. Duby 1968, 122–24; Hatcher and Bailey 2009, 21–28; Brenner 1987, 213–18; Campbell 2016, 61–64.
6. Aston and Philpin 1987.
7. For this narrative in Catalonia, see Vilar 1974; Riera Melis 2011a, 93–94; Savy 2011, 193–94.
8. Campbell 2005, 3–10, and 2016, 61–64, 141–45.
9. Horden and Purcell 2000, 266–68, 273–75; see also Grove and Rackham 2003, 15–16.
10. Jordan 1996, 11–23; Slavin 2019, 11–30.
11. Alfani, Mocarelli, and Strangio 2017, 27–29; Malanima 2012, 96–99; Salrach Marés 2004; Riera Melis 1991. Riera Melis has recently backed away from a Malthusian reading; see Riera Melis 2013b, 36–42.
12. Rubio Vela 1987, 132–36; Laliena Corbera 2011, 292–93; see also Riera i Viader 1989; López Pizcueta 1995; Turull i Rubinat 1986.
13. See the essays in Bourin, Menant, and To Figueras 2014b.
14. Bourin, Drendel, and Menant 2011; see esp. De La Roncière 2011; Drendel 2011b; Furió 2011; see also Benito i Monclús and Riera Melis 2014.
15. Benito i Monclús and Riera Melis 2014; Benito i Monclús, Palermo, and Fara 2018.
16. Slavin 2019, 25–32, 337–55; Curtis 2014, 1–2, 23–38; Benito i Monclús 2013b, 30–32.

17. Collet and Schuh 2018, 9–10; see also Collet 2015.

18. Alfani 2010, 37–40; Campbell 2016, 202–8.

19. Epstein 2000, 49–61; Bernardi 2015, 290–91; Magni 2015, pars. 38–39.

20. Benito i Monclús 2011, 85–86; De La Roncière 2011, 228–32.

21. Hoyle 2010, 974–77; Campbell 2010, 281–83; Ó Gráda 2009, 190–92; see also Franklin-Lyons 2013, 34–36.

22. Ravallion 1996, 7–8; Devereux 2001, 248; Desai 1988, 109–10.

23. Rangasami 1985a, 1749. This idea has been further elaborated by Keen 1994; Edkins 2000, 49–55.

24. Brodman 1998, 28–40, and 2009, 178–86.

25. Rubin 2020, 45–48; Narbona Vizcaíno 2012, 169–73.

26. For the original formulation, see Thompson 1971; for a more recent version, see Sharp 2000.

27. Devereux 2007, 3–11; Ó Gráda 2009, 9–25.

28. For Barcelona, see Càceres Nevot 2006; Serra i Puig 1988. For Valencia, see Rubio Vela 1987 and 1995a; Furió 2011.

29. For Cervera, see Verdés Pijuan 1994; for Tortosa, see Curto i Homedes 1988, 214–15; for Tarragona, see Canyelles Vilar 1996a; see also Martí Arau 2011; Puigferrat i Oliva 2000; Torras i Serra 1994.

30. AHHSCSP, AHPD-LP; ACB-C 13; AMV-LAHC, 349–51; AEV-C, 18–26 and 18–28.

31. Baucells i Reig 1984, 1987, and 1990.

32. López Pizcueta 1998 and 1999.

33. Serrahima i Balius 2012 and 2016; Montoro i Maltas 2019.

34. Echániz i Sans 1988.

35. ACB-PA, B2C, 1343–1683; for a general discussion of the structure of the Pia Almoina record books, see Benito i Monclús 2013a.

36. An article by Pere Ortí i Gost (1992) uses the wheat purchases in the earlier books to chart grain prices during the first half of the fourteenth century.

Several dissertations contain scattered price data from various sources; see Serra i Puig 1967; Gironella i Granés 2013, 981–86; Argilés i Aluja 1993, 230–63.

37. Benito i Monclús 2010; Franklin-Lyons 2013–14.

38. For an overview of weights, measures, and coinage, see Llensa de Gelcen 1951; Spufford 1988; Alsina i Català, Feliu i Montfort, and Marquet i Ferigle 1990.

39. Llensa i de Gelcen 1951, 118–19.

40. Ibid., 100.

Chapter 1

Portions of this chapter appear in slightly different form in Franklin-Lyons 2013–14.

1. For two notable studies on Barcelona, see Bensch 1995; Banegas López 2016.

2. Freedman 2008; Riera Melis 1995–96; Laurioux 2002.

3. Campbell 2016, 145–51.

4. Hoffmann 2014, 341–42, 184–89.

5. Horden and Purcell 2000, 178.

6. Ferrer i Mallol 2001b, 911–17; Barrio Barrio and Cabezuelo Pliego 1999.

7. Rodrigo Estevan 2009, 416–17; Llobet i Portella 1995, 53–58; Banegas López 2016, 65–72.

8. Juncosa Bonet 2016, 97–102; Serra i Puig 1988, 72–75; Ruiz Doménec 1977, 265–76.

9. Serra i Puig 1988, 78–80; Cuvillier 1970, 113–20.

10. Lionello, Malanotte-Rizzoli, and Boscolo 2006, 38–40.

11. Barrio Barrio 2009, 75–86; Cueves Granero 1962, 141–53.

12. Carob beans are also commonly referred to as locust beans and grow particularly well in dry climates. Such foods increased in importance during shortages. AMV-C, J-14, 1374–75, fol. 34r; AMV-MC, A-16, 1371–75, fol. 257r–v; see also Ferrer i Mallol 2001b, 905–10.

13. There are multiple references to these disputes; for a handful of notable instances, see AMV-C, J-12, 1372–73, fols. 39r–v, 46v–47r; AMV-MC, A-16, 1371–75, fol. 81r–v; AMV-CM, g3-3, 1374–75, fols.

8v–9r. See also Banegas López 2016, 92–97.

14. Banegas López 2016, 98–101.
15. Ortega Villoslada 2014, 196–97.
16. Abulafia 2002, 107–10.
17. Ortega Villoslada 2014, 196.
18. Montoro i Maltas 2015, 134–35.
19. Rodrigo Estevan 2009, 415–17.
20. Martín 2004, 73.
21. Comet 1997, 21–24; Fernández Trabal 1995, 162–63.
22. Grove and Rackham 2003, 80.
23. Pliny 1855, 29.
24. Montanari 1994, 85–92; Riera Melis 2011b, 77–85.
25. Riera Melis 1998, 35–38, and 2009, 53–54.
26. Ferrer 1971, 192. The view of barley as fit for animals and its associations with religious asceticism are common tropes in medieval history. See Eiximenis 1977, 46–47; De Voragine 1993, 1:129–30; Martí 1995, 909–13; Renedo i Puig 1995, 922–25.
27. Garcia-Oliver 2004, 305–6.
28. De La Roncière 1982, 821–26; Cáceres Nevot 2006, 40–42.
29. Montoro i Maltas 2015, 137.
30. For the complete set of grain sale prices, see http://www.adamfranklinlyons.com/books/shortageandfamine.
31. Riera Melis 2011b, 83–85, and 2017, 21–30.
32. Le Roy Ladurie 1974, 45.
33. This was not true in England, where the wet climate and colder winters favored oats over barley. See Campbell 2000, 222–23; Reynolds 1997.
34. Rubio Vela 1995a, 170–71.
35. Bertran i Roigé 1979; Camps Clemente and Camps Surroca 1995, 887–88.
36. Lluch Bramon 1996, 570; Lluch Bramon 2006.
37. AEV-C, 14–26, 1352–58, unfoliated; see also Serra i Clota 1996, 530–31.
38. Cueves Granero 1962, 142–45; Curto i Homedes 1988, 35–36, 233–36; Serra i Puig 1967, 34–37.
39. ACB-PA, B3-H, 1382–83, fols. 6r–7r.
40. ACB-PA, B2C, 1351–52, fol. 175r.

41. ACB-PA, B3-H, 1382–83, fols. 6v–7r.
42. ACB-PA, B2C, 1373–74, fol. 73r.
43. ACB-PA, B3-H, 1377, fol. 52. All translations are my own unless otherwise noted.
44. The record states that it was mixed at a 3:2 ratio, wheat to millet. ACB-PA, B3-H, 1377, fol. 53.
45. Ibid., fol. 53, and 1382–83, fol. 5v.
46. Epstein and Galassi 1994; Herlihy and Klapisch-Zuber 1985; Emigh 2005 and 2009.
47. Freedman 1991, 31–32, and 2013, 33–43.
48. Freedman 1991, 166–78; Fernández Trabal and Riera Melis 2004, 139–42.
49. Lluch Bramon 2009, 79–86; Fernández Trabal 1995, 205–11.
50. Freedman 1991, 145–49; Salrach Marés 2001, 96–98; Benito i Monclús 2003, 615–23.
51. Fernández Trabal 1995, 218–23.
52. García Pardo 1989, 50–52; Benito i Monclús 2003, 268–71, 675–77; López Pizcueta 1998, 236–56, and 1999, 157–65.
53. Stalls 1995, 167–78; Barton 2019, 136–40, 148–58; see also Guinot and Torró Abad 2011.
54. Ferrer i Mallol 2001c; Barrio Barrio 2007; Diz Ardid and Sánchez Mateos 2011.
55. Barrio Barrio 1990, 422–26; Soler Millá 2005, 1061–66; Hinojosa Montalvo 1986, 155–57.
56. Fernández Trabal 1995, 161–67.
57. Ferrer i Mallol 2001b, 900–903; Rafat i Segla 1994, 9–11.
58. Bensch 1995, 85–96.
59. Aparisi Romero 2013, 166.
60. Rodrigo Estevan 2013, 145–47.
61. AMSPP-LA 16, 1382, fol. 50r.
62. Barrio Barrio 1990, 420–25.
63. Garcia-Oliver 2004, 317–18.
64. Verdés Pijuan 1994, 56; Turull i Rubinat 1992, 81–86; Milton 2012, 102–3.
65. ASM-P, *manuale* 9, 1373–80, fols. 98r–v, 113r, 127r–128v, 132r–133v; Carrère 1967, 376–78; Torras i Serra 1994, 128–30.
66. Hatcher and Bailey 2009, 21–38.
67. Titow 1972, 30–31.
68. Campbell 2016, 182–98.

69. Slicher van Bath 1966, 89–97; Le Roy Ladurie 1974, 11–19, 289; Duby 1968, 298–311.

70. Georges Duby (1968, 101–3) does note the exceptional fertility of the Artois in France, driven in part by Parisian consumption, which approached yields of 15:1.

71. Demade 2007, 222–24; Scott 2002, 84–85.

72. Duby 1968, 100. Bruce Campbell (2007) tends to peg the average rates for these centuries at around 4:1, with barley faring only slightly better.

73. Furió 2004, 342–43.

74. Duby 1968, 102–3. Guy Fourquin (1964, 117) describes fourteenth-century ratios as the technological maximum available for the next few centuries.

75. For a survey, see Schneider 2011, 25–28.

76. Newfield 2009; Jordan 1996, 35–39; Slavin 2008.

77. Fernández Trabal 1995, 162–64. Similarly, at the Sitges castle near Barcelona, workers who mucked out the animal stalls carried the manure out to the fields. ACB-PA, B3-C4, box 1, 1359, fol. 26r.

78. AMSPP-LA 1, 1356, August payments (unfoliated).

79. ACB-C 13, Hospital Desvilar 1393, fols. 38v–39r. The somada is an old measurement from the Cerdanya originally used for wine, estimated at around 125 kilograms and meant to be as much as one beast could carry; see Bisson 1984, 303–5.

80. ACB-C 13, Hospital d'en Colom, 1375, fol. 43v.

81. Agronomy manuals produced in the Muslim south considered proper manure and the health of the soil the most important aspect of good farming. Some of this knowledge came from Roman writers such as Columella and Palladius; the latter's manual was translated into Catalan in the fourteenth century. However, it is difficult to know what knowledge was available to even the educated overseers in the hospitals

of Barcelona. García Sánchez 1992, 987–99; Capuano 2006.

82. Capuano 2014, 35–41.

83. Gerez Alum 2010–11, 226–27; Bernat i Roca 1998, 97–98.

84. AMV-MC, A-2, fol. 12r; AMV-MC, A-20, 1392–96, fols. 96v–97r; AMV-MC, A-21, 1396–99, fol. 164r; see also Agresta 2020, 379–80.

85. Schneider 2011, 25–28.

86. Many works debate the relative influence on irrigation of Christian, Roman, and Islamic practices; see Glick 1970; Torró Abad and Guinot Rodríguez 2012; Monjo 2012; Guinot Rodríguez 2005; Hinojosa Montalvo 2006; Torró Abad 2013.

87. AMV-MC, A-16, 1371–75, fols. 62v–63r, 81r.

88. Glick tells part of this story, describing attempts to add to the huerta's water supply, efforts that continued into the sixteenth century. Glick 1970, 106–17; see also Martínez Ortiz 1980.

89. AMV-MC, A-17, 1376–78, fols. 38v–39r.

90. Glick 1970, 110–11.

91. AMV-MC, A-17, 1376–78, fol. 38v.

92. Fynn-Paul 2016, 44, 291–93.

93. Monjo 2012; Benito Luna and Monter Domec 1986.

94. Gironella i Granés 2010, 75–104; Fernández Trabal 1995, 164–65; Turull i Rubinat 1992, 68–69; Furió 2004, 347–50.

95. García Marsilla 1993, 41.

96. Glick 1970, 99–100.

97. AMSPP-LA 29, 1397, fol. 49v.

98. Montoro i Maltas 2015, 140–41.

99. Ibn al-'Awāmm 1802, 678–79.

100. Similar structures existed throughout the Atlas Mountains; see Humbert and Fikri 1999; Ruas 2002, 166–71.

101. Bolens 1981, 34–37, and 1979, 107.

102. Fernández Ugalde, Serrano, and Peña-Chocarro 1997; Fernández Ugalde 1997.

103. Cifuentes i Comamala 2013–14.

104. Silo generally appears in Catalan as sitge or sige; see Ibn al-'Awāmm 1802, 680; Ibn Wāfid 2001, 32–34.

105. Martínez Araque 2010, 205–6.

106. More and more of these pits are being unearthed in Christian areas; see Bolens 1979, 106–7; Reynolds 1979, 70–72; Fernández Ugalde, Serrano, and Peña-Chocarro 1997.

107. Curto i Homedes 1988, 53–56; Serra i Puig 1988, 85–86.

108. ACB-PA, B2C, 1343–44, fol. 35r.

109. ASM-AV, *procès* 1383, transcribed in Franklin-Lyons 2018, 296–303; see also Fynn-Paul 2016, 154–55.

110. Puig 2011, 172–73; Montoro i Maltas 2015, 139–41.

111. ASM-AV, *procès* 1383, fol. 8r.

112. Ibid., fol. 6r.

113. Ibid.

114. Puig 2011, 168–74; Cubero i Corpas et al. 2008.

115. ACB-PA, B3-C4, box 2, 1365, fol. 18v, and box 4, 1377, *capbreus extraordinaries*.

116. Franklin-Lyons 2018, 291–92; Miret i Mestre 2005; Codina i Vilà 1995, 36–37.

117. ACB-PA, B3-H, 1377, fol. 73.

118. López Pizcueta 1998, appendix 2, 501; Benito i Monclús 2003, 401–5; Muntaner i Alsina 2013, 90–91; Garcia-Oliver 2004, 305–6.

119. Archives Municipales de Perpignan, AA 5, book 1, fol. 236r.

120. It is unclear why they seem to stop so abruptly in 1411; the small books are often unfoliated and are referred to by their administrative year. ACB-PA, B3-C4, boxes 1–6.

121. AMSPP-LA 1–55.

122. For the complete sowing and harvest records, see http://www.adamfranklin lyons.com/books/shortageandfamine.

123. Càceres Nevot 2006, 161–72.

124. ACB-PA, B3-C4, box 5, 1397, fol. 1v.

125. This ratio is uncertain; one note in the records mentions 2.5 quarters sown, while another notes two quarters purchased for sowing—and four *quartans* (a *quartan* is one-twelfth of a quarter) of that were fed to the chickens. Fifteen quarters were harvested the following year. Assuming that the hospital used half a quarter to supplement the purchased two and then fed some to the chickens, this means that around 2.15 quarters were sown to 15 harvested, or a ratio of roughly 7:1. See ACB-C 13, Hospital dels Malalts, 1379, fol. 29r.

126. Ibid., 1383, fol. 91v.

127. Epstein 2003, 163.

128. These yield numbers accord with comments by Roman writers who tended to assume a normal harvest of somewhere between 8:1 and 10:1 and saw a 15:1 ratio as an exceptional harvest. See Erdkamp 2005, 34–41.

129. Benito i Monclús 2010, 13–18.

130. Stone 2005.

131. Other studies of Catalan agriculture note the importance of both winter and summer cereals. In Pia Almoina documents, winter cereals predominate in the rents from Sitges, Santa Coloma, and Grevalosa. See Ocaña i Subirana 1998, 57–62; Fernández Trabal 1995, 161–64; Furió 2004, 335–38.

132. Surprisingly, these wages changed little over the fifty years covered by these records. Day laborers still received only 2 solidi in 1406 and reached a peak in 1408 of only 2 solidi and 2 denarii.

133. Both the Pia Almoina and the monastery kept a few slaves, although the Pia Almoina slaves worked at the house in Barcelona and rarely did agricultural work. AMSPP-LA 10, 1373, fol. 67r; for one Christmas example, see AMSPP-LA 13, 1377, fol. 58r.

134. AMSPP-LA 7, 1369, fols. 54v–55r; AMSPP-LA 8, 1370, fol. 64r–v; AMSPP-LA 14, 1378, fol. 53r.

135. Benito i Monclús 2010, 22–23.

136. During the harvest of 1377, the overseer in Mogoda hired thirty-two people for the week of the harvest. ACB-PA, B3-H, 1382–83, fols. 37r–39v.

137. For particularly abundant years that required a lot of extra labor, see AMSPP-LA 7, 1369, fol. 48r–v; AMSPP-LA 8, 1370, fol. 64r; AMSPP-LA 45, 1407, fol. 73r–v; see also Richou i Llimona 2015, 19–20.

138. Multiple records mention the spreading of manure (*estampar fems*), generally prior

to planting. ACB-PA, B3-C4, box 6, 1406, November; see also AMSPP-LA 13, 1377, fol. 65r; AMSPP-LA 45, 1407–8, fol. 57v.

139. ACB-PA, B3-C4, box 4, 1377.

140. Ibid., box 2, 1362, fol. 22v.

141. Ibid., box 5, 1400, December.

142. ACB-C 13, Hospital dels Malalts, 1382, fol. 132v.

143. ACB-PA, B3-C4, box 1, 1356, fol. 13r.

144. The records mention garlic, cabbage, chickpeas, and even peach trees and saffron.

145. Stone 2005, 51–58.

146. ACB-C 13, Hospital dels Malalts, 1382, fol. 132v, and 1383, fol. 91v.

147. Ibid., 1383–85, fols. 27v, 94v–95r.

148. Thornton 1991, 188–92.

149. For labor productivity in England, see Apostolides et al. 2008, 25–30.

150. Richou i Llimona 2015, 12–14.

151. Benito i Monclús 2010, 32–36.

152. Unfortunately, the documentation for Mogoda is nowhere near as complete as that for Sitges, making similar studies impossible; see ACB-PA, B3-H, 1377, fol. 51r; ACB-PA, B3, D: Vilafranca de Penedès; 3. Llevadors de Comptes; 1330–1569 (large box II), 1386.

153. Schneider 2011, 29–31.

154. Campbell 2000, 284–92; Campbell 2016, 119–21.

155. Campbell 1995, 92.

156. Hatcher and Bailey 2009, 126–27.

157. Ibid., 23–25. For a survey of literature on England, see Kitsikopoulos 2012.

158. Guilleré 2001a and 2001b; Soldevila i Temporal 2004, 32–38.

Chapter 2

1. For a few examples, especially on the grain trade, see Riera Melis 2017; Iradiel 2017; Sesma Muñoz 2010. For works dealing with famine and the economy, see Benito i Monclús, Palermo, and Fara 2018.

2. AMV-CM, g3-3, 1374–75, fol. 32v.

3. Rubio Vela 2001.

4. Epstein 2000, 49–60.

5. Bourin et al., 2011, 673–74.

6. Spufford 2002; Wolff 1959.

7. Maubert and Vernet 1974, 14–15.

8. For a review of the many problems with these sources, see Feliu i Montfort 2010, 33–35; Sesma Muñoz, Laliena Corbera, and Abella Samitier 2004.

9. Feliu i Montfort 2010, 39–41. The routine death records available in Vic provide a notable exception; see Bautier 1990.

10. Guinot Rodríguez 2003, 28–31.

11. Verdon 2015, 330–35.

12. Barton 2019, 95–98.

13. Ortega Ortega 2009; Barton 2019, 255–57, 290–91.

14. Sesma Muñoz 2003; Ruiz de la Peña Solar 2003; Rubio Vela 1995b.

15. Epstein 2000, 98–101.

16. Feliu i Montfort 2010, 43–44; Santamaría Arández 1992, 379–85; Cruselles Gómez 1999, 59–63.

17. Sesma Muñoz 2004, 388–92; Fernández Trabal 1995, 156–61.

18. Feliu i Montfort 2010, 44–46; Santamaría Arández 1981–84, 171–72.

19. Furió 2010, 418–23.

20. Dyer 2015, 36–40; Bourin et al. 2011, 674–78.

21. Bailey 1989a, 2–7, and 1989b, 191–99, 319–22. See also Bernardi 2015, 290–91.

22. Kathryn Reyerson (1998, 259–60) notes that land within twenty kilometers of Montpellier accounted for 90 percent of all urban land investments.

23. Constans Serrats 1985–93, 3:621.

24. Bertran i Roigé 2013, 134–35.

25. Bourin et al. 2011, 685–90.

26. Eric Thoen and Tim Soens (2015, 215–16) refer to subsistence farming as a "commercial survival economy" and describe the greater integration of exchange as creating a "commercial business economy."

27. Benito i Monclús 2018, 49–51.

28. Furió 2011, 377–84.

29. Eiximenis 2009, 79. See also Reixach Sala 2018, 352; Narbona Vizcaíno 1990, 20–21.

30. Ortí i Gost 2000, 39–44; Reixach Sala 2018, 366–68.

31. Fernández Trabal 1999, 334–35.

32. Narbona Vizcaíno 1990, 24–26; Santamaría Arández 2000, 43–57.
33. Reyerson 1985, 55–58.
34. Cuvillier 1970, 114–20; Rubio Vela 2009, 320–24.
35. Rodrigo Estevan 2009, 414–15.
36. Vicente Navarro 2012, 290–92; Ortega Ortega 2009, 300–304.
37. Ferrer i Mallol 2001b, 894–89.
38. Mott 2012, 184.
39. Tangheroni 1981, 57–60.
40. Zulaica Palacios 1997, 68–72; Curto i Homedes 1988, 39–43.
41. Scott 2012, 71–84.
42. For a survey of grain commerce, see Riera Melis 2017, 89–94, 265–71.
43. Càceres Nevot 2006, 49–51.
44. Soldevila i Temporal 2003, 98–99; Maubert 1980, 127–30; Ferrer i Mallol 2012, 31–33.
45. Curto i Homedes 1988, 39–40; Del Treppo 1976, 308–10; Sarasa Sánchez 1995, 194–95.
46. Furió 2011, 374–78; Rubio Vela 2001, 34–38.
47. Cruselles Gómez 1995, 64–66.
48. Soler Millá 2005, 1064–67, and 2003–4, 142–44.
49. For a few examples, see AMV-CM, g3-1, 1334–37, fols. 4r–v, 26v–27r, and g3-3, 1374–75, fols. 6r–v, 7–8r, 48v, 152v–153r, 165r.
50. Day 2002, 102–7; Murphy 1998, 117–22; Spufford 2002, 104–6; Zorzi 1994, 280–85.
51. Pinto 1985, 632–35.
52. As with trade, there is a large bibliography on legal controls; see Riera Melis 2018, 245–49; Càceres Nevot 2006, 185–91; Dameron 2017, 989–1000.
53. Rubio Vela 2001, 57–59. Italy underwent a similar transformation, although somewhat earlier; see Dameron 2017, 1018–19.
54. Rangasami 1985a, 1748; Edkins 2000, 49–50.
55. Palermo 2013, 59–64.
56. Kelleher 2013; Riera Melis 2017, 198–205.
57. Bajet i Royo 1993, 59; Sevillano Colom 1957, 63–65.
58. One of the stranger regulations specifically banned the sale of chickens in the olive oil market of Barcelona; see Banegas López 2016, 119–34.
59. Jordan 1996, 162–66.
60. AHCB-1B, I-24, 1373–76, fol. 39v.
61. The name of the subsidy is confusing because in Barcelona *ajuda* sometimes referred to a tax levied on the sale of grain, while Valencia and Tortosa both used *ajuda* to refer to the subsidy. Càceres Nevot 2006, 313–15; Curto i Homedes 1988, 79–84.
62. Canyelles Vilar 1996a, 266.
63. Serra i Puig 1967, 25–29.
64. Bruniquer 1912–16, 5:160; Serra i Puig 1967, 72.
65. Tutusaus i Canals 1986, 107.
66. Canyelles Vilar 1996a, 266.
67. *Actes municipals Tarragona* 1984, 61.
68. Curto i Homedes 1988, 70–71.
69. For a few examples, see AMV-C, J-12, 1372–73, fols. 6r–v, 25r–v, 31v.
70. *Actes municipals Tarragona* 1985, 91, 95–97.
71. ACA-RC, Pedro III, *comune* 191, *registro* 774, fols. 47v–48r; see also Tutusaus i Canals 1986, 68.
72. Canyelles Vilar 1996a, 267.
73. Tutusaus i Canals 1986, 98–99.
74. Kelleher 2016, 11–14; see also Mutgé i Vives 2004, 240–42.
75. Larenaudie 1952, 34.
76. Benito i Monclús 2018, 70–71; Tutusaus i Canals 1986, 85.
77. Benito i Monclús 2018, 51–52; Riera Melis 2011a, 141–43.
78. Riera Melis 2018, 259–61.
79. AMV-C, J-13, 1373–74, fol. 31r; AMV-C, J-14, 1374–75, fols. 18r, 20r, 25v; AMV-C, J-19, 1383–84, fol. 29r. Italian cities started using spies and secret guards in the late thirteenth century; see Magni 2015; Dameron 2017, 1000–1001.
80. *Actes municipals Tarragona* 1985, 22, 32, 54; Arxiu Municipal de Vila-Real, Clavaria, 0211, 1372–73, fol. 22v, and 0213, 1374–75, fols. 15r, 26r, and 28v.

81. ACA-RC, Pedro III, *diversorum* 9, *registro* 987, fol. 27r, transcribed in Benito i Monclús 2018, 78.
82. Rubio Vela 2001, 57–59.
83. "No per necessitat, mas per maestria e.n dan de la ciutat." AMV-CM, g3-4, 1378–81, fols. 173v–174r.
84. "Per ser la clau y principal graner de tots los grans qui devallen per Ebro." Bruniquer 1912–16, 3:101.
85. Blanch i Amorós 1991, 26–31; see also Càceres Nevot 2006, 303–8.
86. Blanch i Amorós 1991, 28.
87. AHCB-1B, I-2, 1310–13, fol. 19v–r (bis).
88. Mutgé i Vives 1987, 47–50; Rubio Vela 1982a, 482–86.
89. AMV-MC, A-16, 1371–75, fol. 115v; Baucells i Reig 1974, 110; Bertran i Roigé 1979, 106; Brodman 1998, 22–23; Guilleré 1982, 331. For other poorhouse diets, see Batlle i Gallart 1987, 51–57; Molénat 1984, 316.
90. Guilleré 2009, 130–31.
91. Echániz i Sans 1988, 178–79; López Pizcueta 1998, 27–32.
92. Stouff 1970, 220–30.
93. We learn from the same records that a mule ate through a quarter of grain in fifty days, meaning that mules required only around seven quarters per year. Presumably, their diet was supplemented with hay or forage.
94. ACB-PA, B3-C4, box 2, 1362, fol. 27r–v.
95. Soldevila i Temporal 2004, 58–59; see also Riera Melis 2017, 348–49.
96. Lewis 1975, 21–25; Unger 1980, 181–87.
97. Subsidy payments for large quantities of grain appear in multiple years; for some examples, see AMV-C, J-8, 1368–69, fols. 3v, 9v, 20r; AMV-C, J-12, 1372–73, fols. 14r, 16r; AMV-C, J-13, 1373–74, fols. 2v, 4r.
98. Sevillano Colom 1957, 64–65.
99. Russell 1962, 483–90; García Marsilla 2002, 30–31.
100. Feliu i Montfort 1969.
101. Càceres Nevot 2006, 168–70.
102. Ibid., 316–17.
103. Eiximenis 2009, 234.
104. AMV-MC, A-16, 1371–75, fol. 57v.
105. Ibid., fol. 70r.
106. Banegas López 2016, 42–44.
107. Benito i Monclús 2003, 158–62; Bensch 1995, 85–96.
108. Fernández Trabal 1995, 167–79.
109. Michaud 1998, 279–80.
110. Palermo 1997, 247–48.
111. *Actes municipals Tarragona* 1985, 53; Domingo Rúbies 1997, 82–84; Cuellas Campodarbe and Domingo Rúbies 2015, 107; Iranzo Muñío 2009; Laliena Corbera 2010, 83–84.
112. AMV-MC, A-16, 1371–75, fol. 97r–v.
113. Canyelles Vilar 1996a, 266–67, 270–71.
114. *Actes municipals Tarragona* 1986, 67–68, 161–62, 170, 174, 155.
115. Eiximenis 2009, 230–31.
116. Cruselles Gómez, Cruselles Gómez, and Narbona 1996, 314–17.
117. Epstein 2000, 52–58.
118. Dijkman 2011, 293–99; Dyer 2006, 210–14; Ó Gráda 2015, 120–29.
119. Stouff 1970, 80; Tutusaus i Canals 1986, 63–65; Wolff 1959, 149–51.
120. Càceres Nevot 2006, 152–53; Del Treppo 1976, 279.
121. Tutusaus i Canals 1986, 102–4.
122. AMV-C, J-20, 1384–85, fols. 43r, 44v–45r.
123. AMV-MC, A-16, 1371–75, fol. 12r; AMV-C, J-11, 1371–72, fols. 9r, 32r–33r, 36v–37r.
124. AMV-C, J-12, 1372–73, fol. 6r–v.
125. Ibid., fol. 31v.
126. Ibid., fol. 48v.
127. Ibid., fol. 49r.
128. Abulafia 2002, 105–8.
129. Reyerson 1998, 268–69.
130. Riera Melis 2018, 245–49; Oliva Herrer 2018, 137–39; Barrio Barrio 2009, 75–83; Slavin 2014, 43–48.
131. Eiximenis 2009, 233.
132. Jordan 1996, 136–37.
133. *Actes municipals Tarragona* 1984, 61–62; Riera Melis 2018, 257–59; Curto i Homedes 1988, 70–71.
134. *Aureum opus regalium privilegiorum*, fols. 93r, 95r–v, 120v–121r, 154v–155r.
135. AMV-MC, A-18, 1383–88, fol. 86v.
136. Ibid., fol. 47r–v.

137. AHPB, Antoni Bellver, Llibre Comú, August 22, 1374, and January 28, 1376, fols. 43v–44r, cited as an example of speculating in Richou i Llimona 2013, 132.
138. Richou i Llimona 2013, 151–56.
139. Mummey 2013, 255–57.
140. Smith 1994, 521–22.
141. AMV-CM, g3-3, 1374–75, fol. 11–v.
142. Glénisson 1951, 313–14.
143. Canyelles Vilar 1996a, 268–70.
144. AHCB-1B, I-24, 1373–76, fols. 40r–41v, transcribed in Tutusaus i Canals 1986, doc. 1.
145. Curto i Homedes 1988, 214–15; Soldevila i Temporal 2007, 222–24; Martí Arau 2011, 271–72.
146. ACA-RC, Pedro III, *comune locumtenencie infantis Joannis 23, registro* 1626, fol. 64r–v.
147. Tutusaus i Canals 1986, 68–70.
148. ACA-RC, Pedro III, *sigilli secreti 108, registro* 1240, fol. 119r.
149. ACA-RC, Pedro III, *graciarum 52, registro* 926, fol. 122r–v, transcribed in Tutusaus i Canals 1986, doc. 11.
150. ACA-RC, Pedro III, *diversorum 9, registro* 987, fol. 27r, transcribed in Benito i Monclús 2018, 78.
151. Benito i Monclús 2018, 71–72.
152. Slavin 2019, 169–72, 186–91.
153. Magni 2015, pars. 38–39.
154. Epstein 2000, 8.
155. *Actes municipals Tarragona* 1984, 62; Canyelles Vilar 1996a, 264–65.
156. AMV-CM, g3-3, 1374–75, fols. 7r–v, 161v.
157. Ibid., fol. 86r–v; AMV-C, J-20, 1384–85, fol. 47r.
158. Magni 2015, pars. 3–4.
159. Keys, Brožek, and Henschel 1950, 2:1057–68; Palesty and Dudrick 2006.
160. Ortí i Gost 2007; Abella Samitier 2009; articles in Sánchez Martínez 2009; Tutusaus i Canals 1986, docs. 27–31 and 35–36.
161. Del Pozo Chacón 1996, 219–20.
162. García Marsilla 2002, 39–42.
163. Thoen and Soens 2015, 215–16.
164. Riera Melis 2011a, 103–4, 110–11.
165. Benito i Monclús 2003–4 and 2007.

Chapter 3

1. Furió, Mira, and Viciano Navarro 1994, 85–90.
2. Vinyoles i Vidal 1985, 184–87.
3. AMV-LAHC, *signum* 351, 1375, fol. 3r–v; Argilés i Aluja 1993, 20–21.
4. Doñate Sebastiá 1964, 423–24.
5. Ibid., 435.
6. Quoted in Vinyoles i Vidal 1985, 185–86.
7. AHCB, Miscel·lània 14, December 13, 1414.
8. Vinyoles i Vidal and González i Beltinski 1981, 223–30; Vinyoles i Vidal 2013, 230–36; Brodman 2006, 28–30; Rubio Vela 1982b, 172–73; Otis 1986, 83.
9. Brodman 1998, 117–18.
10. López Beltrán 2010, 49–52.
11. Michaud 2015, 307–8.
12. For a comprehensive look at this dynamic in Marseille, see Michaud 2016, 173–202.
13. Narbona Vizcaíno 2012, 222 (doc. 21), 223 (doc. 22), 226 (doc. 25).
14. AHCB-1B, I-18, 1350–51, fols. 16v–17r.
15. Salicrú i Lluch 2000, 112–30.
16. Bernardi 2015, 282–83; Michaud 2015, 311; De La Roncière 1982, 367–70; Britnell 2009, 20–25.
17. ACB-C 13, Hospital dels Malalts, 1382, fol. 132v; ACB-PA, B3-H, 1382–83, fols. 37r–39v; AMSPP-LA 29, 1397, fol. 49v.
18. Cortina 1970.
19. Arxiu Capitular de València, Pia Almoina accounts, file 5648, vol. 2, 1351, fol. 34r.
20. Benito i Monclús 2003, 385–96.
21. ACB-PA, B3-C4, box 1, 1354, fols. 22r, 30r–v; box 1, 1355, fol. 24r; box 1, 1356, fols. 15r–20r. See also AMSPP-LA 5, 1366, fol. 28v; AMSPP-LA 36, 1402, fol. 24v.
22. ACB-PA, B3-C4, box 1, 1354, fol. 29r–v.
23. Vinyoles i Vidal 1985, 157.
24. ACB-PA, B3-H, 1382–83, fols. 23v–26r; ACB-PA, B3-C4, box 1, 1357, fols. 24v, 28v, and box 4, 1377 and 1378 (unnumbered MSS); AMSPP-LA 6, 1368, fol. 68r; AMSPP-LA 19, 1387, fol. 41r–v.

25. Bourin 2015, 262–63.

26. Michaud 2015, 299.

27. AHPB, Tomàs de Bellmunt (November 12–December 28, 1399), fol. 35r.

28. The Pia Almoina also paid the occasional larger expense, as when a house slave named Ihoan lost an eye and the Almoina paid a barber named Nicolau to come and care for him. ACB-PA, B2C, 1375–76, fol. 115v.

29. AMSPP-LA 9, 1372, fol. 30r; AMSPP-LA 21, 1390, fol. 24v.

30. Batlle i Gallart 2000, 270–72; Soldevila i Temporal 2000, 362–64.

31. Mummey 2013, 112–13, 252–53.

32. Mummey 2014, 128–29.

33. Alfani 2015, 1058–60.

34. Farmer 2002, 125–30, 150–54; Metzler 2013, 154–57.

35. For Barcelona, see Baucells i Reig 1974 and 1980. For Girona, see Guilleré 1982. For la Seu d'Urgell, see Batlle i Gallart 1985. For Tarragona, see Canyelles Vilar 1996b. For Lleida, see Bertran i Roigé 1979.

36. Baucells i Reig 1980, 20–28; Brodman 1998, 28–40.

37. Scholars have argued over the degree to which late medieval charity was secular or religious. Augustín Rubio Vela takes the secularist view, while Brodman argues convincingly for the growing integration of the secular and sacred worlds. Rubio Vela 1984, 33–43; Brodman 1998, 125–34, and 2009, 178–86.

38. AHPB, 29/14 Llibre comú, June 6–December 5, 1375, fols. 39r–40r. For wills written on account of the famine of 1333 and the Black Death, see Batlle i Gallart 1987.

39. Günzberg i Moll 1989 and 2010, 65–73.

40. Eiximenis 2009, 229, 181. Modern English versions highlight the dangers of wealth rather than its opportunity; the Latin Vulgate's term *redemptio* is ambivalent, meaning both redemption and ransom: "redemptio animae viri divitiae suae."

41. Villagrasa Elías 2016, 44–45.

42. Brodman 2009, 245–52.

43. Huguccio, a commentator on Gratian, makes this distinction between voluntary and involuntary (condemning the latter) most clearly; see Tierney 1959, 7–12.

44. Batlle i Gallart and Casas i Nadal 1980; Brodman 1998, 20–21.

45. Narbona Vizcaíno 2012, 199 (doc. 2).

46. Ibid., 169–74.

47. AHCB-1B, I-22, 1365–66, fol. 12v.

48. Narbona Vizcaíno 2012, 226 (doc. 25).

49. AHCB-1B, IV-3, fols. 105r–106r.

50. Eiximenis 2009, 187.

51. AMV-MC, A-17, 1375–83, fol. 8v; AMV-MC, A-18, 1383–88, fol. 63v.

52. Vinyoles i Vidal 1985, 118–19.

53. Constans Serrats 1985–93, 3:311–13 (doc. 847).

54. ACB-PA, B2C, 1368–69, fol. 145r; Santamaría Arández 1983, 386–87.

55. Iranzo Muñío 1997, 106.

56. Villagrasa Elías 2016, 48.

57. AHHSCSP, AHPD-LP 1.1, doc. 1, fol. 3r–v, and doc. 3, fol. 5r. See also Brodman 2009, 146–47.

58. Edkins 2000, 39–40, 68–75. See also De Waal 2005, 141–52.

59. Guglielmi 1998, 47–57.

60. The United Nations (2015, 14–23) classifies people suffering "extreme poverty" as those living on less than $1.25 per day.

61. Brodman 1998, 8.

62. Philip Gavitt (1990, 209) notes that the less impoverished poor sometimes suffered more than the truly destitute because their station made it impossible to resort to begging.

63. *Actes municipals Tarragona* 1984, 80.

64. For a good general overview, see Ward 2016, 81–120.

65. Rodrigo Estevan and Sánchez Usón 2006, 443–45.

66. Herlihy 1990, 157–58.

67. Rodrigo Estevan and Sánchez Usón 2006, 450.

68. AHHSCSP, AHPD-LP 1.1, docs. 1, 2, and 3; AHHSCSP, AHPD-LA 7.1.

69. Brodman 1998, 67.

70. ACA-RC, Alfonso III, *graciarum* 6:2, *registro* 483, fols. 175r–176r; Mutgé i Vives 1987, 159–60.

71. Richou i Llimona 2009, 37–38; Baucells i Reig 1997, 195.

72. Hernando i Delgado 1997, 146–47 (Ripoll de Cortades), 226–27 (Simó Rovira).

73. Arxiu Històric de la Ciutat de Manresa, Fons d'institucions, Hospital de Sant Andreu, *pergamins* 172 (July 27, 1377) and 173 (September 15, 1377); Barnes 1991, 607–8.

74. Rubio Vela 1984, 36–39.

75. Santamaría Arández 1983, 387–88.

76. Brodman 1998, 116.

77. Batlle i Gallart and Casas i Nadal 1980, 136.

78. Batlle i Gallart et al. 2007, docs. 93 and 106.

79. AHCB-IB, I-19, 1354–59, fol. 119r.

80. Ibid.

81. Bruniquer 1912–16, 1:143.

82. AMV-MC, A-17, 1375–83, fol. 23v.

83. There is a similar story in 1373 of Elvira Cornell, a noblewoman from Aragon, who was granted a pension of 330 solidi per year under similar terms. AMV-C, J-12, 1372–73, fol. 38v.

84. AMV-C, J-7, 1367–68, fol. 3r.

85. AMV-C, J-12, 1372–73, fol. 21v. The payment to de Sessa was repeated later; see J-13, 1373–74, fol. 16r.

86. There are other instances of this form of retirement, among them Pere Sagrista, the councilor and treasurer, similarly described as old and infirm, who received a pension in 1381. AMV-C, J-18, 1382–83, fol. 18r.

87. Narbona Vizcaíno 2012, 202–3 (doc. 5).

88. Michaud 2015, 314–15.

89. Brasher 2017, 28–31.

90. Terpstra 1994, 112–13.

91. Pugliese 1990, 109–10.

92. Howe and Devereux 2004, 355–56; Vanhaute 2011, 49–51.

93. Benito i Monclús 2006, 97.

94. This expectation generally rested on the idea of the moral economy as described in Thompson 1971; see also Sharp 2000 and 2013.

95. Fraser and Rimas 2011.

96. Benito i Monclús 2003, 309–10; Ferrer i Mallol 2001a, 190–96.

97. ASM-P, *manuale* 9, 1373–80, fol. 127v.

98. Andrinal and Mora 1993, 433.

99. ACA-RC, Pedro III, *comune* 190, *registro* 773, fol. 119r.

100. Rubio Vela and Ferrando Francés 2003, 1:181–82 (doc. 73).

101. Lübken 2012, 2–4; Black 2001.

102. Brodman 1986, 5.

103. Obradors Suazo 2013, 380–83; Cuadrada Majó 2003, 326–28.

104. AHCB-IB, I-7, 1322–23, fols. 5v–6r; see also Stathakopoulos 2004, 69–70.

105. AHCB-IB, I-21, 1360–63, fol. 65r; for more on the nature of citizenship in the Crown of Aragon, see Navarro Espinach 2010, 167–73.

106. AHCB-IB, I-21, 1360–63, fol. 98v.

107. AHCB-IB, I-24, 1373–76, fol. 72r.

108. Ibid., fol. 132r. The document says February 1375, but the surrounding documents are all from 1376. The scribes did not put in redactions from previous years, so 1375 is probably a scribal error.

109. Ibid., fol. 73r.

110. AHCB-IB, I-19, 1354–59, fol. 52r–v.

111. Jordan 1996, 19.

112. Slavin 2019, 71–73; Slavin 2012, 1239–42.

113. Rangasami 1985b, 1797.

114. Collet and Schuh 2018, 10.

115. Narbona Vizcaíno 2012, 204 (doc. 6).

116. AMV-MC, A-11, 1353–55, fol. 17r–v.

117. AMV-MC, A-17, 1375–83, fols. 63v–64r.

118. Narbona Vizcaíno 2012, 239 (doc. 36).

119. Rubio Vela 1984, 176–82.

120. Muratori et al. 1900, 655.

121. Villani 1979, 144–46.

122. Rodrigo Lizondo and Riera i Sans 2013, 2:719–20 (doc. 648).

123. Vinyoles i Vidal 1984, 408–12, letters 4–6, 7, 9.

124. ACB-PA, B2C, 1373–74, fol. 73r.

125. ACB-PA, B3-C4, box 1, 1358, fol. 8r.

126. García Marsilla 2007, 113–15; Milton 2012, 76–82. For a more pessimistic view of debt, see Smail 2016, 14–25.

127. Ruiz Doménec 1975, 28.
128. Aymard 1983, 1409.
129. García Marsilla 2002, 129; Vela i Aulesa 2007, 142–43; Soldevila i Temporal 2014.
130. Milton 2012, 91–93.
131. AMSPP-LA 12, 1375, fols. 12r, 15r.
132. Ibid., fol. 22v; AMSPP-LA 11, 1374, fol. 18v.
133. Sen 1981, 166; see also Edkins 1996, 549–56.
134. Fairchilds 1976, 27. This passage is widely quoted in works on early modern poverty; see Van Leeuwen 2017, 37–38; Kahl 2005, 96.
135. Bourin, Menant, and To Figueras 2014a, 11–15.

Chapter 4
1. The subject of wealth inequality in preindustrial Europe has not received significant scholarly focus, although a new research project at the Dondena Centre at Bocconi University in Milan aims to produce broad comparative work. See Alfani 2015; Alfani and Ammannati 2017.
2. Collet 2012, 12–15.
3. Jordan 2010, 58–59; Drendel 2011a, 417–18.
4. Pere Benito i Monclús has done considerable work creating chronologies of famines across Europe. See Benito i Monclús 2004 and 2011; see also Alfani, Mocarelli, and Strangio 2017.
5. Ó Gráda 2009, 4.
6. Furió 2011, 412; Curto i Homedes 1988, 231–32.
7. Riera Melis 2018, 249–52.
8. Benito i Monclús 2009, 310–13.
9. Howe and Devereux 2004; Mude et al. 2009.
10. Walsh and Hicks 2018.
11. Edkins 2000, 38–40.
12. Jordan 1996, 15–19; Clark 1985; Alfani, Mocarelli, and Strangio 2017, 25–38.
13. Riera Melis 2007, 125–32; Furió 2011, 349–53.
14. Jordan 1996, 44–47.

15. Newfield 2013, 122–23; Stouff 1970, 81; Ó Gráda 2009, 31–33; Jordan 1996, 17–20; Stathakopoulos 2004, 53–56.
16. Newfield 2013, 122–23; see also Dameron 2017, 987–88.
17. Serra i Puig 1967, 71–107.
18. Rubio Vela 1987, 131–47.
19. The year 1333 lines up with studies of Castile, while 1325, 1347, and 1374 line up with studies of Italy and southern France. See Oliva Herrer 2013, 97–109; De La Roncière 2011, 235–38; Reglero 2011, 309–12; Dameron 2017, 987–89.
20. Garnsey 1988, 17–37; Furió 2011, 412–14.
21. Pere Benito i Monclús (2009, 302–5) and Antoni Reira Melis (2018, 249–52) have suggested that the pairing of *carestía* and *fretura* tends to indicate high prices as well as actual harvest shortages.
22. Marie D'Aguanno Ito (2014, 539–41) has argued that some crises in the Florentine grain market are best understood as economically oriented "market breaks."
23. AMV-C, J-10, 1370–71, fols. 16v, 17r, 36v.
24. Ibid., fol. 22r.
25. Ibid., fol. 22v; see also Soler Millá 2005, 1067–69. There are roughly 2.9 quarters in one Valencian *cafíç*; see Sevillano Colom 1957, 64–65.
26. AMV-C, J-10, 1370–71, fols. 23r, 24r.
27. Ibid., fol. 27r.
28. Ibid., fols. 29v and 41v.
29. Ibid., fol. 43r.
30. Ibid., fol. 36r.
31. Furió 2011, 363–67.
32. AMV-C, J-10, 1370–71, fols. 44r–45r.
33. Ibid., fol. 45r; see also fol. 36v.
34. Furió 2011, 397–98.
35. The documents refer to the destination of de Fonts's trip as the "muntanyes d'en Sarrià," named for one of the major lords of the area, Admiral Bernat de Sarrià. AMV-C, J-10, 1370–71, fol. 37r; see also Hinojosa Montalvo 1992–93, 163–64.
36. AMV-C, J-11, 1371–72, fol. 17v.
37. Ibid., fol. 20r.
38. AMV-MC, A-16, 1371–75, fol. 43v.
39. AMV-C, J-11, 1371–72, fol. 21r.

40. AMV-MC, A-16, 1371–75, fol. 12r.
41. AMV-C, J-11, 1371–72, fol. 28v.
42. Ibid., fols. 28v, 41v.
43. Ibid., fol. 9r.
44. Ibid., fols. 32r, 33r; AMV-C, J-12, 1372–73, fol. 4r–v.
45. AMV-C, J-12, 1372–73, fol. 25r.
46. Navarro Espinach 2010, 167–70; Igual Luis 2012–14, 140–43.
47. AMV-C, J-11, 1371–72, fol. 29r.
48. AMV-MC, A-16, 1371–75, fol. 73r–v.
49. Ibid., fols. 73v–74r.
50. Ibid., fol. 73r.
51. Valencia claimed that this was for the protection of the Genoese, and it probably was, but it also limited the ability of the Genoese to make their own contracts. Ibid., fols. 75v–76r; AMV-C, J-11, 1371–72, fol. 33v.
52. AMV-MC, A-16, 1371–75, fol. 90r–v.
53. Ibid., fol. 92r.
54. AMV-C, J-12, 1372–73, fol. 18r–v.
55. Ibid., fol. 20r.
56. Tangheroni 1981, 114–15.
57. Càceres Nevot 2006, 140–46; Guilleré 2009, 137–38; Curto i Homedes 1988, 213.
58. De La Roncière 1982, 821–23, 827, 835.
59. Wainwright 1987, 134–35, 148–50.
60. AMV-MC, A-16, 1371–75, fol. 109r.
61. Ibid., fol. 116r–v.
62. In February, the council modified this position slightly, stating that laborers could only sell the grain of a single merchant. AMV-MC, A-16, 1371–75, fols. 124v–125r, 134v.
63. Ibid., fol. 144r–v; AMV-C, J-12, 1372–73, fol. 49v.
64. AMV-C, J-12, 1372–73, fol. 6r–v.
65. AMV-MC, A-16, 1371–75, fol. 157r–v.
66. AMV-MC, A-19.
67. Rubio Vela and Ferrando Francés 2003, 1:200–201, letter 87.
68. AMV-MC, A-16, 1371–75, fols. 67r, 97r, 99v.
69. AMV-C, J-17, 1380–81, fols. 22v, 20v, 24v, 37v.
70. Ibid., fols. 10v, 18v, 21v, 22v, 25r, 33v, etc.
71. AMV-MC, A-17, 1375–83, fol. 274v.
72. AMV-MC, A-18, 1383–88, fol. 5v.
73. AMV-C, J-19, 1383–84, fols. 4v–8v.
74. Càceres Nevot 2006, 410 (doc. 45).
75. Bruniquer 1912–16, 1:286.
76. Carmichael 2014, 11–12.
77. Càceres Nevot 2006, 411 (doc. 46).
78. Curto i Homedes 1988, 220.
79. Actes municipals Tarragona 1986, 28–29, 36–37.
80. Richou i Llimona 2013, 145.
81. Actes municipals Tarragona 1986, 73.
82. Curto i Homedes 1988, 220.
83. AMV-C, J-20, 1384–85, fol. 41r–v.
84. Ibid., fol. 26v; AMV-C, J-21, 1385–86, fol. 5r.
85. AMV-C, J-21, 1385–86, fols. 25r, 32v.
86. AMV-C, J-20, 1384–85, fols. 40v, 44v.
87. Richou i Llimona 2013, 156–57; see also Serra i Puig 1967, 81 and doc. 66.
88. Stouff 1970, 62–63, 285.
89. Day, Anatra, and Scaraffia 1984, 284–85; Orsi Lázaro 2008.
90. Tangheroni 1981, 118–20.
91. Càceres Nevot 2006, 159; Actes municipals Tarragona 1985, 41.
92. AMV-MC, A-18, 1383–88, fol. 101r–v.
93. Pere III 1980, 2:600–601; Richou Llimona 2013, 144–45; Silleras-Fernández 2010, 76–78.
94. Larenaudie 1952, 29–30.
95. AHCB-1B, IX, lletres reials originals, ser. B, 26, February 15, 1385.
96. ACB-PA, B2C, 1385–86, unfoliated letter inserted in the cover of the book.
97. AMV-C, J-20, 1384–85, fol. 36r.
98. AMV-MC, A-18, 1383–88, fols. 26v–28r.
99. Actes municipals Tarragona 1986, 25, 126.
100. López Rajadel 1994, 212–13.
101. AMV-C, J-20, 1384–85, fol. 14v.
102. López Rajadel 1994, 194–98.
103. Banegas López 2016, 98–115.
104. AMV-C, J-20, 1384–85, fols. 35r, 36v, 46r, 48r.
105. Ibid., fols. 30r, 41v.
106. AMV-C, J-19, 1383–84, fol. 24v.
107. Records for the fiscal year 1382–83 have not survived; the catalog states that Clavaria J-18 covers the years 1381–83, but the records actually cover the years 1381–82.

108. AHCB-IB, XXVI, *ordinacions originals* 1, no. 27; AHCB-IB, V, *ordinacions especials* (1378–1401), 5, fol. 15r–v.

109. Cohn 2008; Biraben 1975, 1:108–11.

110. Di Coppo Stefani 1783, 64–65.

111. AMCP, Actes Capitulars 2, 1384–85, fols. 2v–3r; AMV-C, J-19, 1383–84, fol. 47r; AMV-C, J-21, 1385–86, fol. 34v.

112. Cohn 2010, chap. 2; Rubio Vela 1979, 76–81; Agresta 2020, 385–90.

113. Bruniquer 1912–16, 1:280; AMV-MC, A-17, 1375–83, fols. 239v–240r; AMV-MC, A-18, 1383–88, fol. 33r.

114. AMV-MC, A-18, 1383–88, fol. 42r.

115. Ibid., fols. 26v–27r.

116. Curto i Homedes 1988, 99–129.

117. Ibid., 207–9.

118. AMV-MC, A-18, 1383–88, fol. 42v. The council eventually agreed to the captain's terms and the ship was relaunched for a three-month period. Ibid., fols. 45r, 46v–47r.

119. Ibid., fols. 66r–67r; AMV-C, J-20, 1384–85, fols. 40v, 48r–v.

120. AMV-C, J-20, 1384–85, fol. 35v.

121. Ibid., fols. 36r, 37v, 42v.

122. *Actes municipals Tarragona* 1986, 84; AMV-C, J-20, 1384–85, fol. 39r.

123. Càceres Nevot 2006, 158–60.

124. AMV-MC, A-18, 1383–88, fols. 137v–138r.

125. Valencia spent another large sum on direct purchases, but the resale value of the grain was not recorded.

126. AMV-C, J-21, 1385–86, fol. 10r.

127. AMV-C, J-20, 1384–85, fols. 29v, 38r, 46v.

128. AMV-C, J-19, 1383–84, fol. 27v; see also Narbona Vizcaíno 2012, 243.

129. Boluda Perucho 1999, 44; Lairón Pla 2001, 26.

130. *Actes municipals Tarragona* 1986, 109–10, 112.

131. Ibid., 116–17.

132. AMV-C, J-21, 1385–86, fols. 4r, 16r.

133. Ibid., fol. 25r; see also AMV-C, J-20, 1384–85, fols. 49v, 53r.

134. AMV-C, J-21, 1385–86, fols. 5r, 21v.

135. AMV-MC, A-18, 1383–88, fol. 110v.

136. AMV-C, J-21, 1385–86, fol. 27r.

137. AMV-C, J-20, 1384–85, fol. 39r.

138. AMV-MC, A-18, 1383–88, fols. 94v–95r.

139. Larenaudie 1952, 29–30.

140. AMV-MC, A-18, 1383–88, fols. 136v–137r.

141. Ibid., fols. 70v–71r.

142. Rohr 2007, 97.

Chapter 5

1. ACB-PA, B2C, 1373–74, fol. 170v.

2. AMV-CM, g3-3, 1374–75, fol. 6r–v.

3. ACB-PA, B2C, 1373–74, fol. 73r.

4. Epstein 2003, 142–43.

5. AMV-MC, A-16 1371–75, fol. 189r–v. They had the news by at least March 10. AMV-C, J-13, 1373–74, fol. 28v.

6. Larenaudie 1952, 32.

7. De La Roncière 1982, 735.

8. Caferro 1998, 3–5, 28; Mollat and Wolff 1973, 134–37.

9. Glénisson 1951, 313–15.

10. Puigferrat i Oliva 2014, 154.

11. Ruiz 2007, 43–44.

12. Mies 1996, 8–9.

13. Josephus 1997, 3:201–19; Marvin 1998.

14. Caferro 1998, 25–30; Larenaudie 1952, 29; Postan 1964, 38–41.

15. Fernández Trabal and Riera Melis 2004, 119–21.

16. Campbell 2016, 332–48; Collet and Schuh 2018; Jordan 1996, 16–19; Le Roy Ladurie 1971, 222–25.

17. Benito Garzón, Sánchez de Dios, and Sáinz Ollero 2007, 121–24; Hoar, Palutikof, and Thorne 2004.

18. Holzhauser, Magny, and Zumbüihl 2005.

19. Horden and Purcell 2000, 120.

20. Glénisson 1951, 311–12.

21. Garnsey 1988, 203–5.

22. The weight of bread loaves decreased from an average of around 750 grams to 531.5 grams. Rubio Vela 1984, 144–46.

23. AMV-C, J-13, 1373–74, fol. 37v; AMV-C, J-14, 1374–75, fols. 38v–39r, 47r; AMV-MC, A-16 1371–75, fol. 267v.

24. ACB-PA, B2C, 1375–76, fol. 246r.

25. ACB, III. Procures, 4. Cisma d'Occident, doc. 77; Vinyoles i Vidal 1995, 122.

26. Miquel i Vives and Domingo Gabriel 1995, 306–7; Stouff 1970, 219–29.

27. AMV-MC, A-16, 1371–75, fol. 234r.
28. Vinyoles i Vidal 1984, 408–10, letters 4–6, and 1995, 121–22.
29. *Crònica del racional* 1921, 148–49.
30. AMV-C, J-14, 1374–75, fol. 41v.
31. Ibid., fol. 50v; see fol. 49v for a similar phrase.
32. AMV-MC, A-16, 1371–75, fol. 263v.
33. AMV-MC, A-17, 1375–83, fols. 57v, 37v.
34. The monastery had contacts in the area and had sent representatives in March as well; see AMSPP-LA 11, 1374, fols. 61v, 66r. For other prices in Castelló d'Empúries, see Gironella i Granés 2010, 320–21, which records prices in solidi per *mitgera*, which is roughly four-ninths of a Barcelona quarter. See also Feliu i Montfort 2004, 14, 22.
35. Unfortunately, we have no records of prices in Castelló d'Empúries for the crucial period between March 1375 and April 1376 to compare with the existing prices for the same time period in Barcelona. Gironella i Granés 2010, 982–84; Martí Arau 2011, 289–96.
36. Puigferrat i Oliva 2014, 153.
37. Ibid., 157–58; Puigferrat i Oliva 2000, 87–88.
38. AEV-C, 14–28, 1374, fol. 9r.
39. Puigferrat i Oliva 2000, 98–100. This work notes that coastal cities had already overcome the crisis through imports, while the interior took longer to recover.
40. Torras i Serra 1994, 126.
41. Ibid., 137.
42. AMV-MC, A-16, 1371–75, fol. 36r. The two types of grain allowed out were *paniç* and *dacça* (or *panís* or *dacsa*), probably referring to millet and sorghum, respectively. Dantí 2008, 96–98.
43. *Actes municipals Tarragona* 1984, 59–61.
44. Benito i Monclús 2009, 307.
45. Curto i Homedes 1988, 163–65.
46. Stouff 1970, 75–76.
47. Larenaudie 1952, 34–35.
48. Glénisson 1951, 321.
49. See Gaillard and Texier 2010, 82–84.
50. Hanska 2002, 170; see also Sharp 2016, 35; Stearns 2009.
51. Hanska 2002, 157; Barriendos Vallvé 2008; Barriendos Vallvé and Martín-Vide 1995.
52. Riera Melis 2018, 254–57; De Vincenti 2018; Chester and Duncan 2010, 85–91; Gerrard and Petley 2013, 1063–66.
53. AMV-CM, g3-1, 1334, fol. 41r.
54. AMV-CM, g3-3, 1375, fol. 3v.
55. Hanska 2002, 9.
56. AMV-MC, A-16, 1371–75, fol. 230v.
57. Bruniquer 1912–16, 1:285–86; see also Tutusaus i Canals 1986, 42–43.
58. AMV-MC, A-16, 1371–75, fol. 208v.
59. Ibid., fols. 189v–190r; AHCB-1B, I-24, 1374–76, fols. 34v–35r.
60. AMV-MC, A-16, 1371–75, fol. 186r. Procession language could be formulaic; see ibid., fols. 44r–v.
61. Ibid., fols. 186v, 230v–231r.
62. *Crònica del racional* 1921, 146.
63. ACB, III. Procures, 4. Cisma d'Occident, doc. 159, cited in Teresa Vinyoles i Vidal 1995, 122.
64. *Petit Thalamus de Montpellier*, n.d. [ca. April 27, June 24, July 23, 1374], fols. 133v–134v, http://thalamus.huma-num.fr/annales-occitanes/annee-1374.html. The *canne*, or rod, in medieval Montpellier was roughly two meters long; see Guilhiermoz 1913, 288.
65. AMV-MC, A-16, 1371–75, fol. 189r–v.
66. Gerrard and Petley 2013, 1062 (quotation), 1065–70. For a survey on risk and forms of mitigation, see Smith 2013; for a look at how religious and secular responses to the plague in Valencia could adapt to changing understandings of disease, see Agresta 2020.
67. Howe and Devereux 2004.
68. Glénisson 1951, 311–12; De La Roncière 1982, 131–32.
69. Perpignan received a privilege to prevent wine imports in 1299; the privilege was modified slightly in 1374 and 1387 but not revoked. Garcia Edo 2010, docs. 67 and 270–73.

70. AMV-MC, A-16, 1371–75, fol. 190v.
71. The restriction lasted from June 16 to September 29, 1377; see AMV-MC, A-17, 1375–83, fols. 148v–149r.
72. AMV-MC, A-16, 1371–75, fol. 202r–v.
73. Jordan 1996, 37–39; Slavin 2012; Newfield 2009.
74. Garnsey 1988, 24–25; Jordan 1996, 19–21.
75. Canyelles Vilar 1996a, 277–78.
76. Arxiu Històric de Protocols de Manresa, vol. 275, February 7, 1375.
77. Sánchez Martínez 2001, 42–44; Martí Arau 2011, 290–94.
78. ACB-PA, B2C, 1373–74, fols. 60r, 102r.
79. Ramon Banegas López provides detailed price data from the records of the Arxiu Històric de la Ciutat de Barcelona that accord closely with the Pia Almoina data; see Banegas López 2008, 315–25 and the appendices that begin on 456; see also Orsi Lázaro 2008, 953–57.
80. The Great Famine is unique in combining a harvest failure with widespread epizootics that killed huge numbers of cattle just as they were most needed. Jordan 1996, 57–58; DeWitte and Slavin 2013.
81. Luongo 2006, 82–83.
82. Tutusaus i Canals 1986, 15–23; Sánchez Martínez 2001, 29–32.
83. Puigferrat i Oliva 2014, 154, 160.
84. Different chronicles present slightly differing versions of Jaume of Mallorca's end. See Sánchez Martínez 2001, 31.
85. ACA-RC, Pedro III, *registro* 775, fols. 97v–98r, cited in Tutusaus i Canals 1986, 19.
86. Tutusaus i Canals 1986, 18–22.
87. Puigferrat i Oliva 2000, 84–85, 154–55.
88. Sánchez Martínez 2001, 34–38.
89. *Actes municipals Tarragona* 1984, 108; see also Morelló Baget 2001, 191.
90. Sánchez Martínez 2001, 39.
91. Pere III 1980, 2:582.
92. Bruniquer 1912–16, 4:319; Jordan 1996, 117–18.
93. Ó Gráda 1995, 13–14.
94. Mokyr and Ó Gráda 1999, 2–4.
95. For diagnosis generally, see Mitchell 2011.
96. Aberth 2001, 16; Carpentier 1962.
97. ASM-P, *manuale* 9, 1373–80, fol. 72r.
98. Caferro 1998, 53.
99. AMV-MC, A-16, 1371–75, fol. 263v.
100. Ibid., fols. 250v–251r.
101. Macrae and Zwi 1994, 95–97; Ressler, Tortorici, and Marcelino 1993, 80–84.
102. For excellent charts of the available information from 1374, see Puigferrat i Oliva 2000, 106–7. For plague deaths, see also Camps Clemente and Camps Surroca 1998, 107–10, 244–46, 332–34; Günzberg i Moll 2002, 40–48.
103. Bautier 1990, 50–52.
104. Benito i Monclús 2009, 301–3.
105. ASM-P, *manuale* 9, 1373–80, fols. 98r–v, 127r–128r.
106. Arxiu Històric de la Ciutat de Manresa, *notularum*, March 26, 1375, cited in Torras i Serra 1994, 116.
107. Pere III 1980, 2:582.
108. The document was recopied by Antoni Vicens of Girona in a compilation of documents from around the region; the original is from the *Noticiari* of Johan Toralles, transcribed in Moliné i Brasés 1917, 214; Puigferrat i Oliva 2000, 79.
109. López Rajadel 1994, 194–98.
110. The city also held religious ceremonies to petition for the end of the Plague, but no mention is made of the shortage. *Petit Thalamus de Montpellier*, n.d. (ca. June 1374–July 1375), fols. 133v–135v, http://thalamus.huma-num.fr/annales-occitanes/annee-1375.html.
111. De La Roncière 1982, 127; Benito i Monclús 2009, 312–13.
112. *Petit Thalamus de Montpellier*, n.d. (ca. June–July 1374), fol. 134r, http://thalamus.huma-num.fr/annales-occitanes/annee-1374.html.

Conclusion
1. Furió 2011, 351.
2. Benito i Monclús and Montoro i Maltas 2017, 502–4.
3. *Petit Thalamus de Montpellier*, n.d. (June 1374), fol. 133v ("cays de fam"), http://thalamus.huma-num.fr/annales-occitanes/annee-1374.html; AMV-C,

J-21, 1385–86, fols. 25r, 32v ("quai extrema necessitat").

4. Benito i Monclús and Riera Melis 2014, 9–11; Drendel 2011b, 265, 270–71; De Waal 2005, 233–36, and 1997, 1–7; Cameron 2018, chap. 5.

5. Collet and Schuh 2018, 7.

6. Edkins 2000, 29–30, 100–102. For a more recent context, see Huyssen 2014, 63–88.

7. Edkins 2000, 103–10; Barrett 2001; Bastagli et al. 2018.

8. AMV-MC, A-16, 1371–75, fols. 252v–253v.

9. Ibid., fol. 253r.

Bibliography

Unpublished Primary Sources
Archives Municipales de Perpignan
  Livres de Provisions (AA 5)
Archivo Municipal de Castellón de la Plana
  (AMCP)
Arxiu Capitular de Barcelona (ACB)
  III. Procures
    4. Cisma d'Occident
  IV. Caritat (C)
    13. Hospitals
  V. Pia Almoina (PA)
    B. Administració, 2. Sortides,
      A. Administració general (B2A)
    B. Administració, 2. Sortides,
      C. Majordomia (B2C)
    B. Administració, 3. Administracions
      foranes (B3)
    C. Sitges, 4. Plecs de Comptes (C4)
    H. Casa de Mogoda (H)
Arxiu Capitular de València
Arxiu de la Corona de Aragon (ACA)
  Real Cancillería (RC)
    Registros del reinado de Pedro III el
      Ceremonioso (Pedro III)
    Comune
    Comune locumtenencie infantis
      Joannis
    Diversorum

    Graciarum
    Sigilli secreti
    Registros del reinado de Alfonso III el
      Benigno (Alfonso III)
Arxiu Episcopal de Vic (AEV)
  Comptes (C)
Arxiu Històric de la Ciutat de Barcelona
  (AHCB)
  Consell de Cent (1B)
    I. Llibres de Consell (I)
    V. Ordinacions especials
    IX. Lletres reials originals
    XXV. Ordinacions originals
  Miscel·lània
  Registre d'Ordinacions (IV)
Arxiu Històric de la Ciutat de Manresa
  (These records are currently in the Arxiu
    Comarcal del Bages, but they follow
    the catalog and organization of the
    city archive developed by Marc Torras
    i Serra in the 1980s)
Arxiu Històric de la Hospital de Santa Creu i
  Santa Pau (AHHSCSP)
  Arxiu de l'Hospital de Pere Desvilar (AHPD)
  Llibres de Porcions (LP)
  Llibre de Actes (LA)
  Porcions de Pere Desvilar (PPD)

Arxiu Històric de Protocols Barcelona (AHPB)
Arxiu Històric de Protocols de Manresa
Arxiu del Monestir de Sant Pere de les
  Puel·les (AMSPP)
  (Accessed on microfilm at the Hill
  Monastic Manuscript Library at St.
  John's University, microfilm reels
  34327–4339)
  Llibres d'abadesses (LA)
Arxiu Municipal de València (AMV)
  Cartas Missivas (CM, g3)

Clavaria (C)
  Series J: Clavaria Comuna (J)
  Llibres d'Administració de l'Hospital d'En
  Clapers (LAHC)
  Llibre de Seguritats (LS)
  Manuals de Consell, series A (MC, A)
Arxiu Municipal de Vila-Real
  Clavaria
Arxiu de la Seu de Manresa (ASM)
  Arxiu del Veguer (AV)
  Peborde (P)

Published Primary Sources

Actes municipals Tarragona. 1984. Col·lecció
  de documents de l'Arxiu Històric
  Municipal de Tarragona, vol. 3 (1369,
  1374–75). Tarragona: Publicacions de
  l'Excm. Ajuntament de Tarragona.
Actes municipals Tarragona. 1985. Col·lecció
  de documents de l'Arxiu Històric
  Municipal de Tarragona, vol. 4 (1378–79,
  1383–84). Tarragona: Publicacions de
  l'Excm. Ajuntament de Tarragona.
Actes municipals Tarragona. 1986. Col·lecció
  de documents de l'Arxiu Històric
  Municipal de Tarragona, vol. 5
  (1384–85, 1385–86). Tarragona:
  Publicacions de l'Excm. Ajuntament
  de Tarragona.
Andrinal, Lorenzo, and Pau Mora, eds. 1993.
  *Diplomatari del monestir de Santa Maria
  de La Real de Mallorca.* Vol. 2 (1361–86).
  Barcelona: Fundació Noguera.
*Aureum opus regalium privilegiorum civitatis et
  regni Valentie: Cum historia cristionissimi
  Regis Jacobi.* 1515. Madrid: Biblioteca
  Digital Real Academia de la Historia.
  http://bibliotecadigital.rah.es/dgbrah/es
  /consulta/registro.cmd?id=44646.
Batlle i Gallart, Carme, Maria Teresa Ferrer
  i Mallol, Maria Cinta Mañé i Mas,
  Josefa Mutgé i Vives, Sebastià Riera i
  Viader, and Manuel Rovira i Solà, eds.
  2007. *El "Llibre del Consell" de la ciutat
  de Barcelona, segle XIV: Les eleccions
  municipals.* Barcelona: Institució Milà i
  Fontanals.
Boluda Perucho, Alfred, ed. 1999. *Els manuals
  de consells medievals de Xàtiva (1376–
  1380).* Valencia: Diputació de València.

Bruniquer, Esteve Gilabert. 1912–16. *Rubricas
  de Bruniquer: Ceremonials dels magnifichs
  consellers y regiment de la ciutat de
  Barcelona.* 5 vols. Barcelona: Ajuntament
  de Barcelona.
Constans Serrats, Luis G., ed. 1985–93.
  Diplomatari de Banyoles. 6 vols.
  Banyoles: Centre d'Estudis Comarcals de
  Banyoles.
"Crònica del racional de la ciutat de Barcelona
  (1334–1417)." 1921. *Recull de documents i
  estudis* 1 (2): 15–191.
De Voragine, Jacobus. 1993. *The Golden
  Legend: Readings on the Saints.* Ca.
  1259–66. Translated by William Granger
  Ryan. 2 vols. Princeton: Princeton
  University Press.
di Coppo Stefani, Marchionne. 1783. *Istoria
  fiorentina di Marchionne di Coppo Stefani.*
  Vol. 11. Florence: Gaet. Cambiagi.
Diz Ardid, Emilio, and Maria Carmen
  Sánchez Mateos, eds. 2011. *El
  repartimiento de Orihuela: Contexto
  histórico y edición facsímil.* Orihuela:
  Ayuntamiento de Orihuela.
Domingo Rúbies, Dolors, ed. 1997. *Pergamins
  de privilegis de la ciutat de Balaguer.*
  Lleida: Edicions de la Universitat de
  Lleida.
Eiximenis, Francesc. 1977. *Com usar bé de
  beure e menjar: Normes morals contingudes
  en el "Terç del Crestià."* Ca. 1379–92.
  Edited by Jorge Gracia. Barcelona:
  Curial.
———. 2009. *Regiment de la cosa pública.*
  1383. Edited by Josep Palomero.
  Valencia: Bromera.

Ferrer, San Vicent. 1971. *Sermons*. Vol. 4. Edited by José Sanchis y Sivera and Gret Schib. Barcelona: Editorial Barcino.

Garcia Edo, Vicent, ed. 2010. *El llibre verd major de Perpinyà (segle XII–1395)*. Perpignan: Fundació Noguera.

Hernando i Delgado, Josep. 1997. "L'ensenyament a Barcelona, segle XIV: Documents dels protocols notarials; 2. Instruments notarials de l'Arxiu de la Catedral de Barcelona i de l'Arxiu Històric de la Ciutat de Barcelona, 1294–1400." *Arxiu de textos catalans antics* 16:131–298.

Ibn al-ʿAwāmm, Abu Zakariya. 1802. *Kitāb al-Filāḥa (Libro de Agricultura)*. Vol. 1. Edited and translated by José Antonio Banqueri. Madrid: La Imprenta Real.

Ibn Wāfid, Ali Ibn al-Husain. 2001. "La traducción castellana del 'Tratado de Agricultura' de Ibn Wāfid." Translated by José María Millás Vallicrosa. In *Agriculture: Texts and Studies; Natural Sciences in Islam*, edited by Fuat Sezgin, 5 vols., 5:1–54. Frankfurt am Main: Institute for the History of Arabic-Islamic Science.

Josephus, Flavius. 1997. *The Jewish War*. Translated by H. St. J. Thackeray. 3 vols. Cambridge: Harvard University Press.

Lairón Pla, Aureliano. 2001. *Libre de diverses statuts e ordenacions fets per lo Consell de la Vila de Algezira*. Valencia: Publicacions Universitat de València.

López Rajadel, Fernando, ed. 1994. *Crónicas de los jueces de Teruel (1176–1532)*. Teruel: Instituto de Estudios Turolenses.

Moliné i Brasés, E., ed. 1917. "Noticiari català dels segles XIV y XV." *Butlletí del Ateneu Barcelonès* 1:211–20.

Muratori, Lodovico Antonio, Giosuè Carducci, Vittorio Fiorini, and Pietro Fedele, eds. 1900. *Rerum italicarum scriptores: Raccolta degli storici italiani dal cinquecento al millecinquecento*; Cronache Senesi. Vol. 15, part 6. Città di Castello: S. Lapi.

Narbona Vizcaíno, Rafael. 2012. "Las leyes de pobres en la metrópolis: Mendigos, miserables, trabajadores en Valencia, 1306–1462." *Clio y crimen* 9:165–284.

Pere III of Catalonia. 1980. *Chronicle*. Translated by J. N. Hillgarth and Mary Hillgarth. 2 vols. Toronto: Pontifical Institute of Mediaeval Studies.

Le Petit Thalamus de Montpellier. Edited by Florence Clavaud. Online edition. http://thalamus.huma-num.fr.

Pliny the Elder. 1855. *The Natural History of Pliny*. Edited by John Bostock and Henry T. Riley. London: H. G. Bohn.

Rodrigo Lizondo, Mateu, and Jaume Riera i Sans, eds. 2013. *Col·lecció documental de la Cancelleria de la Corona d'Aragó: Textos en llengua catalana*. 2 vols. Valencia: Publicacions Universitat de València.

Rubio Vela, Agustín, and Antoni Ferrando Francés, eds. 2003. *Epistolari de la València medieval*. 2 vols. Valencia: Publicacions de l'Abadia de Montserrat.

Varro, Marcus Terentius. 1978. *Économie rurale*. Translated by Jacques Heurgon. Paris: Société d'Édition "Les Belle Lettres."

Villani, Giovanni. 1979. *Nuova cronica*. 1348. Edited by Giovanni Aquilecchia. Torino: G. Einaudi.

Vinyoles i Vidal, Teresa, ed. 1984. "Cartes d'una Catalana del segle XIV al seu marit." *Estudis universitaris catalans* 26 (4): 387–420.

Secondary Literature

Abella Samitier, Juan. 2009. "La deuda pública de los municipios aragoneses en los siglos XIV y XV." *Anuario de estudios medievales* 39 (1): 47–64.

Aberth, John. 2001. *From the Brink of the Apocalypse: Confronting Famine, War, Plague, and Death in the Later Middle Ages*. New York: Routledge.

Abulafia, David. 2002. *A Mediterranean Emporium: The Catalan Kingdom of Majorca*. Cambridge: Cambridge University Press.

Agresta, Abigail. 2020. "From Purification to Protection: Plague Response in Late Medieval Valencia." *Speculum* 95 (2): 371–95.

Alfani, Guido. 2010. "Climate, Population, and Famine in Northern Italy: General Tendencies and Malthusian Crisis, ca. 1450–1800." *Annales de démographie historique* 120 (2): 23–53.

———. 2015. "Economic Inequality in Northwestern Italy: A Long-Term View (Fourteenth to Eighteenth Centuries)." *Journal of Economic History* 75 (4): 1058–96.

Alfani, Guido, and Francesco Ammannati. 2017. "Long-Term Trends in Economic Inequality: The Case of the Florentine State, ca. 1300–1800." *Economic History Review* 70 (4): 1072–1102.

Alfani, Guido, Luca Mocarelli, and Donatella Strangio. 2017. "Italy." In *Famine in European History*, edited by Guido Alfani and Cormac Ó Gráda, 25–47. Cambridge: Cambridge University Press.

Alsina i Català, Claudi, Gaspar Feliu i Montfort, and Lluís Marquet i Ferigle. 1990. *Pesos, mides i mesures dels Països Catalans*. Barcelona: Curial.

Aparisi Romero, Frederic. 2013. "La producción y el consumo de vino en el mundo rural valenciano durante la baja Edad Media." In *Patrimonio cultural de la vid y el vino*, vol. 2, edited by Sebastián Celestino Pérez and Juan Blánquez Pérez, 161–68. Madrid: UAM Ediciones.

Apostolides, Alexander, Stephen Broadberry, Bruce Campbell, Mark Overton, and Bas van Leeuwen. 2008. "English Agricultural Output and Labour Productivity, 1250–1850: Some Preliminary Estimates." Open Research Exeter. https://ore.exeter.ac.uk/repository/handle/10871/13985.

Argilés i Aluja, Maria Caterina. 1993. "Preus i salaris a la Lleida dels segles XIV i XV segons els llibres d'obra de la seu." PhD diss., Universitat de Lleida.

Aston, T. H., and C. H. E. Philpin. 1987. *The Brenner Debate: Agrarian Class Structure and Economic Development in Pre-Industrial Europe*. New York: Cambridge University Press.

Aymard, Maurice. 1983. "Autoconsommation et marchés: Chayanov, Labrousse ou Le Roy Ladurie?" *Annales: Économies, sociétés, civilisations* 38 (6): 1392–410.

Bailey, Mark. 1989a. "The Concept of the Margin in the Medieval English Economy." *Economic History Review* 42 (1): 1–17.

———. 1989b. *A Marginal Economy? East Anglian Breckland in the Later Middle Ages*. Cambridge: Cambridge University Press.

Bajet i Royo, Montserrat. 1993. *Aspectes del comerç a Catalunya en el segle XVI segons els llibres dels mostassas*. PhD diss., Universitat de Lleida.

Banegas López, Ramón Agustí. 2008. "L'aprovisionament de carn a Barcelona durant els segles XIV i XV." PhD diss., Universitat de Barcelona.

———. 2016. *Sangre, dinero y poder: El negocio de la carne en la Barcelona bajomedieval*. Lleida: Editorial Milenio.

Barrett, Christopher. 2001. "Does Food Aid Stabilize Food Availability?" *Economic Development and Cultural Change* 49 (2): 335–49.

Barriendos Vallvé, Mariano. 2008. "Climate and Culture in Spain: Religious Responses to Extreme Climatic Events in the Hispanic Kingdoms (Sixteenth–Nineteenth Centuries)." In *Cultural Consequences of the "Little Ice Age,"* edited by Wolfgang Behringer, Hartmut Lehmann, and Christian Pfister, 379–414. Göttingen: Vandenhoeck & Ruprecht.

Barriendos Vallvé, Mariano, and Javier Martín-Vide. 1995. "The Use of Rogation Ceremony Records in Climatic Reconstruction: A Case Study from Catalonia (Spain)." *Climatic Change* 30:201–21.

Barrio Barrio, Juan Antonio. 1990. "El control del mercado vinícola en Orihuela durante la baja Edad Media, siglos XIII–XIV." In *Vinyes i vins: Mil anys d'història; Actes i comunicacions del III Col·loqui d'Història Agrària sobre mil anys de producció, comerç, i consum de vins i* begudes alcohòliques als Països Catalans, vol. 1, edited by Emili i Giralt Raventós, 419–29. Barcelona: Publicacions Universitat de Barcelona.

———. 2007. "Un repartimiento inédito, el repartimiento de Orihuela de 1330." In *VI estudios de frontera: Población y poblamiento; Homenaje al prof. González Jiménez*, edited by Francisco Toro Ceballos and J. Rodríguez Molina, 79–92. Jaén: Diputación Provincial de Jaén.

———. 2009. "La producción, el consumo y la especulación de los cereales en una ciudad de frontera, Orihuela, siglos XIII–XIV." In *Alimentar la ciudad en la Edad Media: Nájera, Encuentros Internacionales del Medievo 2008, del 22 al 25 de julio de 2008*, edited by Beatriz Arízaga Bolumburu and Jesús Ángel Solórzano Telechea, 59–86. Logroño: Instituto de Estudios Riojanos.

Barrio Barrio, Juan Antonio, and José Vicente Cabezuelo Pliego. 1999. "Rentas y derechos señoriales de las morerías del valle de Elda a finales del siglo XV." In *VII simposio internacional de Mudejarismo, Teruel, 19–21 de Septiembre de 1996*, 43–54. Teruel: Instituto de Estudios Turolenses.

Barton, Thomas. 2019. *Victory's Shadow: Conquest and Governance in Medieval Catalonia*. Ithaca: Cornell University Press.

Bastagli, Francesca, Jessica Hagen-Zanker, Luke Harman, Valentina Barca, Georgina Sturge, and Tanja Schmidt. 2018. "The Impact of Cash Transfers: A Review of the Evidence from Low- and Middle-Income Countries." *Journal of Social Policy* 48 (3): 569–94.

Batlle i Gallart, Carme. 1985. *La Seu d'Urgell medieval: La ciutat i els seus habitants*. Barcelona: Editorial Rafael Dalmau.

———. 1987. *L'assistència als pobres a la Barcelona medieval (s. XIII)*. Barcelona: Rafael Dalmau.

———. 2000. "Els esclaus domèstics a Barcelona vers 1300." In *De l'esclavitud a la llibertat: Esclaus i lliberts a l'Edat Mitjana*, edited by María Teresa Ferrer i Mallol and Josefa Mutgé i Vives, 265–97. Barcelona: C.S.I.C.

Batlle i Gallart, Carme, and Montserrat Casas i Nadal. 1980. "La caritat privada i les institucions benèfiques de Barcelona (segle XIII)." In *La pobreza y la asistencia a los pobres en la Cataluña medieval*, edited Manuel Riu i Riu, 2 vols., 1:117–90. Barcelona: C.S.I.C.

Baucells i Reig, Josep. 1974. "La Pia Almoina de la Seo de Barcelona: Origen y desarrollo." In *A pobreza e a assistência aos pobres na Península Ibérica durante a Idade Média: Actas das 1as Jornadas Luso-Espanholas de História Medieval, Lisbon, 25–30 de setembro de 1972*, 1:73–135. Lisbon: Imprensa Nacional Casa da Moeda.

———. 1980. "Gènesi de la Pia Almoina de la Seu de Barcelona: Els fundadors." In *La pobreza y la asistencia a los pobres en la Cataluña medieval*, edited by Manuel Riu i Riu, 2 vols., 1:2–76. Barcelona: C.S.I.C.

———. 1984. *El baix Llobregat i la Pia Almoina de la Seu de Barcelona: Catàleg del fons en pergamí de l'arxiu capitular de la Catedral de Barcelona*. Barcelona: Departament de Cultura de la Generalitat de Catalunya.

———. 1987. *El Maresme i la Pia Almoina de la Seu de Barcelona: Catàleg del fons en pergamí de l'arxiu capitular de la Catedral de Barcelona*. Barcelona: Departament de Cultura de la Generalitat de Catalunya.

———. 1990. *El Garraf i la Pia Almoina de la Seu de Barcelona: Catàleg del fons en pergamí de l'arxiu capitular de la Catedral de Barcelona*. Barcelona: Departament de Cultura de la Generalitat de Catalunya.

———. 1997. "Limosnas y Pía Almoina: Institucionalización de la caridad para los más necesitados en la área catalana." *Memoria ecclesiae* 11:161–211.

Bautier, Robert-Henri. 1990. "Un nouvel ensemble documentaire pour l'histoire des pestes du XIVe siècle: L'exemple de la ville de Vich en Catalogne." *Ausa* 14 (124): 31–52.

Becker, Marvin. 1972. "Aspects of Lay Piety in Early Renaissance Florence." In *The Pursuit of Holiness in Late Medieval and Renaissance Religion: Papers from the University of Michigan Conference*, edited by Charles Edward Trinkaus and Heiko Augustinus Oberman, 177–99. Leiden: Brill.

Benito Garzón, Marta, Rut Sánchez de Dios, and Helios Sáinz Ollero. 2007. "Predictive Modelling of Tree Species Distributions on the Iberian Peninsula During the Last Glacial Maximum and Mid-Holocene." *Ecography: Pattern and Diversity in Ecology* 30 (1): 120–34.

Benito i Monclús, Pere. 2003. *Senyoria de la terra i tinença pagesa al comtat de Barcelona, segles 11–13*. Barcelona: C.S.I.C.

———. 2003–4. "'Et hoc facimus propter necessitatem famis . . .': Possibilitats de les fonts documentals catalanes per a l'estudi de les crisis alimentàries dels segles X–XIII." *Acta historica et archaeologica mediaevalia* 25:39–62.

———. 2004. "Fams i caresties a la Mediterrània occidental durant la baixa Edat Mitjana: El debat sobre 'les crisis de la crisi.'" *Recerques* 49:179–93.

———. 2006. "Morir de fam a l'Edat Mitjana davant la indiferència de fills, parents i amics." In *Condicions de vida al món rural*, edited by Jordi Bolòs, Antonieta Jarne, and Enric Vicedo, 95–114. Lleida: Institut d'Estudis Ilerdencs.

———. 2007. "'Et si sterilitas, ut solet, in terra illa fuerit . . .': Frecuencia, longevidad y gravedad de las carestías en Cataluña durante la 'fase del crecimiento' de la economía medieval (siglos XI–XIII)." In *Crisis de subsistencia y crisis agrarias en la Edad Media*, edited by Hipólito Rafael Oliva Herrer and Pere Benito i Monclús, 79–110. Seville: Editorial Universidad de Sevilla.

———. 2009. "Carestía y hambruna en las ciudades de occidente durante la Edad Media: Algunos rasgos distintivos." In *Alimentar la ciudad en la Edad Media: Nájera, Encuentros Internacionales del Medievo 2008, del 22 al 25 de julio de 2008*, edited by Beatriz Arízaga Bolumburu and Jesús Ángel Solórzano Telechea, 299–314. Logroño: Instituto de Estudios Riojanos.

———. 2010. "Del castillo al mercado y al silo: La gestión de la renta cerealista de la Almoina de Barcelona en la castellanía de Sitges (1354–1366)." *Historia agraria* 51:13–44.

———. 2011. "Famines sans frontières en Occident avant la conjoncture de 1300: À propos d'une enquête en cours." In *Les disettes dans la conjoncture de 1300 en Méditerranée occidentale*, edited by Monique Bourin, John Drendel, and François Menant, 37–86. Rome: École Française de Rome.

———. 2013a. "L'Almoina de la Seu de Barcelona: Gènesi i formació d'un sistema integrat de comptabilitat (1283–1419)." In *Comptes de senyor, comptes de pagès: Les comptabilitats en la història rural*, edited by Enric Saguer, Gabriel Jover, and Helena Benito, 73–92. Girona: Institut Ramon Muntaner.

———. 2013b. "De Labrousse a Sen: Modelos de causalidad y paradigmas interpretativos de las crisis alimentarias preindustriales." In *Crisis alimentarias en la Edad Media: Modelos, explicaciones y representaciones*, edited by Pere Benito i Monclús, 15–32. Lleida: Editorial Milenio.

———. 2018. "El rey frente a la carestía: Políticas frumentarias de estado en la Europa medieval." In *Políticas contra el hambre y la carestía en la Europa medieval*, edited by Luciano Palermo, Andrea Fara, and Pere Benito i Monclús, 37–80. Lleida: Editorial Milenio.

Benito i Monclús, Pere, and Joan Montoro i Maltas. 2017. "Fams immortalitzades: El 'mal any primer' (1333–1334) dins l'annalística catalana de la baixa Edat Mitjana." In *L'histoire à la source: Acter, compter, enregistrer (Catalogne, Savoie, Italie, XIIe–XVe siècle)*, vol. 1, edited by Guido Castelnuovo and Sandrine Victor, 502–20. Chambéry: Université Savoie Mont Blanc.

Benito i Monclús, Pere, and Antoni Riera Melis, eds. 2014. *Guerra y carestía en la Europa medieval*. Lleida: Editorial Milenio.

Benito Luna, Luis, and María Jesús Monter Domec. 1986. "La acequia de Albalate en el siglo XV: Aproximación al estudio del regadío medieval en el valle del Cinca." *Revista de ciencias sociales del Instituto de Ortega y Gasset* 100:167–76.

Bensch, Stephen. 1995. *Barcelona and Its Rulers, 1096–1291*. Cambridge: Cambridge University Press.

Bernardi, Philippe. 2015. "Quand le bâtiment va . . . : Une facette des rapports ville-campagne: Le marché des matériaux." In *Crisis in the Later Middle Ages: Beyond the Postan-Duby Paradigm*, edited by John Drendel, 273–96. Turnhout: Brepols.

Bernat i Roca, Margalida. 1998. "El manteniment de la salubritat pública a ciutat de Mallorca (segles XIV–XV)." *Acta historica et archaeologica mediaevalia* 19:91–125.

Berthe, Maurice. 1991. *Fams i epidèmies al camp navarrès als segles XIV i XV*. Barcelona: L'Avenç.

Bertran i Roigé, Prim. 1979. "El menjador de l'almoina de la catedral de Lleida: Notes sobre l'alimentació dels pobres lleidatans al 1338." *Ilerda* 40:89–124.

———. 2013. "Mercat i fira a Vilagrassa (S. XII–XIV): De les concessions reials a les tensions amb els municipis veïns." In *Romànic tardà a les terres de Lleida: Estudis sobre Vilagrassa; Actes de la Jornada de Treball XLII, Vilagrassa, 27 novembre de 2011*, edited by Miquel Torres, Joan-Ramon González, Dolors Gabarra, and Josep Sanahuja, 119–52. Lleida: Grup de Recerques de les Terres de Ponent.

Biraben, Jean-Noel. 1975. *Les hommes et la Peste en France et dans les pays éuropéens et méditerranéens*. 2 vols. Paris: Mouton.

Bisson, Thomas N. 1984. *Fiscal Accounts of Catalonia Under the Early Count-Kings (1151–1213)*. Berkeley: University of California Press.

Black, Richard. 2001. "Environmental Refugees: Myth or Reality?" United Nations High Comission for Refugees, New Issues in Refugee Research, Working Paper no. 34. https://www.unhcr.org/research/working/3ae6a0d00/environmental-refugees-myth-reality-richard-black.html.

Blanch i Amorós, Jaume. 1991. "L'alternativa terrestre de la ruta bladera de l'Ebre en el seu tram inferior." *Miscel·lània del centre d'estudis de la Ribera d'Ebre* 1 (8): 17–31.

Bolens, Lucie. 1979. "La conservation des grains en Andalousie médiévale d'après les traités d'agronomie hispano-arabes." In *Les techniques de conservation des grains à long terme*, edited by Marceau Gast and François Sigaut, 105–12. Paris: Éditions de Centre National de la Recherche Scientifique.

———. 1981. *Agronomes andalous de Moyen-Age*. Geneva: Librairie Droz.

Bourin, Monique. 2015. "De nouveaux chemins de développement dans le Languedoc d'avant la Peste." In *Crisis in the Later Middle Ages: Beyond the Postan-Duby Paradigm*, edited by John Drendel, 251–72. Turnhout: Brepols.

Bourin, Monique, Sandro Carocci, François Menant, and Lluís To Figueras. 2011. "Les campagnes de la Méditerranée occidentale autour de 1300: Tensions destructrices, tensions novatrices." *Annales: Économies, sociétés, civilisations* 66 (3): 663–704.

Bourin, Monique, John Drendel, and François Menant, eds. 2011. *Les disettes dans la conjoncture de 1300 en Méditerranée occidentale*. Rome: École Française de Rome.

Bourin, Monique, and François Menant. 2011. "Les disettes dans la conjoncture de 1300 en Méditerranée occidentale." In *Les disettes dans la conjoncture de 1300 en Méditerranée occidentale*, edited by Monique Bourin, John Drendel, and François Menant, 9–33. Rome: École Française de Rome.

Bourin, Monique, François Menant, and Lluís To Figueras. 2014a. "Les campagnes européennes avant la Peste:

Préliminaires historiographiques pour de nouvelles approches méditerranéennes." In *Dynamiques du monde rural dans la conjoncture de 1300: Échanges, prélèvements et consommation en Méditerranée occidentale*, edited by Monique Bourin, François Menant, and Lluis To Figueras, 9–101. Rome: École Française de Rome.

———, eds. 2014b. *Dynamiques du monde rural dans la conjoncture de 1300: Échanges, prélèvements et consommation en Méditerranée occidentale*. Rome: École Française de Rome.

Brasher, Sally Mayall. 2017. *Hospitals and Charity: Religious Culture and Civic Life in Medieval Northern Italy*. Manchester: Manchester University Press.

Brázdil, Rudolf, Oldřich Kotyza, and Martin Bauch. 2018. "Climate and Famines in the Czech Lands Prior to AD 1500: Possible Interconnections in a European Context." In *Famines During the "Little Ice Age" (1300–1800): Socionatural Entanglements in Premodern Societies*, edited by Dominik Collet and Maximilian Schuh, 91–114. Cham: Springer International.

Brenner, Robert. 1976. "Agrarian Class Structure and Economic Development in Pre-Industrial Europe." *Past and Present* 70:30–75.

———. 1987. "The Agrarian Roots of European Capitalism." In *The Brenner Debate: Agrarian Class Structure and Economic Development in Pre-Industrial Europe*, edited by T. H. Aston and C. H. E. Philpin, 213–327. New York: Cambridge University Press.

Britnell, Richard. 2009. "English Agricultural Output and Prices, 1350–1450: National Trends and Regional Divergences." In *Agriculture and Rural Society After the Black Death: Common Themes and Regional Variations*, edited by Richard Britnell and Ben Dodds, 20–39. Hertfordshire: University of Hertfordshire Press.

Brodman, James. 1986. *Ransoming Captives in Crusader Spain: The Order of Merced on the Christian-Islamic Frontier*. Philadelphia: University of Pennsylvania Press.

———. 1998. *Charity and Welfare: Hospitals and the Poor in Medieval Catalonia*. Philadelphia: University of Pennsylvania Press.

———. 2006. "Unequal in Charity? Women and Hospitals in Medieval Catalonia." *Medieval Encounters: Jewish, Christian, and Muslim Culture in Confluence and Dialogue* 12 (1): 26–36.

———. 2009. *Charity and Religion in Medieval Europe*. Washington, DC: Catholic University of America Press.

Burns, Robert Ignatius. 1975. *Medieval Colonialism: Postcrusade Exploitation of Islamic Valencia*. Princeton: Princeton University Press.

Càceres Nevot, Juan José. 2006. "La participació del consell municipal en l'aprovisionament cerealer de la ciutat de Barcelona (1301–1430)." PhD diss., Universitat de Barcelona.

Caferro, William. 1998. *Mercenary Companies and the Decline of Siena*. Baltimore: Johns Hopkins University Press.

Camenisch, Chantal. 2018. "Two Decades of Crisis: Famine and Dearth During the 1480s and 1490s in Western and Central Europe." In *Famines During the "Little Ice Age" (1300–1800): Socionatural Entanglements in Premodern Societies*, edited by Dominik Collet and Maximilian Schuh, 69–90. Cham: Springer International.

Cameron, Sarah. 2018. *The Hungry Steppe: Famine, Violence, and the Making of Soviet Kazakhstan*. Ithaca: Cornell University Press.

Campbell, Bruce M. S. 1995. "Ecology Versus Economy in Late Thirteenth-Century and Early Fourteenth-Century English Agriculture." In *Agriculture in the Middle Ages: Technology, Practice, and Representation*, edited by Del Sweeney, 76–108. Philadelphia: University of Pennsylvania Press.

———. 2000. *English Seigniorial Agriculture, 1250–1450*. Cambridge: Cambridge University Press.

———. 2005. "The Agrarian Problem in the Early Fourteenth Century." *Past and Present* 188:3–70.

———. 2007. *Three Centuries of English Crop Yields, 1211–1491.* https://pure.qub.ac.uk /en./datasets/three-centuries-of-english -crop-yields-1211-1491.

———. 2010. "Nature as Historical Protagonist: Environment and Society in Pre-Industrial England." *Economic History Review* 63 (2): 281–314.

———. 2016. *The Great Transition: Climate, Disease, and Society in the Late-Medieval World.* Cambridge: Cambridge University Press.

Camps Clemente, Manuel, and Manuel Camps Surroca. 1995. "L'alimentació hospitalària a Catalunya a la baixa Edat Mitjana." In *Actes del 1r. col·loqui internacional d'història de l'alimentació a la Corona d'Aragó: Edat Mitjana,* 2 vols., 2:885–906. Lleida: Fundació Pública Institut d'Estudis Ilerdencs.

———. 1998. *La Pesta del segle XV a Catalunya.* Lleida: Edicions de la Universitat de Lleida.

Canyelles Vilar, Núria. 1996a. "L'any de la fam al camp de Tarragona (1374–1376) " In *XIV jornades d'estudis històrics locals: La Mediterrània, àrea de convergència de sistemes alimentaris,* 263–81. Palma de Mallorca: Institut d'Estudis Baleàrics.

———. 1996b. "L'assistència als pobres de Valls: Fi del s. XIII–meitat del s. XIV, a través del cartulari de clàusules pels pobres del bací de Valls." *Historia et documenta* 3:29–59.

Capuano, Thomas M. 2006. "Una nueva versión catalana del *Opus agriculturae* de Palladius." *Romance Philology* 59 (2): 231–40.

———. 2014. "Early Catalan Agricultural Writing and the *Libre o regla o ensanyament de plantar o senbrar vinyes e arbres . . ."* Sciència.cat: Biblioteca Digital. http://www.sciencia.cat/biblioteca /documents/Palladi754_Capuano.pdf.

Carmichael, Ann. 2014. *Plague and the Poor in Renaissance Florence.* 2nd ed. Cambridge: Cambridge University Press.

Carpentier, Elisabeth. 1962. "Autour de la Peste Noire: Famines et épidémies au XIVe siècle." *Annales: Économies, sociétés, civilisations* 17 (6): 1062–92.

Carrère, Claude. 1967. *Barcelone: Centre économique à l'époque des difficultés, 1380–1462.* Paris: Mouton et Cie.

Chester, David K., and Angus M. Duncan. 2010. "Responding to Disasters Within the Christian Tradition, with Reference to Volcanic Eruptions and Earthquakes." *Religion* 4 (2): 85–95.

Cifuentes i Comamala, Lluís. 2013–14. "Els sabers útils al món rural català medieval: Agricultura, menescalia, medicina i conservació dels aliments." *Études roussillonnaises: Revue d'histoire et d'archéologie méditerranéennes* 26:33–40.

Clark, Gregory. 1998. "A Precocious Infant? The Evolution of the English Grain Market, 1208–1770." In *Integration of Commodity Markets in History,* edited by Clara Eugenia Núñez, 17–29. Seville: Editorial Universidad de Sevilla.

Clark, Peter, ed. 1985. *The European Crisis of the 1590s: Essays in Comparative History.* London: Allen and Unwin.

Codina i Vilà, Jaume. 1995. "El gra de la sitja: L'autoconsum alimentari pagès al delta del Llobregat als segles XIV i XV." In *Actes del 1r. col·loqui internacional de l'alimentació a la Corona d'Aragó: Edat Mitjana,* 2 vols., 2:35–51. Lleida: Institut d'Estudis Ilerdencs.

Cohn, Samuel K., Jr. 2008. "Epidemiology of the Black Death and Successive Waves of Plague." *Medical History Supplement* 27:74–100. https://www.ncbi.nlm.nih .gov/pmc/articles/PMC2630035.

———. 2010. *Cultures of Plague: Medical Thinking at the End of the Renaissance.* Oxford: Oxford University Press.

Collet, Dominik. 2012. "'Vulnerabilität' als Brückenkonzept der Hungerforschung." In *Handeln in Hungerkrisen: Neue Perspektiven auf soziale und klimatische Vulnerabilität,* edited by Dominik Collet, Thore Lassen, and Ansgar Schanbacher, 12–26. Göttingen: Universitätsverlag Göttingen.

———. 2015. "Predicting the Past? Integrating Vulnerability, Climate, and Culture During Historical Famines." In *Grounding Global Climate Change: Contributions from the Social and Cultural Sciences*, edited by Heike Greschke and Julia Tischler, 39–57. Dordrecht: Springer International.

Collet, Dominik, and Maximilian Schuh. 2018. "Famines: At the Interface of Nature and Society." In *Famines During the "Little Ice Age" (1300–1800): Socionatural Entanglements in Premodern Societies*, edited by Dominik Collet and Maximilian Schuh, 3–17. Cham: Springer International.

Comet, Georges. 1997. "Technology and Agricultural Expansion in the Middle Ages: The Example of France North of the Loire." In *Medieval Farming and Technology: The Impact of Agricultural Change in Northwest Europe*, edited by Grenville G. Astill and John Langdon, 11–40. Leiden: Brill.

Cortina, Vicent. 1970. "Los trabajadores del campo en la Valencia del siglo XV." In *IV Congreso de historia de la Corona de Aragón: Actas y comunicaciones*, 3 vols., 2:99–113. Palma de Mallorca: Diputación Provincial de Baleares.

Cruselles Gómez, Enrique. 1999. "La población de la ciudad de Valencia en los siglos XIV y XV." *Revista d'història medieval* 10:45–84.

Cruselles Gómez, José Maria. 1995. "Producción y autoconsumo en contratos agrarios de la huerta de Valencia (siglos XIV y XV)." In *Actes del 1r. col·loqui internacional d'història de l'alimentació a la Corona d'Aragó: Edat Mitjana*, 2 vols., 2:61–78. Lleida: Institut d'Estudis Ilerdencs.

Cruselles Gómez, José Maria, Enrique Cruselles Gómez, and Rafael Narbona. 1996. "El sistema de abastecimiento frumentario de la ciudad de Valencia en el siglo XV: Entre la subvención pública y el negocio privado." In *La Mediterrània, àrea de convergència de sistemes alimentaris: XIV jornades d'estudis històrics locals*, edited by Antoni Riera Melis and Maria Barceló Crespí, 305–32. Palma: Institut d'Estudis Baleàrics.

Cuadrada Majó, Coral. 2003. "Barcelona (ss. XIV–XV): Migracions, demografia i economia." In *El món urbà a la Corona d'Aragó del 1137 als decrets de Nova Planta: XVII Congrés d'Història de la Corona d'Aragó*, edited by Salvador Claramunt Rodríguez, 3 vols., 1: 323–32. Barcelona: Edicions Universitat de Barcelona.

Cubero i Corpas, Carmen, Imma Ollich i Castanyer, Montserrat de Rocafiguera i Espona, and Maria Ocaña i Subirana. 2008. "From the Granary to the Field: Archaeobotany and Experimental Archaeology at L'Esquerda (Catalonia, Spain)." *Vegetation History and Archaeobotany* 17 (1): 85–92.

Cuellas Campodarbe, Robert, and Dolors Domingo Rúbies. 2015. "Els principals privilegis de fires i mercats concedits a la ciutat de Balaguer." In *El mercat de Balaguer: Una cruïlla*, edited by Flocel Sabaté i Curull, 105–28. Balaguer: Ajuntament de Balaguer.

Cueves Granero, Maria Amparo. 1962. "Abastecimiento de la ciudad de Valencia durante la Edad Media." *Saitabi: Revista de la facultat de geografia i història* 12:141–67.

Curtis, Daniel. 2014. *Coping with Crisis: The Resilience and Vulnerability of Pre-Industrial Settlements*. Burlington, VT: Ashgate.

Curto i Homedes, Albert. 1988. *La intervenció municipal en l'abastament de blat d'una ciutat catalana: Tortosa, segle XIV*. Barcelona: Fundació Salvador Vives Casajuana.

———. 1995. "El consum de peix a la Tortosa baix-medieval." In *Actes del 1r. col·loqui internacional d'història de l'alimentació a la Corona d'Aragó: Edat Mitjana*, 2 vols., 2:149–66. Lleida: Institut d'Estudis Ilerdencs.

Cuvillier, Jean-Pierre. 1970. "La noblesse catalane et le commerce des blés aragonais au début du XIVe siècle (1316–1318)." *Mélanges de la Casa de Velázquez* 6:113–30.

D'Aguanno Ito, Marie. 2014. "Orsanmichele—The Florentine Grain Market: Trade and Worship in the Later Middle Ages." PhD diss., Catholic University of America.

Dameron, George. 2017. "Feeding the Medieval Italian City-State: Grain, War, and Political Legitimacy in Tuscany, c. 1150–c. 1350." *Speculum* 92 (4): 976–1019.

Dantí, Jaume. 2008. "Els cereals: Retrocés del guaret i conreus intensius." In *Història agrària dels Països Catalans*, vol. 3, *Edat Moderna*, edited by Emili Giralt i Raventós, 91–124. Barcelona: Edicions Universitat de Barcelona.

Davis, James. 2011. *Medieval Market Morality: Life, Law, and Ethics in the English Marketplace, 1200–1500*. Cambridge: Cambridge University Press.

Day, John, Bruno Anatra, and Lucetta Scaraffia, eds. 1984. *La Sardegna medioevale e moderna*. Turin: UTET.

Day, W. R. 2002. "The Population of Florence Before the Black Death: Survey and Synthesis." *Journal of Medieval History* 28 (2): 93–129.

De La Roncière, Charles M. 1982. *Prix et salaires à Florence au XIVe siècle (1280–1380)*. Rome: École Française de Rome.

———. 2011. "Les famines à Florence de 1280 à 1350." In *Les disettes dans la conjoncture de 1300 en Méditerranée occidentale*, edited by Monique Bourin, John Drendel, and François Menant, 225–46. Rome: École Française de Rome.

Del Estal Gutiérrez, Juan Manuel. 1983. "Extrema escasez de pan en Alicante: el año 1333." *Anales de la Universidad de Alicante: Historia medieval* 2:49–62.

Del Pozo Chacón, José Antonio. 1996. "Guerra, fiscalidad y poder local en Vila-Real (1362–1375)." In *El poder real de la Corona de Aragón (siglos XIV–XVI): XV Congreso de historia de la Corona de Aragón*, 5 vols., 4:219–32. Zaragoza: Gobierno de Aragón.

Del Treppo, Mario. 1976. *Els mercaders catalans i l'expansió de la corona catalano-aragonesa al segle XV*. Barcelona: Curial.

Demade, Julien. 2007. "The Medieval Countryside in German-Language Historiography Since the 1930s." In *The Rural History of Medieval European Societies: Trends and Perspectives*, edited by Maria Isabel Alfonso Anton, 173–252. Turnhout: Brepols.

Desai, Meghnad. 1988. "The Economics of Famine." In *Famine*, edited by G. Ainsworth Harrison, 107–38. Oxford: Oxford University Press.

Devereux, Stephen. 2001. "Sen's Entitlement Approach: Critiques and Counter-Critiques." *Oxford Development Studies* 29 (3): 245–63.

———. 2007. "From 'Old Famines' to 'New Famines.'" In *The New Famines: Why Famines Persist in an Era of Globalization*, edited by Stephen Devereux, 1–26. New York: Taylor and Francis.

De Vincenti, Andrea. 2018. "Educationalizing Hunger: Dealing with the Famine of 1770–1771 in Zurich." In *Famines During the "Little Ice Age" (1300–1800): Socionatural Entanglements in Premodern Societies*, edited by Dominik Collet and Maximilian Schuh, 195–208. Cham: Springer International.

De Waal, Alexander. 1997. *Famine Crimes: Politics and the Disaster Relief Industry in Africa*. Bloomington: Indiana University Press.

———. 2005. *Famine That Kills: Darfur, Sudan*. Rev. ed. Oxford: Oxford University Press.

———. 2018. *Mass Starvation: The History and Future of Famine*. London: Polity Press.

DeWitte, Sharon, and Philip Slavin. 2013. "Between Famine and Death: England on the Eve of the Black Death—Evidence from Paleoepidemiology and Manorial Accounts." *Journal of Interdisciplinary History* 44 (1): 37–60.

Dijkman, Jessica. 2011. *Shaping Medieval Markets: The Organisation of Commodity*

Markets in Holland, c. 1200–c. 1450. Leiden: Brill.

Doñate Sebastiá, José María. 1964. "Salarios y precios durante la segunda mitad del siglo XIV." In *VII Congreso de historia de la Corona de Aragón*, 3 vols., 2:417–506. Barcelona: F. Rodríguez Ferrán.

Drendel, John. 2011a. "Conclusion." In *Les disettes dans la conjoncture de 1300 en Méditerranée occidentale*, edited by Monique Bourin, John Drendel, and François Menant, 417–22. Rome: École Française de Rome.

———. 2011b. "Les disettes en Provence." In *Les disettes dans la conjoncture de 1300 en Méditerranée occidentale*, edited by Monique Bourin, John Drendel, and François Menant, 263–75. Rome: École Française de Rome.

Duby, Georges. 1968. *Rural Economy and Country Life in the Medieval West.* Translated by Cynthia Postan. Philadelphia: University of Pennsylvania Press.

Dyer, Christopher. 1995. "Were Peasants Self-Sufficient? English Villagers and the Market, 900–1350." In *Campagnes médiévales: L'homme et son espace; Études offertes à Robert Fossier*, edited by Elisabeth Momet, 653–66. Paris: Publications de la Sorbonne.

———. 2006. "Seasonal Patterns in Food Consumption in the Later Middle Ages." In *Food in Medieval England: Diet and Nutrition*, edited by Christopher Woolgar, Dale Serjeantson, and Tony Waldron, 201–14. Oxford: Oxford University Press.

———. 2015. "Medieval Small Towns and the Late Medieval Crisis." In *Crisis in the Later Middle Ages: Beyond the Postan-Duby Paradigm*, edited by John Drendel, 35–52. Turnhout: Brepols.

Echániz i Sans, María. 1988. "La alimentación de los pobres asistidos por la Pía Almoina de la Catedral de Barcelona según el libro de cuentas de 1283–1284." In *Alimentació i societat a la Catalunya medieval: Anuario de estudios medievales*, Annex 20, 173–262. Barcelona: Institució Milà i Fontanals.

Edkins, Jenny. 1996. "Legality with a Vengeance: Famines and Humanitarian Relief in 'Complex Emergencies.'" *Millennium: Journal of International Studies* 25 (3): 547–75.

———. 2000. *Whose Hunger? Concepts of Famine, Practices of Aid.* Minneapolis: University of Minnesota Press.

———. 2004. "'Famines' or 'Mass Starvations': Victims, Beneficiaries, and Perpetrators." *Humanitarian Practice Network*, July. http://odihpn.org/magazine/%C2%91famines%C2%92-or-%C2%91mass-starvations%C2%92-victims-beneficiaries-and-perpetrators.

Emigh, Rebecca Jean. 2005. "The Great Debates: Transitions to Capitalisms." In *Remaking Modernity: Politics, History, and Sociology*, edited by Julia Adams, Elisabeth S. Clemens, Ann Shola Orloff, and George Steinmetz, 355–80. Durham: Duke University Press.

———. 2009. *The Undevelopment of Capitalism: Sectors and Markets in Fifteenth-Century Tuscany.* Philadelphia: Temple University Press.

Epstein, Stephan R. 2000. *Freedom and Growth: Markets and States in Europe, 1300–1750.* New York: Routledge.

———. 2003. *An Island for Itself: Economic Development and Social Change in Late Medieval Sicily.* Cambridge: Cambridge University Press.

Epstein, Stephan R., and Francesco L. Galassi. 1994. "A Debate on Tuscans and Their Farms." *Rivista di storia economica* 11 (1): 111–137.

Erdkamp, Paul. 2005. *The Grain Market in the Roman Empire: A Social, Political, and Economic Study.* Cambridge: Cambridge University Press.

Fairchilds, Cissie. 1976. *Poverty and Charity in Aix-en-Provence, 1640–1789.* Baltimore: Johns Hopkins University Press.

Farmer, Sharon. 2002. *Surviving Poverty in Medieval Paris: Gender, Ideology, and the Daily Lives of the Poor.* Ithaca: Cornell University Press.

Feliu i Montfort, Gaspar. 1969. "La població del territori de Barcelona en el segle XIV." *Estudis d'història medieval* 1:61–73.

———. 2004. "Les mesures tradicionals catalanes: Un garbuix racional." *Butlletí de la Societat catalana d'estudis històrics* 15:9–30.

———. 2010. "Evolución y asentamiento de la población." In *La Corona de Aragón en el centro de su historia, 1208–1458: Aspectos económicos y sociales*, edited by José Ángel Sesma Muñoz, 31–58. Zaragoza: Grupo C.E.M.A., Universidad de Zaragoza.

Fernández Trabal, Josep. 1995. *Una família catalana medieval: Els Bell-Lloc de Girona, 1267–1533*. Girona: Publicacions de l'Abadia de Montserrat.

———. 1999. "De 'prohoms' a ciudadanos honrados: Aproximación al estudio de las elites urbanas de la sociedad catalana bajomedieval (s. XIV–XV)." *Revista d'història medieval* 10:331–70.

Fernández Trabal, Josep, and Antoni Riera Melis. 2004. "La crisi econòmica i social al camp." In *Història agrària dels Països Catalans*, vol. 2, *Edat Mitjana*, edited by Emili Giralt i Raventós and Josep Maria Salrach Marés, 119–80. Barcelona: Edicions Universitat de Barcelona.

Fernández Ugalde, Antonio. 1997. "El almacenamiento subterráneo y la conquista feudal en la Península Ibérica: Aportaciones de la arqueología." In *Rural Settlements in Medieval Europe: Papers of the "Medieval Europe Brugge 1997" Conference*, edited by Guy de Boe and Frans Verhaeghe, 11 vols., 6:283–89. Zellik: I.A.P. Rapporten.

Fernández Ugalde, Antonio, Elena Serrano, and Leonor Peña-Chocarro. 1997. "Los silos medievales en el reino de Toledo." In *Rural Settlements in Medieval Europe: Papers of the "Medieval Europe Brugge 1997" Conference*, edited by Guy de Boe and Frans Verhaeghe, 11 vols., 6:291–96. Zellik: I.A.P. Rapporten.

Ferrer i Mallol, Maria Teresa. 2001a. "Establiments de masos després de la Pesta Negra." In *El mas català durant l'Edat Mitjana i la Moderna (segles IX–*
XVIII): Aspectes arqueològics, històrics, geogràfics, arquitectònics i antropològics, edited by Maria Teresa Ferrer i Mallol, Josefa Mutgé i Vives, and Manuel Riu i Riu, 189–242. Barcelona: C.S.I.C.

———. 2001b. "Fruita seca i fruita assecada, una especialitat de l'àrea econòmica catalana-valenciana-balear." *Anuario de estudios medievales* 31 (2): 883–944.

———. 2001c. "Repartiments de terres a Oriola després de la conquesta de Jaume II." *Acta historica et archaeologica mediaevalia* 22:509–35.

———. 2012. "Catalan Commerce in the Late Middle Ages." *Catalan Historical Review* 5:29–65.

Fourquin, Guy. 1964. *Les campagnes de la région parisienne à la fin du Moyen Âge: Du milieu du XIIIe au début du XVIe siècle*. Paris: Presses Universitaires de France.

Franklin-Lyons, Adam. 2013. "Modern Famine Theory and the Study of Pre-Modern Famines." In *Crisis alimentarias en la Edad Media: Modelos, explicaciones y representaciones*, edited by Pere Benito i Monclús, 33–45. Lleida: Editorial Milenio.

———. 2013–14. "Grain Yields and Agricultural Practice at the Castle of Sitges, 1354–1411." *Études roussillonnaises: Revue d'histoire et d'archéologie méditerranéennes* 26:65–77.

———. 2018. "Policing the Grain Market in Post-Famine Manresa: A Transcription and Commentary." In *Políticas contra el hambre y la carestía en la Europa medieval*, edited by Luciano Palermo, Andrea Fara, and Pere Benito i Monclús, 283–303. Lleida: Editorial Milenio.

Fraser, Evan, and Andrew Rimas. 2011. "The Psychology of Food Riots: Why Do Price Spikes Lead to Unrest?" *Foreign Affairs*, January 30. https://www.foreignaffairs.com/articles/tunisia/2011-01-30/psychology-food-riots.

Freedman, Paul. 1991. *Origins of Peasant Servitude in Medieval Catalonia*. Cambridge: Cambridge University Press.

———. 2008. *Out of the East: Spices and the Medieval Imagination*. New Haven: Yale University Press.

———. 2013. "Peasant Servitude in Medieval Catalonia." *Catalan Historical Review* 6:33–43.

Furió, Antoni. 2004. "L'utillatge i les tècniques." In *Història agrària dels Països Catalans*, vol. 2, *Edat Mitjana*, edited by Emili Giralt i Raventós and Josep Maria Salrach Marés, 335–60. Barcelona: Edicions Universitat de Barcelona.

———. 2010. "Producción agraria, comercialización y mercados rurales en la Corona de Aragón." In *La Corona de Aragón en el centro de su historia, 1208–1458: Aspectos económicos y sociales*, edited by José Ángel Sesma Muñoz, 363–425. Zaragoza: Grupo C.E.M.A., Universidad de Zaragoza.

———. 2011. "Disettes et famines en temps de croissance: Une révision de la crise de 1300, le royaume de Valence dans la première moitié du XIVe siècle." In *Les disettes dans la conjoncture de 1300 en Méditerranée occidentale*, edited by Monique Bourin, John Drendel, and François Menant, 343–416. Rome: École Française de Rome.

Furió, Antoni, Antonio José Mira, and Pau Viciano Navarro. 1994. "L'entrada en la vida dels joves en el món rural valencià a finals de l'Edat Mitjana." *Revista d'història medieval* 5:75–106.

Fynn-Paul, Jeffrey. 2016. *The Rise and Decline of an Iberian Bourgeoisie: Manresa in the Later Middle Ages, 1250–1500*. Cambridge: Cambridge University Press.

Gaillard, Jean-Christophe, and Pauline Texier. 2010. "Religions, Natural Hazards, and Disasters: An Introduction." *Religion* 40 (2): 81–84.

García Marsilla, Juan Vicente. 1993. *La jerarquía de la mesa: Los sistemas alimentarios en la Valencia bajomedieval*. Valencia: Publicacions Universitat de València.

———. 2002. *Vivir a crédito en la Valencia medieval: De los orígenes del sistema censal*

al endeudamiento del municipio. Valencia: Publicacions Universitat de València.

———. 2007. "Feudalisme i crèdit a l'Europa medieval." *Barcelona: Quaderns d'història* 13:109–28.

Garcia-Oliver, Ferran. 2004. "Els cultius." In *Història agrària dels Països Catalans*, vol. 2, *Edat Mitjana*, edited by Emili Giralt i Raventós and Josep Maria Salrach Marés, 301–34. Barcelona: Edicions Universitat de Barcelona.

García Pardo, Jordi. 1989. *Sant Boi i el Pla del Llobregat a finals de l'Edat Mitjana: Introducció a l'estudi de la seva història econòmica i social a partir de les fonts documentals de l'Arxiu Parroquial de Sant Boi*. Barcelona: El Racó del Llibre de Text.

García Sánchez, Expiración. 1992. "Agriculture in Muslim Spain." In *The Legacy of Muslim Spain*, edited by Salma Khadra Jayyusi, 987–99. Leiden: Brill.

Garnsey, Peter. 1988. *Famine and Food Supply in the Graeco-Roman World: Responses to Risk and Crisis*. Cambridge: Cambridge University Press.

Gavitt, Philip. 1990. *Charity and Children in Renaissance Florence: The Ospedale degli Innocenti, 1410–1536*. Ann Arbor: University of Michigan Press.

Geremek, Bronislaw. 1970. "La lutte contre le vagabondage à Paris aux XlVe et XVe siècles." In *Ricerche storiche ed economiche in memoria di Corrado Barbagallo*, edited by Luigi De Rosa, 3 vols., 2:211–36. Naples: Edizioni Scientifiche Italiane.

Gerez Alum, Pau. 2010–11. "Ús i abús de l'aigua a la Girona baixmedieval." *Estudis d'història agrària* 23:219–29.

Gerrard, Christopher, and David Petley. 2013. "A Risk Society? Environmental Hazards, Risk, and Resilience in the Later Middle Ages in Europe." *Natural Hazards* 69 (1): 1051–79.

Gironella i Granés, Josep Maria. 2010. *Els molins i les salines de Castelló d'Empúries al segle XIV: La mòlta de cereals, el batanatge de teixits, i l'obtenció de sal*

en una vila catalana baixmedieval.
Barcelona: Fundació Noguera.

———. 2013. "La mòlta de cereals i el batanatge de teixits al comtat d'Empúries i al vescomtat de Rocabertí : finals del segle XIII i primera meitat del XIV." PhD diss., Universitat de Barcelona.

Glénisson, Jean. 1951. "Une administration médiévale aux prises avec la disette: La question des blés dans les provinces italiennes de l'état pontifical en 1374–1375." *Le Moyen Âge,* 4th ser., 5–6:303–26.

Glick, Thomas. 1970. *Irrigation and Society in Medieval Valencia.* Cambridge: Harvard University Press.

Gordon, D. T., and Colin Wrigley. 2004. "Whole-Grain Versus Refined Products." In *Encyclopedia of Grain Science,* edited by Colin Wrigley, 424–29. Oxford: Elsevier.

Grove, A. T., and Oliver Rackham. 2003. *The Nature of Mediterranean Europe: An Ecological History.* New Haven: Yale University Press.

Guglielmi, Nilda. 1998. *Marginalidad en la Edad Media.* Madrid: Editorial Biblos.

Guilhiermoz, Paul. 1913. "De l'équivalence des anciennes mesures." *Bibliothèque de l'École des Chartes* 74:267–328.

Guilleré, Christian. 1982. "Une institution charitable face aux malheurs du temps: La Pia Almoina de Gerone (1347–1380)." In *La pobreza y la asistencia a los pobres en la Catlauña medieval: Volumen misceláneo de estudios y documentos,* edited by Manuel Riu i Riu, 2 vols., 2:345–67. Barcelona: C.S.I.C.

———. 1993. *Girona al segle XIV.* 2 vols. Barcelona: Publicacions de l'Abadia de Montserrat.

———. 2001a. "De Torroella de Montgrí á Tossa: Les Catalans et la mer (fin XIIIe–XIVe siècle)." *Quaderns de la Selva* 13:83–108.

———. 2001b. "Le registre particulier d'un marchand de Montepulciano installé à Castelló d'Empúries, Taddeo Brunacini (1336–1340)." *Annales du midi* 236:509–49.

———. 2009. "Prix et salaires en Catalogne au XIVe siècle." In *Sources sérielles et prix au Moyen Âge: Travaux offerts à Maurice Berthe,* edited by Claude Denjean, 123–48. Toulouse: Presses Universitaires du Midi.

Guinot Rodríguez, Enric. 2003. *La baja Edad Media en los siglos XIV–XV: Economía y sociedad.* Madrid: Editorial Síntesis.

———. 2005. "L'horta de València a la baixa Edat Mitjana: De sistema hidràulic andalusí a feudal." *Afers: Fulls de recerca i pensament* 20 (51): 271–300.

Günzberg i Moll, Jordi. 1989. "Las crisis de mortalidad en la Barcelona del siglo XIV." *Revista de demografía histórica* 7 (2): 9–36.

———. 2000. "Crisis agrarias, mortalidad y alimentación en la ciudad y territorio de Barcelona durante la alta Edad Media." *Anuario de estudios medievales* 30 (2): 979–1014.

———. 2002. *Vida quotidiana a la ciutat de Barcelona durant la Pesta Negra, 1348.* Barcelona: Rafael Dalmau.

———. 2010. "Epidemias y mortalidad en la Cataluña medieval: 1300–1500." In *Economic and Biological Interactions in Pre-Industrial Europe from the Thirteenth to the Eighteenth Century: Papers of the "Quarantunesima Settimana de Studi," 26–30 April, 2009,* edited by Simonetta Cavaciocchi, 57–80. Florence: Firenze University Press.

Hanska, Jussi. 2002. *Strategies of Sanity and Survival: Religious Responses to Natural Disasters in the Middle Ages.* Helsinki: Finnish Literature Society.

Hatcher, John, and Mark Bailey. 2009. *Modelling the Middle Ages: The History and Theory of England's Economic Development.* Oxford: Oxford University Press.

Herlihy, David. 1990. "Age, Property, and Career in Medieval Society." In *Aging and the Aged in Medieval Europe: Selected Papers from the Annual Conference of the Centre for Medieval Studies, University of Toronto,* edited by Michael Sheehan,

143–58. Toronto: Pontifical Institute of Mediaeval Studies.

Herlihy, David, and Christiane Klapisch-Zuber. 1985. *Tuscans and Their Families: A Study of the Florentine Catasto of 1427.* New Haven: Yale University Press.

Hinojosa Montalvo, José Ramón. 1986. "El puerto de Alicante durante la baja Edad Media." In *Anales de la Universidad de Alicante: Historia medieval* 4–5:151–66.

———. 1992–93. "Aproximación a la ganaderia alicantina en la Edad Media." *Anales de la Universidad de Alicante: Historia medieval* 9:161–78.

———. 2006. "El aprovechamiento hidráulico en el reino de Valencia durante la Edad Media." *Cuadernos de historia de España* 80:25–54.

Hoar, Mark R., Jean P. Palutikof, and Mike C. Thorne. 2004. "Model Intercomparison for the Present Day, the Mid-Holocene, and the Last Glacial Maximum over Western Europe." *Journal of Geophysical Research* 109 (D8). https://doi.org/10.1029/2003JD004161.

Hoffmann, Richard C. 2014. *An Environmental History of Medieval Europe.* Cambridge: Cambridge University Press.

Holzhauser, Hanspeter, Michel Magny, and Heinz J. Zumbuühl. 2005. "Glacier and Lake-Level Variations in West-Central Europe over the Last 3500 Years." *Holocene* 15:789–801.

Horden, Peregrine, and Nicholas Purcell. 2000. *The Corrupting Sea: A Study of Mediterranean History.* Oxford: Blackwell.

Howe, Paul, and Stephen Devereux. 2004. "Famine Intensity and Magnitude Scales: A Proposal for an Instrumental Definition of Famine." *Disasters* 28 (4): 353–72.

Hoyle, R. W. 2010. "Famine as Agricultural Catastrophe: The Crisis of 1622–4 in East Lancashire." *Economic History Review* 63 (4): 974–1002.

Humbert, André, and Mohammed Fikri. 1999. "Les greniers collectifs fortifiés de l'Anti-Atlas occidental et central." In

Castrum 5: Archéologie des espaces agraires méditerranéens au Moyen Âge, edited by André Bazzana, 361–70. Madrid: Casa de Velázquez.

Huyssen, David. 2014. *Progressive Inequality: Rich and Poor in New York, 1890–1920.* Cambridge: Harvard University Press.

Igual Luis, David. 2012–14. "¿Los mercaderes son egualadors del món? Autóctonos y extranjeros en el comercio bajomedieval de Valencia." *Anales de la Universidad de Alicante: Historia medieval* 18:119–52.

Imamuddin, S. M. 2001. "Farming and Storing in Muslim Spain Under the Umayyads (711–1031)." In *Agriculture: Texts and Studies; Natural Sciences in Islam,* edited by Fuat Sezgin, 5 vols., 4:66–70. Frankfurt am Main: Institute for the History of Arabic-Islamic Science.

Iradiel, Paulino. 2017. *El mediterráneo medieval y Valencia: Economía, sociedad, historia.* Valencia: Publicacions Universitat de València.

Iranzo Muñío, María Teresa. 1997. "Pobreza, enfermedades y símbolos del poder señorial en Híjar: El hospital de la Santa Cruz, 1300–1312." *Aragón en la Edad Media* 13:105–24.

———. 2009. "El mercado urbano del vino en Huesca: Proteccionismo y comercialización." In *Crecimiento económico y formación de los mercados en Aragón en la Edad Media (1200–1350),* edited by José Ángel Sesma Muñoz and Carlos Laliena Corbera, 369–409. Zaragoza: Grupo C.E.M.A., Universidad de Zaragoza.

Jiao, Wu. 2008. "'Don't Blame Us for Food Crisis,'—Minister." *China Daily,* May 8.

Jordan, William Chester. 1996. *The Great Famine: Northern Europe in the Early Fourteenth Century.* Princeton: Princeton University Press.

———. 2010. "The Great Famine: 1315–1322 Revisited." In *Ecologies and Economies in Medieval and Early Modern Europe: Studies in Environmental History for Richard C. Hoffmann,* edited by Scott Bruce, 45–62. Leiden: Brill.

Juncosa Bonet, Eduard. 2016. *La població de Tarragona de la crisi baixmedieval a la de l'antic règim: Aproximació a la demografia històrica*. Tarragona: Arola Editors.

Juneja, Monica, and Franz Mauelshagen. 2007. "Disasters and Pre-Industrial Societies: Historiographic Trends and Comparative Perspectives." *Medieval History Journal* 10 (1–2): 1–31.

Kahl, Sigrun. 2005. "The Religious Roots of Modern Poverty Policy: Catholic, Lutheran, and Reformed Protestant Traditions Compared." *European Journal of Sociology* 46 (1): 91–126.

Kaufman, Frederick. 2011. "How Goldman Sachs Created the Food Crisis." *Foreign Policy*, April 27. https://foreignpolicy.com /2011/04/27/how-goldman-sachs -created-the-food-crisis.

Keen, David. 1994. *The Benefits of Famine: A Political Economy of Famine and Relief in Southwestern Sudan, 1983–1989*. Princeton: Princeton University Press.

———. 2008. *Complex Emergencies*. Cambridge: Polity Press.

Kelleher, Marie. 2013. "Eating from a Corrupted Table: Food Regulations and Civic Health in Barcelona's 'First Bad Year.'" *eHumanista* 25:51–64.

———. 2016. "'The Sea of Our City': Famine, Piracy, and Urban Sovereignty in Medieval Barcelona." *Mediterranean Studies* 24 (1): 1–22.

Kershaw, Ian. 1973. "The Great Famine and Agrarian Crisis in England, 1315–1322." *Past and Present* 59:3–50.

Keys, Ancel, Josef Brožek, and Austin Henschel. 1950. *The Biology of Human Starvation*. 2 vols. Minneapolis: University of Minnesota Press.

Kitsikopoulos, Harry. 2012. "England." In *Agrarian Change and Crisis in Europe, 1200–1500*, edited by Harry Kitsikopoulos, 23–56. London: Routledge.

Labrousse, Camille-Ernest. 1944. *La crise de l'économie française à la fin de l'ancien régime et au début de la Révolution*. Paris: Presses Universitaires de France.

Lakshmi, Rama. 2008. "Bush Comment on Food Crisis Brings Anger, Ridicule in India." *Washington Post*, May 8.

Laliena Corbera, Carlos. 2010. "Dinámicas de crisis: La sociedad rural aragonesa al filo de 1300." In *La Corona de Aragón en el centro de su historia, 1208–1458: Aspectos económicos y sociales*, edited by José Ángel Sesma Muñoz, 61–88. Zaragoza: Grupo C.E.M.A., Universidad de Zaragoza.

———. 2011. "Développement économique, marché céréalier et disettes en Aragon et en Navarre, 1280–1340." In *Les disettes dans la conjoncture de 1300 en Méditerranée occidentale*, edited by Monique Bourin, John Drendel, and François Menant, 277–308. Rome: École Française de Rome.

Langdon, John. 2015. "The Long Thirteenth Century: An Era of Schumpeterian Growth?" In *Crisis in the Later Middle Ages: Beyond the Postan-Duby Paradigm*, edited by John Drendel, 53–71. Turnhout: Brepols.

Langdon, John, and James Masschaele. 2006. "Commercial Activity and Population Growth in Medieval England." *Past and Present* 190:35–81.

Larenaudie, Marie-Josèphe. 1952. "Les famines en Languedoc au XIVe et XVe siècles." *Annales du midi* 64 (17): 23–35.

Laurioux, Bruno. 2002. *Manger au Moyen Âge: Pratiques et discours alimentaires en Europe aux XIVe et XVe siècles*. Paris: Hachette Littératures.

Le Roy Ladurie, Emmanuel. 1971. *Times of Feast, Times of Famine: A History of Climate Since the Year 1000*. Garden City, NY: Doubleday.

———. 1974. *The Peasants of Languedoc*. Urbana: University of Illinois Press.

Lewis, Archibald. 1975. "The Medieval Background of American Atlantic Maritime Development." In *The Atlantic World of Robert G. Albion*, edited by Benjamin Labaree, 18–39. Middletown: Wesleyan University Press.

Lionello, Piero, Paola Malanotte-Rizzoli, and R. Boscolo, eds. 2006. *Mediterranean Climate Variability*. Amsterdam: Elsevier.

Llensa i de Gelcen, Santiago. 1951. "Breve historia de las medidas superficiales agrarias de la antigüedad y estudio particular de aquellas cuyo uso es tradicional en Cataluña." In *Anales de la escuela de peritos agrícolas y de especialidades agropecuarias y de los servicios técnicos de agricultura* 10:66–128.

Llobet i Portella, Josep Maria. 1995. "La producció i el consum de carn a Cervera durant els segles XIV i XV." In *Actes del 1r. col·loqui internacional d'història de l'alimentació a la Corona d'Aragó: Edat Mitjana*, 2 vols., 2:53–60. Lleida: Institut d'Estudis Ilerdencs.

Lluch Bramon, Rosa. 1996. "Els manuals de comptes de l'Almoina del pa de la Seu de Girona: Menjar de pabordes i pa de pobres." In *La Mediterrània, àrea de convergència de sistemes alimentaris: XIV jornades d'estudis històrics locals*, edited by Antoni Riera Melis and Maria Barceló Crespí, 567–77. Palma: Institut d'Estudis Baleàrics.

———. 2006. "Una institució benèfica gironina: L'Almoina del pa." In *Miscel·lània Ernest Lluch i Martín*, edited by Jaume Claret Miranda, 243–52. Vilassar de Mar: Fundació Ernest Lluch.

———. 2009. *Els remences: La senyoria de l'Almoina de Girona als segles XIV i XV*. Girona: Biblioteca d'Història Rural.

López Beltrán, María Teresa. 2010. "El trabajo de las mujeres en el mundo urbano medieval." *Mélanges de la Casa de Velázquez* 40 (2): 39–57.

López Pizcueta, Tomás. 1995. "El 'mal any primer': Alimentación de los pobres asistidos en la Pia Almoina de Barcelona, 1333–1334." In *Actes del 1r. col·loqui internacional d'història de l'alimentació a la Corona d'Aragó: Edat Mitjana*, 2 vols., 2:613–23. Lleida: Institut d'Estudis Ilerdencs.

———. 1998. *La Pia Almoina de Barcelona: Estudi d'un patrimoni eclesiàstic català baixmedieval*. Barcelona: Fundació Noguera.

———. 1999. "El uso del contrato enfitéutico en la gestión del dominio territorial de la Pía Almoina de Barcelona (siglos XIII–XVI)." *Cuadernos de investigación histórica* 17:155–90.

Lübken, Uwe. 2012. "Chasing a Ghost? Environmental Change and Migration in Historical Perspective." *Global Environment: A Journal of Transdisciplinary History* 5 (9): 4–24.

Luongo, F. Thomas. 2006. *The Saintly Politics of Catherine of Siena*. Ithaca: Cornell University Press.

Macrae, Joanna, and Anthony B. Zwi, eds. 1994. *War and Hunger: Rethinking International Responses to Complex Emergencies*. London: Zed Books.

Magni, Stefano G. 2015. "Politica degli approvvigionamenti e controllo del commercio dei cereali nell'Italia dei comuni nel XIII e XIV secolo: Alcune questioni preliminari." *Mélanges de l'École française de Rome—Moyen Âge* 127 (1). http://journals.openedition.org/mefrm/2473.

Malanima, Paolo. 2012. "Italy." In *Agrarian Change and Crisis in Europe, 1200–1500*, edited by Harry Kitsikopoulos, 93–127. London: Routledge.

Martí, Sadurní. 1995. "'Més ne mata la gola que·l coltell.'" In *Actes del 1r. col·loqui internacional d'història de l'alimentació a la Corona d'Aragó: Edat Mitjana*, 2 vols., 2:909–20. Lleida: Institut d'Estudis Ilerdencs.

Martí Arau, Albert. 2011. "Castelló d'Empúries davant la carestia de gra de 1374–1376." *Annals de l'Institut d'estudis empordanesos* 42:263–96.

Martín, José-Luís. 2004. *La ciudad y el príncipe: Estudio y traducción de los textos de Francesc Eiximenis*. Barcelona: Publicacions i Edicions Universitat de Barcelona.

Martínez Araque, Ivan. 2010. "Transmissió del patrimoni i mercat immobiliari urbà: L'habitatge de les famílies artesanes en la vila d'Alzira durant els segles XIV–XV." *Anuario de estudios medievales* 40 (1): 201–21.

Martínez Ortiz, José. 1980. "Precedente histórico del trasvase Júcar-Turia: Un proyecto de construcción del canal y aprovechamiento de las aguas del siglo XIV." In *Primer Congreso de historia del país Valenciano: Celebrado en Valencia del 14 al 18 de abril de 1971*, 4 vols., 2:527–38. Valencia: Publicacions Universitat de València.

Marvin, Julia. 1998. "Cannibalism as an Aspect of Famine in Two English Chronicles." In *Food and Eating in Medieval Europe*, edited by Martha Carlin and Joel Thomas Rosenthal, 73–86. London: Hambledon Press.

Maubert, Claude-Guy. 1980. "La marine catalane et le trafic des grains (1356–1361)." *Mélanges de la Casa de Velázquez* 16:125–40.

Maubert, Claude-Guy, and Robert Vernet. 1974. "Sur les problemes du ravitaillement dans les Pays Catalans: Mouvement des cereales entre la Catalogne et le royaume de Valence pendant l'hiver de 1357–1358." *Cuadernos de historia económica de Cataluña* 12:9–24.

McVaugh, Michael R. 1993. *Medicine Before the Plague: Practitioners and Their Patients in the Crown of Aragon, 1285–1345.* Cambridge: Cambridge University Press.

Meade, Birgit, and Karen Thome. 2019. *International Food Security Assessment, 2017–2027.* U.S. Department of Agriculture, Economic Research Service. https://www.ers.usda.gov/data -products/international-food-security /documentation.aspx.

Menant, François. 2007. "Crisis de subsistencia y crisis agrarias en la Edad Media: Algunas reflexiones previas." In *Crisis de subsistencia y crisis agrarias en la Edad Media*, edited by Hipólito Rafael Oliva Herrer and Pere Benito i Monclús, 17–60. Seville: Editorial Universidad de Sevilla.

Metzler, Irina. 2013. *A Social History of Disability in the Middle Ages: Cultural Considerations of Physical Impairment.* New York: Routledge.

Michaud, Francine. 1998. "The Peasant Citizens of Marseille at the Turn of the Fourteenth Century." In *Urban and Rural Communities in Medieval France: Provence and Languedoc, 1000–1500*, edited by Kathryn L. Reyerson and John Drendel, 275–89. Leiden: Brill.

———. 2015. "Réflexions sur la condition des travailleurs au cours du XIVe siècle à Marseille." In *Crisis in the Later Middle Ages: Beyond the Postan-Duby Paradigm*, edited by John Drendel, 297–322. Turnhout: Brepols.

———. 2016. *Earning Dignity: Labour Conditions and Relations During the Century of the Black Death in Marseille.* Turnhout: Brepols.

Mies, Maria. 1996. *Women, Food, and Global Trade: An Ecofeminist Analysis of the World Food Summit, November 13–17, 1996, Rome.* Bielefeld: Institute für Theorie und Praxis der Subsistenz.

Milton, Gregory. 2012. *Market Power: Lordship, Society, and Economy in Medieval Catalonia (1276–1313).* New York: Palgrave Macmillan.

Miquel i Vives, Marina, and Anna Domingo Gabriel. 1995. "La taula reial a finals del segle XIV." In *Actes del 1r. col·loqui internacional d'història de l'alimentació a la Corona d'Aragó: Edat Mitjana*, 2 vols., 2:293–307. Lleida: Institut d'Estudis Ilerdencs.

Miret i Mestre, Josep. 2005. "Les sitges per emmagatzemar cereals: Algunes reflexions." *Revista de archaeologia de Ponent* 15:319–32.

Mokyr, Joel, and Cormac Ó Gráda. 1999. "Famine Disease and Famine Mortality: Lessons from Ireland, 1845–1850." University College Dublin, Centre for Economic Research Working Papers. https://ideas.repec.org/p/fth/dublec/99 -12.html.

Molénat, Jean-Pierre. 1984. "Menus des pauvres, menus des confrères à Tolède dans la deuxième moitié du XVe siècle." In *Manger et boire au Moyen Âge: Actes du colloque de Nice*, edited by Denis Menjot, 2 vols., 1:313–18. Paris: Belles Lettres.

Mollat, Michel, and Philippe Wolff. 1973. *The Popular Revolutions of the Late Middle Ages.* London: Allen and Unwin.

Monjo, Marta. 2012. "La pervivencia del regadío andalusí en la Aitona bajomedieval." In *Hidráulica agraria y sociedad feudal: Prácticas, técnicas, espacios*, edited by Josep Torró Abad and Enric Guinot Rodríguez, 207–22. Valencia: Publicacions Universitat de València.

Montanari, Massimo. 1994. *The Culture of Food*. Oxford: Blackwell.

Montoro i Maltas, Joan. 2015. "El almacenaje doméstico de grano en la Catalunya de la primera mitad del siglo XIV." In *La civiltà del pane: Storia, tecniche e simboli dal Mediterraneo all'Atlantico*, edited by Gabriele Archetti, 131–45. Spoleto: Fondazione Centro Italiano di Studi sull'Alto Medioevo.

———. 2019. "Caresties, fams i crisis de mortalitat a Catalunya, 1283–1351: Anàlisi d'indicadors i reconstrucció dels cicles econòmics i demogràfics." PhD diss., Universitat de Lleida.

Morelló Baget, Jordi. 2001. *Fiscalitat i deute públic en dues viles del Camp de Tarragona: Reus i Valls, segles XIV–XV*. Barcelona: Institució Milà i Fontanals.

Mott, Lawrence. 2012. "Aspects of Intercoastal Trade in the Western Mediterranean: The Voyage of the Santa María de Natzare." In *Shipping, Trade, and Crusade in the Medieval Mediterranean: Studies in Honor of John Pryor*, edited by Ruth Gertwagen and Elizabeth Jeffreys, 167–95. Burlington, VT: Ashgate.

Mude, Andrew G., Christopher B. Barrett, John G. McPeak, Robert Kaitho, and Patti Kristjanson. 2009. "Empirical Forecasting of Slow-Onset Disasters for Improved Emergency Response: An Application to Kenya's Arid North." *Food Policy* 34 (4): 329–39.

Mummey, Kevin. 2013. "Women, Slavery, and Community on the Island of Mallorca, ca. 1360–1390." PhD diss., University of Minnesota.

———. 2014. "Enchained in Paradise: Slave Identities on the Island of Mallorca, c. 1360–1390." In *Mediterranean Identities in the Premodern Era: Entrepôts, Islands,*

Empires, edited by John Watkins and Kathryn L. Reyerson, 121–38. Burlington, VT: Ashgate.

Muntaner i Alsina, Carme. 2013. "Terra de masos, vila de mar: Vida economia i territori al castell de Sitges i el seu terme entre els segles XIV i XV (1342–1418)." PhD diss., Universitat de Barcelona.

Murphy, Margaret. 1998. "Feeding Medieval Cities: Some Historical Approaches." In *Food and Eating in Medieval Europe*, edited by Martha Rosenthal and Joel Carlin, 117–31. London: Hambledon Press.

Mutgé i Vives, Josefa. 1987. *La ciudad de Barcelona durante el reinado de Alfonso el Benigno (1327–1336)*. Madrid: C.S.I.C.

———. 1988. "L'abastament de peix i de la carn a Barcelona en el primer terç del segle XIV." In *Alimentació i societat a la Catalunya medieval: Anuario de estudios medievales*, Annex 20, 109–36. Barcelona: Institució Milà i Fontanals.

———. 2001. "L'abastament de blat a la ciutat de Barcelona en temps d'Alfons el Benigne (1327–1336)." *Anuario de estudios medievales* 31 (2): 649–91.

———. 2004. *Política, urbanismo y vida ciudadana en la Barcelona del siglo XIV*. Barcelona: C.S.I.C.

Narbona Vizcaíno, Rafael. 1990. "Orígenes sociales de los tres estamentos ciudadanos en Valencia medieval." *Estudis: Revista de historia moderna* 16:7–30.

Navarro Espinach, Germán. 2010. "La presencia de grupos extranjeros en la Corona de Aragón (siglos XIII–XV)." In *La Corona de Aragón en el centro de su historia, 1208–1458: Aspectos económicos y sociales*, edited by José Ángel Sesma Muñoz, 161–90. Zaragoza: Grupo C.E.M.A., Universidad de Zaragoza.

Newfield, Timothy P. 2009. "A Cattle Panzootic in Early Fourteenth-Century Europe." *Agricultural History Review* 57 (2): 155–90.

———. 2013. "The Contours, Frequency, and Causation of Subsistence Crises in Carolingian Europe (750–950 CE)." In *Crisis alimentarias en la Edad Media:*

Modelos, explicaciones y representaciones, edited by Pere Benito i Monclús, 117–72. Lleida: Editorial Milenio.

New York Times. 2008. "The World Food Crisis." Editorial, April 10.

Obradors Suazo, Carolina. 2013. "Council, City, and Citizens: Citizenship Between Legal and Daily Experiences in Fifteenth-Century Barcelona." *Rivista dell'Istituto di storia dell'Europa mediterranea* 10: 371–418.

Ocaña i Subirana, María. 1998. *El món agrari i els cicles agrícoles a la Catalunya vella (s. IX–XIII).* Barcelona: Publicacions Universitat de Barcelona.

Ó Gráda, Cormac. 1995. *The Great Irish Famine.* Cambridge: Cambridge University Press.

———. 2009. *Famine: A Short History.* Princeton: Princeton University Press.

———. 2015. *Eating People Is Wrong, and Other Essays on Famine, Its Past, and Its Future.* Princeton: Princeton University Press.

Ó Gráda, Cormac, and Jean-Michel Chevet. 2002. "Famine and Market in Ancien Régime France." *Journal of Economic History* 62 (3): 706–33.

———. 2004. "Revisiting 'Subsistence Crises': The Characteristics of Demographic Crises in France in the First Half of the Nineteenth Century." *Food and Foodways* 12 (2–3): 165–95.

Oliva Herrer, Hipólito Rafael. 2013. "De nuevo sobre la crisis del XIV: Carestías e interpretaciones de la crisis en la Corona de Castilla." In *Crisis alimentarias en la Edad Media: Modelos, explicaciones y representaciones,* edited by Pere Benito i Monclús, 87–114. Lleida: Editorial Milenio.

———. 2018. "La política de la carestía en Castilla a fines de la Edad Media." In *Políticas contra el hambre y la carestía en la Europa medieval,* edited by Luciano Palermo, Andrea Fara, and Pere Benito i Monclús, 121–41. Lleida: Editorial Milenio.

Orsi Lázaro, Mario. 2008. "Estrategia, operaciones y logística en un conflicto mediterráneo: La revuelta del Juez de Arborea y la 'armada e viatge' de Pedro el Ceremonioso a Cerdeña (1353–1354)." *Anuario de estudios medievales* 38 (2): 921–68.

Ortega Ortega, Julián M. 2009. "Mercado sin competencia: Poblamiento, trashumancia y escenarios de intercambio en el horizonte de 1300; El caso del Aragón meridional." In *Crecimiento económico y formación de los mercados en Aragón en la Edad Media (1200–1350),* edited by José Ángel Sesma Muñoz and Carlos Laliena Corbera, 277–318. Zaragoza: Grupo C.E.M.A., Universidad de Zaragoza.

Ortega Villoslada, Antonio. 2014. "Majorca and the Import of Wheat from the Atlantic Ports (1230–1350)." *SVMMA: Revista de cultures medievals* 3:195–211.

Ortí i Gost, Pere. 1992. "El forment a la Barcelona baixmedieval: Preus, mesures i fiscalitat (1283–1345)." *Anuario de estudios medievales* 22:377–424.

———. 2000. *Renda i fiscalitat en una ciutat medieval: Barcelona, segles XII–XIV.* Barcelona: Institució Milà i Fontanals.

———. 2007. "Les finances municipals de la Barcelona dels segles XIV i XV: Del censal a la Taula de Canvi." *Barcelona: Quaderns d'història* 13:257–82.

Otis, Leah. 1986. "Municipal Wet Nurses in Fifteenth-Century Montpellier." In *Women and Work in Preindustrial Europe,* edited by Barbara A. Hanawalt, 83–93. Bloomington: Indiana University Press.

Palermo, Luciano. 1997. *Sviluppo economico e società preindustriali: Cicli, strutture e congiunture in Europa dal Medioevo alla prima età moderna.* Rome: Viella.

———. 2013. "Di fronte alla crisi: L'economia e il linguaggio della carestia nelle fonti medievali." In *Crisis alimentarias en la Edad Media: Modelos, explicaciones y representaciones,* edited by Pere Benito i Monclús, 47–67. Lleida: Editorial Milenio.

Palermo, Luciano, Andrea Fara, and Pere Benito i Monclús, eds. 2018. *Políticas* contra el hambre y la carestía en la Europa medieval. Lleida: Editorial Milenio.

Palesty, J. Alexander, and Stanley J. Dudrick. 2006. "The Goldilocks Paradigm of Starvation and Refeeding." Nutritional Clinical Practice 21 (2): 147–54.

Piesse, Jenifer, and Colin Thirtle. 2009. "Three Bubbles and a Panic: An Explanatory Review of Recent Food Commodity Price Events." Food Policy 34 (2): 119–29.

Pinto, Giuliano. 1985. "Appunti sulla politica annonaria in Italia fra XIII e XV secolo." In Aspetti della vita economica medievale, atti del convegno (Firenze-Pisa-Prato, 1984), 624–43. Florence: Università degli Studi Firenze.

———. 2011. "Percezione e coscienza delle crisi annonarie nei comuni italiani." In Les disettes dans la conjoncture de 1300 en Méditerranée occidentale, edited by Monique Bourin, John Drendel, and François Menant, 207–21. Rome: École Française de Rome.

Postan, M. M. 1964. "The Costs of the Hundred Years' War." Past and Present 27:34–53.

Pugliese, Olga Z. 1990. "The Good Works of the Florentine 'Buonomini di San Martino': An Example of Renaissance Pragmatism." In Crossing the Boundaries: Christian Piety and the Arts in Italian Medieval and Renaissance Confraternities, edited by Konrad Eisenbichler, 108–20. Kalamazoo: Medieval Institute Publications.

Puig, Carole. 2011. "L'apport de l'étude du stockage à notre connaissance de la conjoncture alimentaire de 1300 (Languedoc, Catalogne)." In Les disettes dans la conjoncture de 1300 en Méditerranée occidentale, edited by Monique Bourin, John Drendel, and François Menant, 159–77. Rome: École Française de Rome.

Puigferrat i Oliva, Carles. 2000. "Fam, guerra i pesta a la plana de Vic, 1374–1376." Ausa 19 (144): 73–107.

———. 2014. "El pas de les companyies de Jaume de Mallorca per la vegueria d'Osona durant la fam de 1374–1376." In Guerra y carestía en la Europa medieval, edited by Pere Benito i Monclús and Antoni Riera Melis, 149–64. Lleida: Editorial Milenio.

Rafat i Segla, Francesc. 1994. "Manresa en l'exportació de safrà durant el segle XIV." In La crisi de l'Edat Mitjana a la Catalunya central, edited by Marc Torras i Serra, 7–26. Bages: Centre d'Estudis del Bages.

Rangasami, Amrita. 1985a. "Failure of Exchange Entitlements Theory of Famine: A Response 1." Economic and Political Weekly 20 (41): 1747–52.

———. 1985b. "Failure of Exchange Entitlements Theory of Famine: A Response 2." Economic and Political Weekly 20 (42): 1797–801.

Ravallion, Martin. 1996. Famines and Economics. New York: World Bank Policy Research Department.

Reglero, Carlos. 2011. "Les disettes dans le royaume de Castille (entre 1250 et 1348)." In Les disettes dans la conjoncture de 1300 en Méditerranée occidentale, edited by Monique Bourin, John Drendel, and François Menant, 309–42. Rome: École Française de Rome.

Reixach Sala, Albert. 2018. "Mundo laboral, política municipal y trends económicos en las ciudades catalanas de la baja Edad Media: El ejemplo de Gerona (1340–1440)." In Trabajar en la ciudad medieval europea, edited by Jesús Ángel Solórzano Telechea and Arnaldo Sousa Melo, 349–78. Logroño: Instituto de Estudios Riojanos.

Renedo i Puig, Xavier. 1995. "Totes artificials laqueries . . . : Dietètica i moral en un capítol del Terç del Crestià de Francesc Eiximenis." In Actes del 1r. col·loqui internacional d'història de l'alimentació a la Corona d'Aragó: Edat Mitjana, 2 vols., 2:921–30. Lleida: Institut d'Estudis Ilerdencs.

Ressler, Everett M., Joanne Marie Tortorici, and Alex Marcelino. 1993. Children in War: A Guide to the Provision of Services; A Study for UNICEF. New York: UNICEF.

Reyerson, Kathryn L. 1985. *Business, Banking, and Finance in Medieval Montpellier.* Toronto: Pontifical Institute of Mediaeval Studies.

———. 1998. "Urban/Rural Exchange: Reflections on the Economic Relations of Town and Country in the Region of Montpellier Before 1350." In *Urban and Rural Communities in Medieval France: Provence and Languedoc, 1000–1500,* edited by Kathryn L. Reyerson and John Drendel, 253–73. Leiden: Brill.

Reynolds, Peter J. 1979. "A General Report of Underground Grain Storage Experiments at the Butser Ancient Farm Research Project." In *Les techniques de conservation des grains à long terme: Leur rôle dans la dynamique des systèmes de cultures et des sociétés,* edited by Marceau Gast and François Sigaut, 70–80. Paris: Éditions de Centre National de la Recherche Scientifique.

———. 1997. "Mediaeval Cereal Yields in Catalonia and England: An Empirical Challenge." *Acta historica et archaeologica mediaevalia* 18:495–507.

Richou i Llimona, Montserrat. 2009. "Els negocis de Ramon de Ganovardes, prevere beneficiat de la Seu de Barcelona." *Estudis històrics i documents dels arxius de protocols* 27:33–51.

———. 2013. "Una dècada d'abastament frumentari a Barcelona: La contribució de la iniciativa privada en els anys setanta del segle XIV." In *Crisis frumentàries, iniciatives privades i polítiques públiques de proveïment a les ciutats catalanes durant la baixa Edat Mitjana,* edited by Antoni Riera Melis, 117–60. Barcelona: Institut d'Estudis Catalans.

———. 2015. "Els comptes de Blanca de Llorach, abadessa de Sant Pere de les Puel·les (1373)." *SVMMA: Revista de cultures medievals* 5:1–23.

Riera i Viader, Sebastià. 1989. "El proveïment de cereals a la ciutat de Barcelona durant 'el mal any primer' (1333): La intervenció del Consell de Cent i de la Corona." In *Història urbana del Pla de Barcelona:*

Actes del II Congrés d'història del Pla de Barcelona, edited by Anna Maria Adroer i Tasis, 2 vols., 1:315–26. Barcelona: Ajuntament de Barcelona.

Riera Melis, Antoni. 1991. "Els pròdroms de les crisis agràries de la baixa Edat Mitjana a la Corona d'Aragó (1250–1300)." In *Miscel·lània en homenatge al P. Agustí Altisent,* 35–72. Tarragona: Diputació de Tarragona.

———. 1995–96. "Jerarquía social y desigualdad alimentaria en el Mediterráneo nor-occidental en la baja Edad Media: La cocina y la mesa de los estamentos privilegiados." *Acta historica et archaeologica mediaevalia* 16–17:181–205.

———. 1998. "'Panem nostrum quotidianum da nobis hodie': Los sistemas alimenticios de los estamentos populares en el Mediterráneo noroccidental en la baja Edad Media." In *La vida cotidiana en la Edad Media, VIII Semana de estudios medievales,* edited by José Ignacio de la Iglesia Duarte, 25–46. Logroño: Instituto de Estudios Riojanos.

———. 2007. "Crisis frumentarias y políticas municipales de abastecimiento en las ciudades catalanas durante la baja Edad Media." In *Crisis de subsistencia y crisis agrarias en la Edad Media,* edited by Hipólito Rafael Oliva Herrer and Pere Benito i Monclús, 125–60. Seville: Editorial Universidad de Sevilla.

———. 2009. "'Tener siempre bien aprovisionada la población': Los cereales y el pan en las ciudades catalanas durante la baja Edad Media." In *Alimentar la ciudad en la Edad Media: Nájera, encuentros internacionales del medievo 2008, del 22 al 25 de julio de 2008,* edited by Beatriz Arízaga Bolumburu and Jesús Ángel Solórzano Telechea, 23–58. Logroño: Instituto de Estudios Riojanos.

———. 2011a. "El mercado de los cereales en la corona catalanoaragonesa: La gestión de las carestías durante el segundo tercio del siglo XIII." In *Les disettes dans la conjoncture de 1300 en Méditerranée occidentale*, edited by Monique Bourin, John Drendel, and François Menant, 87–143. Rome: École Française de Rome.

———. 2011b. "Los sistemas alimentarios de los estamentos populares en el Mediterráneo noroccidental durante la baja Edad Media." In *Comer, beber, vivir: Consumo y niveles de vida en la Edad Media hispánica, XXI Semana de Estudios Medievales, Nájera, del 2 al 6 de Agosto de 2010*, edited by Esther López Ojeda, 57–96. Logroño: Instituto de Estudios Riojanos.

———. 2013a. "El mercat dels cereals a la Corona catalanoaragones: La gestió de les crisis alimentàries al segle XIII." In *Crisis frumentàries, iniciatives privades i polítiques públiques de proveïment a les ciutats catalanes durant la baixa Edat Mitjana*, edited by Antoni Riera Melis, 47–116. Barcelona: Institut d'Estudis Catalans.

———. 2013b. "Pròleg." In *Crisis frumentàries, iniciatives privades i polítiques públiques de proveïment a les ciutats catalanes durant la baixa Edat Mitjana*, edited by Antoni Riera Melis, 11–46. Barcelona: Institut d'Estudis Catalans.

———. 2017. *Els cereals i el pa en els països de llengua catalana a la baixa Edat Mitjana*. Barcelona: Institut d'Estudis Catalans.

———. 2018. "Crisis cerealistas, políticas públicas de aprovisionamiento, fiscalidad y seguridad alimentaria en las ciudades catalanas durante la baja Edad Media." In *Políticas contra el hambre y la carestía en la Europa medieval*, edited by Luciano Palermo, Andrea Fara, and Pere Benito i Monclús, 235–82. Lleida: Editorial Milenio.

Rodrigo Estevan, María Luz. 2009. "Del Pirineo a la cordillera Ibérica: Sistemas alimentarios en las montañas de Aragón (siglos XI–XV)." In *Food, Imaginaries, and Cultural Frontiers: Essays in Honour of Helen Macbeth, Estudios del Hombre*, edited by F. Xavier Medina, Ricardo Ávila, and Igor de Garine, 405–22. Guadalajara: Editorial de la Universidad de Guadalajara.

———. 2013. "Beber vino en la Edad Media: Modos, significados y sociabilidades en el Reino de Aragón." In *Patrimonio cultural de la vid y el vino*, edited by Sebastián Celestino Pérez and Juan Blánquez Pérez, 2 vols., 2:141–59. Madrid: UAM Ediciones.

Rodrigo Estevan, María Luz, and María José Sánchez Usón. 2006. "*Dare victum et vestitum convenienter*: El derecho de alimentos en el Aragón medieval; Entre la norma legal y la obligación moral." *Aragón en la Edad Media* 19:443–60.

Rohr, Christian. 2007. "Writing a Catastrophe: Describing and Constructing Disaster Perception in Narrative Sources from the Late Middle Ages." *Historical Social Research* 32 (3): 88–102.

Ruas, Marie-Pierre. 2002. *Productions agricoles, stockage et finage en Montagne Noire médiévale: Le grenier castral de Durfourt*. Paris: Éditions de la Maison des Sciences de l'Homme.

Rubin, Miri. 2020. *Cities of Strangers: Making Lives in Medieval Europe*. Cambridge: Cambridge University Press.

Rubio Vela, Agustín. 1979. *Peste Negra, crisis y comportamientos sociales en la España del siglo XIV: La cuidad de Valencia (1348–1401)*. Granada: Universidad de Granada.

———. 1982a. "A propósito del 'mal any primer': Dificultades cerealísticas en la Corona de Aragon en los anos treinta del siglo XIV." In *Estudios dedicados a Juan Peset Aleixandre*, 3 vols., 3:475–87. Valencia: Publicacions Universitat de València.

———. 1982b. "La asistencia hospitalaria infantil en la Valencia del siglo XIV: Pobres, huérfanos y expósitos." *Dynamis: Acta hispanica ad medicinae scientiarumque historiam illustrandam* 2:159–91.

———. 1984. *Pobreza, enfermedad y asistencia hospitalaria en la Valencia del siglo XIV*. Valencia: Institución Alfonso el Magnánimo.

———. 1987. "Crisis agrarias y carestías en las primeras décadas del siglo XIV: El caso de Valencia." *Saitabi: Revista de la facultat de geografia i història* 37:131–48.

———. 1995a. "El comsumo de pan en la Valencia bajomedieval." In *Actes del 1r. col·loqui internacional d'història de l'alimentació a la Corona d'Aragó: Edat Mitjana*, 2 vols., 1:153–83. Lleida: Institut d'Estudis Ilerdencs.

———. 1995b. "La población de Valencia en la baja Edad Media." *Hispania: Revista española de historia* 55 (190): 495–525.

———. 2001. "Valencia y el control de la producción cerealista del reino en la baja Edad Media: Orígenes y planteamiento de un conflicto." In *Demografía y sociedad en la España bajomedieval: Aragón en la Edad Media*, 33–65. Zaragoza: Universidad de Zaragoza.

———. 2009. "Trigo de Aragón en la Valencia del trescientos." In *Crecimiento económico y formación de los mercados en Aragón en la Edad Media (1200–1350)*, edited by José Ángel Sesma Muñoz and Carlos Laliena Corbera, 319–67. Zaragoza: Grupo C.E.M.A., Universidad de Zaragoza.

Ruiz, Teofilo F. 2007. *Spain's Centuries of Crisis, 1300–1474*. London: Wiley-Blackwell.

Ruiz de la Peña Solar, Juan Ignacio. 2003. "Ciudades y sociedades urbanas en la España medieval, siglos XIII–XV." In *Las sociedades urbanas en la España medieval: XXIX Semana de estudios medievales, Estella, 15–19 julio, 2002*, 17–49. Estella: Departamento de Educación y Cultura.

Ruiz Doménec, José Enrique. 1975. "Introducción al estudio del crédito en la ciudad de Barcelona durante los siglos XI y XII." *Miscellania barcinonensia* 14 (42): 17–33.

———. 1977. "The Urban Origins of Barcelona: Agricultural Revolution or Commercial Development?" *Speculum* 52 (2): 265–86.

Russell, Josiah C. 1962. "The Medieval Monedatge of Aragon and Valencia." *Proceedings of the American Philosophical Society* 106 (6): 483–504.

Salicrú i Lluch, Roser. 2000. "Entre el reclam de les terres islàmiques i l'escapada septentrional: La institucionalització de la por a les figures d'esclaus a la Catalunya tardomedieval." In *De l'esclavitud a la llibertat: Esclaus i lliberts a l'Edat Mitjana, actas del col·loqui internacional celebrat a Barcelona, del 27 al 29 de maig de 1999*, edited by María Teresa Ferrer i Mallol and Josefa Mutgé i Vives, 87–135. Barcelona: C.S.I.C.

Salrach Marés, Josep María. 2001. "Sociedad rural y mercados en la Cataluña medieval." *Edad Media: Revista de historia* 4:83–111.

———. 2004. "Fam d'ahir, fam d'avui: Anàlisi comparada de les causes." *Estudis d'història agrària* 17:841–60.

Sánchez Martínez, Manuel. 2001. "La presión fiscal en un año difícil: Cataluña, a mediados de 1374–mediados de 1375." *Mayurqa: Revista del Departament de ciències històriques i teoria de les arts* 27:25–45.

———. 2009. *La deuda pública en la Cataluña bajomedieval*. Barcelona: C.S.I.C.

Santamaría Aránděz, Álvaro. 1981–84. "Demografía de Mallorca: Análisis del morabatín de 1329." *Mayurqa: Revista del Departament de ciències històriques i teoria de les arts* 20:155–222.

———. 1983. "La asistencia a los pobres en Mallorca en el Bajomedievo." *Anuario de estudios medievales* 13:381–406.

———. 1992. "La demografía en el contexto de Valencia, siglo XV." *Medievalia* 10:363–86.

———. 2000. *El consell general de Valencia en el tránsito a la modernidad*. Valencia: Direcció General del Llibre.

Sarasa Sánchez, Esteban. 1995. "Los sistemas alimentarios en el reino de Aragón (siglos XII–XV)." In *Actes del 1r. col·loqui internacional d'història de l'alimentació a la Corona d'Aragó: Edat Mitjana*, 2 vols., 1:185–204. Lleida: Institut d'Estudis Ilerdencs.

Savy, Pierre. 2011. "Les disettes en Lombardie d'après les sources narratives (fin XIIIe–début XIVe siècle)." In *Les disettes dans la conjoncture de 1300 en Méditerranée occidentale*, edited by Monique Bourin,

John Drendel, and François Menant, 181–206. Rome: École Française de Rome.

Schneider, Eric. 2011. "Evaluating the Effectiveness of Yield-Raising Strategies in Medieval England: An Econometric Approach." *Discussion Papers in Economic and Social History* 90:1–49.

Scott, Tom. 2002. *Society and Economy in Germany, 1300–1600.* New York: Palgrave.

———. 2012. *The City-State in Europe, 1000–1600: Hinterland, Territory, Region.* Oxford: Oxford University Press.

Sen, Amartya. 1981. *Poverty and Famines: An Essay on Entitlement and Deprivation.* Oxford: Clarendon Press.

Serrahima i Balius, Pol. 2012. "El pa de la busca: Proveïment i consum del blat a Barcelona entre 1450 i 1462." In *Crisi frumentàries, iniciatives privades i polítiques públiques de proveïment a les ciutats catalanes durant la baixa Edat Mitjana,* edited by Antoni Riera Melis, 161–300. Barcelona: Institut d'Estudis Catalans.

———. 2016. "The Almoina of Barcelona During the Catalan Civil War (1462–1472): Changes and Continuities in the Conception of Poor Relief in Late Medieval Europe." In *Approaches to Poverty in Medieval Europe: Complexities, Contradictions, Transformations, c. 1100–1500,* edited by Sharon Farmer, 175–206. Turnhout: Brepols.

Serra i Clota, Assumpta. 1996. "Comportaments alimentaris i factors socioeconòmics en el món rural català a la baixa Edat Mitjana." In *La Mediterrània, àrea de convergència de sistemes alimentaris: XIV Jornades d'estudis històrics locals,* edited by Antoni Riera Melis and Maria Barceló Crespí, 529–42. Palma: Institut d'Estudis Baleàrics.

Serra i Puig, Eva. 1967. "Los cereales en la Barcelona de siglo XIV." Licentiate thesis, Universitat de Barcelona.

———. 1988. "Els cereals a la Barcelona del segle XIV." In *Alimentació i societat a la Catalunya medieval: Anuario de estudios medievales,* Annex 20, 71–107. Barcelona: Institució Milà i Fontanals.

Sesma Muñoz, José Ángel. 2003. "La población urbana en la Corona de Aragón (siglos XIV–XV)." In *Las sociedades urbanas en la España medieval: XXIX Semana de estudios medievales, Estella, 15–19 julio, 2002,* 151–93. Estella: Departamento de Educación y Cultura.

———. 2004. "El poblamiento del espacio periurbano de Zaragoza a comienzos del siglo XIV." In *La población de Aragón en la Edad Media (siglos XIII–XV): Estudios de demografía histórica,* edited by José Ángel Sesma Muñoz, Carlos Laliena Corbera, and Juan Abella Samitier, 385–402. Zaragoza: Leyere.

———, ed. 2010. *La Corona de Aragón en el centro de su historia, 1208–1458: Aspectos económicos y sociales.* Zaragoza: Grupo C.E.M.A., Universidad de Zaragoza.

Sesma Muñoz, José Ángel, Carlos Laliena Corbera, and Juan Abella Samitier, eds. 2004. *La población de Aragón en la Edad Media (siglos XIII–XV): Estudios de demografía histórica.* Zaragoza: Leyere.

Sevillano Colom, Francisco. 1957. *Valencia urbana medieval a través del oficio de Mustaçaf.* Valencia: C.S.I.C.–Instituto Valenciano de Estudios Históricos.

Sharp, Buchanan. 2000. "The Food Riots of 1347 and the Medieval Moral Economy." In *Moral Economy and Popular Protest: Crowds, Conflict, and Authority,* edited by Adrian Randall and Andrew Charlesworth, 33–54. New York: St. Martin's Press.

———. 2013. "Royal Paternalism and the Moral Economy in the Reign of Edward II: The Response to the Great Famine." *Economic History Review* 66 (2): 628–47.

———. 2016. *Famine and Scarcity in Late Medieval and Early Modern England: The Regulation of Grain Marketing, 1256–1631.* Cambridge: Cambridge University Press.

Silleras-Fernández, Núria. 2010. "Money Isn't Everything: Concubinage, Class, and the Rise and Fall of Sibil·la de Fortià, Queen of Aragon (1377–1387)." In *Women and Wealth in Late Medieval Europe*, edited by Theresa Earenfight, 67–88. New York: Palgrave Macmillan.

Slack, Paul. 1995. *The English Poor Law, 1531–1782*. Cambridge: Cambridge University Press.

Slavin, Philip. 2008. "Between Death and Survival: Norfolk Cattle, c. 1280–1370." *Fons luminis* 1:14–60.

———. 2012. "The Great Bovine Pestilence and Its Economic and Environmental Consequences in England and Wales, 1318–50." *Economic History Review* 65 (4): 1239–66.

———. 2014. "Market Failure During the Great Famine in England and Wales (1315–1317)." *Past and Present* 222:9–49.

———. 2019. *Experiencing Famine in Fourteenth-Century Britain*. Turnhout: Brepols.

Slicher van Bath, B. H. 1966. *The Agrarian History of Western Europe, AD 500–1850*. New York: St. Martin's Press.

Smail, Daniel Lord. 2016. *Legal Plunder: Households and Debt Collection in Late Medieval Europe*. Cambridge: Harvard University Press.

Smith, Adam. 1994. *An Inquiry into the Nature and Causes of the Wealth of Nations*. 1776. Edited by Edwin Cannan. New York: Modern Library.

Smith, Keith. 2013. *Environmental Hazards: Assessing Risk and Reducing Disaster*. London: Routledge.

Soldevila i Temporal, Xavier. 2000. "L'esclavitud a Torroella de Montgrí i la seva comarca (1270–1348)." In *De l'esclavitud a la llibertat: Esclaus i lliberts a l'Edat Mitjana*, edited by Maria Teresa Ferrer i Mallol and Josefa Mutgé i Vives, 361–67. Barcelona: C.S.I.C.

———. 2003. "Una vila empordanesa a l'Edat Mitjana: Torroella de Montgrí, segles XII–XIV." *Quaderns de la Selva* 15:89–103.

———. 2004. *Alimentació i abastament al baix Empordà medieval (segles XII–XIV)*. Bisbal d'Empordà: Ajuntament d'Empordà.

———. 2007. "Carestía y crisis de subsistencia en el mundo rural catalán: El baix Empordà en el siglo XIV." In *Crisis de subsistencia y crisis agrarias en la Edad Media*, edited by Hipólito Rafael Oliva Herrer and Pere Benito i Monclús, 221–28. Seville: Editorial Universidad de Sevilla.

———. 2014. "Rural Courts, Notaries, and Credit in the County of Empúries, 1290–1348." *Continuity and Change* 29 (1): 83–114.

Soler Millá, Juan Leonardo. 2003–4. "Relaciones comerciales entre Valencia y el norte de África en la primera mitad del siglo XIV." *Miscelánea medieval murciana* 27–28:125–58.

———. 2005. "'Que ordi ne sia tret la vila d'Oriola ni de son terme': Producción y comercialización de grano en el primer tercio del siglo XIV en la gobernación de Orihuela." In *La Mediterrània de la Corona d'Aragó, segles XIII–XVI i VII centenari de la sentència arbitral de Torrellas, 1304–2004*, edited by Rafael Narbona Vizcaíno, 2 vols., 1:1061–76. Valencia: Publicacions Universitat de València.

Somers, Margaret, and Fred Block. 2005. "From Poverty to Perversity: Ideas, Markets, and Institutions over 200 Years of Welfare Debate." *American Sociological Review* 70 (2): 260–87.

Spufford, Peter. 1988. *Money and Its Use in Medieval Europe*. Cambridge: Cambridge University Press.

———. 2002. *Power and Profit: The Merchant in Medieval Europe*. New York: Thames and Hudson.

Stalls, Clay. 1995. *Possessing the Land: Aragon's Expansion into Islam's Ebro Frontier Under Alfonso the Battler (1104–34)*. Leiden: Brill.

Stathakopoulos, Dionysios Ch. 2004. *Famine and Pestilence in the Late Roman and Early Byzantine Empire: A Systematic Survey of Subsistence Crises and Epidemics*. London: Ashgate.

Stearns, Justin. 2009. "New Directions in the Study of Religious Responses to the Black Death." *History Compass* 7 (5): 1363–75.

Stone, David. 2005. *Decision Making in Medieval Agriculture*. Oxford: Oxford University Press.

Stouff, Louis. 1970. *Ravitaillement et alimentation en Provence aux XIVe et XVe siècles*. Paris: Mouton.

Sullivan, Kevin. 2008. "Food Crisis Is Depicted as 'Silent Tsunami.'" *Washington Post*, April 23.

Tangheroni, Marco. 1981. *Aspetti del commercio dei cereali nei paesi della Corona d'Aragona: La Sardegna*. Pisa: Pacini.

Terpstra, Nicholas. 1994. "Apprenticeship in Social Welfare: From Confraternal Charity to Municipal Poor Relief in Early Modern Italy." *Sixteenth Century Journal* 25 (1): 101–20.

Thoen, Eric, and Tim Soens. 2015. "The Family or the Farm: A Sophie's Choice? The Late Medieval Crisis in Flanders." In *Crisis in the Later Middle Ages: Beyond the Postan-Duby Paradigm*, edited by John Drendel, 195–224. Turnhout: Brepols.

Thompson, E. P. 1971. "The Moral Economy of the English Crowd in the Eighteenth Century." *Past and Present* 50:76–136.

Thornton, Christopher. 1991. "The Determinants of Land Productivity on the Bishop of Winchester's Demesne of Rimpton, 1208 to 1403." In *Land, Labour, and Livestock: Historical Studies in European Agricultural Productivity*, edited by Bruce M. S. Campbell and Mark Overton, 183–210. Manchester: Manchester University Press.

Tierney, Brian. 1959. *Medieval Poor Law: A Sketch of Canonical Theory and Its Application in England*. Berkeley: University of California Press.

Titow, J. Z. 1972. *Winchester Yields: A Study in Medieval Agricultural Productivity*. Cambridge: Cambridge University Press.

Torras i Serra, Marc. 1994. "La carestia de blat de 1374–1376 a Manresa." In *La crisi de l'Edat Mitjana a la Catalunya central*, edited by Marc Torras i Serra, 99–138. Bages: Centre d'Estudis del Bages.

Torró Abad, Josep. 2013. "Canteros y niveladores: El problema de la transmisión de las técnicas hidráulicas andalusíes a las sociedades conquistadoras." *Miscelánea medieval murciana* 37:209–31.

Torró Abad, Josep, and Enric Guinot Rodríguez. 2012. "Introducción: ¿Existe una hidráulica agraria 'feudal'?" In *Hidráulica agraria y sociedad feudal: Prácticas, técnicas, espacios*, edited by Josep Torró Abad and Enric Guinot Rodríguez, 9–20. Valencia: Publicacions Universitat de València.

Turull i Rubinat, Max. 1986. "'El mal any primer' a Cervera: Trasbals sòcio-polític i crisi de subsistència (1333)." *Miscel·lània cerverina* 4:23–54.

———. 1992. "Agricultura i ramaderia a Cervera als segles XIII i XIV." *Miscel·lània cerverina* 8:65–96.

Tutusaus i Canals, Pau. 1986. "Un mal any en la ciudad de Barcelona: 1374–1375." Licentiate thesis, Universitat de Barcelona.

Unger, Richard. 1980. *The Ship in the Medieval Economy, 600–1600*. London: Croom Helm.

United Nations. 2015. *Millennium Development Goals Report 2015*. New York: United Nations. https://www.un.org /millenniumgoals.

United Nations, Department of Economic and Social Affairs. 2011. *Report on the World Situation 2011: The Global Social Crisis*. New York: United Nations Publications.

Vanhaute, Eric. 2011. "From Famine to Food Crisis: What History Can Teach Us About Local and Global Subsistence Crises." *Journal of Peasant Studies* 38 (1): 47–65.

Van Leeuwen, Marco. 2017. "Histories of Risk and Welfare in Europe During the Eighteenth and Nineteenth Centuries." In *Health Care and Poor Relief in Eighteenth- and Nineteenth-Century Northern Europe*, edited by Ole Peter Grell and Andrew Cunningham, 32–66. London: Routledge.

Vela i Aulesa, Carles. 2007. "Les compravendes al detall i a crèdit en el món artesà: El cas dels especiers i els candelers." Barcelona: Quaderns d'història 13:131–55.

Verdés Pijuan, Pere. 1994. "Paisatge agrari i abastament a Cervera (1370–1380)." Miscel·lània cerverina 9:29–67.

Verdon, Laure. 2015. "Les capbreus royaux roussillonnais et la crise malthusienne." In Crisis in the Later Middle Ages: Beyond the Postan-Duby Paradigm, edited by John Drendel, 323–38. Turnhout: Brepols.

Vicente Navarro, Francisco. 2012. "Las actividades económicas de la encomienda de Cantavieja en la frontera entre Aragón y Valencia (siglos XIII–XV)." In La historia peninsular en los espacios de frontera: Las "extremaduras históricas" y la "transierra" (siglos XI–XV), edited by Francisco García Fitz and Juan Francisco Jiménez Alcázar, 279–94. Murcia: Editum.

Viciano Navarro, Pau. 2001. "Els llauradors davant la innovació agrària: El cultiu de l'arròs al País Valencià a la fi de l'Edat Mitjana." Afers: Fulls de recerca i pensament 16 (39): 315–32.

Vilar, Pierre. 1974. "Reflexions sur la 'crise de l'ancien type,' 'inégalités de récoltes' et 'sous-développement.'" In Conjoncture économique, structures sociales: Hommage à Ernest Labrousse, edited by Fernand Braudel, Jean Bouvier, Pierre Chanu, François Crouzet, Adeline Daumard, Georges Dupeux, Claude Fohlen, et al., 37–58. Paris: Mouton.

Villagrasa Elías, Raúl. 2016. La red de hospitales en el Aragón medieval (ss. XII–XV). Zaragoza: Institución Fernando el Católico.

Vinyoles i Vidal, Teresa Maria. 1985. La vida quotidiana a Barcelona vers 1400. Barcelona: Rafael Dalmau.

———. 1995. "Alimentació i ritme del temp a Catalunya a la baixa Edat Mitjana." In Actes del 1r. col·loqui internacional d'història de l'alimentació a la Corona d'Aragó: Edat Mitjana, 2 vols., 1:115–51. Lleida: Institut d'Estudis Ilerdencs.

———. 2013. "Traces of the Destitute Among the Papers of the Hospital of Barcelona." SVMMA: Revista de cultures medievals 2:215–35.

Vinyoles i Vidal, Teresa Maria, and Margarida González i Beltinski. 1981. "Els infants abandonats a les portes de l'Hospital de Barcelona (1426–1439)." In La pobreza y la asistencia a los pobres en la Cataluña medieval: Volumen misceláneo de estudios y documentos, edited by Manuel Riu i Riu, 2 vols., 2:191–285. Barcelona: Institución Milá y Fontanals.

Wainwright, Valerie. 1987. "The Testing of a Popular Sienese Regime: The 'Riformatori' and the Insurrections of 1371." I Tatti: Studies in the Italian Renaissance 2:107–70.

Walsh, Declan, and Tyler Hicks. 2018. "The Tragedy of Saudi Arabia's War." New York Times, October 26.

Ward, Jennifer. 2016. Women in Medieval Europe, 1200–1500. 2nd ed. New York: Routledge.

Wolff, Philippe. 1959. "Un grand commerce médiéval: Les céréales dans le bassin de la Méditerranée occidentale; Remarques et suggestions." In VI Congreso de historia de la Corona de Aragón, 147–64. Madrid: Dirección General de Relaciones Culturales.

Zorzi, Andrea. 1994. "L'organizzazione del territorio in Italia in area fiorentina tra XIII e XIV secolo." In L'organizzazione del territorio in Italia e Germania: Secoli XIII–XIV, edited by Giorgio Chittolini and Dietmar Willoweit, 279–349. Bologna: Società Editrice il Mulino.

Zulaica Palacios, Fernando D. 1997. "Mercados y vías fluviales: El Ebro como eje organizador del territorio e integrador de la economía aragonesa en los circuitos europeos." Aragón en la Edad Media 13:65–104.

Index

Note: Page numbers followed by *f* and *t* refer to figures and tables, respectively. Those followed by n refer to notes, with note number.

Castlar, Francesc, 58
Catala, Berenguer, 147, 152
Catalonia
    agriculture in, 30
    charitable institutions in, 90
    Civil War, 62
    crop data, 11–12
    and demographic regimes of Crown of
        Aragon, 47–48
    diet in, 22
    and dispute over throne of Mallorca, 170
    and famine of 1374–75, 103, 148, 160, 173
    as grain exporter, 8, 118, 121
    grain sources for, 52
    as grain supplier, 53, 118, 120
    land tenure systems in, 24–25
    manure market in, 29
    market regulation in, 59
    markets added in 14th century, 49
    network of cities in, 48
    Plague in (1371–72), 172
    saffron production in, 6, 26, 52–53
    Segre River and, 20
    and shortages of 1384–85, 130, 135–36
    taxes in, 47
    weights and measures in, 12
    years of bad harvest in 1370s, 150
Cathedral of Lleida, pay for salaried workers
    in, 85
cathedrals, and poorhouses, 90
Cerdanya, and famine of 1374–75, and taxes
    to finance defense, 171
Cervelló, Ramon Alemany de, 162
Cervera
    and famine of 1374–75, 148, 157
    small irrigation projects near, 30
charitable institutions, 89–99
    asylum provided by, 98
    care for specific populations, 97–98
    criteria for providing assistance, 94–99
    and deserving vs. undeserving poor, 8,
        91–92, 108–9, 180; donor's salvation
        through good works as reason for dis-
        tinction between, 91, 92, 93–94, 108–9;
        similarities in modern food aid, 182
    donations requiring care of family mem-
        bers, 96
    donations targeting specific populations, 96
    and donors' salvation through good works,
        91, 92, 93–94, 108–9

    and family connections, 97, 98, 108, 109
    and famine of 1374–75: cutting of bread
        handouts, 147, 152, 158, 178; profits from
        rents paid in grain, 153, 178; rural sacri-
        fice to fund urban charity for families of
        well-off, 153; wheat prices in, 153
    feeding of employees in shortages and
        famine, 107
    growth of, 8
    in Italian cities, 99
    moral obligation of wealthy to support,
        90–91
    and poverty and marginality, definitions of,
        94–95, 184n62
    "powerlessness" as criteria for aid from,
        98
    prioritization of citizens first, 96, 97, 102,
        109
    programs for youth, 98–99
    proliferation of, 90
    religious life required of residents, 93–94,
        109
    and residents' loss of agency, 94
    as retirement homes, 97–98
    safety nets used prior to, 91, 95
    stipends and pensions paid by, 98
    and voluntary vs. involuntary poor, 91–92
    See also hospitals; poorhouses
chickpeas, as back-up grain for bad wheat
    years, 3, 153
cities
    debts of: as borrowed from elite to pay
        subsidies to elite, 80; from high cost of
        crisis management, 80
    grain market, impact of shipload of grain
        on, 62–64
    large regional capitals, 48
    medium-sized, web of smaller cities within
        market of, 49
    network of, 48
    per capita grain needs, 63
    political clout of, and ability to control
        grain markets, 48
    poor population in, 89–90
    safety nets as draw for, 84
    See also Italian cities
city governments
    jurors (city officials): and efforts to control
        grain markets, 45, 51; number of, 51
    understanding of famine causes, 45

uniformity of structure, 51
upper, middle, and lower status groups
in, 51–52
urban councils: and efforts to control grain
markets, 45, 51; number of members, 51
city governments' efforts to control grain
markets, 7, 45, 46, 50–53, 55
cities' fierce defense of, 61
and conflict between towns, 49–50
debt from high cost of crisis management,
80
effectiveness of, 62–63
experimentation with, 62
export bans and licenses, 60, 67–68,
75–76, 133–34, 141, 142, 143, 147, 148,
157, 158, 164, 165
and feedback loops in times of shortage,
79–80
fine tuning of, over time, 62
focus on control at borders, 51, 78
goals in normal times, 55
and increased market integration, 46
increase over time, 55, 61, 80
large-scale purchase and resale of grain, 57,
68, 117, 126, 131, 141, 142
methods of control, 55–62
monitoring of supply levels, 57
mostassaf and, 51, 55
motives for, 46, 50, 52
multilevel system of suppliers, creation
of, 53
official price-controlled markets in, 57
political clout of city and, 48
and power to squeeze surplus from rural
areas in time of crisis, 50
price fixing, 56, 59
vs. regulation of meat and wine markets,
62, 65–66
representatives sent to potential exporters,
57–58, 81, 118, 119, 120, 121, 126
and royal mediation between cities, 51
seizure of grain by force (*vi vel gratia*
right), 58–59, 61, 75, 120, 141, 142
self-interest in, 55–56, 61, 62, 65, 66–67
subsidies for grain delivery, 56–57, 64, 68,
71, 117, 119, 121, 123, 124f, 126–27, 129,
130, 131, 132–34, 142
and trade wars, 57
and understanding of market forces, 62,
64–66

civada, 22
Clapers, Bernat des, 90
Clement VII (pope), 140
climate change
as cause of famine, history of theories on,
3, 4, 5, 151
and chronic drought in Valencia, 30
in 14th century: and increased risk of crop
failure, 19, 151; lesser impact on Mediterranean agriculture, 19
Collet, Dominik, 103, 181
Colom, Joan, 90
community, loss of, as marker of famine,
100
Coppo Stefani, Marchionne de, 139
Cortades, Ripoll de, 96
COVID-19, 1–2
credit
extension of, in times of shortages and
famine, 107–8, 109, 179
increased availability in market economy,
49, 50
risks of, 50
crises, modern *vs.* premodern, Labrousse
on, 3
Crónicas de los Jueces de Teruel, 175
crop choice
avoiding shortages as one of several
motives in, 17
culture and, 6, 17, 22–27, 43
crop diversity
as natural effect of Crown of Aragon terrain variations, 19–20
and resilience in agriculture, 19, 21
crop rotation, at Sitges castle, 36
crop yields
in Crown of Aragon, lack of records on,
40–41
effect of manure fertilizer on, 29
effect of weather on, 29
at Sitges castle, 35–36, 36f, 189n125; drop
in, during famine of 1376, 35; variation
with weather, 35
sources on, 11–12
Crown of Aragon
extensive 14th-century records, 9
tax records, 47
usefulness of medieval food shortages in
study of famines, 8–9
culture, and crop choice, 6, 17, 22–27, 43

effect on grain prices, 76, 77*f*
vs. hoarding, 76, 78, 79
and market collapse, 76, 79

Fairchilds, Cissie, 109
families
breakup of, in famines, 100
legal responsibility to care for elderly
members, 95–96
as safety nets for poor, 83, 91, 95, 109
famine
aftershocks of, 103–4, 109
and breakup of families, 100
as complex human disaster, 2, 181
definitions of, 113–14
deserted rural areas in, 101
disease as factor in severity of, 176
epicenters and edges in, 176
levels of suffering in, number of concurrent causes and, 174–76, 180–81
in medieval Europe, rapid onset of, 160
medieval terms for, 116, 174
modern, and mismatch of triggers and
response, 150
multiple contributing factors in, 6, 114–15,
130–31, 137, 150, 179, 180–81
persistence of daily life despite, 182–83
poor persons' selling of goods for food,
167–68
relative rarity of, 114, 180
severity of: at edge *vs.* epicenter, 174, 176,
177, 180; geographic *vs.* temporal scope
in, 115; lack of personal connections
and, 181; lack of political clout and,
181; number of concurrent causes and,
174–76, 180–81; social disjunction level
as measure of, 8; uses for rankings of,
114; war as factor in, 176
vs. shortage, defining features of, 99–100
and shortages in multiple locations:
multiplying effect of, 7, 46, 68, 70–71,
72, 78–79, 81, 176; as necessary to cause
famine, 113, 114, 115, 180
shortages of a few staples as cause of, 166
and socioeconomic entanglements, 103
soil exhaustion and, 27
and spike in wills donating to hospitals, 90
temporal specificity in designation of, 115
years of, in 14th century Crown of Aragon,
115

famine in 14th century
breakdown of social order as component
of, 8
complex factors contributing to, 6, 179,
180–81
three central factors in, 6
famine of 1276, varying impact in different
cities, 81
famine of 1315–1317. *See* Great Famine of
1315–1317
famine of 1333–36
banning of hoarding on, 73
mix of religious and technocratic
responses to, 162
famine of 1374–75
aristocratic diet and, 153
armed ship use in, 147, 164–65
bad grain harvests and, 166, 177
Barcelona's official market grain sales in, 57
and beggars, crackdown on, 3, 154
cathedral grain purchase rights, cutoff of,
147
charities' cutting of bread handouts, 147,
152, 158, 178
and cities' debt from high cost of crisis
management, 80
competition for food in, 75–76, 147–48
credit extended in, 107–8
and disease, role of, 171, 172–74
distant grain sources, use of, 150
economic inequality and, 178
effect on small farmers, 26–27
export bans in, 147, 148, 157, 158, 164, 165;
as counterproductive, 76–77, 78–79;
effect on grain prices, 76, 77*f*
and food distribution channels, shutdown
of, 149
and foreigners, cities' removal of, 3
freeing of slaves to avoid feeding them, 89
harvest failures of 1374–77 and, 148, 154–55
and hoarding, 75, 79
impact, markets' damping of, 69
increased city funding of poor relief during, 153–54
internal conflict in Crown of Aragon and,
149
international conflicts and, 148, 149, 150,
157
and Jews and foreigners, discrimination
against, 95

famine of (*continued*)

King Pere's founding of hospital in, 93

King Pere's increase of shipyard pay during, 106

labor shortages following, 101

large geographical extent, 149, 150, 151, 176, 177, 180

levels of suffering, number of concurrent causes and, 174–76, 180–81

market failures as factor in, 3. 4

memories of, in shortages of 1384–85, 137–39, 144–45

multiple causes of, 2–3

number of deaths in, 178

as one-year event for many, 152, 177

panic and, 160, 177

persistence for second year outside major cities, 152–55

Plague and, 149–50, 172–73, 175, 177

political maneuvering as factor in, 3

poor persons' greater suffering in, 3

poor persons' selling of goods for food, 167–68

prices for food other than grain: meat prices, 166, 167, 167f, 174; stability of, 166–67, 167f; wine prices, 166, 167f, 174

prices of grain in, 153–61, 156f, 166, 167f, 177

recovery by fall of 1375, 150, 177–78

religious responses to, 162–64

representatives sent to potential grain sources, 164

and rural areas: cities' draining of grain reserves from, 155–60; greater suffering in second year, 154–60, 161, 177; return of grain resources to, at end of famine, 159

servants' rations, reduction of, 154

similarities to food shortage of 2007, 2

Sitges castle response to, 36, 38–39

and taxes to finance defense, 171

and threat of starvation for lower ranks, 153–54

variety of factors causing, 150

and wage labor, decline in, 154

war as factor in, 148, 149, 150, 157, 168–71, 173–74, 175, 177, 180–81

wealthy persons' ability to acquire food in, 153

weather and, 2–3, 148, 149, 150–52, 177, 180

weather as factor in, 2–3

in Western Mediterranean, 5

famine of 1376, low grain yields and, 35

famine of 1383, Sitges castle response to, 36

fava beans

as back-up grain for bad wheat years, 153

as crop, 38; at Sitges castle, 39, 39f; yields, 35, 36f, 154

Feliu, Pere, 157–58

Fernández de Híjar, Pedro, 93

Fernando IV of Castile, 102

Ferrandez, Agnes, 98

Ferrandez de Villodres, Garcia, 98

Ferrer, Vincent, 22

fertilizer. *See* manure fertilizer

financial crisis of 2008, food shortage of 2007 and, 2

Flanders

and famine of 1374–75, 152

as grain exporter, 69, 79, 154

Flix, burning of, 62

flood of 1379 in Kingdom of Aragon, 20

Florence

and famine of 1374–75, 149, 160, 167, 168

price fluctuations, 1369–72, 125

and shortages of 1384–85, 145

Foguet, Francesch, 160

Fontelles, Pere, 119, 120

Fonts, Paschual de, 120

food, access to, in normal times

charities and, 89–99

for deserving poor, 83

employer and guild safety nets, 83, 106

estimated annual wage necessary for, 84–85

factors affecting, 83

family support networks and, 83

hospitals' distribution of food, 83

layers of, 83

and multiple wage earners in families, 85

salaried workers and, 85–86

for servants and slaves, 88–89

social hierarchy and, 113

for wage laborers, 83, 86–88, 179

See also charitable institutions

food, access to, in shortages and famine, 99–108

charitable institutions' feeding of employees, 107

grain (*continued*)
    increased price of grain from distant
        sources, 54, 54f
    and price for grain, 47
    See also city governments' efforts to control
        grain markets; grain prices; markets
grain merchants, ships used by, 64
grain prices
    effect of export bans on, 76, 77f
    in famine of 1374–75, 153–61, 156f, 166,
        167f, 177
    fluctuation in famine, 80
    influence of markets on, 47
    Pia Almoina records of, 11
    rising of, in poor harvest years, 68–69
    seasonal fluctuation in, 68–69
grain riots, targeting of urban elites in, 95,
    100
grain storage
    above-ground storage houses, 31–32
    and agricultural resilience, 179
    barley as preferred grain for, 33, 43
    as common in Crown of Aragon, 40
    decline of, with market development,
        32
    as hedge against shortages, 17
    laws on grain sales and, 31, 33–34, 43
    market speculation encouraged by, 17
    private, 31; and spoilage, 32–33; as useful
        for short periods only, 31
    and spoilage, 32–33
    subterranean storage pits, 31; additives
        to prevent bacteria and mold, 32; and
        "increase" of grain, 33; laws forbidding
        sale as seed grain, 33; price drops due
        to added substances, 32; and spoilage,
        32–33
    Taifa kingdom Muslims on, 31–32
    three types of, 31
Great Famine of 1315–1317
    aftershocks of, 103–4
    animal diseases concurrent with, 167,
        200n80
    complex factors causing, 4
    death of livestock in, and diminished
        manure supply, 28
Great Plague, anti-Jewish acts in, 95
Gregory XI (pope), 140, 149, 168–71
Grony family, and wine production, 66
Grove, A. T., 21

Harfleur, grain exports by, 69
Hawkwood, John, 149, 168
Herlihy, David, 95
hoarding
    archival examples of, 74–75
    blaming shortages on, in medieval
        sources, 72
    by cities, effects of, 75–76
    city officials' banning of, 72–73, 79
    vs. export bans, 76, 78, 79
    markets' tendency to eliminate, 73–74
    tendency to reduce rather than worsen
        shortages, 75
Hoffmann, Richard, 19
Horden, Peregrine, 4, 151
Hospital dels Malalts, 35, 38, 39
Hospital of en Colom, 28, 35
Hospital de Sant Andreu, and famine of
        1374–75, 107–8, 159
Hospital Desvilar, 28, 93, 96
Hospital of en Clapers (Valencia), 86, 96,
    152
hospitals
    donations requiring care of family mem-
        bers, 96
    large endowments of, 90
    pay for wet nurses, 86
    preferential treatment for specific popula-
        tions, 96
    records of, 35, 97
    religious life required of residents, 93–94
    and secular/sacred divide, 194n37
    wage labor use, 38
    wills leaving money to, 90
    wills' provisions for masses in donor's
        honor, 90, 93
    See also charitable institutions
Hundred Years' War, and famine, 150
al-ḥurī, 32
Hurricane Katrina, 1

Ibn al-Wāfid, 32
Ibn al-ʿAwāmm, 31–32
irrigation, 29–31
    as common in Crown of Aragon, 40
    as general Catalan practice, 37
    large expense of, 29, 38
    large projects of 14th century, 29–31
    in Manresa, 30–31
    population needed to maintain, 31

as protection against crop failure, 17
Roman and Islamic cultural influences
    on, 29
scholarship on, 29
at Sitges castle, 34
urban economic desires as source of, 29
See also Valencia, irrigation systems in
Italian cities
    charitable institutions in, 99
    and famine of 1374–75, 148–49, 160
    grain exports to Valencia, during shortages
        of 1371, 121–23
    and grain market, 55
    response to migrants in time of famine,
        105–6
    years of bad harvest in 1370s, 150
Italy
    famines of 1328 and 1346, 5
    government measures to control famine,
        56
    and Plague resurgence in 1380s, 139

Játiva, 32, 57, 61, 143
Jaume II (king), 92, 96
Jaume III (king), 169
Jaume IV (king), and dispute over throne of
    Mallorca, 169–70, 175, 176
Jews
    access to food in times of famine, 95
    acts against, in Great Plague, 95
    anti-Jewish violence in Spain (1391), 95
    marginality of, 95
Joan I (king), 101, 135–36, 145
Joanna I (queen of Naples), 135, 140
Johan, Pere, 97–98
Johan I of Prades, 45
Jorba, Antonio, 121
Jordan, William Chester, 103
Juboner, Enrich, 182

Kelleher, Marie, 58–59

labor force on farms
    around Barcelona, 37
    and diminishing returns, 42
    pay, 37, 189n132
    seasonal variation in need for, 42
    women in, 37
    See also wage labor on farms
Labrousse, Ernest, 3

land tenure practices
    blunting of economic incentives by, 41–42
    early incentives for settlers, 25
    effect on agriculture, 24–27
    flexible emphyteusis system around Barce-
        lona and New Catalonia, 24–26, 43
    onerous system of serfdom in northern
        counties (Old Catalonia), 25
lawyers, annual salaries of, 85
Le Roy Ladurie, Emanuel, 23
Little Ice Age, as cause of famine, 4, 151
Lleida
    government of, as model, 51
    as grain exporter, 52
    grain sources for, 19–20
    influence over agricultural management, 41
    irrigation system in, 30
    per capita grain needs, 63
    and Tortosa grain supply, 57
locusts of 1358, impact on food supply, 46
López Pizcueta, Tomás, 10–11

Magni, Stefano, 78
Mallorca
    charitable institution for Jews in, 97
    and colonization, 25
    control over grain market, temporary
        emergency measures, 62
    crop variation by land type, 20
    dispute over throne of, 169–70, 175, 176
    extension of Crown into, 51
    and famine of 1333, 62
    and famine of 1374–75: competition for
        food in, 147–48; labor shortages follow-
        ing, 101; use of armed ships, 147
    as port, and access to grain, 20
    Sardinian slaves, freeing of, in famine of
        1374, 89
    wine-producing interior, dense agricultural
        population around, 49
Manresa
    drought of 1333, 30
    and famine of 1374–75, 157, 158–59, 160,
        174; labor shortages following, 101;
        poor persons' selling of goods for food,
        167–68; and taxes to finance defense,
        171; wine shortages in, 167
    irrigation system in, 30–31
    saffron exports, 52–53
    terms used for famine, 174

manure fertilizer, 27–29, 43, 189–90n138
  benefits of, as well understood, 28, 188n81
  diminished supply of, in Great Famine of
    1315–1317, 28
  effectiveness of, 29
  as general Catalan practice, 37
  at Sitges castle, 34
  trade in, 28–29, 43
marginality, definition of, in 14th century,
    94–95, 184n62
market for agricultural production
  effect on resilience, 18
  routine surpluses from Crown of Aragon
    and, 43–44
markets
  access to, effect on agricultural practices,
    41–43
  and bulk trade in grains, 50
  cities' understanding of, 62, 64–66
  complex set of actors and allegiances in,
    71–72
  and crop choice, 6
  damping of impact from local crop fail-
    ures, 45–46, 47, 49, 50, 68, 69–71, 70f,
    80–81, 113
  and demand for land, 49
  expansion to include northern Europe,
    46–47
  as factor in 14th-century famines, 7, 179
  failures, as factor in famines, 3, 4
  grain imports increase with local short-
    ages, 54–55
  and greater pressure on rural communi-
    ties, 50
  growth of, 49
  and increased availability of money and
    credit, 49, 50
  increased price of grain from distant
    sources, 54, 54f
  increased regulation over time, 55, 61
  and increased use of written contracts, 49
  integration, increase over 14th century, 46,
    68, 78, 80–81, 113
  and marginal land, increased value of, 49
  national and local regulations for, 55
  national measures to control, 51
  and price for grain, 47
  reliance on, and competition for food, 179
  scholarship on, 45
  and severity of shortages, 179

  waypoints profiting from, 53
  See also city governments' efforts to control
    grain markets; food, access to
Marrades, Francesch, 122
Marrades, Pere, 172–73
Marseille
  and shortages of 1384–85, 130, 135
  wages for workers in, 86, 88
  wine production in, 66
Martí, Berenguer, 75
meat market
  regulation of, vs. grain and wine markets,
    62, 65–66
  shortages in Mediterranean region,
    1384–85, 131, 136–37, 139, 145
meat prices
  in Barcelona (1355–1395), 169f
  and famine of 1374–75, 166, 167, 167f, 174
  increases in 14th century, 168, 169f
meat production, modern, as culture-driven
    choice, 17
Medieval Warm Period, famine following
    end of, 4, 151
Mediterranean climate
  characteristics of, 151
  variation within relatively small areas,
    150, 151
Mediterranean territories, shortages of
    1384–85, 130–44
  as both famine and market crisis, 130
  cities' efforts to recover costs following,
    143–44
  cities' use of armed ships in, 139, 141–42
  competition between cities for food, 131,
    133–35, 141
  end of, factors contributing to, 145
  export bans in, 133–34
  geographic range of, as large but limited,
    145
  international political conflict as factor in,
    130–31, 133, 134–35, 139, 140
  meat shortage, 131, 136–37, 139, 145
  memories of famine of 1374 and, 137–39,
    144–45
  multiple problems contributing to, 130–31,
    137
  panic and, 116, 130, 131, 133, 137–40,
    141–43
  and Papal Schism, religious fears raised
    by, 139, 140

peak of crisis, 133
Plague and, 133, 139, 140
political conflict within Crown and, 135–36
and poor, legal restrictions on, 143
poor harvests throughout Crown of Aragon and, 130
price spikes in, 137, 138f
rapid onset of, 160
rapid recovery from, 116, 131–32, 137, 143, 145
residual effects of famine of 1374 and, 139
responses to: as counterproductive, 141; direct purchases, 141, 142; as excessive, 141, 145; export bans and licenses, 133–34, 141, 142, 143; high cost of, 141, 142, 145; import subsidies, 132–34; and overall success of policies, 145–46; religious responses, 132, 133, 140; subsidies, 131, 142; use of force, 141
rising prices and, 130
weather and, 135, 136, 139
wine shortage, 131, 136, 139, 145
Meya, Jofré de, 67
Michaud, Francine, 88
migrants in times of shortage and famine
cities' ability to secure resources as attraction for, 100–101
cities' restrictions on, 100–101, 109
and emptying of countryside, 101
motives of, 102
scholarship on, 102
Milton, Gregory, 107
Mogoda manor
grain storage at, 33, 41
increased labor needs during shortages and famine, 106
as Pia Almoina property, 37
records of, 11, 35
use of wage labor, 37, 189n136
Moià, Ferrer de, 97
Montesa, as grain exporter, 120
Montoro i Maltas, Joan, 31, 32–33
Montpellier
and famine of 1333–36, religious responses to, 164
and famine of 1374–75, severity of impact, 174, 175–76, 177, 180
as grain exporter, 58
as grain importer, 71
Morey, Guillem, 153

mules
food for, 22, 23, 87, 89
as main source of transportation and agricultural traction, 22
Mummey, Kevin, 75–76
Murcia
and famine of 1374–75, severity of impact, 177
reliance on food imports, 148
water supply in, 30
Muslims
access to food in times of famine, 95
marginality of, 95

Nadal, Pere, 32
Naples
and dispute over throne of Mallorca, 169
as grain exporter, 55
and shortages of 1384–85, 134–35, 140
natural shocks, twenty-first century preparations for, 1–2
Navarre, and shortages of 1384–85, 145
Newfield, Tim, 115
North Africa, as grain exporter, 55, 58, 132, 134
northern third of Kingdom of Aragon
as demographic regime, 47
onerous land tenure practices in, 25

oats
as animal food, 24, 87
as back-up grain for bad wheat years, 23, 24
as crop: advantages and disadvantages of, 21, 23; demand for, 29; yields, 27
Ó Gráda, Cormac, 113–14
Orihuela
demographic region of, 48
exports products produced near, 53
and famine of 1374–75, 157, 160, 168
as grain exporter, 118
grain sources for, 20
and shortages of 1384–85, 142
water supply in, 30–31
Osona, and famine of 1374–75, 157, 158
and taxes to finance defense, 171
overpopulation, population and resource model of, 27, 42

Palatia, as grain exporter, 134
Palermo, Luciano, 56, 66
Pallerès, Nicholau, 67

Palma de Mallorca
control over grain market:geographic
advantages of, 60–61; seizure of grain
by force (*vi vel gratia* right), 58; and trade
power, 8
debt problems of, 80
as grain importer, 52
growth of, 49
political clout of, 48
and Sicilian grain shipments, 181
as waypoint profiting from markets, 53, 55
Palou, Ramon de, 118, 119, 121
panic in famine
Mediterranean territories' shortages of
1384–85 and, 116, 130, 131, 133, 137–40,
141–43
reversal of, 80
small shortages and, 80
Papal Schism of 1378, and shortages of
1384–85, 139, 140
Papal States
export bans, 75
and famine of 1374–75, 148, 149, 150, 151,
173–74
Peace of Almazán, 152, 168
peasants, part-time wage labor by, 84
Pellicer, Raimon, 75
Pere Desvilar poorhouse, records of, 10
Pere the Ceremonious (king of Aragon)
and dispute over throne of Mallorca,
169–70
donations to charitable institutions, 93
on export bans, 60
and famine of 1374–75, 101, 148, 149, 174,
176
and financing of defense against Jaume
III, 170–71
on hoarding, 77–78
increase of shipyard pay during shortages
of 1374–76, 106
and market competition between cities,
50
and mediation of food competition
between cities, 76–77
on plague and famine in kingdom, 171
and price controls, 59
and shortages of 1384–85, 135–36
and Sicilian grain supplies, 52
and standardization of measures, 12
Periç, Bernat, 152

Perpignan
and dispute over throne of Mallorca, 170
and famine of 1374–75, 167
influence over agricultural management,
41
laws restricting grain storage, 34
Petley, David, 165
Pia Almoina
administration of, 11
donations requiring care of family members, 96
and famine of 1374–75: cutting of bread
handouts, 147, 152, 178; grain prices in,
153, 155, 157
feeding of employees in times of shortages, 107
grain source and price information, 54, 54*f*
pay for salaried workers, 85
payment of wage workers in kind, 87
per capita grain needs, 63
preferential treatment for specific populations, 96
and price increases of 1371–72, 125
records of, 10–11
and shortages of 1384–85, 137
slaves, food, clothing and care provided
to, 89
use of wage labor, 87
Pia Almoina, agricultural management at,
34–40
advanced practices, 40; as model of best
practices, 42; small landholders' inability to use, 42
benefits of market access, 42
care for growing crops, 38
funds for agricultural improvements, 38
and grain storage, 32, 33, 41
Mogoda manor as property of, 37
planting, 38, 189–90n138
and wage labor, use of, 38, 42
weeding, 38
See also Sitges castle, agricultural practices
at
Pinto, Giuliano, 55
Plague (Black Death)
agricultural changes following, lack of
records on, 40–41
England and, 172
episodes of, in 14th century Crown of
Aragon, 172

and famine, 4, 5, 171–72
and famine of 1374–75, 149–50, 172–73, 175, 177
food shortages after, 5
as general term for disease, 171–72
increased urbanization following, 48–49
increase of adverse weather following, 151
limited effect on market integration, 46
and meat prices, 168
and Mediterranean territories' shortages of 1384–85, 133, 139, 140
outbreaks in 1380s, 133, 139, 140
percentage of population killed by, 48
population slump following, 48; and increased wages, 86–87; and northern lords' efforts to hold on to serfs, 25; and relief from food production pressures, 27
and reduced tax revenue, 173
resurgence in 1380s, 133
seasonal pattern of mortality in, 173
and spike in wills donating to hospitals, 90
in Valencia, and famine of 1374–75, 172–73
Planella, Ramon de, 157
political maneuvering, as factor in Aragon famine of 1374–1375, 3
Pontevedra, as grain exporter, 79
poor, deserving
access to food, 83
cutting of bread handouts in famine, 147, 152, 158, 178
increased handouts to, during shortages, 83–84
shame as mark of, 92
poor, deserving vs. undeserving
and access to charitable institutions, 8, 91–92, 108–9, 180
donor's salvation through good works as reason for distinction, 91, 92, 93–94, 108–9
similarities in modern food aid, 182
poor, undeserving
cities' expulsion of, during shortages, 102, 103, 104, 105
criminalization of, 8, 83–84, 100, 143
as fraudulent recipients of aid, 92
legal restrictions on charity for, 92–93
as marked for acceptable starvation, 91, 94
migrants as, during food crises, 100

turn to begging or crime, 84
types of persons characterized as, 92
poor, urban
increase in, and risk of famine, 84
large number of, 89–90
urban safety nets as draw for, 84
poorhouses
institutions funding, 90
portion of population fed and housed by, 90
records of, 10–11
religious life required of residents, 93–94
poor persons, and systems of poverty as factor in 14th-century famines, 7–8, 179
and deserving vs. undeserving poor, 8
and diversion of suffering to those unable to foment social unrest, 8, 9
and foreigners as undeserving, 8, 95
poor persons' vulnerability to natural shocks
in Aragon famine of 1374–75, 3
and food entitlements (Sen), 4, 8
in food shortage of 2007, 2
14th-century charities and, 8
in modern societies, 1–2
population
population and resource model, 27, 42
size, as poor predictor of famine, 49
population pressure
Black Death and, 48–49
and southward migration, 49
poverty
causes of, 90
definition of, in 14th century, 94, 184n62
prices
of commodities, seasonal fluctuation in, 68–69
inflation from 1350 to 1400, 85
See also food prices; grain prices
Provence, and famine of 1374–75, 160
Pujol, Pere dez, 121
Pujada, Guillem, 121
Purcell, Nicholas, 4, 151

Rackham, Oliver, 21
Ramon, Pere, 121
Rangasami, Amrita, 56, 103
Regiment de la cosa pública (Eiximenis), 64–65
regrating, banning of, 73, 76

religious response to famine
in famine of 1374–75, 162–64
in Mediterranean territories shortages of
1384–85, 132, 133, 140
modern parallels to, 165
modern tendency to dismiss, 161
as not incompatible with technocratic
responses, 162, 165, 181
recent scholarship on, 161–62
in Valencia shortages of 1371–72, 120–21, 129
Renouart, Johan, 71, 121, 126
research on premodern famines
and Brenner debate, 3–4
and definitions, 113–14
difficulty of, 9
focus on pre-Black Death famines, 4
history of theories on causes and effects
of, 3–4
Labrousse and, 3
new scholarship on, 5
and religious responses, 161–62
sources, 9–12
resilience, agricultural. *See* agriculture,
resilience in
resilience of society, functioning of social
support systems as sign of, 100
rice, as back-up grain for bad wheat years, 152
Riera Melis, Antoni, 114
riots during famine, 8, 100
Rodera, Berenguer, 160
Rodrigo Estevan, María Luz, 95
Roials, Berenguer de, 119
Roman Empire
causes of famine in, 150, 152
and irrigation, 29
Roussillon
and famine of 1374–75, 169, 170, 171
as grain exporter, 54
network of cities in, 48
Rovira, Pere, 86–87
Rovira, Simó, 96
Rubio Vela, Augstín, 61, 115, 194n37
Ruiz Doménec, José, 107
rye
as back-up grain for bad wheat years, 23,
147, 152
as crop: advantages and disadvantages of,
21; yields, 27
low rank on social hierarchy of grains, 22
price of, 22, 23, 58

safety nets
in cities, as draw for poor, 84
of employer, confraternity, or guild, 83, 91,
97, 104, 106–7
family as, 83, 91, 95, 109
as first resort before charity, 91, 95
saffron production
and crop failures, impact on small farmers, 26–27
as specialty of central Catalonia, 6, 26,
52–53
Sala, Ferrer, 107–8
Salamó, Guillem and Margarida, 90
salaried workers, pay, by job type, 85–86
Sales, Pere, 107
Salmonia, Johanet, 67
Sánchez Usón, María José, 95
Santa Catarina hospital (Mallorca), 23
Santa Perpètua de Mogoda, 23, 148, 155
Sant Feliu de Llobregat, and famine of
1374–75, 155
Sant Pere de les Puel·les monastery
credit extended to peasants in shortages,
107–8
and famine of 1374–75, 153, 155–57, 159
grain source and price information, 54, 54f
irrigation system, workers required to
maintain, 31
labor force at, 37
manure purchases for fertilizer, 28
records of, 35
reliance on food markets, 41
and shortages of 1384–85, 137
slaves, food, clothing and care provided
to, 89
use of wage labor, 37, 87
wine production, 12, 26, 41
Sardinia
and famine of 1374–75, 148
as grain exporter, 20
and shortages of 1384–85, 131, 135
Schneider, Eric, 29
Schuh, Maximilian, 103, 181
Segre River, flooding of, 20
Sen, Amartya, 4, 7, 89–94, 108
servants
contractual access to food, 88–89
and famine of 1374–75, 154
salaried, pay, 86
Sessa, Johan de, 98

Seu of Urgell, charitable institutions in, 90
Seville
    and famine of 1374–75, 152
    as grain exporter, 55, 79, 148, 152–53, 154,
      181
    shortage of 1361–62, impact, markets' damp-
      ing of, 69, 70f
    shortage of 1384–85. See Mediterranean ter-
      ritories, shortages of 1384–85
    shortage of 2007
      and financial crisis of 2008, 2
      multiple factors causing, 2
      similarities to Aragon famine of 1374–75, 2
shortages
    classifications of, 114
    vs. famine, defining features of, 99–100
    and prisoner's dilemma, 79
    as relatively common, 114
    scholarship on, 116
    temporal specificity in designation of, 115
    years of, in Crown of Aragon, 115
    years of, in Europe, 115
shortages in multiple locations
    increased competition during, 68, 72,
      75–76, 129, 131, 133–35, 141
    multiplying effect of, 7, 46, 68, 70–71, 72,
      78–79, 81, 176, 180
    as necessary to cause famine, 113, 114, 115,
      180
Sicard, Bernat, 58, 121
Sicily
    and famine of 1374–75, 148, 151
    as grain exporter, 20, 35–36, 39, 45, 52, 54,
      54f, 55, 58, 105, 132, 133, 134–34, 148, 154
    and shortages of 1384–85, 130–31, 134
    and Valencia grain shortages (1371–72),
      121–23, 125, 127
Siena, wool carders' riot (1371), 125
Sitges castle
    bad grape harvest (1373), 168
    care for widowed spouses of employees, 107
    and famine of 1361–62, 69
    and famine of 1374–75, 77, 155
    and famine years, response to, 36, 38–39
    per capital grain needs, 63
    as Pia Almoina property, 34
    poor harvests of 1370s, 177
    records of, 11, 18, 34–35
    reliance on food markets, 41
    response to famine years at, 36, 38–39

Sitges castle, agricultural practices at
    as advanced, 34, 40
    and capital for improvements, 34
    case study of, 18
    as common in county of Barcelona, 35
    crop changes after bad harvests, 38–39, 39f
    crop rotation, 36, 38–39, 39f
    crop yields, 35–36, 36f
    fertility of land, 35
    general use in Crown of Aragon, lack of
      records to prove, 40–41
    grain storage, 33
    harvest of 1375, 155
    increased labor needs during shortages
      and famine, 106
    and irrigation, use of, 37
    labor force at, 37
    and manure fertilizer, use of, 37, 188n77
    market access, 34, 37
    partial payment of laborers with food, 88
    price-driven balance of shipping and stor-
      age of grain, 37, 41, 78
    similarity to general Catalan practices, 37
    use of scratch plow, 37
    and wage labor, use of, 34, 36
skilled workers, pay, 86
slaves
    food, clothing and care provided to, 89,
      194n28
    freed, charity fund for destitute members,
      97
    freeing of, in times of famine, 89, 106–7
    reliable access to food, 88–89
Slavin, Philip, 5, 78
Smith, Adam, 76
social breakdown
    famine aftershocks and, 103, 109
    as marker of famine, 100
social support systems, functioning of
    as key to survival of famine, 108
    as sign of society's resilience, 100
    See also safety nets
social unrest during famines of 14th century,
    8, 100
socioeconomic entanglements, 103
soil exhaustion, as cause of famine, theories
    on, 27, 28
sorghum, as back-up grain for bad wheat
    years, 152, 159
sources, 9–12

southern areas of Kingdom of Aragon, as demographic region, 48

spelt, 21–23, 157

Stone, David, 36, 38, 41

storage of food, as hedge against shortage, 31
See also grain storage

Stouff, Louis, 63

Taifa kingdom Muslims
on grain storage, 31–32
land conquered from, as demographic region, 47–48

Tarragona
control over grain market: and export bans, 60; monitoring of supply levels, 57; official markets in, 57, 66–67; and representatives sent to potential exporters, 57, 58; seizure of grain by force (*vi vel gratia* right), 58; subsidies in, 57
and famine of 1374–75: bans on hoarding in, 79; competition for food in, 75–76; discrimination against Jews and foreigners, 95; early alarm, 160; poor persons' selling of goods for food, 167–68; recovery in second year, 177; and taxes to finance defense, 171
grain sources for, 19–20
Plague in (1373), 172
and shortages of 1384–85, 131, 133, 134, 136, 143–44, 145

Tàrrega
and famine of 1374–75, 157
and market competition between cities, 50

Terrades, Ramon de, 90

Teruel
and disputes between farmers and ranchers, 20
and famine of 1374–75, severity of impact, 174, 175, 176, 180
and meat industry, 137
and shortages of 1384–85, 136

Thous, Ambert de, 117

Titow, Jan, 27, 28

Toralles, Johan, 174–75

Tornafort, G. de, 71

Torre Baldovina, records in, 35

Torrella, Pere, 118

Tortosa
control over grain market: Barcelona and, 53–54, 61–62, 148; geographic advantages of, 60–61; and representatives sent to potential exporters, 57; temporary emergency measures, 62
and famine of 1374–75, competition for food in, 76–77, 147
as grain exporter, 118, 121, 123, 127, 148
as grain importer, 121
grain sources for, 19–20
political clout of, 48
and shortages of 1384–85, 131, 133, 134, 141, 144, 160
and Valencia grain supply, 58
as waypoint profiting from markets, 53

Tous, Sereneta and Ramón de, 106–7

Typhus, famine and, 172

Union of Aix, 135

urbanization of 14th century
and agriculture, 43
Black Death and, 48–49

Urban VI (pope), 140

Urgell
and Barcelona's grain supply, 53, 57, 58, 61
and famine of 1374–75, 148, 157; and taxes to finance defense, 171
as grain exporter, 8, 19–20, 32, 43, 54
land tenure laws in, 25, 47, 52

Valencia (city)
archives of, 9–10
Castile's siege of (1365), 168
charitable institutions, pensions paid by, 98
charitable programs for youth, 98–99
control over grain market, 52, 53, 54–55; conflict with Alzira over, 61; economic success due to, 79–80; expansion of territory, 61; and export bans, 60; official markets in, 57;and representatives sent to potential exporters, 57–58, 81, 121; seizure of grain by force (*vi vel gratia* right), 58, 75; subsidies paid by, 71; success of, 61; temporary emergency measures, 62; and trade power, 8
dense agricultural population around, 49
and deserving poor, licensing of, 104
expulsion of undeserving poor during shortages, 104, 105
government of, 52
as grain importer, 52, 55

Valencian shortages (*continued*)
    supplies, 118–19, 141–42; arrangements
        for grain imports, 117; and broaden-
        ing range of shortages, recognition of,
        121; city council report on, 122; direct
        purchases, 126; and failure to anticipate
        shortages of 1374, 129; loans necessary
        to fund, 119–20, 125, 127, 130; petition-
        ing of king for special powers, 118,
        120, 122; power to shift grain markets,
        127, 128f; ramped-up response to crisis
        increase, 120; regional grain purchases,
        126; relaxation of restrictions on
        importers, 121–23; religious response
        to, 120–21, 129; representatives sent to
        potential grain exporters, 118, 119, 120,
        121, 126; restrictions on grain exports,
        117, 118–19; searches for grain inter-
        nationally, 121–22; seizure of grain by
        force (*vi vel gratia* right), 120; subsidies
        for grain imports, 119, 121, 123, 124f,
        126–27, 129, 130; success in avoiding
        crisis, 123, 125–26, 129–30; suspension
        of grain resale, 126
    and grain prices in Barcelona, 125
    lack of broad crisis and, 125
    peak of, 125
    poor harvest of 1370 and, 117
    as separate from famine of 1374–75, 116–17
    as shortage of wheat, not food in general, 118
    social mechanisms used to blunt effects
        of, 116–17
    Valencian control over grain market and, 125
    words used by city officials to describe, 117
    See also Valencia (city); Valencia (kingdom)
Valls
    and famine of 1374–75, and taxes to finance
        defense, 171
    and Tarragona grain supply, 57
Valls, Bonanat de, 97
Vernujols, P. de, 71
vetch, 23, 87
Vic
    charitable institutions in, 90
    and dispute over throne of Mallorca, 170
    and famine of 1374–75, 157–58, 159, 160,
        161; Plague and, 173; severity of impact,
        174–75, 176, 177, 178, 180; and taxes to
        finance defense, 171

Vidal, Guillem and Catarina, 167–68
Vilafranca, Pere de, 97
Vilafranca del Penedès, records in, 35
Vilagrassa, and market competition between
    cities, 50
Villagrasa Elías, Raúl, 93
Villani, Giovanni, 105–6
Villarreal
    control over grain market, and export bans,
        60
    pay for government workers, 85, 86
vineyards
    and crop failures, lesser impact on wealthy
        owners, 26–27
    large operation necessary to run, 26
    and shortages of 1384–85, 136
    as specialized crop, 6
    types of land suitable for, 19, 20
    urban elites' investments in, 26
    See also entries under wine
Vinyoles i Vidal, Teresa, 84–85, 93
vi vel gratia right (seizure of grain by force),
    58–59, 61

wage laborers
    access to food, 83, 86–88, 179
    and famine of 1374–75, 154
    increased need for, during shortages and
        famine, 106
    low level, poverty and starvation of, 83, 84
    pay, by job type, 86–88
    pay increases after Black Death, 86–87
    subsistence wage, estimate of, 84–85
    in towns, 84
    unreliable income of, 87
wage labor on farms
    as advantage for larger farms, 37
    to avoid bottlenecks, 37
    at Hospital dels Malalts, 38
    at Mogoda manor, 37, 189n136
    at Pia Almoina properties, 38, 42
    at Sant Pere de les Puel·les monastery, 37
    at Sitges castle, 34, 36
    as vital for farm efficiency, 42–43
    See also labor force on farms
war
    as factor in famine of 1374–75, 148, 149,
        150, 157, 168–71, 173–74, 175, 177, 180–81
    as factor in famines, 180–81

as factor in Mediterranean territories'
shortages of 1384–85, 130–31, 133, 134–35,
139, 140
as factor in severity of famine, 176
War of the Eight Saints, 149
War of the Two Peters, 152, 154, 181
watering, use of, at Pia Almoina properties, 38
waypoints
profits from markets, 53
and risk of famine-related decline in trade,
53
wealth distribution in medieval society
Christian theology and, 90
as highly unequal, 89
weather
as both trigger and long-term cause of
famine, 150
as cause of most medieval famines, 150,
152
and crop yields, 29, 35
as factor in famine of 1374–75, 2–3, 148,
149, 150–52
and fluctuations of agricultural output in
14th century, 6
in Mediterranean, variation within relatively small areas, 150, 151
poor, crop changes to accommodate, 39
weights and measures in Crown of Aragon,
variations in, 12–13, 13t
Western Mediterranean, famine events of
14th century, 5
wet nurses, pay, 86
wheat
as crop: advantages and disadvantages of,
6, 20, 21; as both staple and cash crop,
19; as cultural choice, 6; demand for,
vs. other crops, 20, 29; at Sitges castle,
38–39, 39f; yields, 27, 35, 36f
crop failure, and potential for food crisis, 18
laws regulating grades and prices, 32
measures for, 12
as preferred grain, 22, 23
price drops after storage, 32

in social hierarchy of grains, 6, 24, 43
See also entries under grain
wheat prices
and bad harvest of 1378, 39
in famine of 1374–75, 153–55, 156f, 166,
167f, 177
See also grain prices
wills
donations to charitable organizations
through, 90
provisions for masses in donor's honor,
90, 93
requirements for care of legator in, 95–96
spike in wills donating to hospitals, during
famine, 90
wine producers, influence with city officials,
66
wine production
flexible land tenure and, 26
and luxury market, development of, 26
protectionist measures, 66
regulation of, vs. grain and meat markets,
62, 65–66
urban elites' investments in, 26
women
aid from charitable institutions, 97
as farm workers, pay, 37
poverty rate, 95
as laborers, pay, 86, 88

Zaragoza
dense agricultural population around, 49
and famine of 1276, 81
government of, as model, 51
as grain exporter, 52
grain sources for, 19–20
influence over agricultural management, 41
irrigation system in, 30
land around, as demographic region,
47–48
and shortages of 1384–85, 131, 132, 133–34,
143, 144
and Tortosa grain supply, 57

CPSIA information can be obtained
at www.ICGtesting.com
Printed in the USA
BVHW091949250222
630059BV00001B/2

9 780271 091747